GENDER
AND
PUBLIC POLICY

GENDER

AND

PUBLIC POLICY

Cases and Comments

edited by

KENNETH WINSTON
Wheaton College

and

MARY JO BANE
Harvard University

WESTVIEW PRESS
Boulder • San Francisco • Oxford

Copyright © 1993 by Westview Press, Inc.

Published in 1993 in the United States of America by Westview Press, Inc., 5500 Central Avenue, Boulder, Colorado 80301-2877, and in the United Kingdom by Westview Press, 36 Lonsdale Road, Summertown, Oxford OX2 7EW

Library of Congress Cataloging-in-Publication Data
Gender and public policy : cases and comments / edited by Kenneth
    Winston and Mary Jo Bane.
        p.   cm.
    Includes bibliographical references.
    ISBN 0-8133-1300-7 — ISBN 0-8133-1301-5 (pbk.)
    1. Women—Government policy—United States.   2. Women—Legal
status, laws, etc.—United States.   3. Women's rights—United States.
I. Winston, Kenneth I.   II. Bane, Mary Jo.
HQ1236.5.U6G45   1993
305.42'0973—dc20   92-24989
                                                                           CIP

Printed and bound in the United States of America

The paper used in this publication meets the requirements
of the American National Standard for Permanence of Paper
for Printed Library Materials Z39.48-1984.

10   9   8   7   6   5   4   3   2   1

Contents

PART VI: MANAGERIAL STYLE AND GOVERNANCE

Preface

This volume consists of selected cases—personal stories, court opinions, historical narratives, managerial decisions, political disputes—designed to facilitate classroom discussion of gender issues that arise in public policy debates. The cases focus on such topics as family, education, reproduction, the workplace, welfare programs, and politics. They reflect no particular theoretical or ideological perspective, but rather enable teachers and students to approach gender issues from many points of view.

In covering such an array of topics, our aim has been to facilitate the examination of certain thematic contrasts that pervade public policy deliberations. These contrasts include those between justice and compassion, autonomy and responsibility, equality and difference, competition and cooperation, public and private, self-interest and the common good. At the same time, each case opens up an area of reflection and inquiry, and by following the suggestions in our comments and recommended readings sections, the reader can pursue each in greater depth. In our own teaching of these materials, we have kept our classes case-focused, but we have also supplemented the cases with background readings. Depending on what we wished to emphasize, we used essays by historians for an overview of developments in policy areas; by philosophers to clarify key concepts and analyze important arguments; or by policy analysts to provide details on budgetary implications, problems of implementation, and the like.

In reviewing currently available texts, we found no public policy casebooks on gender issues and few that even include female protagonists. We took it as a special aim to correct this imbalance and thereby fill a gap in the materials for courses in public policy schools, political science departments, and women's studies programs. Yet, we would emphasize that the focus is on gender issues, not simply women's issues. More than one-third of the cases involve men in some central way. And, though we have made no attempt at a comprehensive treatment of questions of race and ethnicity, people of color are central in five cases.

A word about the overall organization of the volume: In our own teaching, we have found it useful to begin with cases that help students to talk about their own perceptions of the extent to which gender roles are self-assumed or culturally inherited. The materials on marriage (Part I) provide a good vehicle for discussing this question because the elements of choice and self-definition are especially prominent. An individual's understanding of available choices, of course, is a function of whatever constructions of social reality have been previously internalized, and the full story requires reference to that process. Nonetheless, any account that excludes how things appear from a subjective point of view is incomplete. With students we think this is a particularly good starting point.

The theme of self-definition versus social constraint also appears in the materials on reproductive strategies (Part II). In a number of different ways, the cases in this part pose questions about women's control over their life prospects and specifically the use of their body. What is distinctive is that the issues arise, to a large degree, because of recent technological developments, so the central questions come to be framed in terms of women's relation to the "natural lottery," that is, aspects of life formerly beyond anyone's control.

Only in Part III, rounding out the first half of the volume, are cultural institutions introduced in a more explicit way. The cases in this part address the influence of religious, educational, and legal institutions in promoting (or changing) gender identities. Parts IV through VI then concentrate on three large arenas where the impact of gender conceptions is fundamental— and very much in transition: the workplace, the social services sector, and the political sphere.

Other instructors, however, may prefer to approach the materials differently. For example, an instructor who wishes to begin with the cultural context could start with Part III, then move to the more personal issues in the first, second, and fifth parts, and then round out the course with the public and professional issues in the fourth and sixth parts.

*   *   *

Our preoccupation with gender and public policy is long-standing. It began, roughly, in the mid-1970s around the time that we married. Mary Jo became associate director of the Center for Research on Women at Wellesley College and wrote a book about changes in family patterns and their implications for public policy. Ken was teaching philosophy at Wheaton College, the oldest women's college in New England until it became coeducational a few years ago, and getting involved in faculty study groups on feminism and the creation of a gender-balanced curriculum. We both felt the excitement of living during a period of far-reaching cultural transformation, with so many people thinking anew about gender roles. We are indebted to many friends and colleagues for their intellectual companionship and moral support during these years, as well as later. We would like to express particular thanks to Laura Lein, who succeeded Mary Jo as associate director and then became director of the Wellesley Center, and to Ken's Wheaton colleagues Frinde Maher, Kersti Yllö, and especially Trudy Villars, whose premature death from breast cancer was a great loss to the whole Wheaton community.

We are also indebted to many friends and colleagues at Harvard's Kennedy School of Government, where we both held faculty appointments, Mary Jo as professor of public policy and director of the Malcolm Wiener Center for Social Policy and Ken as visiting professor of ethics from 1986 to 1991. During this time Ken received generous financial support from Dennis Thompson, director of the Program in Ethics and the Professions at Harvard, and from Robert Putnam, former dean of the Kennedy School, for the development of case materials on gender issues. Two of his cases—"Fertility and Control: The Case of RU 486" and "A Policewoman's (Non)use of Deadly Force"—are included in this volume. We are grateful to Christopher Sturr and Jillian Dickert for their skillful writing and diligent library work, as well as to Shari Levinson for her ever-cheerful clerical assistance.

In the fall of 1990, Ken joined a Kennedy School committee on the pedagogy of diversity, which met regularly to discuss gender and race in the classroom. Among the faculty members who shared stories of their teaching experiences—their failures as well as their successes, their frustrations as well as their aspirations—were William Apgar, David Ellwood, Robin Ely, Ron Ferguson, Olivia Golden, Glenn Loury, and Harry Spence. These discussions were quite valuable in helping us prepare for our own venture in the spring of 1991 when we cotaught a course on gender and public policy, using most of the cases collected in this volume. Aside from the intellectual excitement that came from attempting to integrate our different perspectives on the issues raised by the cases, our experience in teaching the course encouraged us to believe that the range of materials facilitates productive classroom discussion and creates the moral space for the expression of a wide diversity of views.

In April 1992, Mary Jo became commissioner of social services for the State of New York, after previous assignments as executive deputy commissioner in that department and as a deputy assistant secretary in the U.S. Department of Education. Mary Jo's experiences in making and implementing public policies in two areas of special importance to women deepened our understanding of the practical and political dimensions of these issues. We were both enriched by her many colleagues who taught us so much about "civil service," in the fullest meaning of that term.

In preparing the volume itself, we received special encouragement and support from Amy Gutmann, who read the entire manuscript and offered many helpful suggestions. Finally, we are indebted to our editors at Westview Press: Spencer Carr for his initial enthusiasm and continuing support of the project, Martha Leggett for her attentive supervision of the production process, and Bea Ferrigno for her skillful editing.

Kenneth Winston
Mary Jo Bane

Sources and Credits

PART I

Section A

John Stuart Mill, "Statement on Marriage," March 6, 1851, in John M. Robson, ed., *Essays on Equality, Law, and Education* (Toronto: University of Toronto Press, 1984), p. 37. Reprinted by permission.

Henry B. Blackwell and Lucy Stone, "Protest," *Worcester Spy*, 1855, in Leslie Wheeler, ed., *Loving Warriors: Selected Letters of Lucy Stone and Henry B. Blackwell, 1853–1893* (New York: Dial Press, 1981), pp. 135–136.

Alix Kates Shulman, "A Marriage Agreement," *Redbook* (August 1971): 57 and 138–140. Copyright © 1970, 1971 by Alix Kates Shulman. Reprinted by permission.

Section B

Arlie Hochschild, with Ann Machung, "The Family Myth of the Traditional: Frank and Carmen Delacorte" and "A Scarce Economy of Gratitude: Seth and Jessica Stein," in Hochschild, with Machung, *The Second Shift* (New York: Penguin, 1989), pp. 59–74 and 110–127, respectively. Copyright © 1989 by Arlie Hochschild. Reprinted by permission of Viking Penguin, a division of Penguin Books USA Inc.

PART II

Section A

"Fertility and Control: The Case of RU 486" (C16-90-1021.0). This case was written by Christopher Sturr under the direction of Kenneth Winston, Visiting Professor of Ethics, for use at the John F. Kennedy School of Government, Harvard University. Funding was generously provided by the Program in Ethics and the Professions and by the Harvard Business School. Copyright © 1990 by the President and Fellows of Harvard College. Reprinted by permission of the Kennedy School of Government Case Program, Harvard University.

Section B

Rayna Rapp, "XYLO: A True Story," in Rita Arditti, Renate Duelli Klein, and Shelley Minden, eds., *Test-Tube Women: What Future for Motherhood?* (London: Pandora, 1984), pp. 313–338. Reprinted by permission of Pandora Press, imprint of Unwin Hyman, of HarperCollins Publishers Limited (London).

Anna Quindlen, "Life in the 30s," *New York Times*, May 12, 1988, p. C2. Copyright © 1988 by The New York Times Company. Reprinted by permission.

Section C

"Surrogate Parenting in New York—I," from *Surrogate Parenting in New York: A Proposal for Legislative Reform*, prepared by the staff of the New York State Senate Judiciary Committee, John R. Dunne (chairman) and Roberta Glaros (project director), December 1986.

"Surrogate Parenting in New York—II," from *Surrogate Parenting: Analysis and Recommendations for Public Policy*, by the New York State Task Force on Life and the Law, May 1988.

PART III

Section A

Rebecca E. Klatch, "Portrait of a Social Conservative: Mary Donnelly," in Klatch, *Women of the New Right* (Philadelphia: Temple University Press, 1987), pp. 154–173. Copyright © 1987 by Temple University. Reprinted by permission of Temple University Press.

Section B

Catherine G. Krupnick, "Meadows College Prepares for Men," is being published here for the first time.

Section C

Catharine A. MacKinnon and Andrea Dworkin, "Proposed Ordinance on Pornography," memo to the Minneapolis City Council, December 26, 1983. Reprinted by permission.

Section D

Don Terry, "In Week of an Infamous Rape, 28 Other Victims Suffer," *New York Times*, May 29, 1989, pp. 25 and 28. Copyright © 1989 by The New York Times Company. Reprinted by permission.

PART IV

Section A

Sandi E. Cooper, "Women's History Goes to Trial: *EEOC v. Sears, Roebuck and Company*—Introduction to the Documents," *Signs: Journal of Women in*

Section B

Sara M. Evans and Barbara J. Nelson, "Feminists, Union Leaders, and Democrats: The Passage of Comparable Worth Laws," in Evans and Nelson, *Wage Justice: Comparable Worth and the Paradox of Technocratic Reform* (Chicago: University of Chicago Press, 1989), pp. 69–81 (notes have been deleted). Copyright © 1989 by The University of Chicago. All rights reserved. Reprinted by permission.

Section D

Testimony for and against The Family and Medical Leave Act of 1987 (H.R. 925).

Statement by Schroeder was presented to the House Committee on Small Business, "Hearing Before the Committee on Small Business, House of Representatives," August 4, 1987, Serial No. 100-19 (Washington: U.S. Government Printing Office, 1987), pp. 49–52.

Statement by Norton was presented to the House Committee on Post Office and Civil Service, "Joint Hearing Before the Subcommittee on Civil Service and the Subcommittee on Compensation and Employee Benefits of the Committee on Post Office and Civil Service, House of Representatives," April 2, 1987, Serial No. 100-8 (Washington: U.S. Government Printing Office, 1987), pp. 31–37.

Statements by Sweeney, Schlafly, Lamp, and Kepley were presented to the House Committee on Education and Labor, "Joint Hearings Before the Subcommittee on Labor-Management Relations and the Subcommittee on Labor Standards of the Committee on Education and Labor, House of Representatives," February 25 and March 5, 1987, Serial No. 100-20 (Washington: U.S. Government Printing Office, 1987), pp. 43–47, 185–188, 99–101, and 351–355, respectively.

PART V

Section A

Lucie E. White, "Subordination, Rhetorical Survival Skills, and Sunday Shoes: Notes on the Hearing of Mrs. G.," *Buffalo Law Review* 38 (190): 21–32. Reprinted by permission.

"California Welfare Reform" (C16-87-782.0). This case was written by David M. Kennedy under the direction of Professor José A. Gomez-Ibañez for use at the Kennedy School of Government, Harvard University. This case was made possible in part by funds from the Parker Gilbert Montgomery Endowment for Public Policy. Copyright © 1987 by the President and Fellows of Harvard College. Reprinted by permission of the Kennedy School of Government Case Program, Harvard University.

Section B

"Buying Time: The Dollar-a-Day Program" (C16-90-961.0). This case was written by Nancy Kates at the direction of Professor Marc Roberts, for use at the Kennedy School of Government, Harvard University. Copyright © 1990 by the President and Fellows of Harvard College. Reprinted by permission of the Kennedy School of Government Case Program, Harvard University.

"Cocaine Mothers" (C16-90-944.0). This case was written from public documents by Professor José A. Gomez-Ibañez for use at the Kennedy School of Government, Harvard University. Copyright © 1990 by the President and Fellows of Harvard College. Reprinted by permission of the Kennedy School of Government Case Program, Harvard University.

Section C

Lois Ahrens, "Battered Women's Refuges," in Frederique Delacoste and Felice Newman, eds., *Fight Back: Feminist Resistance to Male Violence* (Pittsburgh: Cleis Press, 1981), pp. 104–109. Reprinted by permission.

Section D

Anita Diamant, "In the Best Interest of the Children," *Boston Globe Magazine,* September 8, 1985, pp. 14, 86–92, 96, and 100. Reprinted by permission.

PART VI

Section A

"Taking Charge: Rose Washington and Spofford Juvenile Detention Center" (C15-89-875.0). This case was written by Anna M. Warrock at the direction of Olivia Golden, Lecturer in Public Policy at the John F. Kennedy School of Government, Harvard University. Funds for development of the case were provided by the Ford Foundation and the Innovation in State and Local Government Program. Copyright © 1989 by the President and Fellows of Harvard College. Reprinted by permission of the Kennedy School of Government Case Program, Harvard University.

Section B

"A Policewoman's (Non)use of Deadly Force" (C16-91-1040.0). This case was prepared by Jillian P. Dickert under the supervision of Kenneth Winston, Visiting Professor in Ethics, for use at the John F. Kennedy School of Government, Harvard University. Copyright © 1991 by the President and Fellows of Harvard College. Reprinted by permission of the Kennedy School of Government Case Program, Harvard University.

Section C

James LeMoyne, "Army Women and the Saudis: The Encounter Shocks Both," *New York Times*, September 25, 1990, pp. A1 and A12. Copyright © 1990 by The New York Times Company. Reprinted by permission.

Colin Nickerson, "In Saudi and US Women, Common Feeling Is Pity," *Boston Globe*, November 13, 1990, p. 11. Reprinted courtesy of *The Boston Globe*.

Colin Nickerson, "Combat Barrier Blurs for Women on the Front Line," *Boston Globe*, November 13, 1990, pp. 1 and 12. Reprinted courtesy of *The Boston Globe*.

Section D

"Among Friends: Lynn Martin, Jerry Lewis, and the Race for the Chair of the House Republican Conference" (C16-89-885.0). This case was written by David M. Kennedy for Martin Linsky, Lecturer in Public Policy, for use at the Kennedy School of Government, Harvard University. Funding for the case was provided by the Center for Leadership Studies. Copyright © 1989 by the President and Fellows of Harvard College. Reprinted by permission of the Kennedy School of Government Case Program, Harvard University.

PART I

FAMILY MATTERS

INTRODUCTION

The terms of marriage are set independently of the wishes of marriage partners. Although marriage is regarded legally as a contract, it is unlike other contracts in that the rights and responsibilities entailed are not negotiated and agreed to by the parties. Typically, in fact, the terms are unknown to them. Most are set as a matter of law; others are stipulated by judges, case by case, when difficulties arise and the parties find themselves attempting to settle their differences in court. Many partners discover only then the inequities that define their relationship.

The nineteenth-century protests by Lucy Stone (in the United States) and John Stuart Mill (in England), both in Section A, are classic repudiations of this state of affairs. Yet, aside from their general egalitarian sentiments, neither of these statements goes as far as Alix Shulman's 1971 "A Marriage Agreement" to formulate alternative terms of marriage in detail. They did not endorse the libertarian idea that couples should be able to arrange the marital relation in whatever way they might choose. The point was to change existing laws, not do away with the social regulation of marriage. In fact, Lucy Stone (unlike Mill) explicitly supported the legal prohibition of divorce, so long as the laws applied equally to women and to men. Even Mill, though he spoke of following one's wishes and will, did not concur with the view—expressed forcefully by Elizabeth Cady Stanton, among others—that the uniform laws of marriage should be repealed altogether, so that marriage could be, in Stanton's words, "subject to the same laws which control all other contracts."[1]

Resistance to abolishing uniform laws may reflect the traditional regard for marriage as a covenant rather than a contract. Covenant conveys the idea of an arrangement of profound social (as well as individual) consequence, involving interests transcending those of the immediate parties. Covenantal obligations are more binding than ordinary commitments even though they are usually more diffuse and open-ended. A contract, by comparison, is typically associated with business transactions between strangers dealing with each other at arm's length. It involves limited commitments, applicable only under specified conditions, for the sake of mutual advantage—not intimate relationships founded on love and trust. In practice, however, as the case of *Graham v. Graham* makes clear (Section A), the diffuse covenantal obligations of marriage reflected well-defined background understandings of gender roles and were enforced by institutional arrangements—whether religious, political, or economic—that sustained male domination. Thus, in egalitarian terms, the partial movement from covenant to contract—from marriage as a sacrament to a personal relationship in the service of individual values and needs—represented a kind of moral progress. Even so, society's interest in the marital relation did not disappear.

Aside from channeling sexual passion, the most obvious social interest in regulating marriage is the well-being of children. The legal duties of care and support of offspring flow from a social decision to allocate responsibility in an individual rather than collective way: Thus society as a whole ensures its own perpetuation. But this rationale for marital regulation lends itself to a common inversion, for the idea that society has an interest in its own preservation leads to the inference that marriage itself has a natural purpose, namely, procreation. Then it is just a step to the view that sexual conduct has certain natural (moral) and certain unnatural (immoral) forms, which it is the business of society to distinguish, promoting the former and prohibiting the latter. This reproductive conception of sexuality is the foundation of the long-standing judicial refusal, exemplified in *Baker v. Nelson*, to grant legal status to gay and lesbian relationships (Section A).

A second and quite different social interest in regulating marriage is to sustain a certain societal self-image. This moralist rationale for regulation involves the imposition on everyone of a single model of marriage, not because uniformity is necessary for achieving a particular social benefit, but because the chosen model embodies an ideal of the proper way to live. On this basis, monogamous marriage is preferred to polygamous, heterosexual marriage to homosexual. The legal treatment of polygamy in the United States offers an instructive example of the moralist rationale at work. Despite the scriptural duty, as interpreted by the Mormon Church, to practice polygamy, the Supreme Court in 1878 observed that polygamy "has always been odious among the northern and western nations of Europe" and, accordingly, held that it is "an offence against society." The Court seemed to be aware that it could make a stronger case for prohibition if it could specify a tangible harm resulting from the practice. But the only claim the Court sets out is that polygamy supports the patriarchal organization of society—and hence despotism—whereas the "principle [of patriarchy]," it asserts, "cannot long exist in connection with monogamy."[2]

Both of these reasons for regulation assume that society's interests in setting the terms of marriage are unitary, but marriage may involve interests that are conflicting as well as interests that are common. Women's interests may diverge to a considerable degree from men's, and the interests of one group of women may differ from those of another. Consider that public policies that help career women realize one conception of gender roles in their lives may undermine the efforts of noncareer women to achieve a very different conception. This conflict is illustrated in Arlie Hochschild's story of the marriage of Carmen and Frank Delacorte (Section B). By her own account, Carmen Delacorte is committed to a traditional division of labor in marriage: men's principal duty is financial support of the family; women's principal duty is service, including housework, child care, and sex. Even though Carmen's actual life does not conform to this ideal, it embodies her aspiration, and she sees factors that prevent its realization as unjust interferences. In her view, women and men should be regarded as equally valuable in their different spheres of competence. Thus, true egalitarianism means equality of status, not that everyone has the same rights and responsibilities. As a result, she resents what she sees as efforts, reinforced by popular culture, to denigrate housewives and to devalue domesticity. (A contrasting view of equality is offered in the second Hochschild story included in Section B, the story of Seth and Jessica Stein.)

Competing ideas of gender roles complicate the question of whether women have an interest in the state's regulation of the marriage contract. If the state is an instrument of male domination, it seems that women would want to bring greater control of the relationship into their own hands. Presumably this concern motivates Alix Shulman's "A Marriage Agreement," but satisfactory negotiation of equitable terms in an enduring relationship depends on a rough equality of bargaining power. Furthermore, without legal enforcement it depends on the good will of the other party. So, in a condition of imbalance between the parties, a better strategy for women would be to turn the authority of the state to their advantage.

This strategy is illustrated in the development of child support laws. When a marriage breaks up, the obligations incurred do not disappear, especially regarding children. In more than 90 percent of divorce cases in the United States, the mother becomes the custodial parent. This means, as Deborah Rhode puts it, that after divorce women typically are single parents whereas men are just single.[3] Moreover, the man's earning power is significantly higher on average. Combining divorced women with never-married mothers (in 1989, the latest year for which figures are available), about 60 percent of women with custody of children received a child support award—hence, 40 percent did not. And of the 60 percent, only about half actually received the full amount. Thus somewhere between 25 and 30 percent of children living with their mothers were supported by their fathers; the rest were not.[4] This phenomenon is a large component of what is called the feminization of poverty. In 1990, more than 50 percent of poor households were headed by women.[5]

Why has this happened? The answer is complicated, but part of it lies in the fact that marriage is regarded as a contract between private parties. As a matter of law, parents have a duty to care for and support their children, whether in residence or not. But because marriage is a contract, court action is required for enforcement. The result is that it is expensive for the custodial parent to obtain child support from the noncustodial parent, if the latter is uncooperative—and each woman has to make the effort individually. Moreover, because child support is only one element among many that need to be settled in divorce proceedings—along with custody, visitation rights, and division of property—what often happens is that everything is open to negotiation. Though the findings are not definitive, some studies indicate that women value custody so highly that they are willing to settle for less child support to avoid the risk of losing care of their children in a legal battle. The consequence is greater likelihood that divorced women and their children will live in poverty.

The federal government has, in a limited way, addressed this concern by enacting certain reforms, including the Family Support Act of 1988. These reforms move proceedings from courts to administrative agencies that are charged with establishing uniform guidelines for determining awards. In this way, opportunities for unfair bargaining are limited. More importantly, this legislation establishes automatic wage withholding (with centralized collection and disbursement) for absent parents.

Although these reforms in child support laws will not guarantee that children of divorced or separated parents can avoid living in poverty, they represent a major advance in holding men accountable for the obligations they incur in marriage. In this respect, they remind us that marriage is not only a relation built on deep affection and intimacy but also a set of enduring commitments, including economic support. Only by keeping the economic arrangement near the center of our attention—as we are encouraged to do by the decision in *O'Brien v. O'Brien* (Section B)—can we expect the inequities that emerge when a marriage is dissolved to be fully corrected.

NOTES

1. Elizabeth Cady Stanton, address to the New York State Legislature (1854), reprinted in *Feminism: The Essential Historical Writings*, edited by Miriam Schneir (New York: Random House, 1972), p. 113.

2. *Reynolds v. U.S.*, 98 U.S. 145 (1878).

3. Deborah Rhode, *Justice and Gender: Sex Discrimination and the Law* (Cambridge: Harvard Univ. Press, 1989), p. 151.

4. Gordon H. Lester, *Child Support and Alimony: 1989* (U.S. Dept. of Commerce, Bureau of the Census, September 1991), p. 4.

5. *Poverty in the United States: 1990* (U.S. Dept. of Commerce, Bureau of the Census, August 1991), p. 20.

SECTION A

The Terms of Marriage

Statement on Marriage
John Stuart Mill

Being about, if I am so happy as to obtain her consent, to enter into the marriage relation with the only woman I have ever known, with whom I would have entered into that state; and the whole character of the marriage relation as constitutued by law being such as both she and I entirely and conscientiously disapprove, for this among other reasons, that it confers upon one of the parties to the contract, legal power and control over the person, property, and freedom of action of the other party, independent of her own wishes and will; I, having no means of legally divesting myself of these odious powers (as I most assuredly would do if an engagement to that effect could be made legally binding on me), feel it my duty to put on record a formal protest against the existing law of marriage, in so far as conferring such powers; and a solemn promise never in any case or under any circumstances to use them. And in the event of marriage between Mrs. Taylor and me I declare it to be my will and intention, and the condition of the engagement between us, that she retains in all respects whatever the same absolute freedom of action, and freedom of disposal of herself and of all that does or may at any time belong to her, as if no such marriage had taken place; and I absolutely disclaim and repudiate all pretension to have acquired any *rights* whatever by virtue of such marriage.

(Signed)   J. S. Mill
6 March 1851

Protest
Henry B. Blackwell and Lucy Stone

While we acknowledge our mutual affection by publicly assuming the relationship of husband and wife, yet in justice to ourselves and a great principle, we deem it a duty to declare that this act on our part implies no sanction of, nor promise of voluntary obedience to such of the present laws of marriage as refuse to recognize the wife as an independent, rational being, while they confer upon the husband an injurious and unnatural superiority, investing him with legal powers which no honorable man would exercise and which no man should possess. We protest especially against the laws which give the husband:

1. The custody of the wife's person.
2. The exclusive control and guardianship of their children.
3. The sole ownership of her personal and use of her real estate, unless previously settled upon her, or placed in the hands of trustees, as in the case of minors, lunatics and idiots.
4. The absolute right to the product of her industry.
5. Also against laws which give the widower so much larger and more permanent an interest in the property of his deceased wife than they give to the widow in that of the deceased husband.
6. Finally, against the whole system by which "the legal existence of the wife is suspended during marriage" so that, in most States, she neither has a legal part in the choice of her residence, nor can she make a will, nor sue or be sued in her own name, nor inherit property.

We believe that personal independence and equal human rights can never be forfeited except for crime; that marriage should be an equal and permanent partnership, and so recognized by law; that until it is so recognized, married partners should provide against the radical injustice of present laws, by every means in their power.

We believe that where domestic difficulties arise, no appeal should be made to legal tribunals under existing laws but that all difficulties should be submitted to the equitable adjustment of arbitrators mutually chosen.

Thus reverencing law, we enter our protest against rules and customs which are unworthy of the name, since they violate justice, the essence of law.

Worcester Spy, 1855   (Signed)   Henry B. Blackwell
                                                       Lucy Stone

---

Graham v. Graham
No. 1181
District Court, E.D. Michigan, N.D.
July 15, 1940

TUTTLE, District Judge.

This is a suit by a man against his former wife upon the following written agreement to have been executed September 17, 1932, by the parties:

Editors' note: This case has been slightly abridged, and most citations have been deleted.

"This agreement made this 17th day of September, 1932, between Margrethe Graham and Sidney Graham, husband and wife. For valuable consideration Margrethe Graham hereby agrees to pay to Sidney Graham the sum of Three Hundred ($300.00) Dollars per month each and every month hereafter until the parties hereto no longer desire this arrangement to continue. Said Three Hundred ($300.00) Dollars per month to be paid to Sidney Graham by said Margrethe Graham directly to said Sidney Graham.

"This agreement is made to adjust financial matters between the parties hereto, so that in the future there will be no further arguments as to what money said Sidney Graham shall receive."

The parties were divorced on July 11, 1933. While the writing itself recites no consideration but merely states that it is made to prevent future arguments as to the amount of money the husband is to receive from his wife, the complaint alleges that the plaintiff had quit his job in a hotel at the solicitation of the defendant who wanted him to accompany her upon her travels, she paying his expenses, and that he was desirous of returning to work but that the defendant in order to induce him not to do so entered into this agreement. The total amount claimed until November 7, 1939, is $25,000, with interest at five per cent per annum from the time each monthly installment of $300 became due. The defendant in her answer alleges that she has no recollection of entering into the agreement; and she denies that she ever induced plaintiff to give up his hotel work, alleging that on the contrary his abandonment of work and continued reliance upon her for support was always distasteful to her. The answer further alleges that at the time of divorce the parties entered into a written settlement agreement under which defendant (plaintiff in the divorce suit) paid plaintiff (defendant in the divorce suit) $9,000 and each party surrendered any and all claims he or she might have in the property of the other.

Subsequent to filing her answer, the defendant filed a motion to dismiss the complaint on the grounds that her promise was without consideration; that the alleged contract was not within the power of a married woman under Michigan law to make; that, since under its express provisions it was to continue only until the parties no longer desired the arrangement to continue, it was terminated by the divorce and settlement agreement; and that in any event any claim under the alleged contract was destroyed by the provision in the settlement agreement releasing all claims of each party to the property of the other and the provision of the decree of divorce restraining the plaintiff (defendant in the divorce suit) from interfering with, molesting, or communicating with the defendant (plaintiff in the divorce suit) in any manner whatsoever. Briefs have been filed upon the legal issues thus raised, to which I have given careful consideration. While in order to present the complete picture of this lawsuit I have set forth the substance of the answer filed by the defendant, I recognize, of course, that, in passing upon the motion to dismiss, the allegations of the answer cannot be taken into consideration; and in disposing of this motion I therefore assume all of the allegations of the bill of complaint to be true.

The claim is made by defendant that since it is apparent that she no longer desires her obligation to continue, it is destroyed under the express terms of the contract. If the proper construction of the agreement is that she is bound only as long as she wills it, then her promise is obviously illusory and the contract is now and was from the beginning void. However, the provision in question would seem to require action of both parties to terminate it, and if that is so the contract is not illusory. A question might be raised as to whether it was not an implied condition of the contract that the obligations were to be effective only so long as the parties remained man and wife so that it would be automatically terminated by divorce; but the defendant does not so argue, and for reasons hereafter stated I deem it unnecessary to decide this question.

A further question is presented as to whether the complaint sets forth any consideration for the alleged contract. As noted, the written contract itself does not recite any consideration. Plaintiff's counsel argues that consideration for defendant's promise is found in the oral agreement of the plaintiff "to give his wife his constant society, to travel with his wife wherever she wished and as frequently as she wished and not to return to work," all of which he was under no duty to do. However, the complaint does not specifically allege that plaintiff made any promise to do these things, but rather states that the desire of defendant to have him refrain from going back to work was the reason or inducement for her making her promise, which, of course, would not necessarily constitute consideration. However, again, it is unnecessary to decide this question, since I am convinced that even if the consideration is what counsel claims, and the plaintiff did agree to refrain from work and accompany his wife on her travels, the contract was not a competent one for married persons to enter into.

In the first place, it is highly doubtful if the alleged contract is within the capacity of a married woman to make under Michigan law. The degree of emancipation of married women with respect to contract and property rights varies widely in the different states. However, it has been repeatedly stated by the Michigan Supreme Court that under the Michigan statutes a married woman has no general power to contract, but can contract only in relation to her separate property. . . . This is admitted by both parties and has been so frequently repeated by the Supreme Court of Michigan that an extended citation of authorities is unnecessary. The limitation applies to contracts of married women with their husbands as well as with third parties. . . . In general, the Michigan Supreme Court in deciding whether an agreement is within a married woman's contractual capacity looks to the nature of the consideration, requiring it to be for the benefit of her separate estate. . . . Where the contract charges specific property belonging to the married woman, the law is not so rigid in requiring that the consideration be for the benefit of her estate. Thus, although a married woman cannot become personally obligated as surety for her husband, a mortgage on her property for the payment of her husband's debts is enforceable. . . . There is a line of Michigan cases which go even beyond this point, however, and which hold a married woman bound on her promise to pay where the consideration is for the benefit either of herself or some member of the family. . . . It appears, however, that all of these cases involve contracts to pay for necessaries in the form of goods or services or for domestic services, in which case there may be good reason to make an exception to the general rule, which clearly has not been abrogated. Since the promise of the defendant here consists of a general executory obligation unrelated to specific property and since the consideration is not for the benefit of her separate estate, but if anything to its detriment, it would appear that the contract is beyond the capacity of a married woman under Michigan law to make.

However, I do not rest my decision on this ground, but rather upon the broader ground that even if the contract is otherwise within the contractual power of the parties it is void because it contravenes public policy. Under the law, marriage is not merely a private contract between the parties, but creates a status in which the state is vitally interested and under which certain rights and duties incident to the relationship come into being, irrespective of the wishes of the parties. As a result of the marriage contract, for example, the husband has a duty to support and to live with his wife and the wife must contribute her services and society to the husband and follow him in his choice of domicile. The law is well settled that a private agreement between persons married or about to be married which attempts to change the essential obligations of the marriage contract as defined by the law is contrary to public policy and unenforceable. While there appears to be no Michigan decision directly in point, the principle is well stated in the Restatement of the Law of Contracts, as follows:

"Sec. 587. Bargain to Change Essential
Obligations of Marriage

"A bargain between married persons or persons contemplating marriage to change the essential incidents of marriage is illegal.
"Illustrations:
"1. A and B who are about to marry agree to forego sexual intercourse. The bargain is illegal.
"2. In a state where the husband is entitled to determine the residence of the married couple, A and B who are about to marry agree that the wife shall not be required to leave the city where she then lives. The bargain is illegal."

Thus, it has been repeatedly held that a provision releasing the husband from his duty to support his wife in a contract between married persons, or those about to be married, except in connection with a pre-existing or contemplated immediate separation, makes the contract void. Garlock v. Garlock, 1939, 279 N.Y. 337. . . .

Similarly, the cases hold that an antenuptial agreement that the parties will not live together after marriage is void. . . . Even in the states with the most liberal emancipation statutes with respect to married women, the law has not gone to the extent of permitting husbands and wives by agreement to change the essential incidents of the marriage contract.

The contract claimed to have been made by the plaintiff and defendant in the case at bar while married and living together falls within this prohibition. Under its terms, the husband becomes obligated to accompany his wife upon her travels; while under the law of marriage the wife is obliged to follow the husband's choice of domicile. . . . Indeed, it is argued by the plaintiff's attorney that this relinquishment by the husband of his rights constitutes consideration for the promise of his wife; but, by the same token it makes the contract violative of public policy. The situation is virtually identical with that set forth in Illustration 2 of Section 587 of the Restatement quoted above. The contract, furthermore, would seem to suffer from a second defect by impliedly releasing the husband from his duty to support his wife, and thereby making it fall directly within the rule of the cases cited supra holding that a contract between married persons living together which contains such a release is void. The present contract does not expressly contain such a release, but if the husband can always call upon his wife for payments of $300 per month he is in practical effect getting rid of his obligation to support his wife. The plaintiff seems to place this construction on the contract since his claim makes no deduction from the promised $300 per month for support of his wife. It is unnecessary to consider in detail the second alleged basis of consideration, namely, the promise of the husband to refrain from working, but it would seem again that a married man should have the right to engage in such work as he sees fit to do, unrestrained by contract with his wife.

The law prohibiting married persons from altering by private agreement the personal relationships and obligations assumed upon marriage is based on sound foundations of public policy. If they were permitted to regulate by private contract where the parties are to live and whether the husband is to work or be supported by his wife, there would seem to be no reason why married persons could not contract as to the allowance the husband or wife may receive, the number of dresses she may have, the places where they will spend their evenings and vacations, and innumerable other aspects of their personal relationships. Such right would open an endless field for controversy and bickering and would destroy the element of flexibility needed in making adjustments to new conditions arising in marital life. There is no reason, of course, why the wife cannot voluntarily pay her husband a monthly sum or the husband by mutual understanding quit his job and travel with his wife. The objection is to putting such conduct into a binding contract, tying the parties' hands in the future and inviting controversy and litigation between them. The time may come when it is desirable and necessary for the husband to cease work entirely, or to change to a different occupation, or move to a different city, or, if adversity overtakes the parties, to share a small income. It would be unfortunate if in making such adjustments the parties should find their hands tied by an agreement between them entered into years before.

It is important to note that the contract here was entered into between parties who were living together at the time and who obviously contemplated a continuance of that relationship. The case is to be distinguished in this respect from those cases which hold that a contract made after separation or in contemplation of an immediate separation which takes place as contemplated is legal, if the contract is a fair one, even though it contains a release of the husband's duty of support. Restatement of Contracts, Sec. 584; Randall v. Randall, 1877, 37 Mich. 563; annotation, 50 A.L.R. 351. In Garlock v. Garlock, supra, where the husband entered into a contract to pay his wife $15,000 per year and she in turn released him from any other duty of support, the court in an excellently reasoned opinion held the contract void as against public policy, but recognized that if the agreement had been made after separation or in contemplation of an immediate separation its decision would have been different. Similarly, in Massachusetts, where, as already indicated, a release of the husband's duty of support invalidates an antenuptial contract, the courts have upheld separation agreements containing such a release. . . . One reason why the courts uphold such separation contracts is that under the laws of most states married persons can secure a judicial separation with a judicial division of their property and a release of the husband's duty of support; and it is therefore felt that the parties should be permitted to enter into a fair agreement between themselves covering the same things upon which they could obtain relief in court. The problem is entirely different, however, where the parties are living together and contemplate a continuance of that relationship.

The case is also to be distinguished from a group of cases which hold that a married woman can properly contract with her husband to work for him outside the home and be compensated by him for her services (although it appears that this is contrary to the weight of authority). . . . The ground on which the contract has been upheld in those cases is that it covered services outside the scope of the marriage contract; the promises did not, as here, involve the essential obligations of the marriage contract, and no question of public policy was therefore involved. There is certainly less reason to hold that a married woman cannot lease property owned by her to her husband for a fair consideration than to hold that the parties cannot contract to refrain from intercourse during marriage; in the former case no abridgement of marital rights or obligations is involved. Admittedly, it is difficult to draw the line in cases not so extreme between contracts involving the personal rights or obligations of the marriage contract and those which involve matters outside its scope; but it is unnecessary here to decide exactly where the line is to be drawn, since in my opinion the promises made in the contract in the case at bar clearly attempt to alter essential obligations of the marriage contract.

While, as stated, there are no Michigan cases exactly in point, there is nothing in them inconsistent with a holding that this contract is invalid, but on the contrary they point toward the same conclusion. In Randall v. Randall, supra, the court in upholding a separation agreement said that there is nothing to prevent a husband and wife from entering into a contract so long as there is no overreaching and no violation of public policy. In Jenne v. Marble, 1877, 37 Mich. 319, however, the court held unenforceable a contract under which a man leased to his wife certain farms, including the family homestead, partly on the ground that to recognize that married persons could contract with each other as freely as strangers would be inconsistent with their disabilities of testimony and the desirability of preventing them from placing themselves "habitually in business antagonism." In Artman v. Ferguson, 1888, 73 Mich. 146, the court held that a husband and wife cannot become partners with each other, largely on the ground that the recognition of the partnership contract would impair the marital relationship by affording opportunity for contentions between them. This case was followed by Root v. Root, 1911, 164 Mich. 638, where a wife was enjoined from competing in business with her husband. Reference may also be made to Michigan Trust Co. v. Chapin, 1895, 106 Mich. 384, where an agreement of a husband to pay his wife $250 a year for her services as housekeeper was held void for want of consideration, since she was obligated to perform such services under the marriage contract. The case is distinguishable from, but at least not inconsistent with, the present one. . . .

A Marriage Agreement
Alix Kates Shulman

When my husband and I were first married, a decade ago, keeping house was less a burden than a game. We both worked full-time in New York City, so our small apartment stayed empty most of the day and taking care of it was very little trouble. Twice a month we'd spend Saturday cleaning and doing our laundry at the laundromat. We shopped for food together after work, and though I usually did the cooking, my husband was happy to help. Since our meals were simple and casual, there were few dishes to wash. We occasionally had dinner out and usually ate breakfast at a diner near our offices. We spent most of our free time doing things we enjoyed together, such as taking long walks in the evenings and spending weekends in Central Park. Our domestic life was beautifully uncomplicated.

When our son was born, our domestic life suddenly became *quite* complicated; and two years later, when our daughter was born, it became impossible. We automatically accepted the traditional sex roles that society assigns. My husband worked all day in an office; I left my job and stayed at home, taking on almost all the burdens of housekeeping and child raising.

When I was working I had grown used to seeing people during the day, to having a life outside the home. But now I was restricted to the company of two demanding preschoolers and to the four walls of an apartment. It seemed unfair that while my husband's life had changed little when the children were born, domestic life had become the only life I had.

I tried to cope with the demands of my new situation, assuming that other women were able to handle even larger families with ease and still find time for themselves. I couldn't seem to do that.

We had to move to another apartment to accommodate our larger family, and because of the children, keeping it reasonably neat took several hours a day. I prepared half a dozen meals every day for from one to four people at a time—and everyone ate different food. Shopping for this brood—or even just running out for a quart of milk—meant putting on snowsuits, boots, and mittens; getting strollers or carriages up and down the stairs; and scheduling the trip so it would not interfere with one of the children's feeding or nap or illness or some other domestic job. Laundry was now a daily chore. I seemed to be working every minute of the day—and still there were dishes in the sink; still there wasn't time enough to do everything.

Even more burdensome than the typical work of housekeeping was the relentless responsibility I had for my children. I loved them, but they seemed to be taking over my life. There was nothing I could do, or even contemplate, without first considering how they would be affected. As they grew older just answering their constant questions ruled out even a private mental life. I had once enjoyed reading, but now if there was a moment free, instead of reading for myself, I read to them. I wanted to work on my own writing, but there simply weren't enough hours in the day. I had no time for myself; the children were always *there.*

As my husband's job began keeping him at work later and later—and sometimes taking him out of town—I missed his help and companionship. I wished he would come home at six o'clock and spend time with the children so they could know him better. I continued to buy food with him in mind and dutifully set his place at the table. Yet sometimes whole weeks would go by without his having dinner with us. When he did get home the children were often asleep, and we both were too tired ourselves to do anything but sleep.

We accepted the demands of his work as unavoidable. Like most couples, we assumed that the wife must accommodate to the husband's schedule, since it is his work that brings in the money.

As the children grew older, I began free-lance editing at home. I felt I had to squeeze it into my "free" time and not allow it to interfere with my domestic duties or the time I owed my husband—just as he felt he had to squeeze in time for the children during weekends. We were both chronically dissatisfied, but we knew no solutions.

After I had been home with the children for six years I began to attend meetings of the newly formed Women's Liberation Movement in New York City. At these meetings I began to see that my situation was not uncommon; other women too felt drained and frustrated as housewives and mothers. When we started to talk about how we would have chosen to arrange our lives, most of us agreed that even though we might have preferred something different, we had never felt we had a choice in the matter. We realized that we had slipped into full domestic responsibility simply as a matter of course, and it seemed unfair.

When I added them up, the chores I was responsible for amounted to a hectic 6 A.M.–9 P.M. (often later) job, without salary, breaks or vacation. No employer would be able to demand these hours legally, but most mothers take them for granted—as I did until I became a feminist.

For years mothers like me have acquiesced to the strain of the preschool years and endless household maintenance without any real choice. Why, I asked myself, should a couple's decision to have a family mean that the woman must immerse years of her life in their children? And why should men like my husband miss caring for and knowing their children?

Eventually, after an arduous examination of our situation, my husband and I decided that we no longer had to accept the sex roles that had turned us into a lame family. Out of equal parts of love for each other and desperation at our situation, we decided to re-examine the patterns we had been living by, and starting again from scratch, to define our roles for ourselves.

We began by agreeing to share completely all responsibility for raising our children (by then aged five and seven) and caring for our household. If this new arrangement meant that my husband would have to change his job or that I would have to do more free-lance work or that we would have to live on a different scale, then we would. It would be worth it if it could make us once again equal, independent and loving as we had been when we were first married.

Simply agreeing verbally to share domestic duties didn't work, despite our best intentions. And when we tried to divide them "spontaneously" we ended up following traditional patterns. Our old habits were too deep-rooted. So we sat down and drew up a formal agreement, acceptable to both of us, that clearly defined the responsibilities we each had.

It may sound a bit formal, but it has worked for us. Here it is:

MARRIAGE AGREEMENT

I. Principles

We reject the notion that the work which brings in more money is more valuable. The ability to earn more money is a privilege which must not be compounded by enabling a larger earner to buy out of his/her duties and put the burden either on the partner who earns less or on another person hired from outside.

We believe that each partner has an equal right to his/her own time, work, value, choices. As long as all duties are performed, each of us may use his/her extra time any way he/she chooses. If he/she wants to use it making money, fine. If he/she wants to spend it with spouse, fine. If not, fine.

As parents we believe we must share all responsibility for taking care of our children and home—not only the work but also the responsibility. At least during the first year of this agreement, *sharing responsibility* shall mean dividing the *jobs* and dividing the *time*.

In principle, jobs should be shared equally, 50-50, but deals may be made by mutual agreement. If jobs and schedule are divided on any other than a 50-50 basis, then at any time either party may call for a re-examination and redistribution of jobs or a revision of the schedule. Any deviation from 50-50 must be for the convenience of both parties. If one party works overtime in any domestic job, he/she must be compensated by equal extra work by the other. The schedule may be flexible, but changes must be formally agreed upon. The terms of this agreement are rights and duties, not privileges and favors.

II. Job Breakdown and Schedule

A) Children

1. *Mornings:* Waking children; getting their clothes out; making their lunches; seeing that they have notes, homework, money, bus passes, books; brushing their hair; giving them breakfast (making coffee for us). Every other week each parent does all.

2. *Transportation:* Getting children to and from lessons, doctors, dentists (including making appointments), friends' houses, park, parties, movies, libraries. Parts occurring between 3 and 6 P.M. fall to wife. She must be compensated by extra work from husband (see 10 below). Husband does all weekend transportation and pickups after 6.

3. *Help:* Helping with homework, personal problems, projects like cooking, making gifts, experiments, planting; answering questions; explaining things. Parts occurring between 3 and 6 P.M. fall to wife. After 6 P.M. husband does Tuesday, Thursday, and Sunday; wife does Monday, Wednesday, and Saturday. Friday is free for whoever has done extra work during the week.

4. *Nighttime (after 6 P.M.):* Getting children to take baths, brush their teeth, put away their toys and clothes, go to bed; reading with them; tucking them in and having nighttime talks; handling if they wake or call in the night. Husband does Tuesday, Thursday, and Sunday. Wife does Monday, Wednesday, and Saturday. Friday is split according to who has done extra work during the week.

5. *Baby sitters:* Getting baby sitters (which sometimes takes an hour of phoning). Baby sitters must be called by the parent the sitter is to replace. If no sitter turns up, that parent must stay home.

6. *Sick care:* Calling doctors; checking symptoms; getting prescriptions filled; remembering to give medicine; taking days off to stay home with sick child; providing special activities. This must still be worked out equally, since now wife seems to do it all. (The same goes for the now frequently declared school closings for so-called political protest, whereby the mayor gets credit at the expense of the mothers of young children. The mayor closes only the schools, not the places of business or the government offices.) In any case, wife must be compensated (see 10 below).

7. Weekends: All usual child care, plus special activities (beach, park, zoo). Split equally. Husband is free all Saturday, wife is free all Sunday.

B) Housework

8. Cooking: Breakfast; dinner (children, parents, guests). Breakfasts during the week are divided equally; husband does all weekend breakfasts (including shopping for them and dishes). Wife does all dinners except Sunday nights. Husband does Sunday dinner and any other dinners on his nights of responsibility if wife isn't home. Whoever invites guests does shopping, cooking and dishes; if both invite them, split work.

9. Shopping. Food for all meals, housewares, clothing and supplies for children. Divide by convenience. Generally, wife does local daily food shopping; husband does special shopping for supplies and children's things.

10. Cleaning: Dishes daily; apartment weekly, bi-weekly, or monthly. Husband does dishes Tuesday, Thursday and Sunday. Wife does Monday, Wednesday and Saturday. Friday is split according to who has done extra work during week. Husband does all the house cleaning in exchange for wife's extra child care (3 to 6 daily) and sick care.

11. Laundry: Home laundry; making beds; dry cleaning (take and pick up). Wife does home laundry. Husband does dry cleaning delivery and pickup. Wife strips beds. Husband remakes them.

*   *   *

Our agreement changed our lives. Surprisingly, once we had written it down, we had to refer to it only two or three times. But we still had to work to keep the old habits from intruding. If it was my husband's night to take care of the children, I had to be careful not to check up on how he was managing. And if the baby sitter didn't show up for him, I would have to remember it was *his* problem.

Eventually, the agreement entered our heads, and now, after two successful years of following it, we find that our new roles come to us as readily as the old ones had. I willingly help my husband clean the apartment (knowing it is his responsibility) and he often helps me with the laundry or the meals. We work together and trade off duties with ease now that the responsibilities are truly shared. We each have less work, more hours together and less resentment.

Before we made our agreement I had never been able to find the time to finish even one book. Over the past two years I've written three children's books, a biography and a novel and edited a collection of writings (all will have been published by spring of 1972). Without our agreement I would never have been able to do this.

At present my husband works a regular 40-hour week, and I write at home during the six hours the children are in school. He earns more money now than I do, so his salary covers more of our expenses than the money I make with my free-lance work. But if either of us should change jobs, working hours or income, we would probably adjust our agreement.

Perhaps the best testimonial of all to our marriage is the change that has taken place in our family life. One day after it had been in effect for only four months our daughter said to my husband, "You know, Daddy, I used to love Mommy more than you, but now I love you both the same."

Baker v. Nelson

Supreme Court of Minnesota, en banc, 1971.
291 Minn. 310, 191 N.W.2d 185, appeal dismissed 409 U.S. 810 (1972).

PETERSON, JUSTICE.

The questions for decision are whether a marriage of two persons of the same sex is authorized by state statutes and, if not, whether state authorization is constitutionally compelled.

Petitioners, Richard John Baker and James Michael McConnell, both adult male persons, made application to respondent, Gerald R. Nelson, clerk of Hennepin County District Court, for a marriage license, pursuant to Minn.St. 517.08. Respondent declined to issue the license on the sole ground that petitioners were of the same sex, it being undisputed that there were otherwise no statutory impediments to a heterosexual marriage by either petitioner.

The trial court, quashing an alternative writ of mandamus, ruled that respondent was not required to issue a marriage license to petitioners and specifically directed that a marriage license not be issued to them. This appeal is from those orders. We affirm.

1. Petitioners contend, first, that the absence of an express statutory prohibition against same-sex marriages evinces a legislative intent to authorize such marriages. We think, however, that a sensible reading of the statute discloses a contrary intent.

Minn.St. c. 517, which governs "marriage," employs that term as one of common usage, meaning the state of union between persons of the opposite sex.[1] It is unrealistic to think that the original draftsmen of our marriage statutes, which date from territorial days, would have used the term in any different sense. The term is of contemporary significance as well, for the present statute is replete with words of heterosexual import such as "husband and wife" and "bride and groom" (the latter words inserted by L.1969, c. 1145, § 3, subd. 3).

We hold, therefore, that Minn.St. c. 517 does not authorize marriage between persons of the same sex and that such marriages are accordingly prohibited.

2. Petitioners contend, second, that Minn.St. c. 517, so interpreted, is unconstitutional. There is a dual aspect to this contention: The prohibition of a same-sex marriage denies petitioners a fundamental right guaranteed by the Ninth Amendment to the United States Constitution, argu-

ably made applicable to the states by the Fourteenth Amendment, and petitioners are deprived of liberty and property without due process and are denied the equal protection of the laws, both guaranteed by the Fourteenth Amendment.[2]

These constitutional challenges have in common the assertion that the right to marry without regard to the sex of the parties is a fundamental right of all persons and that restricting marriage to only couples of the opposite sex is irrational and invidiously discriminatory. We are not independently persuaded by these contentions and do not find support for them in any decisions of the United States Supreme Court.

The institution of marriage as a union of man and woman, uniquely involving the procreation and rearing of children within a family, is as old as the book of Genesis. Skinner v. Oklahoma ex. rel. Williamson, 316 U.S. 535, 541 (1942), which invalidated Oklahoma's Habitual Criminal Sterilization Act on equal protection grounds, stated in part: "Marriage and procreation are fundamental to the very existence and survival of the race." This historic institution manifestly is more deeply founded than the asserted contemporary concept of marriage and societal interests for which petitioners contend. The due process clause of the Fourteenth Amendment is not a charter for restructuring it by judicial legislation.

Griswold v. Connecticut, 381 U.S. 479 (1965), upon which petitioners rely, does not support a contrary conclusion. A Connecticut criminal statute prohibiting the use of contraceptives by married couples was held invalid, as violating the due process clause of the Fourteenth Amendment. The basic premise of that decision, however, was that the state, having authorized marriage, was without power to intrude upon the right of privacy inherent in the marital relationship. Mr. Justice Douglas, author of the majority opinion, wrote that this criminal statute "operates directly on an intimate relation of husband and wife," 381 U.S. 482, and that the very idea of its enforcement by police search of "the sacred precincts of marital bedrooms for telltale signs of the use of contraceptives * * * is repulsive to the notions of privacy surrounding the marriage relationship," 381 U.S. 485. In a separate opinion for three justices, Mr. Justice Goldberg similarly abhorred this state disruption of "the traditional relation of the family—a relation as old and as fundamental as our entire civilization." 381 U.S. 496.[3]

The equal protection clause of the Fourteenth Amendment, like the due process clause, is not offended by the state's classification of persons authorized to marry. There is no irrational or invidious discrimination. Petitioners note that the state does not impose upon heterosexual married couples a condition that they have a proved capacity or declared willingness to procreate, posing a rhetorical demand that this court must read such condition into the statute if same-sex marriages are to be prohibited. Even assuming that such a condition would be neither unrealistic nor offensive under the Griswold rationale, the classification is no more than theoretically imperfect. We are reminded, however, that "abstract symmetry" is not demanded by the Fourteenth Amendment.[4]

Loving v. Virginia, 388 U.S. 1 (1967), upon which petitioners additionally rely, does not militate against this conclusion. Virginia's antimiscegenation statute, prohibiting interracial marriages, was invalidated solely on the grounds of its patent racial discrimination. As Mr. Chief Justice Warren wrote for the court (388 U.S. 12):

> "Marriage is one of the 'basic civil rights of man,' fundamental to our very existence and survival. Skinner v. Oklahoma, 316 U.S. 535 (1942). See also Maynard v. Hill, 125 U.S. 190 (1888). To deny this fundamental freedom on so unsupportable a basis as the racial classifications embodied in these statutes, classifications so directly subversive of the principle of equality at the heart of the Fourteenth Amendment, is surely to deprive all the State's citizens of liberty without due process of law. The Fourteenth Amendment requires that the freedom of choice to marry not be restricted by invidious racial discrimination."

Loving does indicate that not all state restrictions upon the right to marry are beyond reach of the Fourteenth Amendment. But in commonsense and in a constitutional sense, there is a clear distinction between a marital restriction based merely upon race and one based upon the fundamental difference in sex.

We hold, therefore, that Minn.St. c. 517 does not offend the First, Eighth, Ninth, or Fourteenth Amendments to the United States Constitution.

Affirmed.

NOTES

1. Webster's Third New International Dictionary (1966) p. 1384 gives this primary meaning to marriage: "1 a: the state of being united to a person of the opposite sex as husband or wife." Black, Law Dictionary (4 ed.) p. 1123 states this definition: "Marriage * * * is the civil status, condition, or relation of one man and one woman united in law for life, for the discharge to each other and the community of the duties legally incumbent on those whose association is founded on the distinction of sex."

2. We dismiss without discussion petitioner's additional contentions that the statute contravenes the First Amendment and Eighth Amendment of the United States Constitution.

3. The difference between the majority opinion of Mr. Justice Douglas and the concurring opinion of Mr. Justice Goldberg was that the latter wrote extensively concerning this right of marital privacy as one preserved to the individual by the Ninth Amendment. He stopped short, however, of an implication that the Ninth Amendment was made applicable against the states by the Fourteenth Amendment.

4. See, Patsone v. Pennsylvania, 232 U.S. 138, 144 (1914). As stated in Tigner v. Texas, 310 U.S. 141, 147 (1940), and reiterated in Skinner v. Oklahoma ex rel. Williamson, 316 U.S. 535, 540, "[t]he Constitution does not require things which are different in fact or opinion to be treated in law as though they were the same."

The Division of Labor in Marriage

The Family Myth of the Traditional:
Frank and Carmen Delacorte
Arlie Hochschild, with Ann Machung

As he begins his interview with me, Frank Delacorte is speaking from his personal chair, a lounger with armrests and a footrest that extends when he leans back. In this modest living room, it is the only chair with armrests. Some men I interviewed sat in chairs turned closely toward the television set, suggesting a desire for solitary retreat and recovery. Frank's chair faced outward toward the room, suggesting membership, its size and prominence suggesting authority. It is the centerpiece of the room, the provider's chair. I am seated on the sofa, tape recorder beside me, interviewing a man who, as it was to turn out, holds more traditional views on men and women than Evan Holt, but who does more work at home with far less struggle.

Frank is a slender man of twenty-nine with long, ropey muscles in his arms, neatly groomed dark hair, and thoughtful brown eyes. In a modest but deliberate way, he describes himself and his marriage: "I look at myself as pretty much of a traditionalist. It's the way I am inside. I feel the man should be the head of the house. He should have the final say. I don't think he should have the *only* say; my father was the head but a lot of times my mother got her way. But I feel like this is my role in life, and I don't see any reason to want to change it." He pauses and gives a modest but not apologetic shrug of the shoulders. He has chosen his words slowly—as if saying something so fundamental it is normally beyond words.

Franks earns $12,000 a year gluing together the pressboard sides of boxes in a factory. Pressboard isn't the real wood he loves to work with. He dislikes the powerful smell of chemicals in the glue and worries whether they might be hazardous. By trade, he says, he is a cabinetmaker, but when his father-in-law's small cabinetmaking business where he had worked failed, Frank was forced into factory work. Though he was scanning the want ads these days for a better paying job, and had even interviewed for one on a lunch hour, nothing had come through. But his marriage was happy, he thanked God. He has been married for six years to Carmen, now in the bedroom watching a love story on television.

The third of six children in a Nicaraguan working-class family, Frank had moved often, as a child, with his mother and siblings to be near his father, a merchant seaman who worked out of various port cities. He remembers his mother and father—he describes them jointly as "they"—as "stern" and "somewhat cold." He doesn't want to complain, but he feels there had not been enough affection to go around. He considers carefully whether he has the right to complain—because his parents had had a hard life, too—but he tentatively concludes that he wished it had not felt as cold growing up in their home. He wanted to establish a warmer family, and with his marriage to Carmen, he already had.

Frank Delacorte held to the views of most other working-class men I interviewed. Middle-class men often expected their wives to "help" support the family while they themselves expected to "help" at home; and they often supported their wives' work, often thought it was "good for her," and a woman's "right if she wanted it." Middle-class men often saw themselves as "equal" partners playing slightly "different roles." Although their higher salaries gave them greater potential power, it was a point of male honor not to press this economic advantage, not to talk about it, just to have it. Some would occasionally crack jokes about keeping the wife "barefoot and pregnant," or commanding her to "fetch my pipe and slippers," their jokes consolidating the fact that women's oppression was a matter of history.

In contrast, for Frank and many working-class men, there was a different language, of "letting my wife work." For him, it was a point of male honor to show loving consideration toward one whom God had given a subordinate role in marriage. Because the Delacortes needed Carmen's income to live on, Frank actually held less economic power than most middle-class men. Nonetheless, or perhaps because of this, both Delacortes wanted Frank to be "the man of the house," and to have the "final say" over whether Carmen worked. These days, Frank's traditional ideal was too "expensive" for his pocketbook.

Frank did not link his desire to be "the man of the house" with the need to compensate for racial discrimination, a link I sensed in a few other interviews with minority men. Had Frank been Irish or German, rather than Latino, he might have had a better crack at a union job. Most of his coworkers in the nonunion, low-paid jobs at the box factory were Latino. But Frank did not require his relationship with Carmen to make up for racial injustice.

Frank had anticipated a conflict between his pocketbook and his traditionalism even before he married Carmen. With some effort to be candid, he explained:

> I wasn't that ready to get married. Actually, at that time I was feeling inadequate, since I didn't have the kind of job I wanted to have yet. I guess I'm not the most ambitious person in the world [light, nervous laugh]. Yeah, Carmen was much

more anxious to get married than I was. I was really very hesitant for awhile. I felt I might disappoint her, probably financially. Carmen was working at the time. She told me, "If you add our salaries together, really there's plenty to live on. Between the two of us, we shouldn't have any trouble." And that was true! I finally gave in. She really asked me to marry her, rather than me asking her [light laugh].

Frank would marry Carmen when she wanted to marry and she would accept her need to work with good grace, even though she wanted to stay home and be a "milk and cookies mom." The compromise did not take place after the marriage, as it did with the Holts, but before their marriage, as a premise of it. The compromise was not, as it was for the Holts, between a husband's gender ideology and his wife's. The Delacortes agreed on that. Their compromise was between a traditional ideal they shared, on one hand, and a pocketbook too thin to permit them to realize it on the other.

So from the beginning, it was understood that if the fickle fluctuations of the market in wood cabinets made Frank lose his job or take a cut in pay, Carmen would not blame these things on Frank; they would face them together. More important, Frank's inability to earn all the money—to be "male" in that way—would also not be *his* moral burden alone. Carmen would not, like some traditional wives, assume the right to resent having to work. Carmen had a sister-in-law and a cousin, both working mothers, who did resent "having" to work and they made life miserable for their husbands because of it. Not Carmen; to her, the deal was: "We'll need my salary but I won't rub it in." Like most middle-class feminists, Nancy Holt had *wanted* to work, and felt she *should want* to work. It had never occurred to her to reserve a right to resent *having* to work; she insisted on a different right: that she be honored in leisure out of deference for her legitimate career, that her career be considered her work. But Carmen felt strongly that the only "real" work was at home. Having divergent views about womanhood, Nancy and Carmen also held to different notions of what were the right and wrong feelings to have about work or childrearing. And they held different ideas about the proper psychological gifts between a husband and wife.

The two women had opposing "feeling rules." Carmen thought she should dislike her work and feel it as unimportant. Nancy thought she should enjoy her work and find it important. Carmen felt she should feel grateful for whatever extra help Frank gave around the house; Nancy considered 50 percent of the second shift as Evan's rightful job and found it hard to feel grateful for any less.

Carmen, twenty-nine, a pretty, black-haired, heavy-set daycare worker, spoke to me with a spirited voice and dancing hands. She wanted me to know that she did *not* work because she *wanted* to. That was a point of pride. As she explained: "The only reason I'm working is that every time I go to the grocery store the bill is twenty dollars more. I'm not working to develop myself. I'm not working to discover my identity. No way!" She wasn't *that* kind of woman, the new kind, the kind who's off seeking her real self in some office on the thirtieth floor of some high-rise. Ironically, although Carmen didn't want to like her work, she rather did. She chuckled with obvious enjoyment as she described each child she cared for. A few professional women illustrated the opposite dilemma. One struggling feminist writer despondently confessed, "I *want* to love my work, but at the moment I hate it." Ironically, it was a blessing that Carmen *had* to work; she got to enjoy her work even when she wasn't "supposed to."

Carmen referred to her job as a daycare worker as a "business I run out of my home," not to be confused with "being a baby-sitter." Like every daycare worker and baby-sitter I interviewed, Carmen was painfully aware of the low esteem in which the women in America who tend children are held. (I had come to interview her first as the baby-sitter of a two-job couple in the study, but discovering that she and Frank were also a two-job couple, I asked if I could interview them on that account as well.) When I came to her door for our first interview, and explained the project, her first comment was "They don't think you're anything if you're a baby-sitter." For women in more "male" and middle-class occupations, this issue of self esteem didn't arise.

Frank tried to save his pride by explaining to people that Carmen was "really at home." This was not exactly a myth, but it was a slightly misleading way of describing the situation. Sometimes the company he kept made him want to use this phrase. One notch above him in social class, Frank's foreman, Bill, could afford to keep his wife home and to tout the correctness of doing so with a certain cutting conviction. Frank drove to work with Bill every day, and next to rising prices, the topic of women came up most often. Frank coughed and explained with some unease: "We were talking about needing extra money, and I told him about the business that Carmen has, and I said, 'You know, you've got a house. Your wife could have a business like Carmen's. It's not too bad.' His attitude was 'No! No! No! I don't want anybody to say she's taking care of children.' He feels he lives the way most people should live—the husband working, the wife at home." Frank believed that Bill opposed the idea of his wife working not because it was too low for her, but because it was too low for *him*. It would rob him of the one luxury that distinguished a foreman from a worker—the domestic services of a full-time wife. I asked Frank how he felt about his foreman's remark and he said, "I felt put down. Yeah, I definitely felt he put me down."

While she cared for their own year-old child, Delia, Carmen earned about $5,000 a year providing daycare for four two-year-old children of neighboring mothers who worked. She was one of the many women who have become part of an emergent female "underclass" of daycare workers, baby-sitters, maids, au pairs, and companions for the elderly—who accomplish for little pay and status the work performed in a bygone era by the woman of the house. Ironically, it was this declining role of housewife that Carmen, lacking other options, aspired to fill. She, too, was proud to work "at home." Frank never denied that she earned money working at home. But saying "Carmen was home" helped him preserve a notion of himself as provider, as head of the household that was, these days, harder and harder to keep up.

Carmen was an ardent traditionalist. (One woman in my study was so eager to be the traditional wife that she "tried" to get pregnant "by accident" so she could drop out of college and marry, had the word "obey" put back into her marriage ceremony, worked "because my husband told me to," dressed mainly in pink, and named her cat "Pretty Kitty." But even this woman's traditionalism was less ardent than Carmen's.) Carmen very much looked up to Nancy Reagan and very much down on Gloria Steinem. Even within her Catholic, Latino working-class culture of women trapped in low-paid, dead-end jobs, she was far more deeply convinced of her desire to stay home and submit to her husband. Women in her position often wished they worked shorter hours, at better jobs and pay, but most such women nonetheless *did* want to work. Only 10 percent of women in this study could be counted as "traditional" in the sense of not wanting to ever work, although I suspect the numbers nationwide are larger. What so *appealed* to Carmen about being a "traditional woman" was being subordinate to Frank. As Carmen told me excitedly: "I *don't want* to be equal with Frank. I don't want to be equal in work. I want to be feminine. I want to have frilly things. I don't want to compete with men! Heck! I don't want to do what my husband's doing. Let him do it. Maybe that's it—I want to be taken care of."

Carmen further explained: "I want Frank to know more than I do. I don't want my children to be brought up thinking, 'Oh, Mom knows it all, and Dad's just a painting on the wall.' I take pride in Frank knowing more. Maybe that's wrong, but I take pride in it."

A bright but uninspired student in high school, Carmen had gone no farther, but had followed a narrow path of clerical jobs from which daycare seemed a welcome relief. She considered her lack of higher education as a virtue, for she thought it made her inferior to Frank—who "knew more" even though he also had ended his education with a high school diploma. Carmen applied the same principle in bed: the more Frank knew, the more dominant he was, the better. She said: "I don't want to be his equal in bed. I want him to dominate me! I don't want to dominate him. I don't want to say, 'Hey, this is the way you make love to me.'"

Carmen thought that dominating women were committing a serious sin—right up there with homicide and child abuse. One dangerous avenue to female dominance, she felt, was a successful career. Pursing her lips in disgust she told me of an "overly" ambitious sister-in-law who got a Ph.D. in veterinary science—"a Ph.D. in bullshit," she hissed—and as a consequence bossed people around and never married.

Carmen disliked ambitious women partly because she felt they were pushing her kind of women out of style. It was bad enough that rising prices were forcing women out of their homes; what was worse, the daytime soap operas on television she followed avidly while the children took afternoon naps were featuring selfish career women who stole the allure from domestic-minded women. Today, Carmen's kind of women were being portrayed as overweight, depressed, abandoned—as losers. Women who believed in being a housewife were the latest endangered species. Career-minded women were taking over everywhere. She saw the women's movement as an upper-class fad. As Carmen put it, "Betty Ford is for women's liberation, right? But has she mopped the floor yet? Beautiful nails, face lift, hair done, and I'm there nails broken, hair a mess, and I'm thinking, sure, lady, tell me all about it. . . . Instead of parading around, Gloria Steinem should sit down and watch a soap opera. They tell you the way it really is. She should take off her rose-colored glasses and really look."

On the basis of these views it might at first seem that, by temperament, Carmen was a dependent person. But the truth was Carmen *believed* in female dependence. It was part of her gender ideology. She actively, strategically *pursued* it. This was probably because she feared that without some cultural constraint—like the ideal of a woman as wilting violet—she could end up dominating Frank. Carmen reminded me of a student of mine who spoke up a great deal in class, pursued me relentlessly after lectures and in office hours, pressed me to change the "B plus" on her term paper to an "A"—but, when asked about the kind of relationship she hoped to have with her boyfriend, said in a little girl voice, "I want to fit in the palm of my boyfriend's hand, like Thumbelina."

Why did Carmen hold *this* view of the sexes and not some other? Part of the reason was economic. I think it worked like this: in young adulthood, she matched her qualifications with the real world—no college, no typing experience, and few interesting, well-paid jobs out there for women without these. As she explained in exasperation: "I'm not prepared to go out and sit on my butt and be a secretary. I know how to type, but not fifty words a minute. What am I going to do? *Scrub floors*? I should have prepared for such a career [typing] but I didn't, okay? My mother gave me a good education but I didn't take advantage of it. It's my fault, okay? But I'm not on welfare and I'm not on food stamps. I'm trying to help my husband." Carmen couldn't support herself alone without dropping into poverty; better to support herself through marriage. If her husband needed her to work, fine. That's how it was for families these days.

Curiously, several other high school–educated women in this study who were equally trapped in low-paid clerical or sales jobs did want a job they could identify with, and wanted a husband who didn't dominate them and who shared the work at home. Lack of job opportunities didn't totally predict women's views on gender.

A more internal motive seemed to be involved as well. Like Nancy Holt, Carmen wanted to avoid the fate of her mother. If Nancy Holt became a feminist partly in response to her mother's self-belittling response to her life as a housewife, Carmen Delacorte may have become a traditionalist in response to her mother's hard life as an "independent woman." Her mother was a model of a self-made career woman, but to Carmen she was a *dangerous* model. Carmen's mother was a spunky, gifted woman who married at eighteen, got pregnant at twenty, and divorced at twenty-two. The marriage, as Carmen learned from her mother, had been a disaster. Her father never sent child support and called Carmen for the first time in thirty years the day he died of cancer, to ask forgiveness. Carmen described her mother's situation with empathy: "In that society, when a woman becomes divorced or a widow, there is nothing else to do except 'dress the saints' [put clothes on the statues of saints in the church on holidays] for the rest of your life. You don't get married. You don't date. When my mother got divorced, she was a young woman, so her father started to run her life."

Alone with her baby, Carmen's mother ventured to the United States working her way up from assistant file clerk to file clerk to junior auditor and senior auditor in an expanding insurance company. The two lived in a tiny apartment with two other divorced Latino women and their children, until Carmen's mother got remarried (when Carmen was sixteen) to a cabinetmaker who drank too much.

Reflecting on how she would have fared in her mother's situation, Carmen visibly recoiled. *"I would never want my mother's life! Never, never!* I don't think I could be like my mom because my mom didn't have anybody to fall back on."

Gloria Steinem would have drawn entirely different lessons from the struggles of a single mother (and in fact did). The trials of Carmen's mother would have seemed text-book examples of why society should finally prevent wife battery, discourage the double standard, and ensure that divorced men continue to support their children financially and emotionally. But sizing up her personal situation carefully and lacking confidence, Carmen drew a cautionary lesson from her mother's life: don't go out on your own. If her mother had only *submitted* more to her husband, hidden her intelligence, checked her initiative, maybe Carmen's father would have stayed. The equation seemed to be this: it's a cold world for women outside of marriage. So a woman has to marry. If she is to succeed in marriage, she can't be the dominant type. To avoid dominance, she should try to feel subordinate, and if she can, she should project an image that is delicate, fragile, and unburdened by much knowledge. If Carmen could manage to feel or to seem this way, she seems to have reasoned, Frank would always stay. For her, women were by nature as likely to be bright and powerful as men; but it was their duty as women to press their natural personality and I.Q. into the "wilting violet" mold. For her, female subordination was not sexism. It was a *shield* against the sexism a single woman like her mother can face.

Once established, certain things followed from Carmen's gender ideology. One had to do with her relationship with Frank, the other with the second shift. Given her perception of her resources and opportunities, a traditional version of womanhood took on great appeal for her. According to her gender ideology Carmen should be demure, soft-spoken, sweet, passive, and quiet. But, in fact, Carmen had the "wrong" personality for her gender ideology; most of the time she was loud, colorful, engaging, active, willful, and bright. In her occasional heated discussions with Frank, neighbors in the apartment below could hear Carmen's loud voice rising with rhetorical flourish, falling, and coursing through long explanations of something. Then they heard Frank's voice: low, mild, appeasing, steady. In the supermarket, Frank politely followed the unspoken traffic rules of shopping-cart traffic, but Carmen bumped carts that blocked her way. She sometimes took the offensive in family quarrels. She had, for example, pushed Frank to "stand up for himself," when his father chided him for giving up a "promising" job he once had as a bank clerk. But the morning of the day after such occasions, she scolded herself for doing it.

In her youth, she had, as she said, "driven a boyfriend away." She told me: "I had a boyfriend everybody loved, and we thought we were going to marry. But I was awfully dominating. He left me and I always thought he would come back, but he didn't. Mother *always says, 'Don't forget William.'*"

Married life after the first three years was harmonious between Carmen and Frank, but they had one telling showdown. One day, Frank was complaining that Carmen had shown poor judgment in making a payment on a new chair (which could wait) before paying the rent (which could not). According to Carmen, "Frank said to me, 'Since I'm making the most money, I can make most of the decisions.' I said, 'What?! Wait a minute! What?!!' I said, 'Forget it! Just because you're making more money doesn't mean anything. I'm still working.' I told him, 'Do you really believe that?' And he said with a smile, 'Well, not really. I just thought I'd give it a try.'"

All in all, for Frank, the veneer of Carmen's submission would do. He liked Carmen, plucky as she was. Her spunk was no big deal; he wasn't threatened in the least. Getting her personality in line with her ideology was her dilemma, not his.

USING ONE SIDE OF TRADITIONALISM
TO GET AROUND THE OTHER

Carmen wanted to be submissive; that was one side of her traditionalism. She also wanted Frank to earn the bread while she tended the home; that was the second side. When I asked Carmen what she would do with a million dollars, she laughed raffishly and began naming all the pieces of furniture she'd buy and describing the grand apartment house she'd buy for her mother. Then, slowing down, she carefully explained how the money would not affect the *separation* of male and female spheres. She said, "With that kind of money you would have teas, coffees, showers, benefits to go to. Then I'd have the kids over for Kool-Aid. I'd just be a mom." If they had a million dollars, and if Frank didn't have to work, would he stay home? I asked. "Absolutely not! The children would not respect him if he stayed home. He'd hate himself and after a while he'd hate me. And if I didn't want to do the housework, I'd pick on him to do it. At least he should get in the car and play golf for two hours, do *something* outside the house."

But back in the real world a major, practical problem arose: How could Carmen manage all of the second shift? After her first baby was nine months old, Carmen started caring for other children in her home again. Despite her views on women, her needs were no different from those of other working mothers: she desperately needed Frank's help with the work of their household. But this need aroused strongly contradictory feelings.

On one hand, she really *needed* as much help at home as any working mother. On the other hand, the house was supposed to be "her turf." She said she didn't care much about Frank's sharing the second shift—his help might be nice but this sharing was not the great issue feminists were making of it these days. Besides, it might seem dominating of her, she felt, to make him help in the kitchen. Indeed, to the extent that he was *not* in the kitchen, she was proud. When Carmen described their division of housework, it was as if she had to *concede* how much Frank actually helped. She interpreted his involvement in her housework as a failure on her part, and in this respect she differed from the egalitarian women who *boasted* about all their husbands did at home. Carmen described Frank's contribution to shopping, paying the bills, cleaning up, in the manner of a confession: "Okay, Frank and I are equal in the sense that we do some of the housework together." (After saying this, however, she began to talk about the dangers of sexual equality. "Equality" made a wild leap to "competition" and another long leap to antagonism and divorce.)

How was she to manage the contradiction between the desire to keep Frank out of the kitchen and the need to have him in it? First of all, she left her official submissive persona intact by continuing to claim that Frank was "really the boss." But she also "solved" her problem by putting an old female custom to new use: she played helpless. It was a stroke of genius; playing helpless allowed her to remain the submissive wife at the *front* door while also bringing Frank into the kitchen through the *back*. The only cost of this strategy might be the opinion others held of her competence, but that wasn't a problem. She was happy to be seen as helpless. She never asked Frank for help directly, so when he did help, it wasn't because it was his role, but because Carmen couldn't do it. Frank cooked the rice when he got home from work—not because he liked to do it, not because he was especially good at it, but because he could cook the rice better than Carmen could. Frank paid the bills because Carmen paid the wrong ones first. Frank sewed (when Carmen's mother didn't sew for them) because Carmen couldn't sew. Frank worked the automatic teller for Carmen because she "always forgot" the account's code number. Frank drove them on shopping trips because Carmen couldn't drive a car. Responding in this way to one calculated incompetence after another, Frank had come to do nearly half of the second shift. Perhaps Carmen drew the line there, or maybe Frank did. Half would have been unseemly.

According to them, Carmen did "nearly all" of the housework and childcare and Frank "just helped." . . .

A STRATEGY OF INCOMPETENCE

Incompetence was one way to induct traditional men into the second shift. Sickness was another. Carmen has arthritis that "acts up" and prevents her from carrying heavy things. It isn't clear that she "uses" sickness like she uses helplessness. But curiously, other traditional women I talked with seem to get sick more often than egalitarian women. And when they are sick, it follows a certain pattern. Insisting that every task on the second shift is *theirs*, they work heroically until they finally fall ill with exhaustion. *They* don't stop; their illness stops them. Sometimes it's pneumonia, sometimes migraines, a bad back, arthritis. Then their husbands, primed all along to help out in an emergency, "lend a hand." Upon recovering, the woman returns to her double load, plunges full steam ahead, and eventually becomes sick again. Getting sick can have something in common with "getting" incompetent: both are ways of receiving through an indirect strategy (of renegotiating roles) what many egalitarian women receive through a direct strategy—a man's labor in the second shift. The 11 percent of women in this study who reported themselves as traditional all reported being ill more often than their husbands, and more often than other women.

Like many traditional couples, the Delacortes were a curious mixture of old and new. They thought, talked, and felt in traditional ways, but they had to live with the stubborn realities of modern economic life. They aspired to a pattern of male rule, but had backed into a gender democracy. . . .

By discrediting cultural models of female assertion, by strictly confining her tendency to dominate to the "female" sphere, by "remembering William," by raising Frank above her—putting him on a pedestal—Carmen pursued submission as part of a traditional strategy. She squelched her assertion outside the home; she actively magnified any feelings of dependence; these were the psychological moves that kept her soul in line with her strategy.

Their traditionalism fit neither the outer nor the inner realities of their lives. The outer reality was that Frank needed Carmen to earn money and Carmen needed Frank's help with housework and childcare. The inner reality was that Frank was not dominant and Carmen was not submissive. Given the personalities ideal for their ideology, Frank was "too passive," Carmen "too assertive." What contained both contradictions was the family myth that "Frank did little around the house." . . .

A Scarce Economy of Gratitude:
Seth and Jessica Stein

Arlie Hochschild, with Ann Machung

At thirty-six, Seth Stein has been a husband for eleven years, a father for five, a practicing lawyer for eight, and a litigation attorney for the last six. He is tall, with broad, slightly stooped shoulders, and a firm handshake. We sit down for our interview at eight in the evening; normally at this hour, he tells me, he would be unwinding from a ten-hour day, beer in hand, slouched and unmoving in his TV chair, moving his thumb over the buttons of his hand-held remote TV channel control almost randomly. He would have had dinner with his wife and two small children at six-thirty or seven, perched himself on the periphery of his children's activities for three-quarters of an hour, and this, now, would have been the first stretch of time he'd had to himself all day.

His unwinding, I discovered, was usually solitary. Once the children were in bed, his wife, Jessica, who was a lawyer specializing in family law, found herself free at last, and returned to her half-read legal papers, neither joining him in relaxation nor wishing to interfere. ("Sometimes," Seth said later, "I look over the papers in her study and think, 'We're *both* caught up in our professions.'") The living room, with its modern Danish chairs and bright Indian tapestries standing out against white walls, is his private recovery room, a place where he "comes to" after the daily operations of his demanding career. For the first time all day, he takes off his glasses and loosens his tie.

When I ask Seth to describe a typical day, he says:

> I get up at six-thirty. Into the bathroom, shower, get dressed, out of the house by seven-thirty. I might see the kids in passing—"Hi, how are you?" and give a kiss good-bye. Then my morning begins with meetings with my clients, and depending on whether we are in the middle of a big litigation case, I'll meet with the other lawyers on the case, check with the paralegals. I'm at the office until six. I'm generally home by six-thirty at the latest to sit down and have dinner. Then I'll go back at eight or eight-thirty for a few hours. I started coming home for dinner at six-thirty a year ago after realizing I'd missed the first two years of Victor's growing up.

Jessica, a tall, willowy woman of thirty-six, who often dressed in graceful peasant blouses and long floral skirts, had reached that stage in her career, she felt, where she was sure enough of herself as a professional woman that she could abandon the "strong" dark suits she had always worn to work earlier, and still wore in court. She grew up the daughter of a widowed waitress in Texas, and worked her way through the University of Texas law school. But there were few indications of the determination it must have taken to pursue this course of action in the expectant but shy manner with which she approached my questions.

She and Seth had begun marriage intending to honor both law degrees equally. But after many reasonable discussions, Jessica had agreed that Seth's career came first because "litigation law was more demanding." These reasonable discussions did not seem like "moves" in his or her gender strategy, but attempts to "do the best thing" for each person and for the family. Seth was happy about the outcome to these discussions but vaguely unhappy about his marriage. Jessica was unhappy about both.

If Evan Holt resisted his wife's pressure to help at home but gave in on the "upstairs-downstairs" cover story, and if Peter Tanagawa resisted but gave in on his role as the main provider, then Seth Stein resisted and gave up nothing except, very gradually, his wife.

Jessica is one of many women who respond to the exhausting demands of the second shift by trying to induce their husbands to share, and who cope with it when they don't. Nancy Holt tried to sustain her egalitarian identity even as her marriage made it impossible to live up to. Nina Tanagawa, never a "believing feminist," didn't have to do this, but instead coped with the transitional's definition of the family-career problem as "hers." Of the two, Jessica was more like Nancy. She'd begun with an egalitarian dream and had been forced to give it up. Like Nancy, she remained married but, unlike Nancy, Jessica gradually began to detach her feelings from Seth.

Curiously, Seth had none of the traditional man's attitudes toward "women's work." If he'd had the time, he could have done the laundry or sewing without a bit of shame. This was because his manhood was neither confirmed nor denied by what he did at home; what he did at home didn't matter. Instead, his sense of self and of manhood rose and fell with the opinions of his legal community. Loaded as his career was with this meaning for his manhood and self, Seth's career "told" him what he had to do.

Yet, this connection between manhood and career was hard for Seth to see. He actually had little to say about what it meant to "be a man" or about his notion of "manhood." "People are people, that's about it," he would say about these matters. All that occurred to him consciously, it seemed, was how nervous it made him on those rare occasions when he took time off. Meanwhile, fellow lawyers were saying that Seth "had a lot of balls" to break into the fierce competition among lawyers in such a crowded urban market.

While Seth's obsession about his career did not seem desirable to either him or Jessica, it seemed normal and acceptable and had three effects on his family. First, what occurred at the imperial center of his career determined what happened out in the "colony" of his home. Second, although neither of them quite articulated this, Seth's dedication to his career led him to feel he deserved her nurturance more than she deserved his. Because *he* worked the longest hours, and because long hours seemed a manly way of earning nurturance, Seth felt he had "first dibs." Third, his career led him to suppress his emotional attachment to his children, although not his ultimate concern for them. He loved them, but day to day he left it to Jessica to think about what they needed and felt. As he saw it, these were not a result of a gender strategy, but the normal attitudes of a top-notch professional. And actually a gender strategy of resisting the emotional and social work of the second shift *is* built into the very clockwork of male-dominated careers. It is not simply Seth's personal attitudes that are at issue, but the normal hours of work in his office, the calls, the gossip that remind each worker of the overwhelming importance of work to self-esteem, and a whole urgency system based on the exclusion of life at home.

Seth and Jessica had married when they were law students. They share the memory of studying together in the library for exams and being interrupted by a fellow student and friend asking "Shall we go out for Chinese? Italian?" Six years after their marriage, Victor was born, and two years after that, Walter. As with the Tanagawas, the Steins' firstborn strained the couple's energy, but the secondborn provoked a crisis.

Quietly but inexorably a conflict arose between Seth's capitulation to the clockwork of male careers and the enormous demands of his young babies and now-anxious wife. Seth felt Jessica had to handle the second shift. The problem was to prevent her from *resenting* it. To lighten Jessica's resentment, Seth dwelled on his sacrifices of *leisure:* it wasn't so easy to work eleven-hour days. For Jessica, the question was how she could get Seth to want to share. To make a case for sharing the second shift, Jessica focused on the sacrifices she made of her *career:* it wasn't that easy to give up moving ahead in a hard-won career. Their notions of "sacrifice" more and more began to clash. Neither Jessica nor Seth felt anything like gratitude toward the other.

I asked Seth whether he'd ever considered cutting back his ten-hour day while Victor and Walter were young. "It's not a question of what I want," he explained patiently, "I can't. I couldn't share my work with a group of incompetent lawyers just to get a night off. It would blow my reputation! When you come to a desirable area like this, the legal competition is fierce." His conversation moved spontaneously from lawyers who cut back their hours to be with their families to a highly successful lawyer friend of his who one day abandoned law to play second trumpet in a third-rate orchestra, and another friend of his, a brilliant surgeon, who became a cosmetic surgeon at a Beverly Hills "fat farm" for rich socialites. To Seth, these men were spectacular dropouts from their reputable professional establishment, a reminder to Seth of how low a man could fall.

I had begun by asking how he felt about taking time off to be with children, but the topic had slid instead to lawyers who were incompetent and disreputable. Taking time off to be with his child at a play gym seemed to fit into the same mental category in Seth's mind as working at a "fat farm." Both discredited a man's career, and thus the man himself. Both acts cut into a man's good opinion of himself, his source of important compliments. Seth said he didn't know any *good* lawyers who worked reduced hours in order to spend time with their young children: none.

He explained:

> I'd like to get rid of the anxiety I have about being a lawyer. Jessica suggested a long time ago that we could both go into public law. Or we could travel and do things we enjoy. If I could get rid of my anxiety about being a lawyer it would open up a lot of other opportunities. But I *have* to be doing what I am doing. I have to be that guy they turn to when the case is really tough. It's a neurotic drive.

Among his legal colleagues it was almost fashionable to be a "neurotic, hard-driving, Type-A personality" and personally a bit unhappy. Fellow lawyers quietly shared tips about how to resist their wives' pleas that they spend more time at home. Seth told me that one doctor friend had advised, "Promise her you'll take the kids to the zoo this Sunday." Another had said, "I've put my wife off by promising her a four-day vacation this spring." I could imagine these lawyers' wives—Jessica now among them—calling out from the wings, like the chorus in a Greek tragedy, "Your children will only be young once! Young once. Young once . . ." Inside Seth's legal fraternity, the career men sometimes joked about fantasies of taking time off for themselves; but they never talked about it seriously. They talked about it like they talked about cutting out coffee or finally mastering French. Curiously missing from Seth's talk about his long hours was any talk about his children.

Given that his children were so young, why did Seth abdicate to the demands of his career with so little struggle? Why did he have so few serious doubts about it? Perhaps a clue could be found in his boyhood in a highly achievement-oriented Jewish working-class family and neighborhood of New York in the 1950s. He described his sisters as "housewives who weren't brought up to have careers." He described his mother as a housewife and his father as a zealous Russian Jew who threw himself into one cause after another. As he explained, "There was a long period when he would have dinner and then go to a meeting every night. He was the chairman of this and that—Russian war relief, food, clothes to the Russians. Later he was a super-duper Zionist. He was always out there every night."

Even if Seth's childhood had readied him to be an active father (which it had not), even if his legal colleagues had encouraged him (which they did not), in the end it may have been the very unhappiness of his marriage that kept him out of his children's lives. In the meantime, time with them was time-not-doing-law.

In a more internal sense, Seth was frankly addicted to his work. Like a drug addict too hooked really to enjoy a drug, Seth had lost a taste for his work but could see no alternative to working. And since his addiction compensated for something inside, it was also highly rewarding. Seth wanted to see his addiction as a sacrifice to his family. One day when he was feeling especially unappreciated, he burst out to Jessica: "I'm not sailing a yacht. I'm not on the tennis court. I'm not rafting down the Colorado River. I'm not traveling around the world. I'm working my goddamn ass off." But Jessica listened coolly.

JESSICA'S GENDER IDEOLOGY

From the beginning Jessica had been prepared to *balance* her law practice with raising a family. The only legal specialties she seriously considered were those she felt were compatible with taking time for a family; that excluded large firms specializing in corporate law. But she did not want to be marooned in solitary motherhood, as her widowed mother had been while raising her. As she made compromises in her career, she wanted Seth to make them in his.

After their first child, Victor, was born, Jessica established two patterns many women would consider highly desirable "solutions": she cut back her hours at work and she hired a full-time maid. Five years later, when I met her, she would talk cheerfully at dinner parties of having "the best of both worlds"—an adorable three-year-old, a five-year-old, and work she loved. She dropped Victor off at nursery school at nine and went to work. Then she picked him up at noon, gave him lunch, and left him at home with Carmelita, her housekeeper, while she returned to work until five. But there was a certain forced cheer in her account of her day that Seth was the first to explain:

> Jessica has been very disappointed about my inability to do more in terms of the childrearing, and about my not sharing things fifty-fifty. She says I've left the childrearing to her. Her career has suffered. She says she's cut twice as much time from her career as I've cut from mine. She complains that I'm not like some imaginary other men, or men she knows, who take time with their children because they want to and know how important it is. On the other hand, she understands the spot I'm in. So she holds it in until she gets good and pissed off, and then she lets me have it.

Jessica didn't need Seth to help her with housework; Carmelita cleaned the house and even did the weekend dishes on Mondays. Jessica didn't need Seth for routine care of their children either; Carmelita did that, too. But Jessica badly wanted Seth to get more emotionally involved with the children and with her. Even if he couldn't be home, she wanted him to *want* to be. In the meantime, she felt oppressed by his dominating absence. . . .

A SCARCITY OF GRATITUDE

The Steins' different views about their responsibilities at home led them to want to be appreciated, and to appreciate each other in ways that did not correspond. Seth wanted Jessica to identify with his ambition, enjoy the benefits of it—his large salary, their position in the community—and to accept gracefully his unavoidable absence from home. The truth was, Jessica did understand the pressures of his work as only a fellow lawyer could. But he didn't seem to want to be home, and he wasn't. For her part, Jessica wanted to be appreciated for the sacrifices she made in her career, and for her mothering. She worked twenty-five hours a week now, fifteen billable hours, but had been keen to develop a larger family law practice, and perhaps write a book about it.

Seth ignored this sacrifice—indeed, was it a sacrifice? Wouldn't a twenty-five-hour-a-week job be *nice?* He was also too tired at the end of the day to notice much of Jessica's contribution to home and children. . . .

THE NURTURANCE CRUNCH

The Steins' misunderstanding over gifts led to a scarcity of gratitude, and the scarcity of gratitude led to a dearth of small gestures of caring, especially from Jessica to Seth. Increasingly, they were feeling out of touch. When I asked Seth what he was not getting from Jessica that he had expected, he replied in a surprising way, slipping in and out of lower-class grammar:

> Nurturing. She don't take care of me enough. But the deal was so straightforward from day one that I'm not bitter. But when I do reflect on it, that's the thing I reflect on: I ain't got a wife taking care of me. Every once in a while I'll be upset about it and long for someone who might be sitting around waiting to make me comfortable when I get home. Instead, Jessica needs her back massaged just as much as I do. No, she don't take care of my MCP needs—which I can't help having, growing up in this kind of society. I'm just a victim of society—so I can have those needs and not feel guilty. I just can't express them!

Why the sudden ungrammatical English? Did he mean to make a joke? To mock himself? Or perhaps he was conveying a feeling there was something *wrong* with him for wanting what he wanted. And was he not guilty? With a neat little acronym—MCP (male chauvinist pig)—he was summing up the accusations he felt Jessica might throw at him for insisting on his terms of appreciation, his gender ideology.

From time to time, Seth fantasized about having the "right" kind of wife—Jessica without the career motivation, but if not her, someone else. When I asked him, later in our interview, if he ever wished that Jessica didn't work, he shot back: "Yes!" Did he feel guilty for wishing that, I asked. "No!" He wanted Jessica the person and he felt willing and able to appreciate her enormously, on his terms.

In the meantime, each one felt unappreciated and angry: Seth's acquiescence to career demands that left no emotional energy for his children angered Jessica. Jessica's withholding of nurturance angered Seth. Now they avoided each other because they were so angry. The less Seth was around, the less they would face their anger.

WEARING MOTHERHOOD LIGHTLY

Eventually Jessica accepted Seth's long hours and more whole-heartedly colluded in the idea that he was the helpless captive of his profession and his neurotic personality. This was her cover story. But as she did this, she made another emotional move—away from the marriage and family. She did not bolt from motherhood into a workaholism of her own, as some women I interviewed did. But neither did she embrace motherhood. Instead, she wore it lightly. She bought new educational games for Walter and she helped Victor with his piano lessons. But there was a certain mildness in her manner, an absence of talk about the children, an animation when she spoke of times she was away from them that suggested this "solution" of halfheartedness.

If Seth's unconscious move was to remove himself in body and spirit from his children, Jessica's move was to be there in body, but not much in spirit. She would accommodate his strategy on the surface but limit her emotional offerings underneath—give some nurturance to the children, little to Seth, and save the rest for herself, her "separate life."

GETTING HELP

This took some arranging. Jessica had had a history of bad experience with help. First she'd hired a nanny who was a wonderful baby-sitter but refused to do anything else, like pick up toys or occasionally wash breakfast dishes. (Often nannies who were citizens and English-speaking had more exacting standards than illegal aliens.) So Jessica hired a housekeeper to do the housecleaning. Then the two began to quarrel, each calling Jessica at work to complain about the other. At first, Jessica tried to unravel the problem, but she ended up firing the housekeeper. Then she hired a wonderful but overqualified woman for the job, who left after three months. Now she had Carmelita, an El Salvadoran mother of two, who worked at two jobs in order to support her family and send money back home to her aging parents. Carmelita did this by arranging for her sixteen-year-old daughter Filipa to cover for her mornings in the Stein household while Carmelita worked her other job.

Because neither Carmelita nor Filipa could drive a car, Jessica hired Martha, an old high school friend, as an "extra driver-housekeeper." Martha shopped, took Victor to classes, and did Jessica's typing and bookkeeping. Jessica also hired a gardener. Beyond that, she hired another "helper," Bill, a nineteen-year-old student at a local junior college, as a "father substitute." He played ball with Victor, age five, and in general did "daddy-type things." Jessica felt this was necessary for Victor because "Victor suffers the most from Seth's absence." Bill, a cheerful and reasonable young man, had a cheerful and reasonable girl friend who sometimes stayed overnight. It was Bill's barbells that Seth tripped over in the hallway and Bill's girl friend's sweater that sometimes lay on the kitchen table. Sensing that Bill was a "bought father," Victor chose to treat him "just like my brother. He can go with us everywhere." On Saturday afternoons, Jessica wrote checks to pay Carmelita and Filipa; Martha; Bill; the gardener; and other occasional helpers such as plumbers, tree trimmers, and tax accountants.

When I remarked to Jessica that she seemed to have quite a bit of help, she replied, "Well if you want to have children and have a career, I can't think of any other way to do it except to live in a foreign country and have tons of people taking care of you." . . .

Jessica had now completely given up on Seth. Indeed, three years after our first interview, when I asked her again how she felt about Seth's being home so little, she answered with assurance: "Partly it works out so well for me this way because Seth doesn't demand much from me. I don't have to do anything for him. He takes care of himself. Other husbands might do more for the kids, but they would also ask more of me." When I asked what she wanted from her husband, she expressed surprise: "What do I want from him? I think he should let me do what I want to do. Go to New York, Washington, conferences."

A politics of emotional absenteeism had set in. Jessica had stripped down her needs, retracted her demands on Seth. He should let her "do what she wants." And she offered little in return: "just enough" mothering of the children and very little mothering of him. In a dejected tone, she explained: "Last year, I started being home less and less myself. I still shop and tell Carmelita what to make for dinner, but then if I go away for a conference or somewhere else, I don't pay any attention to it. Seth has to do it." Jessica also created for herself a separate world of interest and leisure, where she found nurture for herself:

> I try to do what makes me least dissatisfied, which is going to Seattle on Fridays. I fly there after I put the kids to bed on Thursday evening. I have Friday free for shopping, going to the library, and seeing a psychiatrist I really like who's there, and whom I went to when we lived there. Then I come back that evening. I worry about the kids and my job if I'm here, but going there I have real time to myself. Also, the psychiatrist I am seeing there is really exciting to talk to. I can be fanciful and regressed with him and I'm enjoying that. Plus I have lunch with old friends. That's my perfect day.

With this "perfect day" to make up for the rest of the week, Jessica no longer found Seth's absence so oppressive. After all, Bill was taking Victor to his piano lessons, and Filipa was playing hide and seek with Walter. In the past, when problems with Seth came up, she pried them open, worked on them. Now she'd resigned from that "job" and withdrawn to some other world of "perfect days." . . .

HOLDING IT TOGETHER

"I used to think of us as a couple of really bright, attractive, well-liked people," Seth said softly, at the end of my interview with him, "but the last three years have been tense. When I'm doing an eleven-hour day, I'm sure I'm no fun. When Jessica is bummed out, she's awful to live with."

But at least, they felt, they had their sex life to hold them together. Both Seth and Jessica complained of lack of sexual interest, but thought it was due mostly to fatigue. In a matter-of-fact way, a way beyond sadness, Jessica added slowly: "I would never consider withholding sex, no matter how angry I am. I think both of us realize that if there's no sex, there's no marriage. There's enough else going wrong with the marriage. If I wasn't sexual with him, he'd find somebody else and I wouldn't be surprised at all. I would assume he would and I would move back to Seattle."

Something had gone terribly wrong in the Steins' marriage. Did some early emotional deprivation cause each one to be too anxious about their own needs to take care of the other's? Was Seth too anxious about his self-worth to nurture Jessica, and Jessica too afraid of intimacy? If so, perhaps the Steins would have run into problems regardless of the contradictory pressures of work and family, and regardless of a difference in gender strategy. But Seth nurtured his clients and his ailing father (for whom he had prepared a salt-free lunch each weekday for an entire year). And Jessica was able to develop a close relationship with her psychiatrist and with her friends. The idea of some early psychic injury does not explain why each one expressed their vulnerabilities in this particular way.

Again, perhaps the marriage suffered from a clash of ethnic traditions. Seth Stein came from a closely knit, intensely emotional, first-generation Russian-Jewish family. Jessica came from cooler, more restrained, Midwestern Swedish parents who resembled the parents of Diane Keaton in Woody Allen's film *Annie Hall*. In their book *Mixed Blessings*, Paul and Rachel Cowan suggest that the Jewish man who marries a Gentile woman often seeks a wife who is less intrusive and controlling than his mother, while a Gentile woman seeks, in her husband, the warmth, intensity, and excitement of upward mobility lacking in her cool and collected father. By middle age, the Cowans suggest, the wife may find her husband full of badly expressed needs and the husband may find his wife cool and detached. Perhaps this happened to the Steins. But I found this pattern between workaholic husbands and professionally ambitious wives who combine *other* ethnic and religious traditions as well.

A third interpretation—that there was a clash of gender strategies—may tell us more. With regard to the second shift, Jessica was not a supermom; she had bought herself out of what she could, and cut back her career to do the rest herself. Seth didn't do the "downstairs," like Evan Holt, nor like Peter Tanagawa give his wife enthusiastic support for her role at home. Seth had joined that group of men at the top of much of the business and professional world, men who are married and heterosexual but to whom women and children are not what's basic. In a way, Jessica felt that Seth had "died," like her father.

Disguised by a thin veneer of egalitarian ideology, Seth's view of his fatherhood was pragmatically adapted to the enormous demands of his career. His egalitarian feeling rules didn't conflict with underlying feelings; rather the rules themselves felt inconsequential, light. He "should" care about Jessica's career, but he "couldn't." He should want to engage his children emotionally, but he "couldn't." The "shoulds" were a diminished part of himself; the "coulds" ruled the day.

To the extent that Seth was involved in his family life, he expected to *receive* at home and to *give* at work. Jessica's gender ideology led her to want Seth to *give* at home as well as at work. They differed from other couples in the early motives they attached to their gender ideology and in the moves—mainly outward—they made on behalf of them. If at first Seth stayed late at the office in order to become a successful "man," later he stayed there to avoid conflict at home, all because, the myth went, he was a "hard-driving Type-A guy." Under the guise of balancing motherhood and career, Jessica had withdrawn somewhat from the children, oriented their frustrations toward Seth, and withdrawn almost totally from Seth. . . .

Michael O'Brien v. Loretta O'Brien
Court of Appeals of New York, 66 NY2d 576
Decided December 26, 1985

OPINION OF THE COURT

SIMONS, J.

In this divorce action, the parties' only asset of any consequence is the husband's newly acquired license to practice medicine. The principal issue presented is whether that license, acquired during their marriage, is marital property subject to equitable distribution under Domestic Relations Law § 236 (B) (5). Supreme Court held that it was and accordingly made a distributive award in defendant's favor.* It also granted defendant maintenance arrears, expert witness fees and attorneys' fees (114 Misc 2d 233). On appeal to the Appellate Division, a majority of that court held that plaintiff's medical license is not marital property and that defendant was not entitled to an award for the expert witness fees. It modified the judgment and remitted the case to Supreme Court for further proceedings, specifically for a determination of maintenance and a rehabilitative award (106 AD2d 223). The matter is before us by leave of the Appellate Division.

We now hold that plaintiff's medical license constitutes "marital property" within the meaning of Domestic Relations Law § (B) (1) (c) and that it is therefore subject to equitable distribution pursuant to subdivision 5 of that part. That being so, the Appellate Division erred in denying a fee, as a matter of law, to defendant's expert witness who evaluated the license.

I

Plaintiff and defendant married on April 3, 1971. At the time both were employed as teachers at the same private school. Defendant had a bachelor's degree and a temporary teaching certificate but required 18 months of postgraduate classes at an approximate cost of $3,000, excluding living expenses, to obtain permanent certification in New York. She claimed, and the trial court found, that she had relinquished the opportunity to obtain permanent certification while plaintiff pursued his education. At the time of the marriage, plaintiff had completed only three and one-half years of college but shortly afterward he returned to school at night to earn his bachelor's degree and to complete sufficient premedical courses to enter medical school. In September 1973 the parties moved to Guadalajara, Mexico, where plaintiff became a full-time medical student. While he pursued his studies defendant

---

Editors' note: This case has been abridged.

*The action was originally instituted by plaintiff husband and defendant wife asserted a counterclaim in her answer. Subsequently, the husband withdrew his complaint and reply to the counterclaim and the wife received an uncontested divorce.

held several teaching and tutorial positions and contributed her earnings to their joint expenses. The parties returned to New York in December 1976 so that plaintiff could complete the last two semesters of medical school and internship training here. After they returned, defendant resumed her former teaching position and she remained in it at the time this action was commenced. Plaintiff was licensed to practice medicine in October 1980. He commenced this action for divorce two months later. At the time of trial, he was a resident in general surgery.

During the marriage both parties contributed to paying the living and educational expenses and they received additional help from both of their families. They disagreed on the amounts of their respective contributions but it is undisputed that in addition to performing household work and managing the family finances defendant was gainfully employed throughout the marriage, that she contributed all of her earnings to their living and educational expenses and that her financial contributions exceeded those of plaintiff. The trial court found that she had contributed 76% of the parties' income exclusive of a $10,000 student loan obtained by defendant. Finding that plaintiff's medical degree and license are marital property, the court received evidence of its value and ordered a distributive award to defendant.

Defendant presented expert testimony that the present value of plaintiff's medical license was $472,000. Her expert testified that he arrived at this figure by comparing the average income of a college graduate and that of a general surgeon between 1985, when plaintiff's residency would end, and 2012, when he would reach age 65. After considering Federal income taxes, an inflation rate of 10% and a real interest rate of 3% he capitalized the difference in average earnings and reduced the amount to present value. He also gave his opinion that the present value of defendant's contribution to plaintiff's medical education was $103,390. Plaintiff offered no expert testimony on the subject.

The court, after considering the life-style that plaintiff would enjoy from the enhanced earning potential his medical license would bring and defendant's contributions and efforts toward attainment of it, made a distributive award to her of $188,800, representing 40% of the value of the license, and ordered it paid in 11 annual installments of various amounts beginning November 1, 1982 and ending November 1, 1992. The court also directed plaintiff to maintain a life insurance policy on his life for defendant's benefit for the unpaid balance of the award and it ordered plaintiff to pay defendant's counsel fees of $7,000 and her expert witness fee of $1,000. It did not award defendant maintenance.

A divided Appellate Division, relying on its prior decision in *Conner v Conner* (97 AD2d 88) and the decision of the Fourth Department in *Lesman v Lesman* (88 AD2d 153, *appeal dismissed* 57 NY2d 956), concluded that a professional license acquired during marriage is not marital property subject to distribution. It therefore modified the judgment by striking the trial court's determination that it is and by striking the provision ordering payment of the expert witness for evaluating the license and remitted the case for further proceedings.

On these cross appeals, defendant seeks reinstatement of the judgment of the trial court. Plaintiff contends that the Appellate Division correctly held that a professional license is not marital property but he also urges that the trial court failed to adequately explain what factors it relied on in making its decision, that it erroneously excluded evidence of defendant's marital fault and that the trial court's awards for attorneys and expert witness fees were improper.

II

The Equitable Distribution Law contemplates only two classes of property: marital property and separate property (Domestic Relations Law § 236 [B] [c], [d]). The former, which is subject to equitable distribution, is defined broadly as "*all* property acquired by either or both spouses during the marriage and before the execution of a separation agreement or the commencement of a matrimonial action, *regardless of the form in which title is held*" (Domestic Relations Law § 236 [B] [1] [c] [emphasis added]; *see*, § [B] [5] [b], [c]). Plaintiff does not contend that his license is excluded from distribution because it is separate property; rather, he claims that it is not property at all but represents a personal attainment in acquiring knowledge. He rests his argument on decisions in similar cases from other jurisdictions and on his view that a license does not satisfy common-law concepts of property. Neither contention is controlling because decisions in other States rely principally on their own statutes, and the legislative history underlying them, and because the New York Legislature deliberately went beyond traditional property concepts when it formulated the Equitable Distribution Law (*see generally*, 2 Foster-Freed-Brandes, Law and the Family—New York ch 33, at 917 *et set.* [1985 Cum Supp]). Instead, our statute recognizes that spouses have an equitable claim to things of value arising out of the marital relationship and classifies them as subject to distribution by focusing on the marital status of the parties at the time of acquisition. Those things acquired during marriage and subject to distribution have been classified as "marital property" although, as one commentator has observed, they hardly fall within the traditional property concepts because there is no common-law property interest remotely resembling marital property. "It is a statutory creature, is of no meaning whatsoever during the normal course of a marriage and arises full-grown, like Athena, upon the signing of a separation agreement or the commencement of a matrimonial action. [Thus] [i]t is hardly surprising, and not at all relevant, that traditional common law property concepts do not fit in parsing the meaning of 'marital property'" (Florescue, "Market Value", *Professional Licenses and Marital Property: A Dilemma in Search of a Horn*, 1982 NY St Bar Assn Fam L Rev 13 [Dec.]). Having classified the "property" subject to distribution, the Legislature did not attempt to go further and define it but left it to the courts to determine what interests come within the terms of section 236 (B) (1) (c).

We made such a determination in *Majauskas v Majauskas* (61 NY2d 481), holding there that vested but unmatured pension rights are marital property subject to equitable distribution. Because pension benefits are not specifically identified as marital property in the statute, we looked to the express reference to pension rights contained in section 236 (B) (5) (d) (4), which deals with equitable distribution of marital property, to other provisions of the equitable distribution statutes and to the legislative intent behind its enactment to determine whether pension rights are marital property or separate property. A similar analysis is appropriate here and leads to the conclusion that marital property encompasses a licence to practice medicine to the extent that the license is acquired during marriage.

Section 236 provides that in making an equitable distribution of marital property, "the court shall consider: * * * (6) any equitable claim to, interest in, or direct or indirect contribution made to the acquisition of such marital property by the party not having title, including joint efforts or expenditures and contributions and services as a spouse, parent, wage earner and homemaker, and *to the career or career potential* of the other party [and] * * * (9) the impossibility or difficulty of evaluating any component asset or any interest in a business, corporation or *profession*" (Domestic Relations Law § 236 [B] [5] [d] [6], [9] [emphasis added]). Where equitable distribution of marital property is appropriate but "the distribution of an interest in a business, corporation or *profession* would be contrary to law" the court shall make a distributive award in lieu of an actual distribution of the property (Domestic Relations Law § 236 [B] [5] [e] [emphasis added]). The words mean exactly what they say: that an interest in a profession or professional career potential is marital property which may be represented by direct or indirect contributions of the non-titleholding spouse, including financial contributions and nonfinancial contributions made by caring for the home and family.

The history which preceded enactment of the statute confirms this interpretation. Reform of section 236 was advocated because experience had proven that application of the traditional common-law title theory of property had caused inequities upon dissolution of a marriage. The Legislature replaced the existing system with equitable distribution of marital property, an entirely new theory which considered all the circumstances of the case and of the respective parties to the marriage (Assembly Memorandum, 1980 NY Legis Ann, at 129-130). Equitable distribution was based on the premise that a marriage is, among other things, an economic partnership to which both parties contribute as spouse, parent, wage earner or homemaker (*id.*, at 130; *see*, Governor's Memorandum of Approval, 1980 McKinney's Session Laws of NY, at 1863). Consistent with this purpose, and implicit in the statutory scheme as a whole, is the view that upon dissolution of the marriage there should be a winding up of the parties' economic affairs and a severance of their economic ties by an equitable distribution of the marital assets. Thus, the concept of alimony, which often served as a means of lifetime support and dependence for one spouse upon the other long after the marriage was over, was replaced with the concept of maintenance which seeks to allow "the recipient spouse an opportunity to achieve [economic] independence" (Assembly Memorandum, 1980 NY Legis Ann, at 130).

The determination that a professional license is marital property is also consistent with the conceptual base upon which the statute rests. As this case demonstrates, few undertakings during a marriage better qualify as the type of joint effort that the statute's economic partnership theory is intended to address than contributions toward one spouse's acquisition of a professional license. Working spouses are often required to contribute substantial income as wage earners, sacrifice their own educational or career goals and opportunities for child rearing, perform the bulk of household duties and responsibilities and forgo the acquisition of marital assets that could have been accumulated if the professional spouse had been employed rather than occupied with the study and training necessary to acquire a professional license. In this case, nearly all of the parties' nine-year marriage was devoted to the acquisition of plaintiff's medical license and defendant played a major role in that project. She worked continuously during the marriage and contributed all of her earnings to their joint effort, she sacrificed her own educational and career opportunities, and she traveled with plaintiff to Mexico for three and one-half years while he attended medical school there. The Legislature has decided, by its explicit reference in the statute to the contributions of one spouse to the other's profession or career (*see,* Domestic Relations Law § 236 [B] [5] [d] [6], [9]; [e]), that these contributions represent investments in the economic partnership of the marriage and that the product of the parties' joint efforts, the professional license, should be considered marital property.

The majority at the Appellate Division held that the cited statutory provisions do not refer to the license held by a professional who has yet to establish a practice but only to a going professional practice (*see, e.g., Arvantides v Arvantides,* 64 NY2d 1033; *Litman v Litman,* 61 NY2d 918). There is no reason in law or logic to restrict the plain language of the statute to existing practices, however, for it is of little consequence in making an award of marital property, except for the purpose of evaluation, whether the professional spouse has already established a practice or whether he or she has yet to do so. An established practice merely represents the exercise of the privileges conferred upon the professional spouse by the license and the income flowing from that practice represents the receipt of the enhanced earning capacity that licensure allows. That being so, it would be unfair not to consider the license a marital asset.

Plaintiff's principal argument, adopted by the majority below, is that a professional license is not marital property because it does not fit within the traditional view of property as something which has an exchange value on the open market and is capable of sale, assignment or transfer. The position does not withstand analysis for at least two reasons. First, as we have observed, it ignores the fact that whether a professional license constitutes marital property is to be judged by the language of the statute which created this new species of property previously unknown at common law or under prior statutes. Thus, whether the license fits within traditional property concepts is of no consequence. Second, it is an overstatement to assert that a professional license could not be considered property even outside the context of section 263 (B). A professional license is a valuable property right, reflected in the money, effort and lost opportunity for employment expended in its acquisition, and also in the enhanced earning capacity it affords its holder, which may not be revoked without due process of law (*see, Matter of Bender v Board of Regents*, 262 App Div 627, 631; *People ex rel. Greenberg v Reid*, 151 App Div 324, 326). That a professional license has no market value is irrelevant. Obviously, a license may not be alienated as may other property and for that reason the working spouse's interest in it is limited. The Legislature has recognized that limitation, however, and has provided for an award in lieu of its actual distribution (*see*, Domestic Relations Law § 236 [B] [5] [e]).

Plaintiff also contends that alternative remedies should be employed, such as an award of rehabilitative maintenance or reimbursement for direct financial contributions (*see, e.g., Kutanovski v Kutanovski*, 109 AD2d 822, 824; *Conner v Conner*, 97 AD2d 88, 101, *supra*; *Lesman v Lesman*, 88 AD2d 153, 158-159, *supra*). The statute does not expressly authorize retrospective maintenance or rehabilitative awards and we have no occasion to decide in this case whether the authority to do so may ever be implied from its provisions (*but see, Cappiello v Cappiello*, 66 NY2d 107). It is sufficient to observe that normally a working spouse should not be restricted to that relief because to do so frustrates the purposes underlying the Equitable Distribution Law. Limiting a working spouse to a maintenance award, either general or rehabilitative, not only is contrary to the economic partnership concept underlying the statute but also retains the uncertain and inequitable economic ties of dependence that the Legislature sought to extinguish by equitable distribution. Maintenance is subject to termination upon the recipient's remarriage and a working spouse may never receive adequate consideration for his or her contribution and may even be penalized for the decision to remarry if that is the only method of compensating the contribution. As one court said so well, "[t]he function of equitable distribution is to recognize that when a marriage ends, each of the spouses, based on the totality of the contributions made to it, has a stake in and right to a share of the marital assets accumulated while it endured, not because that share is needed, but because those assets represent the capital product of what was essentially a partnership entity" (*Wood v Wood*, 119 Misc 2d 1076, 1079). The Legislature stated its intention to eliminate such inequities by providing that a supporting spouse's "direct or indirect contribution" be recognized, considered and rewarded (Domestic Relations Law § 236 [B] [5] [d] [6]).

Turning to the question of valuation, it has been suggested that even if a professional license is considered marital property, the working spouse is entitled only to reimbursement of his or her direct financial contributions (*see*, Note, *Equitable Distribution of Degrees and Licences: Two Theories Toward Compensating Spousal Contributions*, 49 Brooklyn L. 301, 317-322). By parity of reasoning, a spouse's down payment on real estate or contribution to the purchase of securities would be limited to the money contributed, without any remuneration for any incremental value in the asset because of price appreciation. Such a result is completely at odds with the statute's requirement that the court give full consideration to both direct and indirect contributions "made to the acquisition of such marital property by the party not having title, including joint *efforts* or expenditures and *contributions and services as a spouse, parent*, wage earner *and homemaker* (Domestic Relations Law § 236 [B] [5] [d] [6] [emphasis added]). If the license is marital property, then the working spouse is entitled to an equitable portion of it, not a return of funds advanced. Its value is the enhanced earning capacity it affords the holder and although fixing the present value of that enhanced earning capacity may present problems, the problems are not insurmountable. Certainly they are no more difficult than computing tort damages for wrongful death or diminished earning capacity resulting from injury and they differ only in degree from the problems presented when valuing a professional practice for purposes of a distributive award, something the courts have not hesitated to do. . . .

*   *   *

MEYER, J. (concurring).

I concur in Judge Simons' opinion but write separately to point up for consideration by the Legislature the potential for unfairness involved in distributive awards based upon a license of a professional still in training.

An equity court normally has power to " 'change its decrees where there has been a change of circumstances'" (*People v Scanlon*, 11 NY2d 459, 462, *on second appeal* 13 NY2d 982). The implication of Domestic Relations Law § 236 (B) (9) (b), which deals with modification of an order or decree as to maintenance or child support, is, however, that a distributive award pursuant to section 236 (B) (5) (3), once made, is not subject to change. Yet a professional in training who is not finally committed to a career choice when the distributive award is made may be locked into a particular kind of practice simply because the monetary obligations imposed by the distributive award made on the basis of the trial judge's conclusion (prophecy may be a better word) as to what the career choice will be leaves him or her no alternative.

The present case points up the problem. A medical license is but a step toward the practice ultimately engaged in by its holder, which follows after internship, residency and, for particular specialties, board certification. Here it is undisputed that plaintiff was in a residency for general surgery at the time of the trial, but had the previous year done a residency in internal medicine. Defendant's expert based his opinion on the difference between the average income of a general surgeon and that of a college graduate of plaintiff's age and life expectancy, which the trial judge utilized, impliedly finding that plaintiff would engage in a surgical practice despite plaintiff's testimony that he was dissatisfied with the general surgery program he was in and was attempting to return to the internal medicine training he had been in the previous year. The trial judge had the right, of course, to discredit that testimony, but the point is that equitable distribution was not intended to permit a judge to make a career decision for a licensed spouse still in training. Yet the degree of speculation involved in the award made is emphasized by the testimony of the expert on which it was based. Asked whether his assumptions and calculations were in any way speculative, he replied: "Yes. They're speculative to the extent of, will Dr. O'Brien practice medicine? Will Dr. O'Brien earn more or less than the average surgeon earns? Will Dr. O'Brien live to age sixty-five? Will Dr. O'Brien have a heart attack or will he be injured in an automobile accident? Will he be disabled? I mean, there is a degree of speculation. That speculative aspect is no more to be taken into account, cannot be taken into account, and it's a question, again, Mr. Emanuelli, not for the expert but for the courts to decide. It's not my function nor could it be."

The equitable distribution provisions of the Domestic Relations Law were intended to provide flexibility so that equity could be done. But if the assumption as to career choice on which a distributive award payable over a number of years is based turns out not to be the fact (as, for example, should a general surgery trainee accidentally lose the use of his hand), it should be possible for the court to revise the distributive award to conform to the fact. And there will be no unfairness in so doing if either spouse can seek reconsideration, for the licensed spouse is more likely to seek reconsideration based on real, rather than imagined, cause if he or she knows that the nonlicensed spouse can seek not only reinstatement of the original award, but counsel fees in addition, should the purported circumstance on which a change is made turn out to have been feigned or to be illusory.

COMMENTS AND
RECOMMENDED READINGS

John Stuart Mill's "Statement on Marriage" was written two months before he married his dear friend and regular companion, Harriet Taylor. Though Mill's views were quite advanced for their time, Taylor was both more libertarian and more egalitarian. She advocated abolition of the laws regulating marriage and, contrary to Mill, believed that married women did not have to regard care of their homes and children as their primary occupation. The joint and separate writings of Mill and Taylor on marriage and the status of women are collected in *Essays on Sex Equality* (Chicago: Univ. of Chicago Press, 1970), edited with an extended introduction by Alice S. Rossi. Like Mill and Taylor, Lucy Stone and Henry Blackwell entered marriage with a public statement of principles; their "Protest" was read aloud during their marriage ceremony. For this document as well as selected correspondence, see *Loving Warriors: Selected Letters of Lucy Stone and Henry B. Blackwell, 1853–1893* (New York: Dial Press, 1981), edited and introduced by Leslie Wheeler.

Despite the legal regulation of marriage, the rhetoric of contract pushes marriage partners in the direction of a relation based on individual consent, with specific terms reflecting "the will and wishes" of the parties. The idea of individually negotiated contracts received a flurry of attention in the late 1960s and early 1970s. In its first year of publication, *Ms.* magazine ran several articles on the subject, including Susan Edminston's "How to Write Your Own Marriage Contract" (Spring 1972, pp. 66–72). In June 1973, *Ms.* published the complete contract of Harriet Mary Cody and Harvey Joseph Sadis (pp. 62ff.), which served as a model for many individuals. The most comprehensive and considered treatment of the subject came several years later with the publication of *The Marriage Contract: Spouses, Lovers, and the Law* (New York: Free Press, 1981) by Lenore J. Weitzman. This volume remains the most useful guide to the issues, including the legal—or, rather, nonlegal—status of such contracts.

Not everyone who enters a marriage or marriage-like relation adopts the same conventional assumptions about its proper form. The story of polygamy in the United States offers an instructive variation. For a review of the legal history, see John T. Noonan, Jr., *The Believers and the Powers That Are* (New York: Macmillan, 1987), Chapter 9. The question of polygamy has come to the fore again recently in a number of adoption and child custody cases. Most importantly, in March 1991, the Utah Supreme Court ruled that a family cannot be automatically prohibited from adopting children simply because it is polygamous.

Another variation is represented by same-sex marriage. Although Justice C. Donald Peterson's opinion in *Baker v. Nelson* reflects current law, several avenues have opened recently for indirect public recognition of nontraditional domestic partnerships. In New York City, for example, rent-control laws have been interpreted so as to include long-standing same-sex unions, and in 1990 couples in California began to use the state's official registry for unincorporated nonprofit associations as a symbolic declaration of their commitment. The registration confers no legal benefits, but registrees receive a certificate from the state. For a provocative and personal defense of gay and lesbian rights, see Richard D. Mohr, *Gays/Justice: A Study of Ethics, Society, and the Law* (New York: Columbia Univ. Press, 1988).

Arlie Hochschild (with Ann Machung, *The Second Shift* [New York: Penguin, 1989]) aptly refers to the majority of couples she interviewed as "transitional" between traditional and egalitarian conceptions of marriage. (This category is represented in our readings by the story of Seth and Jessica Stein.) In many instances, transitional also means precarious, especially for women. In the absence of full economic power (a condition reinforced by persistent wage differentials and occupational segregation), women are more likely than men to experience dependency and poverty. Although recent legal reforms have enhanced women's status considerably, equity is still a distant goal. For a comprehensive discussion of gender inequities in law, see Deborah Rhode, *Justice and Gender: Sex Discrimination and the Law* (Cambridge: Harvard Univ. Press, 1989). The specific case of divorce reform is discussed in Lenore J. Weitzman, *The Divorce Revolution: The Unexpected Social and Economic Consequences for Women and Children in America* (New York: Free Press, 1985). A comparative perspective—and the argument that Europeans generally have enacted more sensible family policies, from which Americans have much to learn—is offered by Mary Ann Glendon in *Abortion and Divorce in Western Law: American Failures, European Challenges* (Cambridge: Harvard Univ. Press, 1987).

The issues of child support and divorce settlements are placed in the context of other policy reforms by Marian Wright Edelman in *Families in Peril: An Agenda for Social Change* (Cambridge: Harvard Univ. Press, 1987), and David T. Ellwood, *Poor Support: Poverty in the American Family* (New York: Basic Books, 1988).

PART II

REPRODUCTIVE STRATEGIES

INTRODUCTION

A major objective of the women's movement has been to enhance or facilitate reproductive choice. In large part, the aim is to overcome "biological determinism," the inevitability of a motherhood-centered life. By decentering—without necessarily eliminating—the option of motherhood, women are better able to pursue occupational opportunities and other public activities. But this shift requires control over reproductive functions. Hence, there is an openness to new reproductive technologies, as well as to novel conceptions of family life.

Not all women have welcomed these developments. Some women feel they violate a self-image rooted in traditional family arrangements. Even more sharply than in the case of dual-career marriages, the debate on reproductive technologies seems to set women against each other in a struggle over appropriate ideals. Just as Carmen Delacorte (see Part I, Section B) felt that her life-concept was devalued by ambitious, upper-class women whose concerns dominated the women's movement, so motherhood-centered women feel that use of the new technologies devalues the ethic of nurturance that defines their lives. They see themselves as protectors of a comprehensive moral vision in which biological determinism is not to be overcome but rather to be appreciated. Women *are* closer to the reproductive process and to caretaking than men, in this view. Thus, any development that undermines the separation of spheres—that demotes motherhood from a sacred calling and makes childbearing a matter of convenience—must be resisted. This stance is evident among the activists working to block introduction into the United States of the new "contragestive" pill, RU 486, which might make abortion easier to perform and more private. It also disposes them against prenatal testing. (On these matters, see the cases in Sections A and B.)

Overcoming biological determinism means attempting to manage the "natural lottery" by controlling the occurrence (or nonoccurrence) of certain qualities in embryos. These qualities may range from genetic defects to intelligence, athletic ability, and sex. Managing the production of human qualities is not entirely new, of course; that is what education is largely about. (Most forms of legal liability and moral accountability are based on a presupposition that human qualities can be managed and/or developed.) The new technologies, however, facilitate such control in unprecedented ways. Perhaps the worry here is simply a fear of the unknown: What will human life be like when a person's qualities result from deliberate choice, not chance? The deeper question, however, is: How do we avoid devaluing the "less than perfect" child?

This question is sharply put in the debate over amniocentesis, which the pro-life movement has described as a procedure for selective genocide against the disabled (see Section B). Rayna Rapp, in her moving account of a late second trimester abortion (after amniocentesis indicated she was carrying a Down's syndrome fetus), speaks of the need for feminists to affirm that the lives of the disabled are worth living. Yet it is not obvious that one can sustain the idea of the intrinsic worth of the most disadvantaged among us and still support abortion for whatever reason. Perhaps, as Anna Quindlen suggests, it is one thing if a fetus is discovered to have Tay-Sachs disease, which leads to blindness, paralysis, and death in early childhood; another, if it has Turner's syndrome, which produces mildly unusual facial features, short stature, and infertility; yet another if it is female rather than male.

A different worry about reproductive technologies has to do with self-alienation. Women's liberation from traditional norms and arrangements may require wrenching detachment from the emotional networks that formerly sustained them. As women attempt to gain deliberate control over reproductive choices, a certain distancing from self and others may occur in the process of redefining conventional attachments and commitments. This phenomenon is especially salient in the cases arising from commercial surrogate motherhood (see Section C), which is not itself a new technology—though it makes use of artificial insemination or in vitro fertilization—but a new kind of relationship. In surrogacy, reproduction becomes a service—one of many formerly performed, for the most part, by women within marriage—that can now be purchased on the market by either women or men. This situation has led to a certain loss of bearings for the surrogate, for the child, and for society.

The surrogate may experience the transaction as degrading, in the specific sense that she is treated in accordance with norms applying to creatures of lower rank. The service she provides is associated with the high status of motherhood, but she is a stranger in a contractual relationship. So, regardless of any potential harm to her, it may seem inconsistent with her self-respect to engage in such a transaction. Confusion about motherhood is also involved in concerns about the child, specifically the child's not knowing who his or her real mother is. This confusion appears to be intrinsic to surrogacy, in which there are three possible mothers: the genetic mother whose egg is fertilized to begin the biological process; the gestational mother who carries the embryo to term; and the caretaker mother who rears and nurtures the child. This profusion of possibilities is considered psychologically damaging to the child unless there is a single definite answer to the question of who the mother is. (Those who insist on a definite answer usually select the gestational mother.) The difficulty with this view is that it construes a matter of public policy—What is the best way to arrange these relationships?—as an ontological question: What is the correct description of reality?

The same point applies to society's concern that if it permits surrogacy it is condoning baby selling. The claim that surrogacy is a form of baby selling actually begs the question. Selling is a transfer to or exchange with one party (for consideration) of what belongs to another party. But in surrogacy a central point of contention is to whom the baby belongs. The genetic link is one possible basis for a claim of right; the gestational link is another. For some people, whether the surrogacy is done by artificial insemination or by in vitro fertilization is crucially different, because in the former case the surrogate has a genetic tie to the baby and in the latter case she does not. Again, these issues cannot be settled as matters of ontology but only as matters of policy. The question is whether important social values are served—or disserved—by permitting such commercial transactions. How significant are the benefits to be achieved for infertile couples by condoning surrogacy arrangements? How important are the rights of reproductive freedom and of privacy—and do they encompass this kind of transaction? On the other side, what are the risks of exploitation? How likely is it that at the time of birth a surrogate will regret her agreement because of the difficulty of anticipating her feelings? What are the risks that less-than-perfect children will be abandoned?

SECTION A

Contraception/Abortion

Fertility and Control: The Case of RU 486
Christopher Sturr

INTRODUCTION

In September of 1988, a French pharmaceutical company, Groupe Roussel-Uclaf, began marketing RU 486, a drug which induces abortion in early pregnancy. When used in conjunction with another drug, a prostaglandin, it is 90–95 percent effective in causing a miscarriage in the first trimester, with few serious side effects. Since its introduction, RU 486 has been used for abortion by over 34,000 French women. Testing of the drug has also shown it to have properties which may make it effective for uses other than abortion, including the treatment of breast cancer, some kinds of brain tumors, and Cushing's syndrome, an often fatal disease caused by adrenal malfunctioning. But RU 486 has not been marketed in the United States, nor has any pharmaceutical company or other group even sought approval for the drug from the Food and Drug Administration for any of its potential uses.

RU 486 would undoubtedly make abortion easier and more private, and possibly more commonplace. Not surprisingly, a survey of the growing literature on RU 486—including articles in newspapers and general news magazines, political and law journals, women's magazines, religious and business publications, pharmaceutical and medical journals, and government documents—reveals that many groups have taken an interest in whether the drug becomes available in the US. Given the changes an abortion drug could bring to the practice of abortion, the question of which of these groups will control the availability of RU 486 is central to the abortion debate.

THE DEVELOPMENT OF RU 486

RU 486 was developed as a result of a joint effort of the French government, private industry, and members of the medical and scientific communities.

But the personal efforts of one man, Etienne-Emile Baulieu, were perhaps most important in the discovery of the pill. A medical doctor by training and a highly successful research biochemist specializing in the study of steroid hormones, Baulieu was chiefly affiliated with INSERM (the National Institute of Health and Medical Research), a laboratory run by the French government, but he combined this work with teaching biochemistry at the university level and consulting in the pharmaceutical industry. Baulieu made his mark early in his career with his discovery in 1959 of soluble steroids secreted by the adrenal glands, which led to advances in the treatment of adrenal cancer. His early success brought him to research labs in the US where, after a time, he worked with Gregory Pincus, a biochemist at Boston University who had played a major role in the development of the contraceptive pill. As Pincus' associate, Baulieu was involved in testing the contraceptive pill, and served on a World Health Organization committee on contraception. Pincus's mentorship was financial as well as intellectual: he was instrumental in getting funding from the Ford Foundation for the research Baulieu was to do at INSERM in the 1960s.[1] That research combined Baulieu's earlier work on steroids with his new interest in reproductive technology, and built on the concept demonstrated by Pincus in the development of the contraceptive pill: that fertility control was achievable by tinkering with the operation of the reproductive hormones.

The development of the contraceptive pill grew out of the observation that the levels of certain hormones varied at particular stages in the menstrual cycle, and appeared to be associated with physiological change. By altering certain of those levels—specifically of estrogen and progesterone—over the course of a monthly cycle, the pill proved to be a highly effective way of preventing ovulation and, hence, fertility. In a similar, but entirely mechanical way, some intrauterine devices (IUDs) appear to inhibit production of progesterone, which is necessary for implantation of the fertilized egg in the uterus. (Other IUDs prevent implantation simply by irritating the uterine lining.) Both methods of contraception, however, carried side effects, some of them serious. Elevated levels of estrogen from the pill could produce nausea, weight gain, blood clotting, and increased risk of heart attack, among other effects. IUDs had had an even more troubled history due to the risk of uterine or tubal infection, which could lead to infertility. Because of these side effects, IUDs were illegal in many countries, and the pharmaceutical companies which produced the kinds of IUDs that most commonly led to infection faced costly lawsuits.

In his research on reproductive hormones, Baulieu sought to map out new territory in a couple of ways. First, he focused on progesterone alone. Unlike estrogen, which is associated with ovulation—i.e., with points in the reproductive process before fertilization—progesterone plays a significant role *after* the egg has been fertilized. High levels of progesterone are associated with two stages in the reproductive cycle: the preparation of the uterus for pregnancy and the period after a fertilized egg has been successfully implanted in the womb. In the latter case, the hormone is associated with the suppression of other hormones which would normally trigger a new ovulatory cycle, and hence lead to menstruation—and to the discharge of the gestating embryo. A method of fertility control that involved progesterone alone, rather than progesterone and estrogen, would somehow have to keep progesterone from inhibiting menstruation and thereby prevent a fertilized egg from becoming implanted or, if the egg has already been implanted, cause it to be expelled with the lining of the uterus in menstruation. The resulting product would be, in Baulieu's words, a "contragestive," because it would impede gestation rather than conception.[2]

In addition, Baulieu sought to avoid controlling fertility by manipulating hormone levels in the body, which, as the pill had shown, could lead to risky side effects. Instead, Baulieu's research focused on finding a way to inhibit the effects of progesterone on the menstrual and gestational processes by interfering with its ability to signal the uterus to prepare for pregnancy. His efforts began to pay off in 1970, when he and his researchers were able to isolate the receptors within the cells of the uterus that receive messages from progesterone. From that point, the search was on to find a progesterone "antagonist," or antiprogesterone—i.e., a substance that would replace progesterone in those receptors and hence prevent them from getting the hormone's signals to commence or continue gestation.[3] Eventually, Baulieu and his research team were joined in that search by chemists at the Groupe Roussel-Uclaf, the leader among pharmaceutical companies in steroid biochemistry. Their tests, using a method developed by Roussel's chief chemist, ultimately led to the discovery in 1978 of a progesterone antagonist registered as Roussel-Uclaf 38486, which was assigned the trade name "mifepristone" but became more commonly known as RU 486.[4]

Over the next several years, RU 486 underwent extensive testing, the results of which confirmed its effectiveness as an abortive agent, particularly when used in conjunction with prostaglandin, a hormone which causes the uterus to contract. Prostaglandin, which is naturally active during menstruation, had itself been tested as an abortion drug, with rates of success as high as those for RU 486, though with more side effects. Combined with RU 486, it both raised the success rate of the new drug and reduced such side effects as heavy uterine bleeding and painful contractions.

The extensive testing of RU 486 revealed some other properties of the drug which could potentially prove extremely useful. It was found that besides blocking progesterone receptors, RU 486 also blocked the receptors for the glutocorticoid hormone, which fulfills a wide variety of functions unrelated to reproduction. As a result of this property, scientists have studied or suggested a number of applications for RU 486, including treatment of Cushing's syndrome (which is caused by excess cortisone production), treatment of glaucoma, and local treatment of wounds, burns, and skin abrasions.[5] Moreover, the drug's antiprogesterone action was considered potentially useful in the treatment of certain cancerous breast tumors and menangiomas (benign brain tumors which seem to depend on progesterone), as well as in inducing labor in difficult births (thereby reducing the need for Caesarian sections).

It was also possible that RU 486 could be used as a form of birth control very much like the contraceptive pill. When RU 486 was first written about in the popular press, it was more often referred to as a "once-a-month pill" than as an "abortion pill." The earliest tests of the pill on monkeys showed it to be 100 percent effective in preventing advanced pregnancy if administered once a month. The effect of taking a monthly dose of RU 486 would be to cut off the supply of progesterone for whatever role it would have in incipient gestation—whether in enabling implantation of an egg or in staving off continued ovulation and menstruation. But while Baulieu and others expressed the hope that RU 486 might someday be commonly administered as a "once-a-month pill," this use of the pill was not tested as extensively as its use in first-trimester abortion; consequently, the pill was marketed only for its abortive properties.[6]

In those properties, supporters of RU 486 saw a potential answer to a growing crisis in world health care. A December 1986 article on the drug in the *New England Journal of Medicine* laid out the argument that was to be repeated many times in the debate on RU 486:

> Demographic surveys estimate that there are approximately 90 million births worldwide each year and 40 to 50 million abortions. . . . Thus, unfortunately, in the last quarter of the 20th century, abortion, with its risks and sequelae, is the most widely used method of fertility regulation. The need for a safe, convenient, and effective method of preventing or terminating pregnancy is obvious.[7]

But this argument would bring supporters of RU 486 in direct conflict with another group which also expressed concern about surgical abortions but sought a different solution: the anti-abortionists, who vocally opposed abortion in any form, including that induced by a pill, and sought to stop or suppress any agent that would make abortion possible.

MARKETING RU 486 IN FRANCE

The company that would market RU 486, Groupe Roussel-Uclaf, was a subsidiary of Hoechst A.G., a German pharmaceutical conglomerate. Hoechst A.G., whose yearly revenues in the US alone totaled over $6 billion,[8] owned 54.5 percent of Roussel-Uclaf; the government of France owned another 36.25 percent. Roussel had participated in the development of RU 486 both because of its specialization in the manufacture of steroids and related drugs and because of the interest of the company chairman, Edouard Sakiz, in the product. A native of Turkey and a biochemist by training, Sakiz had been involved in the research and testing of RU 486, and had even co-signed a scientific article on the drug. He was also a personal friend and former classmate of Baulieu, who had been employed at Roussel since the mid-sixties as an "independent and exclusive" consultant.[9]

Sakiz, like Baulieu, had a longstanding interest in reproductive technology. In Sakiz's case, this interest had a corporate side: he remembered Roussel's decision in the 1960s not to produce the contraceptive pill, a response to then-prevailing societal attitudes toward the pill. Said Sakiz in an interview: "We lost the market for contraceptives even though we were the most important steroid company in the world. And now contraceptives are considered natural; they aren't at all controversial." [10]

Sakiz was aware of the potential for controversy in RU 486; but after his experience with the contraceptive pill, he did not intend to let his company cave in to political sentiments about the new drug which, like those about the contraceptive pill, he thought likely to wane. This optimism about ultimate public acceptance of RU 486 in part grew out of the way both Sakiz and Baulieu viewed the drug—i.e., not primarily as a new abortion technology, but as an advance in fertility control. RU 486 was, in fact, not unlike other methods of birth control which manipulated hormones: the only difference was the point in the reproductive process that it took effect. It was perhaps easier for those who favored RU 486 to make such comparisons with other forms of birth control when it was still thought to have potential as a "once a month" pill. If the pill were used in this way, it would blur the distinction between abortion and contraception: a woman who took the drug would not really know what was an induced miscarriage and what was simply heavy menstruation.

Later, when this use of RU 486 was played down, the reluctance to emphasize the abortive properties of the drug persisted; Baulieu continued to refer to it as a "contragestive," not as an "abortifacient." "I resent when people present the very early interruption of pregnancy as killing a baby, morally or physically," he said. [11] But to those who opposed RU 486, the distinction Baulieu and others tried to make between a contragestive and an abortifacient was nonexistent, and they set their sights on Roussel in an effort to prevent the drug from being marketed.

Early Opposition. Pressure against Roussel for its involvement in RU 486 in fact started long before the drug was ready for marketing. In late February of 1988, more than seven months before Roussel gained approval to market the pill, the *New York Times* reported that US companies were receiving threats that they would be boycotted should they sell or even do research on abortion-inducing drugs like RU 486. The article further reported that representatives of Hoechst-Roussel, the American subsidiary of Roussel's parent company, had stated that their firm would not pursue approval for RU 486 from the US Food and Drug Administration. [12]

Protest had also reached Roussel-Uclaf itself. By June of 1988, Sakiz was receiving threatening letters daily. "Assassins, stop your work of death," exhorted one letter. "Your pill kills babies and you will suffer the consequences," warned another. Opponents of abortion had also begun to picket the company's headquarters on the Boulevard des Invalides in Paris. They handed out leaflets calling RU 486 a "chemical weapon" that would "poison the still-tiny children of a billion Third World babies." [13]

One particularly disturbing tactic took advantage of the history of Roussel's parent company, Hoechst A.G., to make its point. The ancestor company of Hoechst, I.G. Farben, had been a manufacturer of cyanide gas for the Nazis' gas chambers. (It is likely, also, that this manufacture was done using concentration-camp labor.) Anti-abortion protesters used this fact to compare the product of Hoechst's subsidiary to the Holocaust. "The protestors told us, 'You are changing the uterus into a death oven,'" Sakiz told the *Times*.[14]

Indictments such as these were beginning to wear on the morale of Roussel's employees. On June 23rd, a rally of hundreds of anti-abortion protesters took place in front of Roussel's headquarters during the company's annual meeting. The centerpiece of the meeting was to have been Sakiz's announcement of a rise in Roussel's profits, which had brought the company out of a three-year slump, but the protest eclipsed the chairman's report. Instead, Xavier Dor, a member of the board of directors who opposed abortion, made the new drug the focus of discussion. Foes of the pill within the company most frequently cited the threats of boycott they had received from anti-abortion forces as the reason behind their opposition.[15]

The opposition within the company foreshadowed a change of heart in Sakiz. An article in the *New York Times Magazine* later reported:

> The key development that seemed to force Sakiz's about-face came when Alain Madec, an ambitious 41-year-old executive vice president, and the No. 3 man at Roussel, announced that he was against RU 486. He was the third of Roussel's five-man executive committee to throw his weight against the pill, joining two other executive vice presidents. Sakiz had withstood their opposition because they were due to retire soon. But with Madec's announcement, he began to worry that Madec might be currying favor with Hoechst to stage a palace coup.

These pressures began to wear on Sakiz. If they did not erode his enthusiasm for the drug, they at least made him less eager to push the cause within the company.

ROUSSEL'S REVERSAL

Events in the fall of 1988 soon brought things to a head for Sakiz. On September 8, as a result of testing on RU 486 sponsored by the World Health Organization, the government of China gave its approval for Roussel to market the drug there. This was the first step in an arrangement Roussel had made with the World Health Organization for distribution of RU 486 at cost to Third World countries. Then, on September 23, Claude Evin, the French minister of health, approved the drug for a trial period of marketing in France. The French government would fully fund the distribution of the pill to certain approved clinics throughout France, where women seeking abortions could obtain free treatment with RU 486.

Sakiz had hoped that the protests against the drug were aimed mostly at preventing this approval, but if he had expected any abatement in the controversy over RU 486, he was soon proven wrong. Over the next month, protests from opponents of abortion increased, strengthened by the Catholic Church, which came out publicly against the pill: Jean-Marie Lustiger, then the Archbishop of Paris, called RU 486 "extremely dangerous."[16]

By the end of October, less than one month after RU 486 was approved, the mounting pressures against the pill from within and without the company finally wore Sakiz down. The *New York Times* later reported his "unexpected move":

> At an Oct. 21 meeting, he surprised members of the management committee by calling for a discussion of RU 486. There, in Roussel's ultra-modern board room, the pill's long-standing opponents repeated their objections: RU 486 could spark a painful boycott, it was hurting employee morale, management was devoting too much of its energy defending itself in this controversy. Finally, it would never be hugely profitable, because much would be sold on a cost basis to the third world.
>
> After two hours, Sakiz again stunned the committee by calling for a vote. When he raised his own hand in favor of suspending distribution of RU 486, it was clear that the pill was doomed.
>
> "We have a responsibility in managing a company," he later explained in an interview. "But if I were a lone scientist, I would have acted differently," he added, even afterward unable to keep his inner conflicts from bubbling to the surface.

A few days later, on October 25, the company informed its employees of the decision to suspend distribution of the pill. The decision became public the next day, when Roussel announced "that it was suspending distribution of the drug because of pressure from anti-abortion groups." On October 27, the *New York Times* ran a front-page story on Roussel's decision. "Drug Maker Stops All Distribution of Abortion Pill; Pressure of Foes Cited," the headline read. "French Company's Decision in Face of 'Polemic' Stuns the Pro-Choice Groups."

Because of a fortuitously-timed meeting of the World Congress of Gynecology and Obstetrics in Rio de Janeiro, response from the medical community to Roussel's decision to suspend distribution of RU 486 was almost immediate. Led by Baulieu, who was attending the session, physicians from around the world made Roussel's decision the focus of their discussion. A petition condemning Roussel's action circulated at the meeting, and Baulieu himself spoke out loudly against his own company. The story again made the front page of the *Times*. "Doctors Protest Company's Action on Abortion Pill; Withdrawal Denounced," the October 28 headline began. "Paris Concern Is Assailed at Health Parley in Rio for Yielding to Pressure."

Baulieu's actions, however, did not necessarily indicate a rift with the chairman of Roussel. In an interview with the *Times*, Baulieu said that Sakiz had encouraged him and others to speak out against Roussel's decision. That decision, at least as far as Sakiz was concerned, was provisional: he hoped that, just as anti-abortionists had made themselves felt when the drug seemed likely to proceed as planned, pro-choice forces and the medical establishment would support the drug now that the tide had turned. Another story in the October 28 edition of the *Times* underscored that hope: "Maker says Pressures Could Revive Abortion Pill." Roussel officials, the paper reported, had said publicly that they might resume distribution "if the atmosphere becomes peaceful again."

The day after the protest in Rio, the French government, acting to protect the investment it had made in the pill, both in the initial research at INSERM and through Roussel (of which it was one-third owner), stepped in. French Health Minister Claude Evin summoned Pierre Joly, Roussel's vice chair, to his office to say that if the company did not resume distribution, the government would transfer the patent for RU 486 to another firm. "I could not permit the abortion debate to deprive women of a product that represents medical progress," said Evin in his public statement. "From the moment Government approval for the drug was granted, RU 486 became the moral property of women, not just the property of the drug company." Roussel bowed to the government's wishes: the public trial period, which the government had agreed to finance, would go on.

Some observers later expressed suspicions that the whole sequence of events—Roussel's decision to stop distribution, the protest in Rio, and Evin's order—had been staged to take the pressure off Roussel and put it on the French government, which was less vulnerable, but both Evin and Sakiz strongly denied this.[17] In any case, it was clear that some at Roussel were not displeased with the outcome. The government's order, the *New York Times*, noted,

> delighted Sakiz. It was the trump card that defeated his opponents and took the onus off his company. Roussel officials had dropped RU 486 because they believed its future had become a public matter, too large for a private company to decide. Now the Government had decided the question for them.[18]

On the day that Evin's order was made public, Pierre Joly, speaking for Roussel, said that the company was pleased with the result: "We are relieved of the moral burden weighing on our group. For us the problem is now solved."[19]

Over the next year and a half, RU 486 was tested in clinics in France and, on the basis of the results of that study, the French government gave final approval for the drug. RU 486 would no longer be distributed free, but instead would be subsidized by 80 percent under France's socialized medical program, as were surgical abortions. Meanwhile, Groupe Roussel-Uclaf and Hoechst A.G. began seeking approval to market their product in Britain, Holland, and Scandinavia. However, the company refused to seek approval for the drug in the United States, or to let another company or group do so. Since a drug could be approved for marketing in the US only if a company initiated the approval procedures through the Food and Drug Administration, the prospects for RU 486 in the US appeared slim at best. But Etienne-Emile Baulieu, who was lecturing around the world to promote his invention, predicted that the success of RU 486 in France, and coming successes in other countries, would inevitably lead to the drug's approval in the US. Others felt differently.

ABORTION IN THE US

The history of abortion as a major political issue in the US is relatively short, but intense. While many states began to liberalize their abortion laws in the 1960s, it was the landmark 1973 *Roe v. Wade* Supreme Court decision, ruling that states could not restrict access to abortion during the first trimester, that kicked off the "pro-life" movement which came to wield considerable political force in the US. Still, despite the prominence of the abortion question in American political debate, and the staunch pro-life position of the Reagan administration, general public sentiment was not clear.

By one measure, at least, abortion could be said to be, in a sense, "popular" in the US. The US had one of the highest abortion rates among developed countries: each year, around 28 of every 1000 women of childbearing age had abortions. In 1985 alone, 1.6 million abortions were performed in the US; since the late sixties, the total number of legal abortions exceeded 24 million—which amounted to about one quarter of all pregnancies in the nation.[20]

Pro-life activists sought to stem the tide of abortion using a number of high visibility tactics—picketing or blocking abortion clinics and the offices of doctors who performed abortions, producing graphic films on the physiology of abortion, and even bombing some clinics—which captured considerable media attention. Most people agreed that, whatever their ultimate effect on political opinion about the legality of abortion, these tactics at least succeeded in making many Americans uncomfortable about abortion. Roussel was cognizant of the force of the pro-life movement in the US. "The pressure groups in the United States are very powerful, maybe even more so than in France," said Pierre de Rible, an official at Roussel. "We see that in the American presidential campaign abortion is a major subject of debate, but in France people speak less and less about it."[21]

But supporters of abortion in the US responded with political pressure of their own, not only organizing marches and lobbying campaigns, but launching a "self-help abortion movement," which, the *Times* reported, taught women "how to perform abortions on themselves and each other."[22] To such groups, RU 486 would presumably seem to be a logical extension of the "self-help" spirit. Moreover, the appeal of new technology like RU 486 would not necessarily be limited to people who were vocally pro-choice. Tony Kaye speculated in *The New Republic* very early on in the debate about RU 486 that the pill might have a broader appeal:

> If RU-486 became the abortion method of choice in this country, the abortion debate would be over for many people who now consider it an open question. Polls show that the pro-life movement hasn't succeeded in increasing the number of Americans supporting a legal ban on abortion. They have succeeded in

making Americans queasy about abortion generally. This soft support is very vulnerable to RU-486 because polls also show that Americans oppose early abortions less fervently and in fewer numbers than late abortions. For many of them, a six-week-old embryo is still closer to a fertilized ovum than a human being.[23]

Other evidence appeared to bear out Kaye's prediction of general popular support for RU 486. In a November 9, 1988, letter to the *New York Times,* Humphrey Taylor, president of the Harris polling group, asserted that, by fearing reprisals in the US, Roussel had "seriously misread American public opinion." Taylor's group had been commissioned to conduct a poll on RU 486. Fifty-nine percent of those polled, Taylor reported, had said they would favor "a new birth control method . . . to terminate unintended pregnancy in its first few weeks by taking a pill."

Kaye's analysis of the appeal of RU 486 spoke directly to the main fear pro-lifers had about the drug (besides its abortifacient qualities): that it would deflate their methods. If, as some predicted, RU 486 would render the abortion clinic obsolete, then pro-life activists would be unable to picket them. Anti-abortionist forces also charged that by describing RU 486 in such terms as "birth control," "contraceptive," and "contragestive," supporters of the drug were obscuring the fact that the drug caused abortion. At least one pro-life organization loudly announced its intention of finding other methods to publicize and fight abortions that could take place in the privacy of the home. In February 1988, the *New York Times* reported that "National Right to Life and other groups opposed to abortion have served notice to drug companies that if any company sold an abortion-inducing drug the millions of Americans who oppose abortion will boycott all the company's products."[24]

BOYCOTTING ABORTION DRUGS

RU 486 was not the only abortion drug to appear, at least on the horizon, in the US, nor was Roussel the only firm to experience opposition from anti-abortion activists. Several pharmaceutical companies had already faced boycotts, or the threat of one, because they were doing research on, or had marketed, abortion-related drugs. The National Right to Life Committee, for example, had called on its members to boycott the Upjohn Company of Kalamazoo, Michigan, because it sold prostaglandin analogues. Three drugs, Prostin F2 Alpha, Prostin 15M, and Prostin E2, were marketed by Upjohn for termination of second-trimester pregnancy, and for treating congenital heart defects in newborns. In 1985, after a two-year boycott by members of National Right to Life, fertility research in Upjohn's labs ceased altogether, but the NRTL kept up its boycott because the company continued to market Prostins—even though, an Upjohn spokesman pointed out, the market for the prostaglandins they produced was small: "More than 95 percent of all abortions are done in the first trimester," he told the *Times.*[25]

Another prostaglandin analogue, Cytotec, was a target of concern, though not yet of a boycott, by anti-abortion forces. Cytotec was developed by G.D. Searle Co. for its anti-ulcer properties, and was tested, approved by the FDA, and marketed for that purpose. Like the other prostaglandins, however, Cytotec could effect a developing fetus: a normal dose of the drug induced abortion in one out of 10 pregnant women. What made Cytotec significant was that, in contrast to other prostaglandins such as Upjohn's Prostin drugs, which were administered by injection or suppository, Cytotec was a pill—which made it resemble RU 486 more than other drugs of its kind.[26]

However, Cytotec was intended mostly for arthritis sufferers who took large doses of aspirin and other non-steroidal anti-inflammatory drugs, which could cause ulcers. Since most arthritis users were beyond child-bearing age, Cytotec's counterindication for pregnant women was deemed to be outweighed by the potential benefit of preventing life-threatening ulcers.[27] The FDA approved Cytotec on December 27th, 1988, but only with the provision that the drug be specially labelled to warn patients and doctors that it could cause miscarriage. Nevertheless, anti-abortion activists opposed the approval of Cytotec by the FDA not only because of the potential danger it posed to fetuses if it were inadvertently misused, but also because of its potential intentional use as an abortifacient. John Willke, president of the NRTL, questioned the FDA's reasoning that the benefits of Cytotec outweighed its potential risks, by challenging the notion that Cytotec was more effective than existing anti-ulcer drugs;[28] and Mary Jo Kahler, director of Human Life of Washington State, an affiliate of the NRTL, suggested that Searle intended Cytotec to be used for abortions all along: "Searle can cover up the real purpose of Cytotec as an abortifacient by marketing it as a drug for stomach ulcers," she said. "Marketing it as a drug for stomach ulcers gives it credibility in the public's mind."[29]

Perhaps because of such comments, other companies took a cautious approach to abortion-related drugs. Such appeared to be the case with Winthrop Sterling USA of New York after it developed a drug called "Epostane," which had abortive properties similar to those of RU 486. Epostane acted by preventing the ovaries from producing progesterone (instead of blocking progesterone, as RU 486 did). Dr. Marinus Crooij, a researcher at the Free University in Amsterdam who studied the drug, told the *Times* that he thought Epostane might prove to be more effective than RU 486, in combination with prostaglandins, since Epostane worked well eight weeks into pregnancy, while RU 486 became less effective after six weeks.[30] However, a spokesperson for Sterling insisted that the company had no plans to market Epostane, because doing so "is not consistent with Sterling's strategic goals." National Right To Life President John Willke reported early in 1989 that Sterling was in communication with the NRTL, and

> has given us written assurances that they are removing this drug from the scene completely. They will not do any more research on it. They will not give or sell the license for it to any other company. They will not allow any other research

to be done on the drug. In effect, it has been put in a deep freeze. For this, we are deeply grateful to the Winthrop Sterling Drug Company and to its owner, Eastman Kodak.[31]

Against this backdrop, it was perhaps not surprising that Hoechst-Roussel, Groupe Roussel-Uclaf's American subsidiary, denied early on that it would market RU 486, apparently because of threats. A spokesman for Hoechst-Roussel said: "We're not in that business—we don't want to get into it." On September 29, 1988, the *Times* reported rumors that a New Jersey company, Gynopharma Inc., would apply for permission to market RU 486 in the US. Gynopharma's only other product, the *Times* noted, was an intrauterine device called Paragard. The company therefore fit into the category of firms which some had speculated would be best suited to market RU 486. Small companies with few products had less to fear from boycotts, it was felt, and certainly a company that marketed an IUD would have fewer pro-life consumers than most pharmaceutical companies. However, Laura Giles, a spokeswoman for Gynopharma said that the company "is not currently planning" to develop the drug (while also noting that the firm "does not comment on any project in progress or which is or has been under internal review"). An earlier press release stated that "Gynopharma does not have an agreement, nor is the company involved in negotiations with" Roussel.

Most observers and, privately, representatives of pharmaceutical companies agreed that this degree of caution stemmed from a fear of boycotts. This wariness was, to all appearances, uniform and industry-wide: one of the roles of the Pharmaceutical Manufacturers Association was to "develop positions on public policy issues affecting the industry," yet it had formulated no policy regarding abortion-inducing drugs on the grounds that it was not an industry-wide matter.[32]

DRUG APPROVAL:
"AN ADVERSE CLIMATE"

Other factors than boycotts alone, however, were considered responsible for the unavailability of drugs like RU 486—as the Upjohn case indicated. Upjohn itself had publicly denied that it had stopped its fertility research because of the boycott, attributing its action instead to "an adverse regulatory climate" in the US. "It is very difficult to get fertility drugs approved," an Upjohn spokesman said. "And there is a litigious climate. Litigation is terribly expensive, even if you win."[33] Notwithstanding Upjohn's obvious stake in not appearing to cave in to boycott threats, the point the company made was clear: a number of complex and interrelated factors had contributed to the difficulties of making drugs like RU 486 available in the US.

Approval of new drugs in the United States is the province of the Food and Drug Administration, which is part of the Department of Health and Human Services. According to the stringent provisions of the Food and

Drug Act of 1962, the FDA is required to approve only those drugs which are demonstrated, through extensive and documented testing, to be "safe and effective" for the intended purpose. The drug-approval process has four stages. In the first, a potential drug is tested on animals. This stage is designed to determine whether a drug is safe for testing on human beings. After these initial tests, the sponsor of the drug submits an Investigational New Drug (IND) application, essentially informing the FDA that the drug will be tested on human beings within thirty days unless the FDA objects.

Clinical tests of drugs on human beings are divided into three phases. Phase I involves a small number of research subjects (under 100), and seeks to establish the toxicity and safe dosages for the drug. This phase lasts around one year. Phase II entails more detailed study of the safety of the drug, and begins to examine its efficacy; it involves between 100 and 1000 subjects who have the disease or syndrome which the drug purports to treat, and can take between two and three years to complete. The final stage of testing, Phase III of clinical trials on humans, seeks to test efficacy and detect any rare or long-term side effects of the drug in question. This phase involves several thousand subjects and can take several years. After Phase III has been completed, the sponsor submits a New Drug Application (NDA) for approval by the FDA.

All told, then, the process of getting a drug approved, from research to final approval, takes between six and 10 years. Furthermore, only a fifth of drugs for which INDs are submitted are eventually approved. In recent years, AIDS advocates, contending that the federal government had not acted quickly enough to develop an AIDS vaccine or drugs to combat the diseases associated with AIDS, successfully pressured the FDA into bending its rules somewhat. As a result, in July 1988 the agency issued new guidelines allowing drugs which were available abroad but had not been approved for use in the US by the FDA to be imported through the mail for personal use by people with "life-threatening conditions like AIDS and cancer."[34]

However, the FDA also signaled its unwillingness to extend such waivers to RU 486. On September 26, 1988, wary of the potential applicability of its directive to RU 486, Burton I. Love at the FDA made a special exception to the new rule:

> "RU486" or "Mifepristone" manufactured by Roussel Uclaf Laboratories, Paris France has been approved in France and in China. The drug is used to induce abortion and can be used up to 49 days after a woman's last menstrual period.
>
> This drug will not be allowed entry under the "Pilot Guidance for Release of Mail Importations" which was issued on July 20, 1988, because it does not meet the criteria in the policy statement.

Making this exception was superfluous, since RU 486 was not yet used for the treatment of a "life-threatening condition"; the care Love took to specify the exception indicated how "adverse" the "regulatory climate" was for the drug.

In fact, the "adverse regulatory climate" and "litigious climate" cited by Upjohn described the climate in the US for the development and marketing of *any* drugs having to do with reproduction, including contraceptives. As a result, of seventeen major companies doing research on contraceptives before the 1980s, only one, Ortho Pharmaceutical Corp., continued such research a decade later.[35] No new contraceptive methods had been introduced in the US for thirty years, since the introduction of the oral contraceptive pill and intrauterine devices. Most observers cited as a reason for this decline in contraceptive research and development the same factor impeding abortion drugs: the virulence of the abortion debate.

A panel formed by the National Academy of Sciences issued a report in February of 1990 which gave the strongest voice to concern about the state of contraceptive technology in the US. The panel's report, which was summarized in an article in the February 15, 1990, issue of the *New England Journal of Medicine*, emphasized that:

- the slowing pace of research in the development of contraceptives had left the US far behind Europe;
- the number and kind of contraceptives available to people in the United States had not changed substantially in thirty years (since the introduction of the oral contraceptive and the IUD);
- the abortion rate, and the number of people who were choosing sterilization early in their reproductive lives, were both increasing;
- there were "shortcomings of existing products, including characteristics related to health risks, effectiveness, and convenience as well as to other user preferences."

Although several highly effective contraceptive methods were available in the US, including the oral contraceptive pill, IUDs, and "barrier methods" such as condoms and diaphragms, the panel's report saw these as inadequate, particularly for teenagers and people in their early twenties. Behavioral difficulties made these methods less effective with this age group. Also, women who could not use a particular method for health reasons (many women, for example, could not safely take the pill) had few alternatives. Moreover, because of lawsuits in the 1970s, only two pharmaceutical companies were still producing intrauterine devices; and many doctors refused to prescribe IUDs out of fear of litigation.[36] "Although the pill and the IUD have been modified to increase their safety and effectiveness," the National Academy of Sciences panel concluded, "they are still not suitable for use by all couples in all circumstances."

The panel's report advanced several reasons for the inadequacy of contraceptive research in the US, including the cost of getting a drug approved (at a time when, increasingly, non-profit groups were doing research on contraceptives), the "liability crisis," and, prominently, the FDA's stringent drug approval process. The report called on the FDA to change its procedures for evaluating contraceptive drugs, in particular by taking into ac-

count the comparative safety of new drugs for people with counterindica-
tions for existing contraceptives. However, few saw much likelihood that
the FDA, sensitive to the administration's pro-life stance, or the drug companies, fearful of boycotts and litigation, would actively seek to modify the
climate for research and development on fertility control.

THE ABORTION DEBATE AND DOCTORS

Members of the medical profession were as affected by concern about litigation as were the pharmaceutical companies. For this reason, fears on the
part of pro-life groups that doctors would prescribe drugs like Cytotec for
their abortifacient properties seemed unlikely to be realized. Once a drug
was approved for any indication, it could be used for any other legal purpose; however, a doctor could be liable for harm done to a patient who was
prescribed a drug for an untested use.

But what was perhaps more crucial for the prospects of RU 486 was the
impact on doctors of the abortion debate. The growing reluctance on the
part of physicians to provide surgical abortions indicated that they, too,
were affected by the virulence of the abortion debate. Between 1982 and
1985, the number of abortion providers in the US declined by five percent
(from 2,908 to 2,680), and continued to decline thereafter.[37]

Physicians themselves offered a number of reasons to explain this trend.
Some doctors simply opposed abortions, viewing them as antithetical to the
goals of the medical profession. Dr. Curtis E. Harris, head of the American
Academy of Medical Ethics, a group of doctors that favored restricting the
availability of abortions, referred to abortion as "a real contradiction," in
light of the fact that "[m]ost gynecologists work to bring a child into the
world in a healthy state."[38]

Other doctors were intimidated by vocal public opposition to abortion.
Facing daily picketing and harassment and occasional acts of violence led
some doctors who did not oppose abortions in principle to decline to perform them. Several physicians told the New York Times that the medical community ostracized doctors who performed abortions. They were ostracized,
moreover, by doctors who were pro-choice as well as those who were not:
abortionists were simply stigmatized. As a result, many doctors who believed that abortions should be available felt ambivalent about offering to do
abortions themselves, because of the strong emotions performing them
aroused.

Dr. Louise Tyrer of Planned Parenthood offered another explanation for
the decreasing interest in performing abortions: "The older doctors like myself who used to see women by the hundreds in hospitals suffering complications of illegal abortions and even dying were highly motivated to change
that." Younger doctors, she said, "have not seen any of that—they're not
aware of the horrors."[39]

Whatever the cause, a consequence of this reluctance to perform abortions was the increasing inaccessibility of surgical abortions in all but urban

areas.[40] Doctors who did provide abortions were distributed unevenly geographically: in 1985, 82 percent of counties in the US had no doctors who
performed abortions, while these counties accounted for 30 percent of
women of childbearing age. Doctors who performed abortions tended to be
heavily concentrated in cities: only two percent of abortions in 1985 took
place outside of metropolitan areas. Dr. Constance J. Brumm, a gynecologist
in the small town of Pullman, Washington, told the *Times* that, while she
strongly felt that abortions should be legal and available, "as long as there
is someone else to provide abortions, I'd rather not do it." Brumm, the paper
reported, explained that

> she feared that her 2-year-old son would be taunted; that she dreads the inevi-
> table harassment; that she thought that if she did abortions she would lose pa-
> tients who now come to her for gynecological care.

Since no one else offered abortions in Pullman, women seeking abortions
had to travel to Spokane, 90 miles away, or even farther. "We send about
100 women out of the community every year for abortions," Brumm said.

Precisely because of these trends, many in the medical profession have
come out in support of RU 486. Just as women who wanted access to abortion welcomed the privacy that RU 486 would bring, so did doctors. In the
case of doctors, however, the drug offered them refuge from the increasing
stigma of being an abortionist. Thus the strong support for RU 486 shown
at the meeting of the World Congress of Gynecology and Obstetrics in Rio,
though undoubtedly largely on behalf of women's health, may have arisen
in part from these motives.[41]

Technology like RU 486 would likely accelerate the trend of physicians
abandoning surgical abortion. This could be a particularly significant consequence, since the failure rate of the drug requires the availability of surgical abortion as a backup. Some also fear that the new pill would bring with
it increasing problems of accessibility for women, especially the rural poor,
who already have little access to abortion.[42]

THE ABORTION DEBATE
AND GOVERNMENT

In the abortion debate, the US federal government had been a prominent
voice, on the pro-life side, since Ronald Reagan assumed the presidency in
1980. Under regulations issued by the Reagan administration, the federal
government was prohibited from funding any research related to abortion,
and federal money could not be used through Medicaid to pay for abortions
for poor women (a decision President Bush reaffirmed when he vetoed
funding for abortion for victims of incest or rape). The government's influence on the abortion debate, moreover, was felt beyond the shores of the
US, when the Reagan administration acted to cut off funds to international
organizations—such as the United Nations Fund for Population Activities

and International Planned Parenthood—on the ground that they financed abortion clinics. Such a move cast a chill on the involvement of the World Health Organization in the distribution of RU 486. Although the WHO's Human Reproduction Unit had been engaged in trials of the drug, it had been reluctant to sponsor distribution of the pill because, Baulieu charged, its director "says he's afraid that American money will be cut off if an RU 486 program comes under the WHO umbrella."[43]

In Congress, there was more divergence of opinion about abortion and, hence, about RU 486. Representative Robert Dornan (R-Calif.) as early as 1986 was taking action to block development of what he termed the "death pill." In a "Dear Colleague" letter, he announced his intention of submitting an amendment to the Health and Human Services appropriations bill which would have barred FDA funding for testing RU 486. "The proponents of abortion," Dornan wrote in his letter,

> want to replace the guilt suffered by women who undergo abortion with the moral uncertainty of self-deception. Imagine, with the "death pill," the taking of a pre-born life will be as easy and as trivial as taking aspirin.

Dornan's amendment did not pass, but his voice did not go unheard, at least by officials in the Bush administration. On June 9, 1989, FDA Commissioner Frank E. Young wrote to Dornan and to 11 other congressmen—in response to concerns they had expressed in a letter the previous month—to assure them that the agency would not permit RU 486 to be imported into the US for personal use.[44]

Others in Congress, however, expressed deep frustration over the continuing unavailability of RU 486, particularly in a nation where research on contraceptives had all but stopped and the abortion rate continued to be high. According to the National Research Council, *The New Republic* reported in November 1990, somewhere between 1.2 and 3 million unwanted pregnancies occurred in the US annually, and about half of the 1.5 million abortions performed each year were due to contraceptive failure.[45] In view of such statistics, as well as the potential benefits of RU 486 in the treatment of a number of diseases, some members of Congress saw an urgent need for study of the drug. Writing in a 1989 report of the House Committee on Government Operations, Representative Ted Weiss (D-NY) argued:

> Given the many possible benefits of RU-486, it is unconscionable that political considerations in the United States have interfered with the scientific study and availability of this drug. Given the legality of abortion and the large number of abortions nationwide, it is unjustifiable that NIH research on the contraceptive and abortifacient use of RU-486 is not permitted.

PROSPECTS FOR THE FUTURE

Back in December 1988, Roussel had devised a set of five "mandatory prerequisites" a country must meet before RU 486 could be marketed there:

abortion must be legal; abortion must be accepted by public, medical, and political opinion; prostaglandin must be available; distribution of the drug must be strictly controlled; and patients must sign a consent form agreeing to undergo surgical abortion if the drug treatment failed. On two of those criteria, the US was a problematic market for RU 486. First, Sulprostone, the synthetic prostaglandin used in conjunction with RU 486, and manufactured by the German pharmaceutical firm of Schering A.G., had not been approved for use in the US. It was not clear whether prostaglandins already being sold in the US would be adequate substitutes; nor, given the troubled history of Cytotec and Upjohn's Prostins, was the outlook promising for introducing a new product. Second, and most crucially, while the majority of Americans appeared to support legal abortion, the degree of public acceptance Roussel sought would be hard to meet. "By 'accepted by public opinion,'" one commentator wrote, "the company clearly means 'uncontroversial' . . ."—a standard that the vocal pro-life advocates made virtually unattainable in the US.[46]

Still, as 1990 drew to a close, the voices in favor of bringing RU 486 to the US were growing more insistent. Studies released in the spring of that year had given increasing evidence of the safety of the drug when used to induce abortion, and some physicians argued that the pill appeared to be both safer and cheaper than surgical abortion. In June, one of the most powerful medical groups in the nation—the American Medical Association—endorsed testing of RU 486 and supported efforts to persuade Roussel to release it in the US. Meanwhile, a number of researchers had been complaining about the difficulty of obtaining RU 486 to study its effects on Cushing's syndrome, breast cancer, glaucoma, and brain cancer, as well as contraception; the National Institute of Health had abandoned clinical tests on patients with Cushing's syndrome because it could not acquire RU 486 in sufficient quantities to sustain the effects of treatment. In light of these developments, some members of Congress had begun to take steps to remedy the situation. In July, for instance, 70 members, led by Rep. Barbara Boxer (D-Calif.), signed a letter urging Roussel to make RU 486 available for testing in the US, hoping thereby to convince Roussel that the pro-life movement did not, as The New Republic put it, "represent . . . the will of the public at large."[47] And in November, Rep. Ron Wyden (D-Ore.) announced that the Small Business Subcommittee on Regulation, Business Opportunity and Energy would hold hearings to investigate why "important clinical trials of this new drug are being shut down all over the country."[48]

At the same time, Baulieu was exerting pressure on Roussel to make RU 486 available to Third World countries, while decrying the chilling effect US policy on abortion had on groups like the World Health Organization. Calling the US "a major obstacle, an indecent obstacle" to distribution of RU 486 in poor countries, Baulieu asked, "How can we ignore that 500 women die every day as a result of badly executed abortions?"[49]

Roussel did seem to be inching toward a more liberal policy regarding distribution of RU 486. In the spring of 1990, in what the May 24 edition of the *International Herald-Tribune* described as a "surprise move," Roussel announced its intention to begin selling the drug in Britain and Scandinavia, despite the reluctance of its parent company. Hoechst, Baulieu told the paper, "is not enthusiastic about it, [b]ut the Roussel people are determined to go ahead."

These signs of growing demand for RU 486 notwithstanding, no one expected the drug to be anything but controversial in the US. Despite promising study results, groups on both sides of the abortion issue questioned the safety of RU 486. National Right To Life officials charged that recent test results in fact supported their contention that RU 486 was unsafe. They worried particularly about "anemic, malnourished women" in the Third World who might be administered the drug under Roussel's agreement with WHO. "The company is promoting this drug as safe," said one official, "but we don't have any idea of what the long-term effects will be." [50] Similar sentiments were voiced by Cindy Pearson of the National Women's Health Network (NWHN), an organization supporting abortion and the "self-help abortion movement." In a 1988 discussion paper, Pearson questioned the safety of RU 486 in comparison to currently accepted techniques (especially suction, the most common method of abortion). [51] These concerns were shared by other women's advocates, especially in light of the readiness with which other treatments, like the pill and the IUD, which turned out not to be as safe as was thought, had been hailed in the name of women's health.

Pearson also foresaw possible political and moral consequences for women and the "women's health movement" if RU 486 became the abortion method of choice. "Do we lose perceived power in society if we go back behind closed doors to have abortions?" she asked.

> Does the personal become less political when it is a miscarriage alone at home vs. an abortion in a setting where other women are experiencing the same thing? Women will experience the cramping and pain of a miscarriage over several hours compared to a ten-minute suction abortion. They will lose the support given by abortion clinic counselors, who reaffirm that abortion is a moral decision and who help women get through the pain of the suction procedure.

The effect of RU 486, Pearson worried, could be to "encourage an already-existing trend of making women feel guilty about abortion."

Meanwhile, Roussel's parent company kept a weather eye on its bottom line. The threat of boycott was apparently undiminished. John Willke of the National Right To Life had declared that if RU 486 ever came to the US, he would mount a worldwide boycott of every product made by Roussel and Hoechst. "It'll be a whopper," he warned. [52] In the US, at least, Hoechst would be particularly vulnerable to NRTL action. In addition to Hoechst-Roussel, its pharmaceutical company in New Jersey, the firm owned Hoechst Celanese corporation which, *The New Republic* reported, "produces everything from carpet fibers to tire cord," with revenues running to about $6 billion. In view of these facts, it was perhaps not surprising that a spokeswoman for Roussel told the *New York Times* in July 1990 that "[s]elling in the United States is out of the question at the moment." Responding to criticisms Baulieu had directed at the company, she pointed out that Baulieu "is a scientist and not an industrialist. Hoechst has interests in the United States and cannot do any old thing. It can't close its eyes to this reality."[53]

NOTES

1. Jeremy Cherfas and Joseph Palca, "The Pill of Choice?" *Science* (Sept. 22, 1989), p. 1324.

2. Dorothy Wickenden, "Drug of Choice," *The New Republic*, November 26, 1990, p. 24.

3. Cherfas, p. 1324.

4. Ibid.

5. Cherfas, p. 1322.

6. Ibid.

7. Beatrice Couzinet, Nelly Le Strat, Andre Ulmann, Etienne-Emile Baulieu, and Gilbert Schaison, "Termination of Early Pregnancy by the Progesterone Antagonist RU 486 (Mifepristone)," *New England Journal of Medicine*, December 18, 1986, p. 1565.

8. Reproductive Health Technologies Project, "RU 486: The New French Abortion Pill" ("media kit"), 1989.

9. Cherfas, p. 1323.

10. Steven Greenhouse, "A New Pill, A Fierce Battle," *New York Times Magazine*, February 12, 1989, p. 24.

11. Greenhouse, p. 26.

12. Gina Kolata, "Boycott Threat Blocking Sale of Abortion-Inducing Drug," *New York Times*, February 22, 1988, p. A1.

13. Greenhouse, p. 24.

14. Ibid.

15. Greenhouse, p. 24, and *Le Monde*, June 24, 1988, p. 38. No mention of the protest appeared in the *Times* in June 1988. The article in *Le Monde*, which appeared the day after the meeting, reported the rise in Roussel's profits announced at the meeting, and enthusiastically listed RU 486 as one of the projects of the company, but included no mention of the protest.

16. Greenhouse, p. 26.

17. Ibid.

18. Ibid.

19. Greenhouse, "France Ordering Company to Sell its Abortion Drug," *New York Times*, Sept. 29, 1988, p. 1.

20. Alan Guttmacher Institute, *Facts in Brief: Abortion in the United States* (2 pp. pamphlet), 1989.

21. Greenhouse, "Maker Says Pressures Could Revive Abortion Pill," *New York Times*, October 28, 1988, p. A9.

22. Kolata, "Self-Help Abortion Movement Gains Momentum," *New York Times*, October 23, 1989, p. B12.

23. Tony Kaye, "Are You for RU 486?" *The New Republic*, January 27, 1986, pp. 13–15.

24. Kolata, "Boycott Threat Blocking Sale of Abortion-Inducing Drug," p. A1.

25. Ibid.

26. Bonnieclare Erling, "The 'New Abortion Pill': Will the drug shift attention away from abortion clinics?" *Seattle Weekly*, April 12, 1989, pp. 24–25.

27. Ibid.

28. John C. Willke, "Abortion Drugs—What's The Situation Now?" *National Right To Life News*, January 22, 1989, p. 3.

29. Erling, op. cit.

30. Kolata, "Boycott Threat Blocking Sale of Abortion-Inducing Drug," p. A13.

31. Willke, "Abortion Drugs—What's The Situation Now?," p. 3. However, the company's spokesperson was reported in the *Times* in February as suggesting that Winthrop Sterling might sell the patent to another company to market. Kolata, "Boycott Threat Blocking Sale of Abortion-Inducing Drug," p. A13.

32. Ellen Benoit, "Why Nobody Wants $1 Billion: How a small band of activists has intimidated some of the world's biggest companies," *Financial World*, June 27, 1989, p. 35.

33. Ibid., and Kolata, "After Large Study of Abortion Pill, French Maker Considers Wider Sale," *New York Times*, March 8, 1990, p. B10.

34. Since this directive was issued, AIDS groups have also had success in getting the FDA to modify its process to speed up the approval of AIDS drugs.

35. "Birth-control group urges more research," *Boston Globe*, January 30, 1990, p. 8.

36. Ibid.

37. Alan Guttmacher Institute, *Facts in Brief: Abortion in the United States*, 1989.

38. Quoted in Kolata, "Under Pressures and Stigma, More Doctors Shun Abortion," *New York Times*, January 8, 1990, p. A1.

39. Ibid.

40. Guttmacher Institute, *Facts in Brief: Abortion in the United States*.

41. Marlise Simons, "Doctors Protest Company's Action on Abortion Pill," *New York Times*, October 28, 1988, p. A1.

42. Cindy Pearson, "RU 486: What will it mean for the women's health movement?" (3 pp. discussion paper for the Board of Directors of the National Women's Health Network), November 12, 1988.

43. Alan Riding, "Abortion Politics Are Said To Hinder Use Of French Pill," *New York Times*, July 29, 1990, p. 1.

44. *Science*, September 22, 1989, p. 1321.

45. Wickenden, p. 27.

46. Ibid., p. 25.

47. Ibid.

48. Judy Foreman, "Work on new uses for abortion pill reported blocked," *Boston Globe*, November 19, 1990, p. 6.

49. Riding, p. 1.

50. Kolata, "After Large Study of Abortion Pill, French Maker Considers Wider Sale," p. B10.

51. Cindy Pearson, "RU 486: What will it mean for the women's health movement?"

52. Wickenden, p. 25.

53. Riding, p. 15.

SECTION B

Amniocentesis

XYLO: A True Story
Rayna Rapp

Mike called the fetus XYLO, X-Y for its unknown sex, LO for the love we were pouring into it. Day by day we fantasized, as newly, first-pregnant people do, about who this growing cluster of cells might become. Would it have Mike's thinning hair or my thick locks? My rubbery skin or his smooth complexion? Day by day, we followed the growth process in the myriad of books that surrounds modern pregnancy for the over-35 baby boomlet. Products of our time and place, both busy with engrossing work and political commitments, we welcomed this potential child with excitement, fantasy, and the rationality of scientific knowledge. As a women's movement activist, I had decided opinions about treating pregnancy as a normal, not a diseased condition, and we were fortunate that adequate health insurance and good connections netted us a health care team—obstetrician, midwives, genetics counselor—who were eager to answer our questions, but believed, as we did, that most pregnancies required little intervention.

The early months of the pregnancy passed in a blur of exhaustion and nausea. Preoccupied with my own feelings, I lived in a perpetual underwater, slow-motion version of my prior life. As one friend put it, I was already operating on fetal time, tied to an unfamiliar regimen of enforced naps, loss of energy and rigid eating. Knowing the research on nutrition, on hormones, and on miscarriage rates among older pregnant women, I did whatever I could to stay comfortable, and relaxed. Neither romanticism nor rationalism would see us through these months—we just had to accept the major changes in my body and our lives that a late, desired pregnancy brings.

*   *   *

I was thirty-six when XYLO was conceived, and like many of my peers, I chose to have amniocentesis. Both Mike and I knew about prenatal diagnosis from our friends' experiences, and from reading about it in newspapers and magazines. Each year, more than 20,000 American women choose amniocentesis, and the number is growing rapidly. The test is performed between the sixteenth and twentieth weeks of pregnancy (counted from the last menstrual period). Most obstetricians, mine included, prefer to send their pregnant patients directly to hospital-associated genetics Centers, where counseling is provided, and the lab technicians are specialists in the procedure. This, of course, ups the already considerable cost of quality pregnancy care. Amniocentesis requires complex laboratory work, and is priced between $400 and $1000 in the state of New York, where my test was performed. In New York, medicaid covers the costs and the City lab, a model of its kind, has a sliding scale fee for women not covered by private or government health plans and outreach services in several languages. But since the Hyde amendment's cut-off of medicaid funds for abortion at the federal level, very few states still fund the procedure. And of those that fund abortion, even fewer fund amniocentesis for eligible, low-income women. So accessibility of the test varies widely throughout this country, depending on healthcare economics, state welfare law, and on the attitudes of obstetricians, who may or may not refer patients, depending on how current their knowledge of the literature is, and how they feel about genetics, genetic diseases, and the decision to abort an affected fetus. Given these mazeways of resources, medical services, and public health information, the majority of women undergoing amniocentesis are like me—consumers of expensive healthcare services, late childbearers, middle-class, and white. But we aren't the only group of women who need to know about the test.

Three groups of women are 'at risk' (to use the epidemiological language) of carrying genetically damaged fetuses, and might therefore want to seek out prenatal diagnosis. The first is women who've already borne a child with a genetic disease or birth defect, or have such children in their own or their partner's family. The second includes women and their partners from extended families or ethnically specific communities in which the incidence of certain inherited diseases is known to be relatively high. And the third is older women, or women with older partners since the risk of bearing a Down syndrome child increases with age. While prenatal diagnosis can only reveal a certain number of genetic diseases and fetal anomalies, not by any means all of the conditions known to occur, it can detect ones such as:

- dominant gene conditions that affect one of the two parents, like a type of very serious inherited high cholesterol with a predisposition to heart disease;
- recessive gene conditions in which parents are carriers but never manifest the problem themselves, such as thalassemia, Tay Sachs and sickle-cell anemia;
- X-linked (sex-linked) diseases for which the woman is the carrier, and only male offspring are affected, like Duchenes's muscular dystrophy, .and hemophilia (bleeders' disease) (in most X-linked conditions, there

is no specific test for the disease, only for the sex of the fetus. So the parents must face the possibility that a male fetus is 50 percent likely to be affected, and 50 percent likely not);

• neural tube defects such as anencephaly (a missing portion of the brain) and spina bifida (caused by a prenatal lesion in the neural tube, this disease may leave a person differentially paralyzed, depending on where the lesion occurs);

• chromosomal anomalies in which the 'wrong number' of chromosomes leads to a series of different conditions, like Turner's syndrome, Kleifelter's syndrome, and, most commonly, Down syndrome.

While all of these conditions are relatively rare, certain groups are at greater than average risk of having offspring affected by them: neural tube defects are more likely among Anglo-Irish couples, Tay Sachs afflicts Ashkenazi Jews, sickle-cell anemia is most prevalent among people of African origin, and thalassemia is a Mediterranean disease. Down syndrome increases with the age of the pregnant woman and, to a lesser degree, with the age of her partner as well. At the age of thirty, a woman's chances of giving birth to a Down syndrome child are about one in 885; at thirty-five, they increase to one in 365, and at forty, they're about one in 109 (Hendin and Marks, 1979; Consensus Development Conference, 1979; President's Commission, 1983).

The increased risk of Down syndrome has something to do with aging. Perhaps we ovulate with more 'mistakes' during cell reproduction, perhaps accumulated environmental assaults affect relatively more of our eggs, perhaps our bodies become less able to 'slough off' genetically anomalous fetuses as early miscarriages. Men's semen is also affected by age, but their contribution to Down seems to go up much more slowly.

It was the fear of Down syndrome which sent us to seek prenatal diagnosis of XYLO. Down syndrome produces a characteristic physical appearance—short, stocky size, large tongues, puffy eyes and skin folds pointed upwards—and is a major cause of mental retardation, world-wide. People with Down syndrome are quite likely to have weak cardiovascular systems, gastrointestinal problems, and run a much higher risk of developing childhood leukemia. While the majority of Down syndrome infants used to die very young, a combination of antibiotics and infant surgery enables modern medicine to keep them alive. And programs of childhood physical-mental stimulation and cosmetic surgery may facilitate their assimilation. Down syndrome is caused by an extra chromosome, of the pair that geneticists label as number 21, and is sometimes called 'trisomy 21' for that reason. There is no cure for Down syndrome. A pregnant woman whose fetus is diagnosed as having the extra chromosome can either prepare to raise a mentally retarded and physically very vulnerable child, or decide to abort it.

Initially, in the mid-to-late 1960s, women over forty were counselled to have the test. Then, the age dropped to thirty-eight, and currently it's recommended for women who are thirty-five or older when they conceive (President's Commission, 1983; Sadovnick & Baird, 1981). We're thus witnessing two social processes at work: the routinization of a frontier of medicine is being extended more deeply into the population at the same time that an increasing number of women are choosing to delay childbearing. As these two trends intersect, amniocentesis becomes a new pregnancy ritual among people like me, with great implications for our lives, and the lives of other women as well.

*   *   *

Some of these facts about chromosomes I could vaguely dredge up from a college course on the February morning when Mike and I arrived at a local medical center for genetic counseling, in my nineteenth week of pregnancy. Nancy Z., our social-work trained counselor, took a detailed pedigree (or family tree) from each of us, to discovery any rare diseases or birth defects for which we could be tested. She then gave us an excellent genetics lesson, explained the amniocentesis procedure and the risks, both of amniocentesis, and of discovering a serious genetic defect. Less than 1 percent of pregnancies miscarry after amniocentesis. That's a low risk, but it isn't no-risk, and during pregnancy we all feel very concerned and vulnerable about anything that might cause damage or death to our fetuses. Most women feel fine after the test, but a certain percentage (perhaps 10 percent) experience uterine cramping or contractions, and are told by doctors to rest until they subside. Overall, about 98 percent of the women who go for amniocentesis will be told that no fetal defects or anomalies have been found. So the overall rate of genetic defect detection (about 2 percent) and of miscarriage following the procedure (less than 1 percent) are both very small, but also very similar.

After counseling, we descended to the testing area, where an all-female team of radiologist, obstetrician, nurses and staff assistants performed the tap. In skilled hands, and with the use of sonogram equipment, the tap is a rapid procedure. I spent perhaps five minutes on the table, belly attached to sonar electrodes, Mike holding my feet for encouragement. The radiologist flipped off 'polaroid' pictures of XYLO, and we went home with our first 'baby album'—grey blotches of a head and spine of our baby-in-waiting. The radiologist located the placenta, which enabled the obstetrician to successfully draw a small, clear sample of amniotic fluid (less than one-eighth of a cup). The tap felt like a crampier version of drawing blood. It wasn't particularly painful or traumatic. We marched the fluid back to the genetics lab where it would be cultured, and went home.

The waiting period for amniocentesis results is a long one, and I was very anxious. Cells must be cultured, then analyzed in intensive lab examination, and this process of karyotyping takes two to four weeks. While we are all told that 'no news is good news,' it's a hard period to endure. Caught between the late date at which sufficient amniotic fluid exists to be tapped (sixteen to twenty weeks), the experience of quickening, when the woman feels the fetus move (roughly, eighteen to twenty weeks), and the legal limits of abortion (few abortions are performed after twenty-four weeks in the USA), we all have terrible fantasies, and many of us report distressing dreams.

For the 98 percent of women whose amniotic fluid reveals no anomaly, reassurance arrives by phone, or, more likely, by mail, confirming a negative test. When Nancy called me twelve days after the tap, I began to scream as soon as I recognized her voice; in her lab, only positive results (very negative results, from a potential parent's point of view) are reported by phone. The image of myself, alone, screaming into a white plastic telephone is indelible. Although it only took twenty minutes to locate Mike and bring him and a close friend to my side, time is suspended in my memory, and I replay the call, and my screams echo for indefinite periods. Results are not formally communicated by phone, but with a bit of intervention from our midwives and obstetrician, we learned that a tentative diagnosis of a male Down syndrome fetus had been made. Our fantasies for XYLO, our five months' fetus, were completely shattered.

Mike and I had discussed what we would do if amniocentesis revealed a serious genetic condition long before the test. For us, the diagnosis of Down syndrome was reason to choose abortion. Our thinking was clear, if abstract, long before the concrete horror became reality. We were eager to have a child, and prepared to change our lives to make emotional, social, and economic resources available. But the realities of raising a child who could never grow to independence would call forth more than we could muster, unless one or both of us gave up our work, our political commitments, our social existence beyond the household. And despite a shared commitment to co-parenting, we both understood that, in this society, one was likely to be the mother. When I thought about myself, I knew that in such a situation, I would transform myself to become the kind of twenty-four-hour-a-day advocate such a child would require. I'd do the best and most loving job I could, and I'd undoubtedly become an activist in support of the needs of disabled children. But even if we *did* totally transform our lives to raise a Down syndrome child, other stark realities confronted us: to keep a Down syndrome child alive through potentially lethal health problems is an act of love whose ultimate consequences are problematic. As we ourselves age, to whom would we leave the person XYLO would become? In a society where the state provides virtually no decent, humane services for the mentally retarded, how could we take responsibility for the future of our dependent Down syndrome child? In good conscience, we couldn't choose to raise a child who would become a ward of the state. The health care, schools, various therapies that Down syndrome children require are inadequately available and horrendously expensive in America, and no single family can take the place that a decent health and social policy may someday extend to physically and mentally disabled people. In the meantime, while struggling for such a society, we did not choose to bring a child into this world who could never grow up to care for himself.

Other genetic diagnoses may present less, or more, clear choices to potential parents. If your fetus has Tay Sachs, it's a 100 percent childhood death sentence, while the disabilities associated with spina bifida range from quadraplegic, but mentally alert, to both much milder physical, and much harsher mental, diagnoses. A disease like sickle-cell anemia is episodic, and ranges from life-threatening to livable, depending on severity. It nearly always involves intense bouts of pain. Diseases like hemophilia can now be medically managed to allow for livable, if restricted lives. The diagnosis of Down syndrome spells mental retardation, but the detection of an extra chromosome can't tell us if our specific Down syndrome fetus will grow up to have the mental age of three or seven, learn articulate speech or toilet training. So both the kind of genetic anomaly, and the range of its potential severity make the choices surrounding prenatal diagnosis a parental nightmare.

Most women who've opted for amniocentesis are prepared to face the question of abortion, and many of us *do* choose it, after a seriously disabling diagnosis is made. Perhaps 95 percent of Down syndrome pregnancies are terminated after test results are known. Reports on other diseases and conditions are harder to find, but, in one study, the diagnosis of spina bifida led to abortion about 90 percent of the time. These were all women who'd borne and raised a previous spina bifida child. (Hook, 1978a, 1978b; Brock, 1977; Lawrence and Morris, 1981).

In shock and grief, I learned from my obstetrician that two kinds of late second-trimester abortions were available. Most common are the 'installation procedures'—saline solution or urea is injected into the uterus, prostaglandins are injected into the woman's veins to bring on labor, and sometimes pitocin, a labor-enhancing drug, is also used. The woman then goes through labor to deliver the dead fetus. 'Giving-birth-to-death' (as one woman who'd chosen an abortion after a Down syndrome diagnosis described the process) is emotionally draining on both the woman and her mate, who is often allowed to stay with her through the labor. Sedation may or may not be available. The second kind of mid-trimester abortion, and the one I chose, is a D and E—dilation and evacuation. Performed in the operating room of a hospital after the cervix has been dilated with laminaria (sterile seaweed sticks that absorb fluid, inserted twenty-four to forty-eight hours in advance), the D and E demands more active intervention from a doctor, who vacuums out the amniotic fluid, and then removes the dismembered fetus manually. A general anesthetic or heavy sedation is used. From the medical team's point of view, the D and E requires some intense, upsetting work, but it's over in about twenty minutes, without putting the woman through labor.

Either way, all the women I've spoken to found this a very tough abortion to endure. Like me, they'd wanted the pregnancy, or they would have ended it at a much earlier stage. Both forms of late abortion entail increasing maternal risks as the fetus grows—the later, the riskier, although both are still quite safe. But the psychological pain is enormous. Deciding to end the life of a fetus you've wanted and carried for most of five months is no easy matter. More than 90 percent of abortions in America are performed in the first trimester, long before fetal life is felt by the pregnant woman. The number of relatively late second-trimester abortions performed for genetic reasons is very small, perhaps about 400 a year in the USA. It's an almost inconsequential number, unless you happen to be one of them.

Making the medical arrangements, going back for counseling, the pretests, and, finally, the abortion, was the most difficult period of my adult life. I was then twenty-one weeks pregnant, and had been proudly carrying my expanding belly. Telling everyone—friends, family, students, colleagues, neighbors—seemed an endless nightmare. But the rewards of making our decision public were very great. Friends streamed in from all over to teach my classes: I have scores of letters expressing concern, and the phone never stopped ringing for weeks. There were always flowers being delivered to our door, and everyone eased my return back to work. Our community of friends was invaluable, reminding us that our lives were rich and filled with love despite this terrible loss. My parents flew a thousand miles to sit guard over my hospital bed, answer telephones, shop and cook. Filled with sorrow for the loss of their first grandchild, my mother told me of a conversation she'd had with my father. Despite their grief, they were deeply grateful for the test. After all, she reasoned, we were too young and active to be devastated like this; if the child had been born, she and my dad would have taken him to raise in their older years, so we could get on with raising other children. I can only respond with deep love and gratitude for the wellspring of compassion behind that conversation. But surely, no single woman, mother or grandmother, no single family, nuclear or extended, should have to bear all the burdens that raising a seriously disabled child entails. It points out, once again, the importance of providing decent, humane attention and services for other-than-fully-able children (and adults).

And, of course, parents of disabled children are quick to point out that the lives they've nurtured have been worth living. I honor their hard work and commitments, as well as their love, and I think that part of 'informed consent' to amniocentesis and selective abortion (as my experience is antiseptically called in medical jargon) should include information about groups for parents of Down syndrome children, and social services available to them, not just the individual, medical diagnosis of the problem. And even people who feel they could never choose a late abortion may none the less want amniocentesis so they'll have a few extra months to prepare themselves, other family members, friends, and special resources for the birth of a child with special, complex needs.

Recovering from the abortion took a long time. Friends, family, coworkers, students did everything they could to ease me through the experience. Even so, I yearned to talk with someone who'd 'been there.' Over the next few months, I used my personal and medical networks to locate and interview a handful of other women who'd opted for selective abortions, and in each case, I was the first person they'd ever met with a similar experience. The isolation of this decision and its consequences are intense. Hard as it is to break the barriers of privacy that surround sex, birth control, pregnancy and childbirth in our culture, the feminist in me ardently champions their demise. Only when women (and concerned men) speak of the experience of selective abortion as a tragic but chosen fetal death can we as a community offer the support, sort out the ethics, and give the compassionate attention that such a loss entails. I was fortunate, probably more fortunate than most women, to receive that kind of attentiveness throughout this experience.

For two weeks, Mike and I breathed as one person. His distress, loss, and concern were never one whit less than my own. But we were sometimes upset and angered by the unconscious cultural attitudes which precluded acknowledgment of his loss. He was expected to 'cope,' while I was nurtured through my 'need.' We've struggled for male responsibility in birth control, sexual mutuality, childbirth and childrearing, and I think we need to acknowledge that those men who do engage in such transformed practices have mourning rights during a pregnancy loss, as well.

And yet, having spent fifteen years arguing against biological determinism in my intellectual and political life, I'm compelled to recognize the material reality of this experience. Because it happened in my body, a woman's body, I recovered much more slowly than Mike did. By whatever mysterious process, he was able to damp back the pain, and throw himself back into work after several weeks. For me, it took months. As long as I had the 14 pounds of pregnancy weight to lose, as long as my aching breasts, filled with milk, couldn't squeeze into bras, as long as my tummy muscles protruded, I was confronted with the physical reality of being post-pregnant, without a child. Mike's support seemed inadequate; I was still in deep mourning while he seemed distant and cured. Only much later, when I began doing research on amniocentesis, did I find one small study of the stresses and strains selective abortion engenders. In a tiny sample, a high percentage of couples separated or divorced following this experience (Blumberg, Golbus and Hansen, 1975; Sorenson, 1974). Of course, the same holds true after couples face serious childhood disablement, and child death. Still, I had no idea that deep mourning for a fetus could be so disorienting. Abortion after prenatal diagnosis is so medicalized, so privatized, that there is no common fund of knowledge to alert us as individuals, as couples, as families, as friends, to the aftermath our 'freedom of choice' entails.

Which is why I've pierced my private pain to raise this issue. Amniocentesis raises many questions which women should be thinking about. We need to discuss this experience, analyze its ethics and politics, its social dimensions, its freedoms and responsibilities. We must not leave this discourse solely to medical technicians, health economists, bioethics experts, or the forces of rightwing politics which would outlaw genetic research and funding because, in its view, amniocentesis leads to abortion. As 'consumers' of this service, and as feminists concerned for the future and quality of women's reproductive freedom, we need to face amniocentesis, and discuss it in our own fashion, as we have discussed sexuality, birth control and abortion, pregnancy, childbearing and childrearing, which similarly get appropriated as 'technical,' or 'medical,' rather than fully social and political issues.

A beginning check-list of feminist questions about amniocentesis might include:
  • Who gets the test, and under what conditions? The few studies we
    have of 'underutilization' by low-income women—often Black, Hispanic or Asian—suggest they'd use amniocentesis. In practise, how-

ever, the high cost of a test rarely covered by medicaid, rushed and sometimes insensitive prenatal care, lack of medical staff trained to use their languages and cultural categories when confronted with hard questions often get in the way. Health care in America is stratified in this, as in all other experiences, by race and class as well as sex (Marion, Kassam et al., 1980; Sokal, Byrd, et al., 1980; Hook, Schreinemachers and Cross, 1981);

- What does 'informed consent' mean, and how can we expand and insure its use? A coercive referral for amniocentesis so that a doctor won't face a malpractice suit is *not* reproductive freedom. And the opposite problem—a doctor who doesn't offer information about the test to eligible women because he/she doesn't believe in abortion—is also a curtailment of our right to decide for ourselves the conditions under which we'll bear our children;

- How can we insure that the availability of amniocentesis doesn't conflict with our commitment to build a better world for disabled people? The disability rights movement has raised the question of eugenics, and the goal of making it 'cheaper' and 'more acceptable' to screen for genetically 'perfect' fetuses than to support the services disabled children need. While health economists may find amniocentesis and abortion more 'cost effective' than caring for special-needs children, as feminists we need to acknowledge that such lives are worth living. At the same time, we know that a woman needs access to abortion *for whatever reason* she chooses not to bear a specific pregnancy to term. Our commitment to abortion goes hand-in-hand with an equally feminist commitment to decent prenatal care, child care, education and health services for the children women *do* bear. The same connections must be made in support of disability rights. *Any* woman may decide she will not bear a specific fetus, once prenatal diagnosis reveals a serious disability she does not want to live with. But *every* feminist should support the rights, based on special needs, of disabled children and adults;

- How can women who opt for amniocentesis learn the social, as well as the medical 'facts' of the diagnoses their fetuses receive? Genetics counselors and doctors necessarily focus their limited time and resources on explaining technical and medical questions. But we as 'consumers' and potential parents need to reach out and establish networks of information so that a woman confronting the diagnosis of Down syndrome or sickle-cell anemia, or any other serious prenatal diagnosis, can meet other parents and children living with these conditions, and learn realistically about the quality, cost, and availability of the services that make such lives better.[1] Such a network would socialize an otherwise-too-private set of problems;

- How can we make second trimester abortions less devastating for the women who choose them? As feminist health activists, we need to insure that abortion laborers aren't placed on delivery floors with live-birthing mothers. We also need to establish self-help networks of

women who've recovered from selective abortions and are willing to speak with those undergoing the process. Again, public discussion, not private misery, can benefit future users of selective abortion;
- How can we insure that accurate, up-to-date information about prenatal diagnosis, explained in clear, non-jargon language is available to women? As many feminists have pointed out, the legal, medical, and ethical practices surrounding childbearing and 'fetal rights' are usually out of our control.

*   *   *

Our justified cynicism about the medical establishment should not prevent us from obtaining, scrutinizing and using the most accurate scientific information we can find. With embryo transplants, test-tube babies, and cloning making front-page headlines continuously, feminists desperately need scientific literacy. What we don't know *can* hurt us. And the solution is certainly not to leave such issues to the Right to Life, which would defund fetal and genetic research since, in their view, it leads to abortion. Medical professionals and ethicists often counter this argument by pointing out that the availability of selective abortion allows people who are at risk for a serious disease, and might therefore never have reproduced, to have children. This is a necessary, but hardly a sufficient response from a feminist perspective. We need to develop our own informed support for prenatal diagnosis programs, beginning with the defense of abortion rights and incorporating the kinds of questions whose surfaces I've barely touched on here.

As feminists, we need to speak from our seemingly private experiences toward a social and political agenda. I'm suggesting we pierce the veil of privacy and professionalism to explore issues of health care, abortion, and the right to choose death, as well as life, for our genetically disabled fetuses. If XYLO's story, a true story, has helped to make this a compelling issue for more than one couple, then his five short months of fetal life will have been a great gift.

NOTES

1. Such networks of support and information are frequently mentioned by genetics counselors, but it is hard to track them down. Newsletters, such as *Down's Syndrome*, report the activities of parents' and advocates' groups. Local health departments often have listings of parents' groups. See, too, the list of resources in *Ms*, April 1984.

REFERENCES

Blumberg, B. D., M. S. Golbus and K. H. Hansen. 1975. 'The Psychological Sequelae of Abortion Performed for Genetic Indication.' *American Journal of Obstetrics and Gynecology*, 122: 799–808.
Brock, D. J. H. 1977. 'Antenatal Diagnosis of Spina Bifida and Anencephaly.' In H. A. Lubs and F. de la Cruz, eds. *Genetic Counseling*. Raven Press, New York.

Consensus Development Conference. 1979. *Antenatal Diagnosis*. NICHHD Report; NIH pub. no. 79-1973.

Hendin, D. and J. Marks. 1979. *The Genetic Connection*. Signet, New York.

Hook, E. B. 1978a. 'Differences Between Rates of Trisomy 21 (DS) and Other Chromosomal Abnormalities Diagnosed in Live Births and in cells cultured after Second Trimester Amniocentesis.' *Birth Defects*, 14: 249–267.

Hook, E. B. 1978b. 'Spontaneous Deaths of Fetuses with Chromosomal Abnormalities Diagnosed Prenatally.' *New England Journal of Medicine*, 299: 1036–1038.

Hook, E. B., D. M. Schreinemachers and P. K. Cross. 1981. 'Use of Prenatal Cytogenetic Diagnosis in NY State.' *New England Journal of Medicine*, 305: 1410–1416.

Lawrence, K. M. and J. Morris. 1981. 'The Effect of the Introduction of Prenatal Diagnosis on the Reproductive History of Women at Increased Risk from NTD.' *Prenatal Diagnosis*, 1: 51–60.

Lipkin, M. and P. T. Rowley, eds. 1974. *Genetic Responsibility*. Plenum Press, New York.

Lubs, H. A. and F. de la Cruz, eds. 1977. *Genetic Counseling*. Raven Press, New York.

Marion, J., G. Kassam et al. 1980. 'Acceptance of amniocentesis by 100 low-income patients in an Urban Hospital.' *American Journal of Obstetrics and Gynecology*, 138: 11–15.

President's Commission for the Study of Ethical Problems in Medicine and Biomedical and Behavioral Research. 1983. *Screening and Counseling for Genetic Conditions*. US GPO 83-600502.

Sadovnick, A. D. and P. A. Baird. 1981. 'A Cost Benefit Analysis of Prenatal detection of Down syndrome and Neural Tube Defects in Older Mothers.' *American Journal of Medical Genetics*, 10: 367–378.

Soka, D. G., J. R. Byrd et al. 1980. 'Prenatal Chromosomal Diagnosis: Racial and Geographic Variation for Older Women in Georgia.' *Journal of American Medical Association*, 244: 1355–1357.

Sorenson, J. 1974. 'Genetic Counseling: Some Psychological Considerations.' In M. Lipkin and P. T. Rowley, eds. *Genetic Responsibility*. Plenum Press, New York.

Life in the 30s
Anna Quindlen

"This child I carry, like my other two, is wanted. Healthy or not."

It's interesting to note the way medical miracles can go from brave new world to simple acceptance almost overnight. Once it was a major news event when a heart from one person was placed in the chest of another. Once it stopped the presses when a baby was born of an egg fertilized outside a woman's body. Today, there have been many heart transplants and many babies conceived in vitro, and people speak knowledgeably of donating organs, or of infertility.

It was not so many years ago that few of us could pronounce, much less talk about, amniocentesis. It is a procedure in which amniotic fluid is withdrawn with a needle from the uterus of a pregnant woman; the fluid is then tested to see if the child within has certain abnormalities.

The procedure is now routinely recommended to women over the age of 35, and almost everyone has heard of it. I know this because I am almost 36 years old, I am expecting a baby and soon after "Congratulations" and "Was it an accident?"—this is, after all, my third child in a 1.8 children per family country—I am sure to be asked whether I am having amnio, as it is now familiarly called. The assumption is that I am.

The reality is that I am not. I have had a good long time to think about it, knowing since the birth of my second that I wanted more and that I would slip into the danger zone over 35 before I became pregnant again. My husband and I have had some good long talks about it, too, about how much stress and disappointment our family could stand, about when life begins and under what circumstances it should be ended.

*   *   *

This has nothing to do with our being Roman Catholics, although people always seem to suspect that our religion and our decision are inextricably linked. For while some people use amniocentesis to prepare for bad news, for most it is an issue of abortion. You have the test so that you can find out if the child will be impaired. And if it will, you can . . . well, what I'm supposed to write here is terminate pregnancy. But that's not what I feel. If I were talking about doing something as clinical as "terminating" something as disembodied as "a pregnancy," I wouldn't have a problem.

It's interesting how we have managed to move the bottom line of the question to the back of our minds. The other day, I was talking to a woman who said that she never let her mind get that far; that she underwent the procedure for peace of mind and forced her thoughts to make a sharp S-curve around the possibility that the results would not be soothing.

I think that's natural. There are two questions here, and both are terrifying. One is about abortion itself, and about when and why we can bear it. Some of my friends have suggested that I have a new diagnostic test, something called chorionic villi sampling, that gives earlier results than amnio, and so allows for earlier abortion. But timing is not truly my concern. Perhaps if this child were unwanted, I could think of it as a fetus. But my children—three of them now—have all been wanted; they were babies from the moment I knew they were coming. I do not know what it would take for me to stop their lives.

What would it take? That is the other question. If a test could tell that the child I carry is schizophrenic or autistic, conditions that are my two personal demons, what would I do then? Or if I were Jewish and a carrier of Tay-Sachs, the vile disease that reduces children to insensate husks before they die at the age of 3 or 4? I suspect I might make a different decision here.

But for Down's syndrome, in which the baby would be moderately to severely retarded and have medical problems ranging from persistent ear infections to heart disease? Or spina bifida, which can cause lifelong paralysis and often necessitates corrective surgery? Trying to explain to my doctor, who is wise and sensitive, I raised my arms from the too-large armholes of the paper gown as though I were begging him to finish my sentence. "It's not . . . It's not . . ." I repeated. "Sufficient impediment?" he said. Right as usual.

How much can you handle? People tell me that's the real question: whether a family has sufficient resources, both emotional and financial, to fit the extraordinary needs of a handicapped child into its web. But here's the real answer: I haven't a clue what I could handle. I do know that I would have blighted my life if I had turned away from all the things I thought I was not big enough to do.

I once tried to have my tubes tied because I was convinced I could never handle children. On a bad night, when my children were young, I have been convinced I couldn't handle another. And despite our decision, I pray that the third will be as wonderful and healthy as the first two have been—in, I should add, that order.

*   *   *

It all comes down to our other children. If I decided to abort this baby because it was going to be retarded, or unable to walk, or in need of extraordinary amounts of medical care, I could not find the words to explain it to them. The only compelling argument anyone has made to us for amnio, which is not entirely without risk, was made by my doctor, who asked us to consider the possibility that we could not devote sufficient time to the needs of the children we have now if we're looking after those of someone so much needier. We considered that argument, and let it go. Having more than one child always means a willingness either to give less to the others or to stretch yourself more.

The first two children have taught us that, and they have taught us that life is nothing but hard questions, and that we answer them as best we can. In some sense, the future's already writ. This child is already something: boy, girl, healthy, ill—perhaps, if you are a devotee of nature over nurture, even good or bad. I do not know yet. I know only one thing now. This child is ours, for better or for worse, in sickness and in health.

SECTION C

Surrogacy

Editors' note: The first report reproduced here was written in 1986 by the staff of the New York State Senate Judiciary Committee in support of legislation that would have recognized surrogate motherhood contracts as legal and irrevocable in New York. The second report, written by a task force appointed by Governor Mario M. Cuomo, and issued in 1988, advocated the opposite view. At the request of the governor, Assemblywoman Helene Weinstein of Brooklyn and Senator John Marchi of Staten Island introduced a bill in 1991 to enact most of the task force's recommendations. The bill was approved by both houses of the legislature at the close of the 1992 session.

Surrogate Parenting in New York—I
New York State Senate Judiciary Committee

EXECUTIVE SUMMARY

Many American couples, experiencing the problem of infertility, are turning to surrogate parenting to help them create families. It is estimated that over five hundred surrogate births have occurred in the United States, most of them in the last few years. The purpose of this report is to examine the questions presented by surrogate parenting and to determine the appropriate public policy response.

Generally, surrogate parenting involves an agreement between a married couple who cannot have a child and a fertile woman who agrees to be artificially inseminated with the sperm of the husband of the couple, to carry the child to term, and then to surrender all parental rights. The biological father establishes paternity, and his infertile wife legally adopts the child. A fee, as well as all necessarily incurred costs, is paid to the surrogate, and often a fee is paid to an infertility center or other third-party intermediary for making the arrangements.

This process, by itself, involves little or no state involvement. However, the development of surrogate parenting has outpaced the development of law. Consequently, when the courts are called upon to interpret and enforce these agreements, they must decide issues, such as the status of the child, without the guidance of statutes or caselaw.

National attention has focused on cases involving breaches of surrogate parenting agreements. In 1983, a child conceived as the result of a surrogate parenting agreement was born defective, and neither party wanted to accept parental responsibility. More recently, the case of "Baby M," now pending in the New Jersey superior court, involves a surrogate mother's refusal to relinquish parental rights to the child.

In July 1986, Nassau County Surrogate Court Judge C. Raymond Radigan, in the course of an adoption proceeding, ruled on the legality of a surrogate parenting agreement. The major issue was whether the agreement violated state law which prohibits payment of compensation other than medical expenses in adoptions. Judge Radigan concluded that New York State's current laws are ambiguous and provide little guidance to the courts in deciding cases involving surrogate parenting arrangements. In a letter to the chairmen of the judiciary committees of both the Senate and the Assembly, he urged that the legislature examine this issue.

In response to Judge Radigan's request, the Senate and Assembly judiciary committees held a joint hearing in October 1986 to determine what action, if any, the legislature should take in regard to the practice of surrogate parenting. Nineteen witnesses, including legal experts, ethicists, and representatives of religious and feminist groups, provided extremely valuable testimony on the moral, ethical, and legal implications of surrogate parenting. In addition, several witnesses recounted their personal experiences with the practice.

Following the hearing, the Senate Judiciary Committee chairman instructed the committee staff to review hearing testimony, to conduct further research on the subject and to make recommendations regarding legislation to carry out the appropriate public policy. This report outlines the findings of the committee staff and makes recommendations to the legislature with regard to determining a public policy response to the practice of surrogate parenting in New York State.

Findings and Recommendations

After a careful analysis of the testimony presented to the committee at its hearing and after a careful review of the literature and research into the practice of surrogate parenting, the committee staff recommends that the state recognize surrogate parenting contracts as legal and enforceable. The first and foremost concern of the legislature must be to ensure that the child, born in fulfillment of a surrogate parenting agreement, has a secure and permanent home and settled rights of inheritance. The prospects for achieving this goal will be enhanced if there is informed consent on the part of all parties to the agreement. In addition, legislation should be designed to prevent exploitation of the parties and excessive commercialization of the practice.

The foregoing recommendations are based on the following findings:

1. Surrogate parenting is perceived as a viable solution to the increasingly common problem of female infertility. Thus, the practice is likely to continue in the foreseeable future.

2. In fashioning a response, the legislature must consider the implications of the practice for the parties and for society as a whole. Specifically, the challenge to accepted societal values, the possible physical and psychological harm to participants, and the potential for fraud, manipulation, and coercion of the parties by entrepreneurs must be examined.

3. Clearly, surrogate parenting presents the legislature with the problem of adapting the law to social and technological change. Contract law, adoption law, and constitutional law obliquely touch upon the subject and provide some basis for legal issues raised by the practice of surrogate parenting. The gaps and deficiencies of the law result in the uncertain status of the child born of a surrogate parenting arrangement.

4. In light of the state's interest in ensuring the status of children born under surrogate parenting arrangements, recognition and regulation of the practice is the most appropriate legislative response.

Legislative Action

The following recommendations are submitted as a framework for correcting the imbalance between the current state of the law and the developing practice of surrogate parenting.

The Role of the Courts

The keystone to any legislation relating to surrogate parenting must be judicial approval of the surrogate parenting contract prior to insemination of the surrogate mother. The purpose of the court proceeding should be to ensure that the parties are fully aware of their rights and obligations under the agreement. In order to achieve informed consent, the legislation should require that the parties have the benefit of independent legal representation and the availability of counseling by a licensed mental health professional.

Legislation regulating surrogate parenting should also provide for judicial approval of the fees paid to the surrogate mother, attorneys, and the infertility center. In reviewing surrogate parenting contracts, the court should apply a standard of "just and reasonable compensation" to determine that all fees and compensation are equitable, appropriate to the services rendered, and without coercive effect.

Provisional Approval

The health and safety of the child and of the surrogate mother require that insemination be performed by a physician licensed by the state and that tests for sexually transmitted diseases be completed before each insemination. For this reason, the court's approval of the contract should be provisional until it receives notice from a licensed physician that he or she has tested the natural father and the surrogate mother for sexually transmitted diseases, that the surrogate has been inseminated with the semen of the intended father, and that conception has occurred. The court's approval of the contract should then become final.

Effect of Court Approval

Any proposed legislation should make explicitly clear that a child born to a surrogate mother, in fulfillment of a contract approved by the court prior to insemination, shall be deemed the legitimate, natural child of the biological father and his wife. This would supplant any requirement that the wife of the biological father adopt the child. The statutory determination of parenthood may be rebutted by the intended father if paternity tests show conclusively that he is not biologically related to the child.

Remedies for Breach

The surrogate mother's agreement to waive parental rights should be irrevocable and enforced at the birth of the child. Prior to delivery, the surrogate mother should be deemed to have full control of the decisions relating to her pregnancy. Surrender of the child should be enforceable through the remedy of specific performance.

Parental obligations, such as support, should be enforceable against the intended parents from the time of conception. Breach of contract, e.g., refusal to accept parental responsibilities, should result in a judgment of support against the intended parents, since they, by operation of the statute, will be the legal parents of the child.

Eligibility

Given the scarcity of empirical evidence about how the surrogacy process affects those involved, it is recommended that the courts recognize as enforceable only those contracts concluded between a surrogate mother and a couple, the female of whom is medically certified as infertile. Legislation should provide for a measure of proof by which medical necessity can be demonstrated to the court. The petition for court review of the contract should be accompanied by the written statement of a licensed physician that the intended mother has a condition which makes conception or birth of a child unlikely or which creates a likelihood that a child of the intended mother will have a mental or physical impairment or disability.

Conclusion

These recommendations provide a framework for an effective legislative response to the legal void surrounding the practice of surrogate parenting. Enforcement of the surrogate contract by the state will secure the welfare of children born under surrogate parenting arrangements. Regulation, based on the principle of informed consent, will address the risks associated with the practice. Judicial review and approval of the surrogate parenting contract prior to insemination is crucial to enforcement, regulation, and informed consent and should be considered the keystone of any proposed legislation. . . .

THE DEVELOPMENT OF
SURROGATE PARENTING

Surrogate parenting developed as a response to the desire of infertile couples to have a child with a genetic link to one parent. Its growing popularity is due to recent increases in the incidence of female infertility and to the development of infertility centers which facilitate the process. An examination of the phenomenon of increasing infertility supports the conclusion that, because surrogate parenting meets a perceived need, it will continue to gain in popularity in the foreseeable future.

Infertility and Its Causes

According to recent studies, infertility is currently on the rise. A 1976 study found that "one in ten couples failed to conceive after at least one year of marriage during which no contraceptives were used."[1] By 1983, however, "one in eight American married couples failed to conceive after one year of trying."[2] Statistical studies generally set the infertility rate at from 12 to 15 percent of the couples wishing to conceive. These figures may be conservative since they generally include only those couples who seek clinical assistance for infertility. They do not include cases in which the couple chooses not to conceive for genetic reasons, the female can conceive but habitually miscarries, the female has had an early hysterectomy, or the female can conceive but would experience a high risk pregnancy.[3]

Medical experts attribute the rising rate of female infertility to a combination of factors. Changing work roles and the availability of contraception have led many women to postpone childbearing. Delaying childbearing allows age-related biological factors to increase the rate of infertility. In addition, the widespread use of intrauterine devices for the purposes of birth control and changing sexual practices have increased the incidence of pelvic inflammatory disease, a leading cause of female infertility.[4]

Increases in infertility in the United States have occurred at a time of moral emphasis on the family. There is some indication that the values of the pro-family movement have "reinforced the social image of infertility as a major health problem."[5] Mental health experts agree that the inability to beget, bear, and raise children has grave psychological and emotional implications for many infertile men and women.[6] As one scholar put it, "infertility often implicates the most fundamental feelings about one's self and one's relationship to the familial unit, and may leave persons feeling handicapped or defective in an area that is central to personal identity and fulfillment."[7] Infertile couples often experience isolation, guilt, marital strife, and a loss of confidence and self-worth.

The Options of the Infertile Couple

Infertile couples wishing to create families are faced with a limited number of choices. Conventional medical treatments, including hormonal drug therapies and surgical procedures, cure a certain percentage of infertility. Yet, in 1983, it was estimated that some 500,000 American women had either an absence or blockage of the fallopian tubes or oviducts.[8] Surgical procedures to correct this condition are sometimes recommended, but in a significant number of cases, surgery is unsuccessful.[9]

When conventional medical treatment fails, the infertile couple is faced with two options: adoption or the less conventional medical treatment of artificial conception. Traditionally, adoption has been the primary means of relieving childlessness. For many couples, however, adoption is no longer a satisfactory alternative. Professionals involved in child welfare and adoption attribute this to a decreasing supply of healthy infants available for adoption. According to the National Committee for Adoption,[10] several factors may have contributed to the decrease: (1) the accessibility of birth control, (2) the legalization of abortion, (3) the closure of many comprehensive maternity homes, and (4) greater social acceptance of single mothers and greater willingness of single mothers to rear their own children. Due largely to social acceptance of single mothers, the number of adoptions decreased by 32.4 percent between 1972 and 1982, despite a 13 percent increase in the number of live births and a 77.4 percent increase in out-of-wedlock births.[11]

Reduced availability has resulted in longer waiting periods and more stringent applicant requirements. According to Nassau County Surrogate Judge C. Raymond Radigan, waiting periods in New York State can be as long as seven years.[12] Such waits are typical nationwide.[13]

The combined factors of increasing infertility and decreasing availability of healthy infants for adoption are causing more and more couples to seek nonconventional medical treatment of infertility. Nonconventional or alternative reproductive technologies offer the infertile couple the hope of having a child with a genetic link to one or both partners. The two most common techniques, artificial insemination and *in vitro* fertilization, involve the transfer of the sperm or egg out of the body which produced it to another body or medium in order to facilitate fertilization.

Artificial insemination is the introduction of sperm into an ovulating woman for the purposes of fertilization. The technology is simple; it requires only the mechanical introduction of the sperm into the uterus. For this reason, artificial insemination has a relatively high rate of success and has been common practice for several decades.

In vitro fertilization involves the capture of a mature egg before ovulation and the transfer of that egg to an external medium, such as a petri dish or test tube, where it can be exposed to sperm. If fertilization occurs, the fertilized egg is placed in an incubator until it is developed enough to be implanted in the mother. *In vitro* fertilization is the indicated treatment in cases where scarring of the fallopian tubes prevents natural conception. It has severe disadvantages, however. The overall success rate is about 10 percent, a relatively low figure when compared to artificial insemination. In addition, the procedure can be physically and emotionally stressful for the infertile woman. Cost estimates range from $38,000 to $50,000.[14]

Surrogate Motherhood—A Viable Alternative

Surrogate parenting is not a distinct type of artificial conception technology. Rather, it involves a different application of artificial insemination in order to produce a child when the female of the couple is infertile. The distinguishing feature of surrogate parenting is the involvement of the surrogate mother as the third person.[15]

The use of a surrogate mother is indicated when the wife has a condition which makes the conception or birth of a child unlikely or which creates a likelihood that the child will have a serious mental or physical impairment. In most cases, infertile couples resort to the use of a surrogate only after they have exhausted all other medical options and have been discouraged from adopting by long waiting periods and increasingly stringent requirements.

For some couples, a surrogate mother provides the only means to have a child genetically related to one of them. The waiting period is much shorter than in traditional adoptions, and the infertile wife can participate with her husband in choosing a surrogate agreeable to both. The child born of a surrogate arrangement is reared by a couple who so wanted him that they were willing to participate in a novel process with potential legal and other risks.[16]

The process offers potential benefits for the surrogates as well. A recent study[17] found that the motivations of women applying to become surrogate mothers are complex. Approximately 85 percent indicated that they would not participate without compensation but that money was not their sole motivation. Other factors influencing their decisions included the enjoyment of being pregnant, the desire to give the gift of a baby to an infertile couple, and an emotional need to work through the previous loss of a child by abortion or adoption. A significant number of those studied were sympathetic to the problems of infertility, and some had, themselves, been adopted as children by infertile couples. For many, surrogacy represents an alternative income option. For example, some divorced women with young children have chosen to be surrogates in order to support their children and to remain at home to care for them.[18]

The Role of the Entrepreneur

For the couple wishing to create a family through surrogate parenting, the most difficult and important step is finding a suitable surrogate mother. In some cases, the surrogate is a close friend or relative of the couple, and the agreement is private and informal. In other cases, the couple advertises for a surrogate, usually in suburban and university campus newspapers. But, increasingly, childless couples are turning to infertility centers to help them make their surrogate parenting arrangements.

The first infertility center was opened in the 1970s in Los Angeles by an obstetrician, two lawyers, and a psychologist. Over the past ten years, entrepreneurs have responded rapidly to the market opportunity presented by increased infertility. Major centers have opened in Detroit, Philadelphia, Louisville, Columbus, Topeka, and suburban Washington, D.C. Two infertility centers are currently operating in New York City, and one recently opened in Buffalo. A Long Island center, opened in 1983 and managed by a photographer, is apparently no longer in business.[19] Since the practice is not recognized or regulated by any state, there is no reliable information on the number of centers in existence at any one time, the qualifications of the entrepreneurs, or the number of surrogate births arranged by each center.

The couple's first contact with a center is likely to involve a preliminary interview, during which they may discuss their particular problem and receive information and counseling regarding infertility. If they decide to proceed with surrogate parenting, they sign a contract with the center and gain access to its files on available surrogate mothers. When the couple becomes interested in an individual surrogate, the center coordinates an interview, arranges for medical and psychiatric evaluation of the surrogate, and provides legal representation for the couple in contract negotiations. When a contract is concluded, the center arranges a schedule for the insemination of the surrogate. If conception occurs, the center coordinates the legal steps necessary to establish the natural father's paternity and to finalize adoption of the child by the infertile wife.

The most important service provided by the center is recruitment of potential surrogate mothers. Selection and screening practices vary widely from center to center. Some centers carefully interview applicants and require a waiting period of several months between the time the surrogate is interviewed and the signing of a contract with an infertile couple. Other centers keep files on prospective surrogates but regard them as independent agents. In these cases, medical and psychological testing are included as part of the surrogate parenting agreement and are paid for by the infertile couple.

A surrogate parenting contract generally contains three major provisions: (1) the surrogate agrees to bear the child and surrender parental rights at birth; (2) the natural father agrees to accept responsibility for the child; and (3) the natural father agrees to pay all medical expenses incurred and the fees of both the surrogate and the infertility center.[20] Secondary provisions may include agreements regarding counseling; medical, psychiatric and genetic screening; amniocentesis or other tests to detect genetic defects in the fetus; restrictions on such behavior as smoking, drinking, or drug use by the surrogate; and provision for changes in the fee structure in the event of miscarriage or stillbirth. Despite the fact that the contracts may not be enforceable, they make provision for legal remedies in case of breach.[21]

After the surrogate gives birth, the wife of the natural father adopts the child, often travelling to a jurisdiction which has an accommodating step-parent adoption statute. For example, the Florida Step-Parent Adoption Act[22] does not include a residency requirement or a requirement for disclosure of any fee or expense involved in the adoption. Taking the baby out of state for adoption is often viewed as necessary because twenty-four states prohibit the payment of any consideration other than medical expenses in adoptions.[23] Recently, however, contracts developed by infertility centers are signed only by the natural father, the surrogate mother, and her husband, if any. One center operator argues that under this arrangement, the wife of the natural father is not responsible for any of the payments made to the surrogate. Therefore, she can petition to adopt in the state of her residence regardless of any prohibition against compensation in adoptions.[24] . . .

OPTIONS FOR GOVERNMENTAL RESPONSE

There are three possible legislative responses to the practice of surrogate parenting: inaction, prohibition, and regulation. This section will examine the public policy and constitutional aspects of each option.

Laissez Faire: "Let Well Enough Alone"

As discussed in the previous section, New York law does not address the issues raised by surrogate parenting. Although certain aspects of existing law may apply to such arrangements and, to some extent, may serve to resolve the question of the status of the child and to define the rights and duties of the parties, there is no certainty.

Some argue that an absence of settled law regarding surrogate parenting does not require immediate remedial action. They argue that in issues where there are deep-seated controversies or unknown factors, it is best to allow the law to develop without legislative intrusion.[56]

The laissez faire approach ignores the fact that without legislative action, the rights of the child, including the right to a permanent and stable home environment, are at risk. Breaches of an agreement may result in familial upheaval and protracted custody battles. Therefore, the question of contract enforceability should not be left to the "uncertainties of evolutionary legal development."[57]

Hearing testimony and published articles make it clear that legal experts, ethicists, and mental health professionals, whether they oppose or support surrogate parenting, agree that the legislature should fill the legal void that surrounds the practice.

Prohibition

In deciding whether the practice of surrogate parenting should be prohibited, the state must first determine whether such a prohibition would deny a fundamental constitutional right. If a fundamental right is involved, any attempt to impair this right will likely be struck down as unconstitutional, absent any compelling state interests.

Neither the United States nor the New York constitution contains language explicitly stating that a person has a right to have a child. Decisions relating to procreation and self autonomy, however, have been discussed within the context of the "right to privacy,"[58] which has been defined as containing ". . . only personal rights that can be deemed 'fundamental' or 'implicit in the concept of ordered liberty.'"[59]

It is arguable that the desire to have a child falls within this concept of "ordered liberty." The Supreme Court, in dicta, has repeatedly discussed the right of procreation in the same context as marriage and marital intimacy.[60] In *Skinner v. Oklahoma*,[61] the Supreme Court struck down Oklahoma's Habitual Criminal Sterilization Act, which provided for the sterilization of criminals convicted of two or more crimes involving moral turpitude. The Court ruled that the statute denied equal protection in that the phrase, "crimes of moral turpitude," was too vague. In its decision, the Court stated that, "[t]his case touches a sensitive and important area of human rights. Oklahoma deprives certain individuals of a right which is basic to the perpetuation of a race—the right to have offspring."[62] Furthermore, "[t]he right of procreation without state interference has long been recognized as 'one of the basic civil rights of man . . . fundamental to the very existence and survival of the race.'"[63] In a later case, *Eisenstadt v. Baird*,[64] the Court stated: "[i]f the right of privacy means anything, it is the right of the individual, married or single, to be free from unwarranted governmental intrusion into matters so fundamentally affecting a person as the decision whether to bear or beget a child."[65] In 1977, the Supreme Court in *Carey v. Population Services, Inc.*,[66] found unconstitutional a statute which prohibited the sale or advertising of contraception because, "[t]he decision whether or not to bear or beget a child is at the very heart of this cluster of constitutionally protected choices. That decision holds a particularly important place in the history of the right of privacy. . . ."[67] Most recently, the Court has even hinted that the promotion of child birth, rather than abortion may, in fact, be a legitimate state interest.[68]

From the foregoing, there appears to be ample precedent that the right to have a child is a fundamental right protected by the constitutional right of privacy and that attempts to outlaw surrogate parenting would be construed as unconstitutional interference with that right. The question still remains, however, whether this right of privacy extends to the use of surrogate parenting as a means of procreation. The right of privacy has not yet been interpreted to include a third party,[69] but to prohibit an infertile couple from using a viable alternative such as surrogate parenting may, in fact, preclude those persons from the only reproductive mechanism possible, and, thereby, indirectly deny those persons the right to have a child.

While it is not suggested that the state should encourage the practice of surrogate parenting, it should not prohibit the practice *in toto*, since such a prohibition would perpetuate the legal vacuum which now exists to the detriment of children born of these arrangements.

Regulation

If it is accepted that the use of surrogate parenting falls within the protections of the right of privacy, then surrogate parenting may only be restricted or denied if there exists a compelling state interest which necessitates such a restriction or denial. "Compelling is, of course, the key word; where a decision as fundamental as . . . whether to bear or beget a child is involved, regulations imposing a burden on it must be narrowly drawn to express only those interests."[70]

The Supreme Court has noted, however, that the right of privacy "is not absolute, and certain state interests may, at some point, become sufficiently compelling to sustain regulation of factors that govern the right. . . ."[71] Surrogate parenting, if accepted as a part of the fundamental right of privacy, involves the interests of several different parties, all of whom may present the state with compelling interests to protect.

Identifying the Interests

The state's principal interest, once it decides to allow surrogate parenting, is to ensure the status of the child who is born of the arrangement. The state's interest in protecting the child would be best met if the status and legitimacy of the child were secured upon birth, thus avoiding the possibility of a protracted custody battle.

Aside from the infertile couple's decision whether to have a child, the surrogate mother's benefits and potential risks should also be assessed. Under the *Roe v. Wade* analysis, the surrogate mother has the right to decide whether or not she will give birth to a child. Under current law, the state does not limit her decision concerning who should inseminate her, nor does it prevent her from giving the child up for adoption. The state has traditionally refrained from interfering with these personal decisions.

The state does, however, have an interest in the health, safety, and welfare of the mother because of a mortality rate involved with bearing a child, a risk of transmission of disease, and the psychological and emotional ramifications of giving up a child.

Finally, the state has an interest in preventing the potential abuses which may accompany the commercialization of childbearing. The abuses of this technique would most likely be associated with the use of surrogate parenting by couples who are biologically capable of producing their own offspring but wish their children to have superior genetic traits or wish to avoid the inconvenience of pregnancy and childbirth.

The state may, in addition to other regulations, justifiably limit the use of surrogacy to couples where the female is infertile. A "medically necessary" standard has been employed before and has constitutional precedence. In the case of *Maher v. Roe*,[72] the Court upheld a Connecticut statute which limited Medicaid reimbursement for abortions to those which were "medically necessary." The Court considered whether the medically necessary distinction resulted in a denial of equal protection under the constitution, in that indigent women who wanted to have a medically unnecessary abortion might be precluded from doing so. The Court upheld the Connecticut regulation because it "placed no obstacles—absolute or otherwise—in the pregnant woman's path to an abortion. An indigent woman who desires an abortion suffers no disadvantage as a consequence of Connecticut's decision to fund childbirth; she continues as before to be dependent on private services she desired."[73]

Similarly, a requirement that the couples using surrogate parenting demonstrate medical necessity does not infringe upon the right of fertile couples to have children, since they may do so naturally. Additionally, couples who wish to use surrogate parenting outside of the recommended statutory framework will not have the benefit of court enforcement of their contracts.

In summary, it is the committee staff's decided conclusion that surrogate parenting is a logical extension of the right to procreate, and accordingly, a part of the constitutional right of privacy. There are state interests and parties to be protected within the surrogate parenting arrangement, which necessitates state regulation of the surrogate parenting process. These restrictions, however, must be narrowly drawn to address the specific concerns of the state.

RECOMMENDATIONS

The fundamental issue considered in this report is whether the state should recognize the surrogate parenting contract as legal and enforceable and, thereby, ensure the legal status of the child. Based on the foregoing findings and analysis, the committee staff recommends that the legislature grant enforceability to surrogate parenting contracts and regulate the practice as set forth below.

The Role of the Courts

Judicial approval of the surrogate parenting agreement prior to insemination of the surrogate mother is the keystone of any legislation relating to the practice of surrogate parenting. For a contract to be enforceable, the parties should be required to apply to the Surrogate or Family Court, prior to insemination, to have the terms of the agreement reviewed and approved by the court.

Promoting the Interests of the Child

Recognition of the contract as legal and enforceable will ensure the legal status of the child born of a surrogate parenting arrangement for the purposes of determining parental responsibilities and rights of inheritance. If the state grants enforceability to the contract, it has an interest in determining before the agreement is concluded that the child will have a stable and suitable home. For this reason, legislation should authorize the court, at its discretion, to order an independent investigation prior to approval of the agreement. This investigation may include the following information:

(a) the marital and family status, as well as the history, of the intended parents;

(b) the physical and mental health of the intended parents;

(c) the property owned by and the income of the intended parents;

(d) whether either parent has ever been respondent in any proceedings concerning allegedly neglected, abandoned or delinquent children; and

(e) any other facts relating to the familial, social, emotional and financial circumstances of the intended parents which may be relevant to the judge's decision.

Ensuring Informed Consent

Parties to a surrogate parenting contract agree to acts that have irrevocable consequences and involve physical and psychological risks. Accordingly, the state has an interest in ensuring that the parties are fully aware of their rights and responsibilities under the agreement and have sufficient information to intelligently weigh the risks against the benefits. Informed consent will help to assure that the transfer of parental rights at birth does not produce disruptions in the home environment of the child.

Before approving the surrogate parenting contract, the court should determine the following:

(1) that a physician licensed by the state has examined the surrogate mother and advised her of the physical risks she may assume in the course of insemination, pregnancy, and delivery;

(2) that a licensed mental health professional[74] has determined that the surrogate and her husband, if any, are capable of consenting to the termination of their parental rights and have been counseled about the potential psychological consequences of their consent;

(3) that the surrogate's husband consents to the artificial insemination of the surrogate;

(4) that the surrogate mother and her husband agree to assume parental rights if it is later determined, on the basis of paternity tests, that the intended father named in the agreement is not the true biological father of the child;

(5) that a licensed mental health professional has counseled the intended parents and determined that they fully understand the consequences and responsibilities of surrogate parenting and are prepared to assume parental responsibilities for the child born to the surrogate, regardless of the condition of that child;

(6) that each of the parties has had the advice of independent legal counsel in negotiating the terms of the agreement.

Preventing Exploitation

Legislation should allow payment of a reasonable fee to the surrogate mother. A prohibition of compensation would, as a practical matter, be a *de facto* prohibition of the practice itself. According to both hearing testimony and recent studies, most surrogate mothers would not participate in the arrangement without compensation.[75]

Payment of a fee to the surrogate mother does not fall within the scope of Section 374 of the Social Services Law. The prohibition is intended to prevent the coercion of women who are already pregnant or who have already given birth to the child. The surrogate mother arrangement is distinguishable, since the surrogate mother's agreement to relinquish her parental rights occurs prior to conception. In addition, payment is made, not by some third party, but by the biological father who then gains custody of the child. Since the surrogate parenting contract is an agreement between the natural parents of a child, it should be exempted from statutory prohibitions against payment of compensation in adoptions.

Fees paid to the surrogate mother, attorneys, and infertility centers should be subject to judicial approval. In reviewing surrogate parenting contracts, the court should apply a standard of "just and reasonable compensation" to determine that all fees and compensation are equitable, appropriate to the services rendered, and without coercive effect.

Provisional Approval

The health and safety of both the child and the surrogate mother require that insemination be performed by a licensed physician and that tests for sexually transmitted diseases be completed before each insemination. For this reason, the court's approval of the contract should be provisional until the court receives a physician's certification that the natural father and the surrogate mother have been tested for sexually transmitted diseases, that the surrogate has been inseminated with the semen of the intended father, and that conception has occurred. The court's approval of the contract would then become final.

Effect of Court Approval

The legislation should provide that any child born to a surrogate mother, in fulfillment of a contract approved by the court prior to insemination, shall be deemed the legitimate, natural child of the biological father and his wife. This statutory determination of parenthood would supplant any requirement that the wife of the natural father adopt the child. The intended father, named in the agreement, may rebut the statutory determination if paternity tests show conclusively that he is not biologically related to the child.

If either the natural father or his wife dies before the birth of the child, the terms of the contract should not be altered and the statutory determination of legal parenthood should remain in effect as to the survivor. If both intended parents die, the surrogate's consent to relinquish parental rights should be voidable at her option. If she elects to claim parental rights, the child would have inheritance rights from the natural father, but not from his wife. The intended parents should be encouraged to nominate a guardian for the child in the event they both die and the surrogate chooses not to claim parental rights.

Contract Enforcement and Remedies for Breach

The surrogate mother's agreement to waive parental rights must be irrevocable and enforced at the birth of the child. Prior to delivery, the surrogate mother is deemed to have full control of the decisions relating to her pregnancy. Surrender of the child should be enforceable through the remedy of specific performance.

Parental obligations, such as support, should be enforceable against the intended parents from the time of conception. Breach of contract, e.g., refusal to accept parental responsibilities, should result in a judgment of support against the intended parents, since they will be the legal parents of the child by operation of the statute.

Breach of other provisions of the contract may be handled as the parties see fit in the terms of the contract. It is very important, however, that the monetary damages for breach of these provisions be limited to the amounts contained in the contract. No cause of action should be created for emotional distress or mental anguish due to the conduct of the parties during the contract period.

Eligibility

Surrogate parenting is the only solution to infertility for a couple when the woman cannot conceive or carry a child to term or would pass on a genetic defect. The same cannot be said for the use of a surrogate mother when the female of the couple is fertile. Although there are not documented cases of surrogacy for nonmedical reasons, the possibility exists that a couple may choose to employ a surrogate as a matter of convenience.

Given the scarcity of empirical evidence about how the surrogacy process affects those involved, it is recommended that the courts recognize only those contracts concluded between a surrogate mother and a couple, the female of whom is medically certified as infertile. Legislation should provide for a measure of proof by which medical necessity can be demonstrated to the court. The petition for court review of the contract should be accompanied by a statement signed by a licensed physician that the intended mother has a condition which makes conception or birth of a child unlikely or which creates a likelihood that a child of the intended mother will have a mental or physical impairment or disability.

CONCLUSION

Any surrogate parenting law must recognize the benefits the practice provides for infertile couples and resolve the present uncertainties regarding the legal status of the child. In order to ensure the smooth and peaceful transition of parental rights at birth, the law must ensure that all parties know, in advance, their rights and obligations under the agreement so that they may give informed consent to its provisions. In addition, the law must attempt to limit the possible abuses of the practice while preserving, to the greatest extent possible, the right of privacy in reproductive matters. It is submitted that the foregoing statutory recommendations meet these requirements.

NOTES

1. Aral and Cates, *The Increasing Concern with Infertility*, 250 J.A.M.A. 2327 (1986).

2. Center for Disease Control, *Infertility, United States, 1983*, 34 *Morbidity and Mortality Weekly Report* 197 (1985).

3. Ontario Law Reform Commission, *Report on Human Artificial Reproduction and Related Matters* 10–11 (1985).

4. Aral, *Supra* note 1, at 2329.

5. *Id.* at 2330.

6. Menning, *The Emotional Needs of Infertile Couples*, 34 Fertility and Sterility 313, 314–315 (1980).

7. Robertson, *Embryos, Families and Procreative Liberty: The Legal Structure of the New Reproduction*, 59 S. Cal. L. Rev. 939, 945 (1986).

8. Grobstein, Flower, Mendeloff, *External Human Fertilization: An Evaluation of Policy*, 222 Sci. 127 (1983).

9. *Id.*

10. National Committee for Adoption, *Adoption Factbook: United States Data, Issues, Regulations and Resources* 18–19 (1985).

11. *Id.* at 18.

12. *In Re Baby Girl L.J.*, 123 Misc. 2d 972 (1986).

13. There is some indication that such long waiting periods can be shortened to as little as three to nine months when the adoption is arranged individually rather than through a public or private agency. According to the National Committee for Adoption, individually arranged adoptions are more likely now than they have been in the past fifteen to twenty years. Groups, such as the National Committee for Adoption, are concerned that quicker placements may be achieved by eliminating the safeguard procedures used by public and private agencies.

14. Grobstein, *supra* note 8, at 130.

15. Another form of surrogacy involves the surrogate gestational mother, who provides the gestational, but not the genetic, component of reproduction. The wife's egg is fertilized with her husband's sperm through *in vitro* fertilization, and the resulting pre-embryo is transferred to another woman who gestates and gives birth to the infant for the infertile couple. In these cases, the child is biologically related to both the husband and the wife, but not to the surrogate. This application of technology is indicated in cases where the wife has certain uterine problems, implantation difficulties, chronic miscarriage, or health problems that would make pregnancy harmful or lethal.

16. American Fertility Society, Ethics Committee, *Ethical Considerations of the New Reproductive Technologies*, 46 Fertility and Sterility, Supplement 1, 1s, 64s (1986).

17. Parker, *Motivation of Surrogate Mothers: Initial Findings*, 140 Am. J. Psychiatry 117, 118 (1983).

18. American Fertility Society, *supra* note 16, at 64s.

19. *New York Times*, Nov. 20, 1983, at 18.

20. The following fee structure is common: $6,500 to $10,000 for the infertility center, $10,000 for the surrogate mother, all medical expenses not covered by a surrogate's health insurance, $300 for psychiatric evaluation of the surrogate, travel expenses for the surrogate, term life insurance for the surrogate, $400 for an attorney for the surrogate, $400 for maternity clothes, $500 for paternity tests, and $500 in attorney's fees for the adoption.

21. Brophy, *A Surrogate Mother Contracts to Bear a Child,* 20 J. Fam. L. 263, 264 (1981–82).

22. Florida Step-Parent Adoption Act, F.S. Sec. 63.04 (2) (d).

23. Katz, *Surrogate Motherhood and the Baby-Selling Laws,* 20 Colum. J. L. & Soc. Prob. 1, 8 (1986).

24. Brophy, *Supra* note 21, at 264.

. . .

56. Graham, *Surrogate Gestation and the Protection of Choice,* 22 Santa Clara L. Rev. 291, 318 (1982).

57. Ontario Law Reform Commission, *supra* note 3 at 103.

58. *Griswold v. Connecticut,* 381 U.S 479 (1965), in which the court struck down a statute making it a crime for a married couple to use contraceptives.

59. *Roe v. Wade,* 410 U.S. 113, 152 (1973). (A Texas statute which outlawed abortions was found unconstitutional as it related to abortions performed throughout the entire term of pregnancy.)

60. *Ibid.,* at 159.

61. 316 U.S. 535 (1942).

62. *Ibid.,* 536.

63. *Maher v. Roe,* 432 U.S. 464, 472 (1977), citing *Skinner v. Oklahoma,* at 541.

64. 405 U.S. 438 (1972).

65. *Ibid.,* at 453.

66. 431 U.S. 678 (1977).

67. *Ibid.,* at 678.

68. *Harris v. McRae,* 448 U.S. 297, 325 (1980).

69. *Griswold v. Connecticut, Roe v. Wade, supra.*

70. *Carey v. Population Services, Inc., Id.* at 683.

71. *Carey, Id.* at 683.

72. *Supra* 432 U.S. 464.

73. *Ibid.,* at 474.

74. A mental health professional may be a psychiatrist, psychologist, clinical social worker, or a marriage, family, and child counselor.

75. Parker, *supra* note 17, at 118.

Surrogate Parenting in New York—II
New York State Task Force on Life and the Law

EXECUTIVE SUMMARY

Part I: The Medical, Legal and Social Context

Surrogate parenting is not a technology, but a social arrangement that uses reproductive technology (usually artificial insemination) to enable one woman to produce a child for a man and, if he is married, for his wife. Surrogate parenting is characterized by the intention to separate the genetic and/or gestational aspects of child bearing from parental rights and responsibilities through an agreement to transfer the infant and all maternal rights at birth.

The well-publicized Baby M case has given surrogate parenting a prominent place on the public agenda. Nonetheless, the reproductive technologies used in the arrangements—artificial insemination and, increasingly, in vitro fertilization—also pose profound questions about the ethical, social and biological bases of parenthood. In addition, the procedures to screen donors raise important public health concerns. The Task Force will address these issues in its ongoing deliberations and recognizes that they form part of the context within which surrogate parenting must be considered.

Legal questions about surrogate parenting, although novel in many respects, arise within the framework of a well-developed body of New York family law. In particular, policies about surrogate parenting will necessarily focus upon two basic concerns in all matters involving the care and custody of children—the protection of the fundamental right of a parent to rear his or her child and the promotion of the child's best interests.

The Supreme Court of New Jersey has ruled that paying a surrogate violates state laws against baby selling. Surrogacy agreements may also be found invalid because they conflict with comprehensive statutory schemes that govern private adoption and the termination of parental rights.

In New York, it is uncertain whether surrogate parenting contracts are barred by the statute that prohibits payments for adoption. If not, it is probable that the surrogate could transfer the child to the intended parents by following private adoption procedures. If a dispute about parental rights arises before the surrogate consents to the child's adoption, custody would probably be determined based on the child's best interests. Regardless of the outcome, the court ordinarily will have no basis for terminating the parental status of either the surrogate or the intended father.

The right to enter into and enforce surrogate parenting arrangements is not protected as part of the constitutional right to privacy. Surrogate parenting involves social and contractual—rather than individual—decisions and arrangements that may place the rights and interests of several individuals in direct conflict. The commercial aspects of surrogate parenting also distinguish the practice from other constitutionally protected private acts. Constitutional protection for the right to privacy is diminished when the conduct involved assumes a commercial character.

The social and moral issues posed by surrogate parenting touch upon five central concerns: (i) individual access and social responsibility in the face of new reproductive possibilities; (ii) the interests of children; (iii) the impact of the practice on family life and relationships; (iv) attitudes about reproduction and women; and (v) application of the informed consent doctrine.

Surrogate parenting has been the subject of extensive scrutiny by public and private groups, including governmental bodies in the United States and abroad, religious communities, professional organizations, women's rights organizations and groups that advocate on behalf of children and infertile couples. Of the governmental commissions that have studied the issue, many concluded that surrogate parenting is unacceptable. In this country, six states have enacted laws on surrogate parenting, four of which declare surrogate contracts void and unenforceable as against public policy.

Part II: Deliberations and Recommendations
of the Task Force

As evidenced by the large body of statutory law on custody and adoption, society has a basic interest in protecting the best interests of children and in shielding gestation and reproduction from the flow of commerce.

When surrogate parenting involves the payment of fees and a contractual obligation to relinquish the child at birth, it places children at risk and is not in their best interests. The practice also has the potential to undermine the dignity of women, children and human reproduction.

Surrogate parenting alters deep-rooted social and moral assumptions about the relationship between parents and their children. The practice involves unprecedented rules and standards for terminating parental obligations and rights, including the right to a relationship with one's own child. The assumption that "a deal is a deal," relied upon to justify this drastic change in public policy, fails to respect the significance of the relationships and rights at stake.

Advances in genetic engineering and the cloning and freezing of gametes may soon offer an array of new social options and potential commercial opportunities. An arrangement that transforms human reproductive capacity into a commodity is therefore especially problematic at the present time.

Public policy should discourage surrogate parenting. This goal should be achieved through legislation that declares the contracts void as against public policy. In addition, legislation should prohibit fees for surrogates and bar surrogate brokers from operating in New York State. These measures are designed to eliminate commercial surrogacy and the growth of a business community or industry devoted to making money from human reproduction and the birth of children.

The legislation proposed by the Task Force would not prohibit surrogate parenting arrangements when they are not commercial and remain undisputed. Existing law permits each stage of the arrangement under these circumstances: a decision by a woman to be artificially inseminated or to have an embryo implanted; her voluntary decision after the child's birth to relinquish the child for adoption; and the child's adoption by the intended parents.

Under existing law on adoption, the intended parents would be permitted to pay reasonable expenses associated with pregnancy and childbirth to a mother who relinquishes her child for adoption. All such expenses must be approved by a court as part of an adoption proceeding.

In custody disputes arising from surrogate parenting arrangements, the birth mother and her husband, if any, should be awarded custody unless the court finds, based on clear and convincing evidence, that the child's best interests would be served by an award of custody to the father and/or genetic mother. The court should award visitation and support obligations as it would under existing law in proceedings on these matters.

To date, few programs have been conducted by the public or the private sector to prevent infertility. Programs to educate the public and health care professionals about the causes of infertility and the measures available for early detection and treatment could spare many couples from facing the problem. Both the government and the medical community should establish educational and other programs to prevent infertility. Resources should also be devoted to research about the causes and nature of infertility. . . .

DEVISING PUBLIC POLICY ON
SURROGATE PARENTING

The Framework for Public Policy

Contemporary American society is characterized by its pluralism. That pluralism embraces the rich and varied threads of different religious, moral and ethnic traditions. It requires a continued effort to express one's own world view and to understand those of others.

One hallmark of a pluralistic society is its commitment to individual freedom and to the right of individuals to choose their own path among the many different traditions and values that make up our social fabric. In particular, certain freedoms considered basic to the expression of personal identity and selfhood are accorded special deference. In the framework of our Constitution, this deference is shown by requiring government neutrality or non-interference with rights deemed fundamental, unless government can show a compelling interest.

Our social policies and law, however, reflect more than the celebration of individual liberty. A broad if seldom articulated consensus of shared values shapes and enriches our common experience. We therefore acknowledge society's interest in protecting and promoting those social values and institutions it deems primary to its collective life. The issue of surrogate parenting confronts society with the need to weigh the competing claims of individuals involved in the arrangements and to strike an appropriate balance between the individual's freedom to make reproductive choices and other social and moral values.

Decisions about family life and reproduction are intensely private. The rights of adults to make reproductive choices have therefore been granted special protection and status.

Proponents of surrogate parenting assert that the right to enter into such an arrangement is part of the fundamental right to reproduce. They maintain that there is no conclusive or compelling evidence that surrogacy causes tangible harm to individuals. They argue that, without such evidence, society lacks any legitimate basis for intervention. In assessing what constitutes "tangible" harm, proponents dismiss appeals to shared norms and values as vague or symbolic, and hence inappropriate as the basis for public policy. Finally, proponents suggest that pluralism is best promoted by safeguarding and extending the rights of individuals.

The Task Force does not accept these assumptions as the basis for public policy for surrogate parenting. The surrogate contract is not part of a fundamental right supported on constitutional grounds or defensible as a basic moral entitlement. The claims of surrogates and intended parents to reproductive freedom in the context of surrogate arrangements are attenuated in several ways: by the commercial nature of the arrangements; by the potential conflicts between the rights of parties to the surrogate contract; and by the risks of harm to other individuals.

Many individual rights, like freedom of speech or the right of consenting adults to engage in sexual relations, are constrained when they enter the stream of commerce. They lose their strictly private or privileged stature and the claim they exert on society to non-interference and deference. The same holds true for the decision to conceive and bear a child. Society protects that choice when made privately and without financial incentives. Consistent with that protection, society is free to deny women the opportunity to make money from their gestational capacity and to deny others the right to pay someone else to reproduce.

Unlike privacy protections guaranteed to single individuals, surrogate parenting contracts involve potentially conflicting claims between individuals. These potential conflicts may place the surrogate's right to bodily integrity in conflict with a contractual obligation to submit to invasive medical procedures. Most obviously, the surrogate and the intended parents may have competing and irreconcilable claims to parental status and rights. The Task Force concluded that surrogate parenting arrangements also carry the risk of harm to others. Most serious are the potential risks to the children born from such arrangements. Members of the surrogate's family, including the surrogate's other children, might also be harmed.

Once it is recognized that surrogacy is outside the scope of the basic right to reproduce, the arguments by the proponents of surrogacy lose much of their force. Since the right to enter into a surrogate contract is not a fundamental right, society has no obligation to marshall evidence of tangible harm before devising policy on surrogate parenting arrangements. Proponents of surrogacy correctly point out that the risks to children or to the surrogates are unproven—no empirical data exists to confirm these predictions because the practice is so novel. Nonetheless, society can conclude that the potential or likely risks of a practice outweigh the benefits conferred without awaiting broad-scale social experimentation.

Moreover, surrogate parenting touches upon basic values and relationships in our private and collective lives: the interests of children, the role of the family, attitudes about women, and the potential commercialization of human reproduction. Society need not cast aside widely held norms or values about these issues in formulating public policy on surrogate parenting. As long as fundamental rights are not infringed, society can promote and protect a broadly shared vision of the public good. Indeed, our existing laws relating to such areas as the family, medical treatment and criminal sanctions, embody shared social values. Through these laws, society establishes a widely accepted framework within which individuals pursue a more particularized vision of the goods of life.

When no fundamental right exists, the possibilities for government intervention are broad. However, the possibility of such intervention does not render it desirable. Indeed, some strongly favor governmental neutrality on all issues when harm to individuals cannot be demonstrated. Under liberal political theory, this neutrality is viewed as the best assurance that individuals will be unhindered in pursuing their own moral choices.

Yet, even if society wished to adopt a neutral stance with regard to all social policies it is clear that "neutral" alternatives for policy on surrogate parenting cannot be fashioned. Legislation that upholds the contracts lends the authority of both the courts and the legislature to enforce the agreements. Alternatively, legislation to void the contracts and withdraw the state's active involvement from the arrangements also cannot be considered neutral. Finally, government inaction, while neutral in theory, is not neutral in practice. When disputes arise, the parties will seek relief from the courts, forcing the articulation of public policy on a case-by-case basis. More significantly, however, the practice will proliferate through the existing commercial channels that have sprung up to promote it. The vacuum left by the absence of publicly articulated goals and values will be filled by the practices and mores of the marketplace. The result will not be neutral in any sense nor will the impact be limited to the commercial sector. Instead, the attitudes and practices that guide our most private relationships will be refashioned by commercial standards.

Society has a basic interest in protecting the best interests of children and in shielding gestation and reproduction from the flow of commerce, as evidenced by the large body of statutory law on custody and adoption. A "neutrality" that would leave such fundamental goods vulnerable to the dictates of the marketplace is contrary to the public interest.

An Assessment: The Social and Moral
Dimensions of Surrogacy

The Task Force deliberated at length about the social, moral and legal issues posed by surrogate parenting. Its members began the deliberations with a wide diversity of opinion.

Ultimately, they reached a unanimous decision that public policy should discourage surrogate parenting. Divergent and sometimes competing visions form the basis for this conclusion. Their judgments are informed by different values, concerns and beliefs. The unanimous support for the conclusion reached is no less remarkable because of the diversity of opinion that underlies it.

The Task Force members share several basic conclusions about surrogate parenting. First, when surrogate parenting involves the payment of fees and a contractual obligation to relinquish the child at birth, it places children at risk and is not in their best interests. Second, the practice has the potential to undermine the dignity of women, children and human reproduction. Many Task Force members also believe that commercial surrogate parenting arrangements will erode the integrity of the family unit and values fundamental to the bond between parents and children.

The Task Force concluded that state enforcement of the contracts and the commercial aspects of surrogate parenting pose the greatest potential for harm to individuals and to social attitudes and practices. The conclusions and concerns expressed below relate primarily to these two aspects of surrogacy.

The Interests of Children

The Sale of Babies. Many Task Force members view surrogate parenting as indistinguishable from the sale of children. They reject the practice as morally and socially unacceptable because it violates the dignity of children and the societal prohibition against the purchase and sale of human beings. That prohibition rests on basic premises about the nature and meaning of being human and the moral dictates of our shared humanity. One such premise is respect for the inherent dignity and equality of all persons. Allowing one person to purchase another contravenes this premise and should be rejected regardless of the intentions or motivations of those involved.

The fact that it is the child's father who purchases the child from the child's mother (or, at the least, purchases her right to have a relationship with her child) does not change the character of the arrangement. Euphemisms like "womb rental" or "the provision of services," developed in part as marketing techniques, disserve the public by seeking to obscure the nature of the transaction. The intended parents do not seek a pregnancy or services as the ultimate object of the arrangement; they seek the product of those "services"—the child.

The surrogacy contracts themselves make this intent unmistakably clear. For example, the contract between Mary Beth Whitehead and the Sterns specified that the Infertility Center would hold $10,000 in escrow for Mary Beth Whitehead. If Mary Beth Whitehead had suffered a miscarriage prior to the fifth month of pregnancy, she would not have received any money under the contract. If she had a miscarriage subsequent to the fourth month of pregnancy or if the child died or was stillborn, her compensation would have been $1,000, an amount completely unrelated to the "services" performed. Likewise, if testing indicated that the fetus had genetic or congenital anomalies and Mary Beth Whitehead had refused to have an abortion and had carried the child to term, she would have received little or no compensation. Finally, all doubt about the nature of the contract is removed by virtue of the fact that Mary Beth Whitehead was not entitled to any compensation for her "services" alone; she was only entitled to compensation if she surrendered the product of those services—the child.

The Risks Posed. The Task Force concluded that surrogate parenting presents unacceptable risks to children. First, the fact that the practice condones the sale of children has severe long-term implications for the way society thinks about and values children. This shift in attitudes will inevitably influence behavior towards children and will create the potential for serious harm.

Surrogacy also poses more immediate risks to children. Under the arrangement, children are born into situations where their genetic, gestational, and social relationships to their parents are irrevocably fractured. A child may have as many as five parents, or, frequently, will have at least four—the mother and her husband and the father and his wife. Where the birth mother has no genetic link to the child, the child has two mothers.

In contemporary family life, many children are denied the benefit of an ongoing relationship with both their biological parents. High divorce rates and the growing number of unwed mothers leave many children with a close connection to only one parent. When remarriage occurs, children are raised in a reconstituted family unit that does not share the bonds of genetic relationship. The same has always been true for children relinquished at birth or thereafter and raised by adoptive parents. Although some children thrive in these situations, others face greater risk of emotional harm or loss.

Unlike divorce or adoption, however, surrogate parenting is based on a deliberate decision to fracture the family relationship prior to the child's conception. Once parenthood is fragmented among persons who are strangers to one another, there is no basis to reconstruct the family unit or even to cope with alternative arrangements in the event conflict arises.

A child may be caught in the cross-fire of a fractious and lengthy court battle between his or her parents during the early years of the child's life, when stability and constant nurturing are vital. Alternatively, where the bonds of kinship are attenuated, children who are born with physical or mental anomalies are far more likely to be abandoned by both parents. Potentially, neither parent will have a bond with the child at birth; the mother because she successfully preserved her emotional distance and the father because he has not shared the pregnancy and has no relationship to the child's mother. While legislation or contractual agreements can apportion financial responsibility, they cannot compensate for the high risk of emotional and physical abandonment these children might face. Other potential dangers for children include the harm from knowing their mothers gave them away and the impact on brothers and sisters of seeing a sibling sold or surrendered.

Advocates of surrogate parenting suggest that any risks to children are outweighed by the opportunity for life itself—they point out that the children always benefit since they would not have been born without the practice. But this argument assumes the very factor under deliberation—the child's conception and birth. The assessment for public policy occurs prior to conception when the surrogate arrangements are made. The issue then is not whether a particular child should be denied life, but whether children should be conceived in circumstances that would place them at risk. The notion that children have an interest in being born prior to their conception and birth is not embraced in other public policies and should not be assumed in the debate on surrogate parenting.

The Dignity of Women and Human Reproduction

The gestation of children as a service for others in exchange for a fee is a radical departure from the way in which society understands and values pregnancy. It substitutes commercial values for the web of social, affective and moral meanings associated with human reproduction and gestation. This transformation has profound implications for childbearing, for women, and for the relationship between parents and the children they bring into the world.

The characterization of gestation as a "service" depersonalizes women and their role in human reproduction. It treats women's ability to carry children like any other service in the marketplace—available at a market rate, based on negotiation between the parties about issues such as price, prenatal care, medical testing, the decision to abort and the circumstances of delivery. All those decisions and the right to control them as well as the process of gestation itself are given a price tag—not just for women who serve as surrogates, but for all women.

The Task Force concluded that this assignment of market values should not be celebrated as an exaltation of "rights," but rejected as a derogation of the values and meanings associated with human reproduction. Those meanings are derived from the relationship between the mother and father of a child and the child's creation as an expression of their mutual love. Likewise, the meaning of gestation is inextricably bound up with the love and commitment a woman feels for the child she will bring into the world.

In a surrogate arrangement, the intended parents seek a child as a way to deepen their own relationship and to establish a loving bond with another human being. In the process, however, the birth mother uses the child as a source of income and, in turn, is used by the intended parents as a vehicle to serve their own ends. They seek the biological components of gestation from her while denying the personal, emotional and psychological dimensions of her experience and self. If she succeeds in denying her emotional responses during this profound experience, she is dehumanized in the process. If she fails, her attachment to the child produces a conflict that cannot be resolved without anguish for all involved.

Proponents of surrogate parenting urge that neither the surrogate nor the intended parents should be denied their right to choose the arrangement as an extension of their claim to reproductive freedom. Yet protection for the right to reproduce has always been grounded in society's notions of bodily integrity and privacy. Those notions are strained beyond credibility when the intimate use of a third person's body in exchange for monetary compensation is involved.

Women who wish to serve as surrogates would not be limited in their private choices to conceive and bear children—they would only be denied the opportunity to make money from their gestational capacity. Some Task Force members believe that this limitation is justified by the possibility of exploitation, especially in relation to poor women inside and outside of this country. They fear the creation of a class of women who will become breeders for those who are wealthier.

Other Task Force members concluded that the risk of exploitation could be minimized, but remained concerned about the potential loss to society. They believe that societal attitudes will shift as gestation joins other services in the commercial sphere; the contribution and role of women in the reproductive process will be devalued. Abstracted from the family relationships, obligations and caring that infuse them with meaning, gestation and human reproduction will be seen as commodities. Advances in genetic engineering and the cloning and freezing of gametes may soon offer an array of new social options and potential commercial opportunities. An arrangement that transforms human reproductive capacity into a commodity is therefore especially problematic at the present time.

The Family

The Family Unit. The family has long been one of the most basic units of our society—a repository of social and moral tradition, identity and personality. It provides the structure and continuity around which many of our most profound and important relationships are established and flourish.

Social and economic forces have challenged the traditional family unit. At the same time, high divorce rates and the incidence of unwed parents have changed the permanence of the family in the lives of many. Yet, these trends do not alter the importance of the family in our personal and communal lives.

Surrogate parenting allows the genetic, gestational and social components of parenthood to be fragmented, creating unprecedented relationships among people bound together by contractual obligation rather than by the bonds of kinship and caring. In this regard, surrogate parenting, like prenuptial agreements, has been viewed as an extension of a more general social movement from status (or kinship) to contract as a basis for ordering family relationships and the reproductive process.

Although some individuals now choose to shape aspects of their personal relationships with the principles and tools of contract law, society should not embrace this trend as a prescriptive standard. It embodies a deeply pessimistic vision of the potential for human relationships and intimacy in contemporary society. It promotes legal obligations as the touchstone for our most private relationships instead of fostering commitments forged by caring and trust. Rather than accept this contractual model as a basis for family life and other close personal relationships, society should discourage the commercialization of our private lives and create the conditions under which the human dimensions of our most intimate relationships can thrive.

The Relationship of Parent and Child. Surrogate parenting alters deep-rooted social and moral assumptions about the relationship between parents and children. Parents have a profound moral obligation to care for their offspring. Our legal and social norms affirm this obligation by requiring parents to care for their children's physical and emotional well-being.

Surrogate parenting is premised on the ability and willingness of women to abrogate this responsibility without moral compunction or regret. It makes the obligations that accompany parenthood alienable and negotiable.

Many of the Task Force members concluded that society should not promote this parental abdication or the ability of some women to overcome the impulse to nurture their children. Some Task Force members reject all third party donation to the reproductive process because it encourages adults to relinquish responsibility for biological offspring. Other Task Force members distinguish surrogacy from gamete donation because of the surrogate's direct and prolonged relationship to the child she bears.

Surrogate parenting also severs the second prong of the legal relationship that binds parents and children—parental rights. In fact, the practice involves unprecedented rules and standards for terminating both parental status and rights, including the right to a relationship with one's own child. Under existing law, parental rights cannot be denied without a showing of parental unfitness. This high standard embodies society's respect for the rights that flow from parenthood and the relationship those rights seek to protect.

Surrogate parenting rejects that standard in favor of a contract model for determining parental rights. Many Task Force members view this shift as morally and socially unacceptable. The assumption that "a deal is a deal," relied upon to justify this drastic change in public policy, fails to recognize and respect the significance of the relationships and rights at stake.

The Relationship Between the Spouses. Some Task Force members reject surrogate parenting and all third party donation to the reproductive process because they violate the unity and exclusivity of the relationship and commitment between the spouses. According to this view, procreation reflects the spiritual and biological union of two people; children born of that union manifest the uniqueness of the marital relationship. The involvement of a third person as surrogate or as gamete donor contravenes the spiritual and human values expressed in marriage and in the procreative process.

Some Task Force members also believe that an imbalance may be created in the marital relationship when only one parent is genetically related to the child. This imbalance may generate tension in the family unit rather than enrich the relationship between the spouses.

The Waiver of Fundamental Rights

Under the laws of New York and other states, parental rights and status cannot be irrevocably waived in advance of the time the rights will be exercised. By placing these rights as well as others beyond the reach of an advance agreement that is legally enforceable, society seeks to preserve those rights and the values they embody.

Many Task Force members believe that parental rights, including the right to a relationship with one's own child, deserve this special status. They do not view this as a limitation of individual freedom, but as a societal judgment about how that freedom is best protected.

The Task Force's proposal is consistent with existing adoption laws, which provide that a woman cannot consent to her child's adoption until after the child is born. Surrogate parenting should not be allowed to dislodge this long-standing public policy.

Informed Consent

Many of the Task Force members support the nonenforceability of surrogate contracts, in part because they believe that it is not possible for women to give informed consent to the surrender of a child prior to the child's conception and birth. Some commentators have argued that this conclusion diminishes women's stature as autonomous adults. The Task Force members reject that assertion.

The debate on surrogate parenting focuses on the ability of women to make informed choices—not because women differ from men in making important life decisions, but because women alone can bear children. The inability to predict and project a response to profound experiences that have not yet unfolded is shared by men and women alike. This inability often stems from the capacity for growth and an openness to experience in our relationships with others. These qualities are a positive and dynamic part of our humanness.

Denying women the opportunity to change their minds does not accord them respect; it limits their options and freedoms. Other avenues exist to inform or influence social attitudes about women. These avenues can be explored without penalizing women by demanding a degree of certainty and irrevocability we do not demand of men or women in making other vital life choices.

Many Task Force members believe that enforced removal of a child from the child's birth mother under a surrogate contract involves severe consequences for the birth mother. Studies have shown that many women who voluntarily relinquish children for adoption face a lingering and deep sense of loss. The harsh consequences of a poorly informed decision to relinquish one's child require a rigorous standard for consent before consent should be considered truly informed. This is why the adoption laws do not permit an expectant mother to surrender her child for adoption and insist that she await the child's birth before making such a decision. While some women have been able to anticipate their response in advance of the child's conception, the long gestational process and the child's birth, others have not. Our policies must recognize that many women may not be able to give informed consent in these circumstances.

Recommendations for Public Policy

At the outset of its discussion about surrogate parenting, the Task Force recognized that society could choose any one of five broad directions for public policy, subject to constitutional constraints that might apply. Essentially, society could seek to prohibit, discourage, regulate or promote the practice or could take no action.

The Task Force proposes that society should discourage the practice of surrogate parenting. This policy goal should be achieved by legislation that declares the contracts void as against public policy and prohibits the payment of fees to surrogates. Legislation should also bar surrogate brokers from operating in New York State. These measures are designed to eliminate commercial surrogacy and the growth of a business community or industry devoted to making money from human reproduction and the birth of children. They are consistent with existing family law principles on parental rights and reproduction.

The Task Force proposes that surrogate parenting should not be prohibited when the arrangement is not commercial and remains undisputed. The Task Force concluded that society should not interfere with the voluntary, non-coerced choices of adults in these circumstances. Existing law permits each stage of these voluntary arrangements: a decision by a woman to be artificially inseminated or to have an embryo implanted; her decision after the child's birth to relinquish the child for adoption; and the child's adoption by the intended parents. The proposed legislation would also not bar the payment of reasonable medical and other expenses to surrogates, if the payment is made as part of an adoption and is permitted by existing law.

The Task Force evaluated and rejected the option of upholding the contracts under the regulatory models proposed in many states. This regulatory approach squarely places the state's imprimatur on the surrogate arrangement. It employs the authority of both the legislature and the courts to uphold the contracts. Through these two powerful branches of government, society would be enmeshed in a long series of dilemmas and problems posed by the practice.

The regulatory approach has been justified and supported as the only way to protect the children born of surrogate parenting. The practice is seen as a trend that cannot be inhibited given the existence of the underlying technologies and the intense desire of infertile couples to have children, a desire that now fuels a growing black market in the sale of children. According to this view, regulation does not facilitate surrogacy, but merely accepts and guides its inevitable proliferation.

The Task Force found this justification for regulating and upholding the practice unpersuasive. The difficulty of discouraging a practice does not dictate social acceptance and assistance. Society has not legalized the purchase and sale of babies to establish a better marketplace for that activity despite the fact that both the children and intended parents might be better protected. The laws against baby selling embody fundamental societal values and doubtlessly minimize the practice even if they do not eliminate it.

Public policy on surrogate parenting should also reflect basic social and moral values about the interests of children, the role of the family, women and reproduction. A commitment by society to uphold the contracts removes the single greatest barrier to those considering the practice. In contrast, voiding the contracts, banning fees, and prohibiting brokering activity will drastically reduce the number of persons who see a commercial surrogate arrangement. Given the potential risks to the children born of surrogacy, children are best served by policies designed to discourage the practice.

The Task Force members feel deep sympathy for infertile couples, many of whom experience a profound sense of loss and trauma. Nevertheless, the Task Force concluded that society should not support surrogacy as a solution. The practice will generate other social problems and harm that reach beyond the infertile couples who seek a surrogate arrangement.

While treatment is increasingly sought by and available to infertile couples, few initiatives to prevent infertility have been taken by the public or the private sector. The Task Force recommends that measures should be undertaken to reduce the incidence of infertility through public education and public support for research about its causes. Broader awareness among health care professionals and members of the public about the causes of infertility, especially infertility related to sexually transmitted diseases, could prevent some couples from ever facing the problem. Other couples would benefit from an increased understanding of the causes of infertility and new treatments for it.

APPENDIX:
PROPOSED SURROGATE PARENTING ACT

1. Definitions

(a) *Birth mother* shall mean a woman who gives birth to a child pursuant to a surrogate parenting contract.

(b) *Genetic father* shall mean a man who, by virtue of his provision of sperm, is the father of a child born pursuant to a surrogate parenting contract.

(c) *Genetic mother* shall mean a woman who, by virtue of her provision of an ovum, is the mother of a child born pursuant to a surrogate parenting contract.

(d) *Surrogate parenting contract* shall mean any agreement, oral or written, whereby a woman agrees either:

(i) to be inseminated with the sperm of a man who is not her husband; or

(ii) to be impregnated with an embryo that is the product of an ovum fertilized with the sperm of a man who is not her husband,

and to surrender the child.

2. Public Policy

Surrogate parenting contracts are hereby declared contrary to the public policy of the State of New York and are void and unenforceable.

3. Commercial Surrogacy Prohibited

(a) No agency, association, corporation, institution, society, organization, or person shall request, accept or receive any compensation or thing of value, directly or indirectly, in connection with any surrogate parenting contract; and no person shall pay or give to any person or to any agency, association, corporation, institution, society or organization any compensation or thing of value in connection with any surrogate parenting contract.

(b) This subdivision shall not be construed to prevent a person or other entity from accepting, receiving, paying or giving money or other consideration

(i) in connection with the adoption of a child provided such acceptance or payment is also permitted by section 374.6 of the Social Services Law and paid pursuant to section 115.7 of the Domestic Relations Law; or

(ii) to a physician for reasonable medical expenses for artificial insemination or in vitro fertilization.

(c) Any person or entity who or which violates the provisions of this subdivision shall be guilty of a misdemeanor for the first such offense. Any person or entity who or which violates the provisions of this subdivision, after having been once convicted of violating such provisions, shall be guilty of a felony. . . .

COMMENTS AND
RECOMMENDED READINGS

The case of RU 486 offers two alternative foci of discussion. First is the decision by Edouard Sakiz, chair of Groupe Roussel-Uclaf, to proceed with marketing the new pill—and his subsequent reversal when opposition developed both within and outside the company. Sakiz's position was complicated because he played three different roles, which carried different (and potentially conflicting) obligations: medical researcher, advocate for reproductive freedom, and manager of a business corporation. The assessment of priorities among these roles determines whether his reversal is seen as an evasion of responsibility, a judicious compromise, or simply the correct decision. To sort through the questions raised by such role obligations, see David Luban, *Lawyers and Justice: An Ethical Study* (Princeton: Princeton Univ. Press, 1988), chapters 6 and 7. Although Luban is especially concerned with legal ethics, his analysis applies to all role moralities. For a general discussion of corporate social responsibility and the obligations of managers, see Patricia H. Werhane, *Persons, Rights, and Corporations* (Englewood Cliffs: Prentice-Hall, 1985).

The second focus is the question of who controls—and who ought to control—the availability of RU 486 in the United States. Several identifiable groups have large stakes in this debate, including women's organizations (especially pro-choice and anti-abortion activists), the medical community, pharmaceutical companies, and the Food and Drug Administration. Each group has its own interests, its own resources, and its own vulnerabilities. For an overview reflecting one side of the debate, see Lawrence Lader, *RU 486: The Pill That Could End the Abortion Wars and Why American Women Don't Have It* (Reading: Addison-Wesley, 1991). Appropriate cautions against overly optimistic expectations for the pill are offered by Dorothy Wickenden, "Drug of Choice," *The New Republic,* November 26, 1990, pp. 24–27.

In her account of amniocentesis, Rayna Rapp observes that "feminists desperately need scientific literacy" if they want to exercise their reproductive freedom and not be at the mercy of biomedical technocrats. Other feminists are less sanguine about the possibility of keeping the technological imperative at bay and repudiate it altogether. For reflections on the worries raised by recent medical advances, see Jean Bethke Elshtain, "Technology As Destiny," *The Progressive,* June 1989, pp. 19–23. A clearly written, accessible account of prenatal medical screening, including a discussion of ethical concerns, appears in *Before Birth: Prenatal Testing for Genetic Disease* (Cambridge: Harvard Univ. Press, 1990) by Elena O. Nightingale and Melissa

Goodman. Of course, the physical condition of the fetus is not the only information revealed by screening; it also reveals the sex, which itself could become the basis for interrupting the reproductive process. This prospect is alarming to those who ponder the preferential treatment accorded male over female infants in many parts of the world. Yet sex selection has its defenders among feminists who see it as an important component of reproductive freedom. See especially Mary Anne Warren, *Gendercide: The Implications of Sex Selection* (Totowa: Rowman and Allanheld, 1985).

The use of RU 486 or of amniocentesis cannot be discussed without entering into the controversy on abortion. A useful selection of opposing viewpoints is contained in *The Problem of Abortion*, 2d edition (Belmont: Wadsworth, 1984), edited by Joel Feinberg. Much of the abortion debate centers on apparently undecidable questions, such as whether a fetus is a person, which generate unending controversy. An alternative is to focus on the role of women in society, specifically the relation between occupational choice and motherhood, from which a view on abortion may be derived as a natural consequence. So, at least, Kristin Luker argues in *Abortion and the Politics of Motherhood* (Berkeley: Univ. of California Press, 1984). This is not to say that the controversy disappears. But when it is focused on basic choices about how to live, there may be more room for allowing a diversity of choices—and thereby for reaching a social compromise on the abortion question.

The literature on surrogacy primarily addresses the legal issues. Of central importance is the fact that a legal contract is rarely enforceable by specific performance, that is, by coercing the party breaching the contract to hand over the good or perform the service. The usual remedy for a breach, rather, is monetary compensation. Here the law regarding adoption is a close analogy: A pregnant woman who contracts to give up her child for adoption is nonetheless permitted as a matter of law to change her mind upon birth of the child. For an overview, see Martha Field, *Surrogate Motherhood: The Legal and Human Issues* (Cambridge: Harvard Univ. Press, 1988). A brief against surrogacy is offered by Elizabeth Anderson, "Is Women's Labor A Commodity?" *Philosophy and Public Affairs* 19:1 (Winter 1990). For a sustained defense, see Carmel Shalev, *Birth Power: The Case for Surrogacy* (New Haven: Yale Univ. Press, 1989). On all the issues raised by the cases on reproductive strategies, see the collection of essays in *Gender in Transition: A New Frontier* (New York: Plenum Medical Book Co., 1989), edited by Joan Offerman-Zuckerberg.

PART III

CULTURE

INTRODUCTION

As a category of distinction, gender is as prominent and as compelling as race, class, or ethnicity and has fateful consequences in every human society. Although there is no universal agreement on just what the distinction is, two views are easily rejected: that there are no significant differences between females and males, and that there are no significant similarities. The real question is the degree of overlap and here people tend to divide into two camps: gender maximalists and gender minimalists.

Gender maximalists hold that differences are large and deeply entrenched and therefore the overlap is small. Some maximalists favor biological explanations of gender difference; they focus especially on women's capacity to give birth and include the accompanying physiological and hormonal effects. In this view, the sexual differentiation inherent in reproduction, although conditioned by culture, is not reducible to culture. Women's giving birth connects them in a special way to other human beings (as fetuses and infants) and thus provides a natural foundation for the development of distinctive traits and a distinctive point of view. Gender differences are not only anatomical but also intellectual, including cognitive development, moral orientation, and aesthetic sensibility. Conversely, men's disconnection from the process of birth gives rise to different—some would say opposite—traits. This biological account is reinforced, for some maximalists, by the evolutionary history of human beings in nomadic hunter-gatherer societies, which allowed sufficient time for natural selection to establish a genetically based sexual division of labor. (It should be noted, however, that sociobiologists are not necessarily committed to the inevitability of separate spheres. Sarah Hrdy's work on primates demonstrates that a sociobiologist can also be a gender minimalist.[1])

Other maximalists account for patterns of gender identity formation on the basis of social, as opposed to biological, facts. One view, elaborated in the work of Nancy Chodorow, is captured in the phrase "mothering reproduces mothers." The idea, briefly, is that children develop a close attachment to primary caretakers of the same sex and distance themselves from caretakers of the opposite sex. Close attachment involves development of a self-concept that embodies affective connections with specific others that are exhibited by the primary caretaker. Because most primary caretakers are women, girls tend disproportionately to develop the dispositions associated with caretaking, that is, they become mothers.[2] It is worth adding that gender differences that arise from the process of socialization, such as the one Chodorow describes, may be no less deeply entrenched than biologically based differences—hence no more (or less) easy to change. In fact, given recent advances in genetic engineering, human biology may be more easily manipulated than social conditioning.

For gender minimalists, maximalism leads to spurious or exaggerated dichotomies between females and males. At its worst, it fosters "essentialism," the view that there are inherent and immutable gender differences. For minimalists, on the contrary, the range of variation in traits is greater within one gender than between genders. Further, what differences exist are often contingent and malleable. They may indeed be situational, that is, female or male traits may have more to do with the different activities, opportunities, and obstacles encountered than with any constitutional differences. As women and men put themselves (or find themselves) in situations previously dominated by the other gender, their traits will tend to converge.

Some radical minimalists claim that many gender differences have no ground at all other than the human tendency to magnify slight variations. Aspects of social experience become gender-coded by association predominantly with one gender or the other, without there being any intrinsic gender difference or any functional necessity for such a division. This "gratuitous gendering," as Jane Mansbridge calls it,[3] leads individuals to develop self-images (as females or males) that have no basis in any actual features of themselves or the world. (Of course a belief that has no real basis may still have real effects; people do develop expectations about themselves and others because of these gratuitous distinctions.)

Although neither maximalism nor minimalism has secure empirical support, it is appropriate to ask what interests are served by holding one position or the other. The answer is not very clear. It may be thought that dominant groups (such as males) will tend to be maximalists, magnifying difference in order to enhance their claim to dominance. Then qualities associated with the subordinate group (females) will be viewed as less functional for the work to be done in the public world. A corollary of this position is that the subordinate group will tend to be minimalists, emphasizing similarities between themselves and the dominant group, in order to ease their own entry or assimilation into public life. In this view, gender differences arise only because women have been denied opportunities available to men.

These hypotheses about whose interests are served, however, can be overturned: The subordinate group may emphasize difference (hence be maximalist) to demonstrate the partiality and nonrepresentativeness of the dominant group and establish the legitimacy of its own entry into the public world to achieve balance. Or, pushing a little farther, it could be said that women's distinctive attributes—especially their superior moral sensibilities—are needed to purify or redeem public life. (Julia Ward Howe and Jane

Addams, among others, offered this rationale for women's political equality.[4]) Similarly, the dominant group may adopt minimalism in order to establish that its dominance is not based on an arbitrary trait (maleness) but rather on individual merit.

Despite the inconclusiveness of this debate, it is clear that one's understanding of the sources and the depth of gender difference will strongly affect one's assessment of the possibilities of change—and hence what public policies one supports as likely to have salutary consequences.

Of the three principal cases in this part, maximalism is most evident in "Portrait of a Social Conservative" (Section A). Mary Donnelly's commitment to separate spheres is derived from a profoundly religious upbringing that stressed women's specialness, particularly as preservers of moral order in the face of men's difficulty in exercising self-restraint. Politics aside, many of her observations could have been made by a feminist maximalist.

Gender minimalism is presupposed by the videotape project described in "Meadows College Prepares for Men" (Section B). This study of coeducational classroom dynamics at a former women's college aimed to develop techniques for equalizing women's participation in class discussion. The assumption was that in an ideal world gender would bear no relation to a student's likelihood of participation. Thus the differences that currently exist on other coeducational campuses, where male dominance of classroom discourse is well documented, must reflect contingent factors that can be manipulated to produce different results.

Finally, the readings on pornography and rape (Sections C and D, respectively) suggest that the whole maximalism-minimalism debate is simply a diversion from the central question raised by gender difference: patterns of domination. For Catharine MacKinnon and Andrea Dworkin, authors of the Minneapolis ordinance, pornography is defined by the depiction of female subordination, not by the traditional criteria of prurient interest and absence of social value. Pornography, in their view, creates a climate of constant sexual harassment and subjugation in every social setting. Thus the central issue is less sexual arousal (of men) than discrimination (against women). Pornography is a special focus of attention not, or not only, because of the possible connection to sexual crimes, such as rape, but also because it depicts the pervasive cultural fact of male dominance in its most graphic and, in a sense, most basic form. The concern is about internalization of gender conceptions from a culture built on female degradation. The maximalist-minimalist debate, so it may be claimed, does not address this concern.

NOTES

1. Sarah Blaffer Hrdy, *The Woman That Never Evolved* (Cambridge: Harvard Univ. Press, 1981).

2. Nancy Chodorow, *The Reproduction of Mothering: Psychoanalysis and the Sociology of Gender* (Berkeley: Univ. of California Press, 1978).

3. Jane Mansbridge, "Feminism and Democratic Community," in *Democratic*

Community, edited by John W. Chapman and Ian Shapiro (New York: New York Univ. Press, forthcoming).

4. Jessie Bernard, "Women As Voters: From Redemptive to Futurist Role," *Sex Roles and Social Policy,* edited by Jean Lipman-Blumen and Jessie Bernard (Newbury Park: Sage Publications, 1979), pp. 279–286.

Learning Gender Roles

Portrait of a Social Conservative:
Mary Donnelly*
Rebecca E. Klatch

The interview with Mary took place at her husband's office building in downtown Boston, a large, prestigious insurance company. Mary, fifty-nine, was dressed in a floral print dress and a raincoat that had a baby's feet pin on the lapel, symbol of pro-life. Her grey-streaked shoulder-length brown hair was pulled back by a gold headband. She began by pulling out some things she brought to show me, beginning with a photo of her entire family. She explained who everyone was—her husband and seven children—three daughters, four sons. Then she gave me a paper her daughter Carol had written for college about Mary's and Mary's mother's lives. She explained: "Carol's paper will give you the background of how I was raised—my mother's philosophy—and my life. She compares me to Betty Friedan; we're about the same age. She explains how although we grew up at the same time, we are different. She says this is because we had such different mothers and upbringings. You can see for yourself." Excerpts from her daughter's paper appear below, as block quotations, as a counterpoint to Mary's comments.

UPBRINGING

I majored in chemistry in college. I went to an all-girl's Catholic college, St. Theresa's. We were really brought up to think there wasn't anything we couldn't do. That's why I couldn't believe these women saying we're second-class citizens. I never thought I was second class. I thought we were first-class citizens, that we could do anything. My mother raised us that way, too.

---

*Names and details have been changed to protect the identity of the women interviewed.

I was raised to believe life is serious. I wasn't raised frivolous. It was that life is serious and you are responsible for your actions. I read *The Feminine Mystique* and I suppose a lot of it was true. But I was never brought up to believe things were going to be easy. I knew that the Lord didn't just hand us a rose garden. It depends on your perspective, the way you were raised. I thought it would be hard for both women *and* men.

My mother describes the Catholicism of her youth as "More hellfire and brimstone. . . . We feared God, but fear implied respect. God was not simply all-loving. He was also all-judging, all-just, and also all-rewarding. Hell and final judgment were constantly on people's minds." My grandmother was a daily churchgoer, and the only organized non-home activities she participated in were church-based; she was part of prayer groups, participated in novenas and special periods of group prayer and sacrifices. My mother, as early as seventh grade, taught religion to the young children, and often attended daily Mass with my grandmother.

Religion [was] the center of family life. My grandmother recalls that the whole family used to pray together at home several evenings a week and they were part of several church-related organizations. . . . Acts of self-restraint at all times of the year were considered "spiritual exercises," a way to show how few earthly things one needs to survive. . . . Most of all, the emphasis on self-denial and personal, spiritual preparedness was in preparation for the Day of Judgment. My grandmother lived with a constant awareness that one day she would stand alone and be judged. All her life she has been readying herself for that day. . . . In my grandmother's family, life was not centered around earthly gains and material pleasures; spiritual goals superseded tangible, material rewards.

MARRIAGE AND FAMILY

Things were different then. For example, let me tell you about how I met my husband—what a story! My mother had arranged for me to meet this Harvard boy; she was interested in me getting married. I took a flight to Boston, the first time I had flown alone. You see, then [1945] it was scandalous for a woman to travel alone. That just shows you how much times have changed. But my mother agreed to let me go meet this boy. So on the flight I met my husband! I was sitting there and I saw this man walk down the aisle. He was dressed in his naval officer's uniform and I thought, "How handsome, how distinguished he looks." He had stripes all along his jacket. I thought he must be an admiral. He began to talk to me and at first I thought he was so interesting. But then he asked me about myself, and before I could say much, he interrupted and talked on about himself. So that was it, I thought, "Oh, he's one of those kind that goes on and on about himself." I still thought he was handsome and all, but I just forgot about him. Well, I had told him what college I was at. So one day he called me there and asked if he could see me. I was so surprised. It turned out this young man who I was going out with at the time didn't like Greek plays. There was a Greek play that night so I said, "Okay, you can come to the

Greek play tonight out on the lawn." Well, it turned out he loves Greek plays. Shakespeare is his favorite. So he was in seventh heaven. . . .

In May '45 I graduated college. In July I began working as an analytic chemist at a pharmaceutical company. Let's see—we got married in May of '47. Then in November of '47 my husband decided to leave the Navy to go into insurance in Boston. So we had to move. So I ended up quitting my job. I think sometimes that if we hadn't moved, I would have kept on working. That was a great job. . . .

I was infanticipating, my first child. I had baby number one in March of '48. I had five kids in six years, so I was very busy. It was marvelous. I loved it. My husband's attitude was: "That's your area of expertise just like I have mine at work. I'll run mine and you run yours." That was a wonderful time. I'd do exactly the same again. I had a diaper service for ten consecutive years! We had this great barn with grounds for the children to play on. And this wonderful caretaker who would bring armfuls of lilacs. And he would always be there to help whenever I brought a new baby home. It was great. I couldn't write the script. . . .

Let's see. I was involved then with the Sodality, a church group. I was program chairman. We'd get speakers on current events. I was always involved in something. The next thing would be the Brownies; I was Brownie leader for my daughters. I wanted them to join, but there wasn't anyone to lead it. I planned everything but the mothers helped, too. I'm always an innovator. It was great fun. I did that for two or three years. When my mother heard that I was doing that she said, "Boy, you're going from the frying pan into the fire. Why don't you play cards or something?" But I'm not a cards type.

My husband would always be setting dates to get away. He called me every day and would say, "Let's go out tonight." And I'd have to say, "There's no need to go out. We have everything." Great reverse psychology; that was very smart because I never felt like a martyr staying at home. We went out a lot. We always went out to eat. . . . We always had sitters. Then every afternoon we had a girl from the high school come in and take all the young children out to the beach. . . . And every summer we had a girl who would live in and help out.

It's wonderful raising children. Every one is an individual with strong and weak points. They learned to get along. We wanted them to know that they are here to try to get along and to recognize that each one has strengths and weaknesses. But it's funny; I was talking to one of my daughters the other day . . . and she was saying that this friend of hers just had a baby—just one—and she didn't know what to do. She said to me, "We both can't understand how you did it. She only has one and you had seven!" They're both around thirty. It's different. I didn't have a whole lifestyle entrenched. I was twenty-three when I got married. And then things were different.

My mother—I wish there were more mothers like her in the world today. She waited up for me every night no matter what. Whenever I'd go out on dates, the boys would have to walk past her to say goodnight. And I lived at home most of college! So that we thought marriage was heaven. Finally, we didn't have to walk past my mother! Marriages were a different lifestyle then. Previously, you only had a smattering of privacy. Families were very careful of their daughters; they didn't want them to get abused. So they were very protective. You weren't on your own much before marriage. So marriage was heavenly. [Do you think marriage was more romantic then?] Yes, definitely. And you had real honeymoons. Which was great for the man—and the woman. Today you have the honeymoon before you're even married! It's nothing. The men come in and out so the honeymoon doesn't even mean anything. But we'll never go back to that way.

OCCASIONS OF SIN AND
RELIGIOUS FAITH

Do you know what occasions of sin are? They'd speak of occasions of sin then. Occasions of sin were an offense against God. For example, the trip to Boston could have been an occasion of sin. If you, with the full consent of your will, did something which committed an offense against God, that was a serious sin, the death of your soul. For example, if you went out with a man and he was drinking—I didn't touch the stuff much—and he drank a few and then the next drink he had he was going to be too drunk to drive home, but he did it anyway, willfully, that is an occasion of sin. And that might put a man in an uncontrollable circumstance; that is a sin. So you were not to abuse the mores, not to give a scandal. It was better if you hadn't been born or—like a millstone around your neck you walked into the water—if you give scandal. If Mary is seen in a questionable place or at a questionable time, then that could give a scandal. Because if someone might see Mary, and Mary was known to be brought up in this way, they might think it was okay to be seen this way. So that might influence others. And then those others might do the same act and if someone saw them, that might influence still others. So then I would be held responsible for that person and all the others. . . .

Now, then . . . where was I? I taught high school CCD [Confraternity of Christian Doctrine] for ten years. I quit about five years ago. I thought, "I'm getting such satisfaction out of this—let someone else get the same satisfaction." So I quit. Then the Church got into psychology and all of that—no longer taught right and wrong. So I began to think that teaching was a way that I could influence and educate. So then I went back to teaching. . . .

I know from facts that suicide increased two hundred times in the last fifteen years. Suicide increased because all the restraints have been removed from kids. I would have known, when I was growing up, that the Lord didn't promise us a rose garden. I didn't expect to be given anything. But kids today do. So then they're dissatisfied. I was told [snaps fingers] that's this life, and then there's eternity. This life is just preparing us for eternity. But kids today don't know about eternity. They're very materialistic. I have absolute faith.

[My mother told me,] "I was never allowed to sleep past eight in the morning and had to account for all of my time. . . . My father came home every night at exactly ten before six and dinner was eaten and dishes were done by seven-fifteen *every night without fail; I never* went anywhere in a car alone with a boy. I *always* obeyed my mother and father no matter how much I disagreed; they were my parents. . . . It was easier to control people then because nobody really thought to resist or question things. For instance, the whole 'today' emphasis on the 'rebellious teen years' was unheard of. Kids didn't control their parents the way they do now. There was so little to draw us away from the way of life our parents wanted us to live."

I lost the faith for awhile. With my daughter's death, I felt, "How could the Lord let this happen?" Here was a young person so full of life and every-thing. She was beautiful and so popular and had everything. I saw her go from this strong, bright girl to like a little puppy. She would lie on her bed and cower; that's what chemotherapy does. She would be startled by a car going by or a noise in the room. And I thought, "How could the Lord cut down a young life like this?" It was terrible. Then in the middle of this—right when she was so sick—my son Patrick came to me one day and said he had an assignment for school that he had to look up all these biblical quotes. He had to do it by the next day, so he asked if I would help him. I said, "Sure." So one of the quotes was: "Why are you so fearful? Oh, you of little faith." I'll tell you where that came from. It was when the Lord was out on a fishing boat with the apostles. He fell asleep and a storm came. They got very frightened and so they woke Him up. He turned to them and He said, "Why are you so fearful? Oh, you of little faith." And that spoke to me. I was in a boat in the middle of the storm, and I thought He had fallen asleep. That gave me such strength. After that everything was easy. . . . After she died, we got all kinds of messages and notes from people all over the country. . . . Many sent all kinds of biblical passages to tell us what got them through their troubles. I keep these quotes now. And I have those mosaics you hang in windows—I have a bunch of them with a boat on them to remind me. If you have faith, you can do anything. Without it, you can't.

SPREADING THE WORD

So I was teaching at St. Matthew's. They used to bus the children one after-noon a week for religious training. My children must have been at First Communion age by then, about second grade. You know, now that I think about it, another girl from the all-girls' college ended up as the head of the League of Women Voters; just to illustrate what girls can take on when they're brought up at a girls' college. Anyway, the priest asked me to take on the religious training; he knew I went to St. Theresa's. This was the pe-riod of anti-Establishment. The students decided they wanted to write their own curriculum. So I teamed up with another girl. Also the girls wanted to meet with the boys; before, they had been separated. They wanted to dis-cuss the Vietnam war, abortion, drugs—all of these in the religion course. So we spent hours trying to become knowledgeable. I'd call her up and we'd

try to plan. So we could present both sides of the Vietnam issue, for example. The one valuable thing I got out of that experience was that I read
the Pope's encyclical "Humanae Vitae." The message of that was responsible
parenthood. It points out the road ahead for artificial contraception—teenage pregnancies, promiscuity, et cetera. It says it all there. That renewed my
faith in the infallibility of the Pope, particularly on moral issues.

Another thing my mother always said to me was, "To whom much is
given, much is expected." I was given this marvelous education, and I had
to help spread the word of God. I was not to keep this education for myself. . . . I'm still teaching. . . . but I've noticed over the five years I was away
that the kids don't respect the teachers anymore. When I complained, the
others said, "You think the kids are bad here. You should see them in public
school." All I can say is they must be very casual about school these days.

> During my mother's childhood, structure and discipline were emphasized at
> home and at school. From the very beginning grades teachers stressed things
> like penmanship, neatness, and orderly conduct and work; school . . . was not
> an extended playpen. A teacher's authority was respected and was never
> doubted or challenged. . . . It was this rigidness, this unchallenged structure
> and order that leads my mother to say that, "High school was serious. . . .
> People seemed more mature than they do now. We respected our school and
> our teachers."

[Mary gets out her resume to give me; we look at her various activities.
I comment on her involvement with the League of Women Voters.] Yes, I
was one of the charter members of the League of Women Voters, but I'm too
busy now. I can't just sit around at meetings and make light conversation.
I'm not that type; I have to be doing something. I joined again around 1976
or '77 because I thought it would be a good way to meet others of a different
philosophy. I had surrounded myself with everyone with the same philosophy as me. I thought it might look scandalous to some, but then I thought
that, if enough women joined like me, we could change things. Also, I was
interested in doing the study of the urban crisis. They were investigating
federal money being spent, HUD and all the others. The League was trying
to decide which federal programs to hang on to. It was amazing to see how
many federal programs there were; so many should have stayed here at the
state level. We send these programs out to the federal to be laundered. All
of our tax money goes down there. Each state should keep the money and
use it. This is what our friend Reagan is doing, to make states stronger. After
I worked on this—and I learned a lot—I bowed out. . . . but it did open up
doors with those people in the community who I hadn't talked with before.
I had been labelled. I think it made them see that there was more to me than
one issue. There were other things I was interested in.

POLITICAL AWAKENING

[When did you first get involved in politics?] In 1973 I was involved with the
Mass. Citizens for Life. I helped get out a newsletter. [Did you get involved

through the Church?] No, it was after the Supreme Court legalized abortion. I had been watching that, keeping track. Because when we lived in New York I had seen how Rockefeller vetoed the anti-abortion legislation. The "Humanae Vitae" foresaw all of this. Once again, "To whom much is given, much is expected." I had to get involved. We raised people's consciousness. . . .

When ERA came along we saw that it was part of the same parcel, the same people were pushing it. Bella Abzug said that the ERA would seal in abortion. We knew the amendment would legalize abortion. [How did it do this?] The Massachusetts ERA makes us have to pay for abortions for the poor women. I've heard some naive people say you can be pro-life and also pro-ERA. But that's not true; ERA ensures abortion. [How?] There are clever lawyers of ERA who wouldn't publicize that the state ERA is causing Massachusetts to pay for abortions to the poor. In very simple terms, if a man can get any medical procedure, the ERA guarantees that women have to be allowed to get any medical procedure. What is an abortion anyway? It's a medical procedure. So women would be guaranteed the right to abortion under the ERA.

I have files on everything—the ERA, abortion, Secular Humanism, sex education. I first heard the ERA debated by a college classmate of mine who was head of the ERA. A large number of NOW women got into the League to have the League study the abortion issue and take a stand. I understand that they changed the rules. . . . They used every possible means to educate about the necessity of abortion. After that, a lot of people bowed out of the League.

The Mass. Citizens asked someone to speak against ERA. . . . We never had that meeting. But the Republican Town Committee had a debate. That was the beginning for me. I could see what we were in for. There were two females. One saw it as the greatest thing ever done, and the other saw how ambiguous the ERA was, how it wouldn't do anything. . . . Then I saw in the church bulletin that the League was sponsoring a woman speaking for the ERA. I said to myself, "This is the one place that I should be." So I went and she spoke for the ERA. During the question period, I shot up my hand and I said, "I think to be fair to the citizens here we should hear the other side of the issue. There is a whole other side." And I explained some points about the ERA. Well, you would have thought that I had said something just awful! One woman finally stood up and said, "I think she's right. We should hear the other side." Afterwards I asked the woman who defended me how it was that she was supporting me. She said, "I get the Phyllis Schlafly newsletter. I believe in this." And I said, "*You do?*"

We decided—the Mass. Citizens for Life—that we had an insurmountable task ahead of us. The League refused to consider the opposition. I came up with the idea of hiring a hall and selling tickets. . . . We sold two hundred fifty tickets to hear the women speak. Then one of the women said we should organize another one. This time we sold three hundred tickets. But it was only a month before the election. It was like taking on Goliath. New York and New Jersey had defeated the ERA the year before, so we tried to figure out how to meet the women who were successful there. I saw in

Parents magazine a letter written by one of the women against ERA from New York—Westchester, I think. So we got her on the phone and you know what she said? She said, "We were trying to reach *you*." They had been trying to reach us because they heard there were people in Massachusetts fighting the ERA. I didn't know what we could do in that short a time, but thought we'd try.

This priest gave us a hall for free. So we talked with the woman in New York and she sent this, what she called, a "bomber" of a woman. It turned out it was Dotty Burlow, who was in my class at college! I said, "Now I know why New York was defeated, if Dotty was working on it!" We tried to get the press to cover this, but they didn't want to come.

And do you know what the missing link was in Massachusetts that New York had that made it win? Guess. [I have no idea.] Just guess. Who in New York would you suppose is so influential as to make a difference? [I don't know.] Jewish women! It was Jewish women working in a group called Operation Wake-Up who made the difference. They're still meeting; they monitor all the legislation in Albany to inform voters.

CONTINUING ACTIVISM

I went to the International Women's Year conference in Houston, the White House Conference on the Family. I can't tell you what I've seen. The IWY in Houston in '77—the delegates were supposed to be democratically elected. State elections were held. A group of forty-two women planned it in Washington; they were appointed by Carter. Only one of those women represented me. The rest were pro-ERA, pro-abortion. When we found out how much of our tax money, how many organizations in Washington were supporting this. . . . do you know only two people in all of the New England states were elected who were on my side? Two pro-life people from Springfield, Massachusetts. Those forty-two women only told their friends, and their friends organized the conventions to choose delegates. We never even heard about it. It shows you how easily things can be controlled. . . . I wrote it up for the local papers.

So I went as an official observer to the IWY. Each congressman had two official observer passes to be given out. So I called up my congressman and said, "I'm now officially applying." He didn't even know he had them. They didn't pay for anything, but they got me in. I got sick when I saw all those presidents' wives in pastel suedes. And the charade of voting. There was no way they could lose on any plank. They went through all the parliamentary procedures. And then women just shrieked when they passed the Reproductive Rights—as if there was any way they could lose. I was sitting in the Astrodome watching all of these females and you know what I did? When I give you this litany, you won't believe it. . . . I thought of this National Right-to-Life man I saw who dressed up like Bella Abzug and went out to where Bill Baird and all of his paid demonstrators were marching for abortion. He started marching with them and he chanted: "Got to keep up the killing!

Got to keep up the killing!" Bill Baird had to pack up and leave. So I stood up and I just started to yell in all directions, "We've got to keep up the killing!" Because that's what they want, after all, to kill. Well, people couldn't believe it. I got spit on and elbowed. I really hit them with that [excited, gleefully]. I was only one and they were all of one mind. And for the American public to think that this is the average American woman, why I think that's the greatest travesty. . . .

Reagan says it best. When someone questions him on ERA he says, "I'm for the E and the R but not the A." That's me. I have three daughters so of course I want equal rights for them. I just don't want them saddled with having to be like a man. . . .

> My mother was raised by a mother and father who saw the job of homemaking as a great responsibility, a vocation that tapped a woman's mental and physical faculties and demanded creativity. In that same household she came to value personal, spiritual strength and independence more than material, monetary security. Judging from the example of her own mother, my mother saw the role of wife and mother as ideal for herself; she grew up with a great respect for motherhood and home-making. My mother knew that it was a selfless occupation in which a woman made constant material and emotional sacrifices, but also reaped many spiritual rewards. My mother grew up seeing the value of a life of give and take, a life in which "nothing worthwhile comes easy . . . the future belongs to those who prepare for it . . . and, sweet are the uses of adversity."

A few years ago Joan Kennedy and Margaret Heckler had a big event for the ERA extension, to raise money. I was invited somehow so I called up two of the most attractive females I know and a priest and a couple of others and we all went. I remembered there was a back door; it was the Copley. We snuck in so we didn't have to pay. The priest decided to just picket in front. So my friend and I were standing around talking. Some women recognized me and I'm sure they were wondering, "What is she doing here? What trouble is she going to cause?" After awhile I was tired of polite conversation. I said to my friend, "We came here for one thing, to talk to Tip O'Neill." So we went up to him. There was a circle around him and we waited politely. Finally, he turned to me. I introduced myself and then I said, "My aunt lives on Russell Road and her children are your constituents." We talked about that. He loved that because he always talks about Russell Street, where he grew up. His face lit up and then I said, "You know, we aren't a part of this organization that is running this event." And he said, "Well, I'm pro-ERA." And I said, "Do you know who is sponsoring this event?" He said, "I'm here for the ERA." And I said, "If you don't know who is sponsoring it, I'll tell you—the National Organization for Women. And they're for abortion and contraception for minors without parental consent and they're for homosexual rights." He was absolutely livid! He said—without moving his lips—"Get out of here. How dare you act so friendly and then try that. . . ." Well, he was so mad I didn't know what to do. I just stood there. Then the one person in the world who could help me was sent by the Lord. Who do you think that was? Who was the one woman of any-one who could help me in this circumstance? [I don't know.] Well, this leg-islature is unique in the country; it's the only one who has elected an avowed lesbian to office. Right then and there Elaine Noble came running down to say hello to Tip. It was perfect! Right after I said all of those things. He was so mad.

Then a friend noticed that the return address for this invitation was on Ethan Allen Road. She said to me, "Do you know what Ethan Allen Road is? It's the headquarters for Planned Parenthood." They had been asking for donations to be sent there, to Planned Parenthood, without telling anyone. Here was Tip O'Neill, supposedly a pillar of the Church, supporting Planned Parenthood. So this friend sent this packet of information to Tip O'Neill. . . . but he never answered, not a word. So once I was in Washing-ton and I went to his office and left word, "Tell Tip O'Neill the woman who took him on at the Copley came to see him." I think he probably worries when he's out on the street that I'll come up to him [laughs]. But I'm thank-ful to the Lord that I had the courage. . . .

REFLECTIONS

I still write letters to people. But I'm weary. You're labelled. People think I'm a fanatic. And with the Moral Majority. The Moral Majority is only say-ing what the Catholic Church has been saying all along. Vatican II said what a Catholic is—someone who goes to church, who doesn't engage in pre-marital sex, et cetera. But now there's a lack of guidance. Now the Moral Majority is doing a lot of guiding where it is needed.

[Is your husband supportive of what you do?] Yes, my husband is very good. He and I think alike. [Does he do political work as well?] Well, he'll speak for me when I'm not there. Sometimes he says to me when we're going out, "Let's not get into it tonight." And then I'll hear him across the table arguing—the same things I think.

My father always told me, "Don't even go out with non-Catholics." It's so important to marry someone who is from a similar background as you. It makes a marriage so much more secure. You know, out of the two hundred girls who graduated at St. Theresa's with me, I can count on one hand the number of marriages which have broken up. That's how prepared we all were for marriage. Something is missing today. That *was* another era. . . .

But my daughter Carol said to me that she doesn't know any one of her friends at Princeton with parents who are divorced. So you know how I explain that? I figure if you're at Princeton you must be a kid with high achievement, the ability to stick it out. And that can only come from strong parents. That must be because of a strong home.

St. Theresa's was an upper crust school, but there were also blacks there. . . . The nuns were so inspiring. Every year the top ten women in every class—the most brilliant and the prettiest women—would go into the Church to become nuns. The nuns today—I laugh—they were all brought up on the whole women's lib. . . . They want to do mass and everything. It's so sad. [She picks up the program from her commencement and begins to read from the commencement speech]:

"Tomorrow, when the sun is set on this campus, you, my dear young women, leave Alma Mater, your loving Mother, and you begin to walk— alone. It is all important then that you take with you a reliable sense of values. . . . The power of a good woman in the world has been extolled by philosophers as one of the greatest forces in life, sublimating mankind to the beautiful, the true, the holy and the ideal. . . . Woman has been entrusted with human life and all that affects it in the tender and most receptive years of its growth and development. . . . For this reason God made woman instinctively holy, pure, kind, tender, sympathetic, and religious. God has endowed her with gifts necessary for the good of the human race and the salvation of souls. The preservation of these feminine gifts is woman's highest prerogative and her greatest responsibility. . . .

"[The] de-feminization of woman as we see it today, began with the crazy crusade for her emancipation. Towards the end of the last century women yelled loudly for the equality of the sexes, for the abolition of the double standard of morality. It's a man's world they said 'and we want to get into it.' With the drastic lowering of standards, women got into man's world; they got equality but at the awful price of their superiority. . . .

"Woman has unfortunately . . . been reduced to a state where she was before Mary graced this earth. . . . She has bartered her charm for what she calls emancipation. This so-called emancipation has been a boomerang, because it emancipated men from old time loyalties and enforced deference. Those women who want the new equality with men can no longer enjoy their old superiority to them. . . . In the quest of something she more than possessed but did not realize, woman has cheapened herself for she can never be man's equal, she must be either greater as God intended, or less as she determines. . . ."

That's the way we were brought up. . . . It was a different world. . . . What we had to lean on!

TODAY'S WORLD

Our wonderful president is trying to bring voluntary prayer back to the schools. Do you know who took prayers out of the schools? Madeline Murray O'Hair. She went to Russia to try to become a citizen, but they wouldn't take her. So she came back and when she put her children in school she said, "I couldn't send my children to a school with prayers." She was an atheist. But in May of this year the President called a National Day of Prayer. And Madeline's son was in the audience. He repudiated his mother and had embraced a Christian religion. He is giving his whole life to compensate for the harm he feels his mother did. He brought a petition signed by a million plus people. . . .

I also spend a lot of time trying to figure out what is going on. I read

Human Events, Conservative Digest, The Wanderer. . . . I saw a survey where pollsters in New York—very recently—questioned two hundred forty people in the media. They asked twenty-five questions. When they asked, "Are you affiliated with any Church?," only five percent were affiliated! Most had never darkened the door of a church. And 90 percent were pro-abortion, 90 percent were for homosexual rights, and under 10 percent had voted for Reagan. So I remember this when I read the newspapers.

[At this point Mary's husband interrupts to tell her their daughter Carol is waiting to be picked up. He turns to me and says, "How do you like this chick? Pretty interesting, eh? And she's my first wife!" Mary laughs and says, "I adore him."]

Reverend Wildmon—have you heard of him? He started the National Federation of Decency. He brought all the national TV stations to the bargain table and threatened a boycott. So he got them to say that in six months they would clean up their shows. They began to monitor the shows. This little guy from Toobalo, Mississippi. But he should have brought on the boycott; they haven't changed. . . . I heard from a friend of mine in New York that he would be calling me. He wanted my support when he came here. . . . What one person can do! He has a newsletter and all kinds of clout.

Then I went in 1979 to the big gala event held in Washington at the expiration of the seven years for ERA. Dr. Voth from the Menninger Clinic was there. And this retired general, Gatsis. He gave so many facts. He told us that Liz Carpenter—you know, who Carter appointed—she was at the Pentagon and she was trying to get women into all echelons of the military. Well, he gave us the facts: a high percent of women in the military are pregnant, such-and-such a percent never finish.

We were so turned on after we'd heard him that we went right over to Congress. And who should we see, a cadre of naval officers coming down the hall. So I took it upon myself to say to them, "We just heard that women are being railroaded into the military to make women being drafted more palatable." We knew this would mean that women would have to enter combat, because once women are in, some smart guy will say, "I'm not going to combat unless she goes." They didn't know what hit them! A few of them walked on. But some said that they were totally with me and that their wives were with me. They gave us the names of people to talk to at the Armed Forces. So we went right over. . . . We found out that what that general had been saying was true. The Commander-in-Chief, the President, was giving orders and he's for the ERA. What does a good officer do? He doesn't question. . . . So this was what was happening. . . . This was being done by a group of women. The military was being used by the women pushing for ERA. . . .

ON WOMEN'S ROLES

It's not that I don't want things to change. . . . I don't expect them to stay the same. I just don't want them forced. I want it to be evolution. . . . Women's liberation is a small group of women who have forced themselves on us. . . . I think: "Why them and not me? What have I been doing?" I'll tell you. I was raising seven children. What were they doing? Hardly any of them are in an ongoing marriage. Kate Millett, Shulamith Firestone—they are blaming society for their own failure. I don't think society has failed me. They had time and a strong motivation. It became so obvious at the IWY that women with children who were at home don't have the time to do this. . . .

My mother is going on eighty-nine. . . . She has three kids and felt totally fulfilled. I have a brother with six kids—all of whom have their master's [degrees]. Five of them are married with kids. . . . All of them pay taxes, all of them are well balanced, all of them are contributors. Then I have a sister—she was named outstanding Catholic woman of the year in Tennessee. All her children are contributors, all well balanced. So you look at the results of a fulfilled woman in the home . . . and how society profits. . . . And you look at how society fails with women half in the home and half out. . . . Kids don't feel they have to honor their mother and father. Did I vandalize the schools? Did I talk back to my parents?

> My grandmother saw her role, her domestic responsibilities, as God-given; she would someday be held accountable for the way she ran her household and raised her children. As the financial organizer of the family, she meticulously kept records of all expenses and kept all expenditures to a bare minimum. . . . For my grandmother, staying at home and raising a family was anything but a submissive, passive existence. While some women might see their home-oriented life as stifling and unfulfilling, my grandmother saw her role in the home as a responsibility before God. Her home was her domain to control and shape, the "stage" where she would "perform" for God.

My mother earned it. My mother had to develop everything on her own. It was the Depression. Mother had to stretch everything. She even made my father's pajamas. She canned everything, too. She was an authority on good food; we never had a piece of white bread in the house. She made a real career out of her home. . . . You owe an awful lot to a home like that. . . . Now we have labor-saving devices. My mother used to do all of her own wash. She'd take a whole day to do ironing. And she only had three children. Sometimes I think I could have three children and take care of them with my hands tied behind my back. . . . I don't think women should stay inside. . . . It's natural evolution that they don't—especially with only three children.

> My mother told me, "The way people say 'just a housewife' is new since the feminist philosophy became popular. It somehow implies that a woman in the home is taking it easy and shirking responsibility by not earning money at the same time that she raises a family. The feminist movement is not improving the status of women by making motherhood look like the easy way out."
> In addition, my mother sees the "Wages for Housework" campaign as an example of the excessively materialistic nature of the feminist movement. Her

family experience taught her that the sacrifices and hard work that motherhood demands reaped rewards that money cannot buy: personal satisfaction, security, and the approval of God. "Putting a price tag on the work of a mother would make home-making seem just like any other job, which it definitely is not," says my mother. She goes on to say: "It is a career, however. It is a career and it is a great responsibility. Mothering has rewards all its own. To pay a mother for raising children would be degrading, for it would take motherhood out of the 'unique responsibility' category and turn it into a job; the sacred title of 'mother' would have to be changed to 'worker.' Women would gain money, but they would also lose a source of pride and identity."

Do you know what the father at St. Theresa's said to us all the time? He said, "Beware that you are not perfect. No human is perfect. And beware of the guy who likes to hang curtains. Look for the masculine guy. And you be as feminine as you can. Longevity depends on a happy marriage." And every week he repeated to us, "Get married, get pregnant. Get married, get pregnant. Then your husband will mature and be doing the most masculine of acts—supporting you. And you will be doing the most feminine of acts—nurturing. And you will mature. And you will be secure."

Unlearning Gender Roles

Meadows College Prepares for Men
Catherine G. Krupnick

Do men get more for their money than women when they invest four years and tens of thousands of dollars in a college education? Close examination of videotapes of college classroom interactions reveals that they generally do. For example, men are more likely than women to get the attention of faculty members; thus men tend to dominate supervised practice in the subject under discussion. This situation results in part from gender differences in reaction time that are quite marked. Should a teacher choose the first volunteer to answer a question (as often happens), that student will most likely be male. Moreover, videotapes disclose that men talk at greater length, interrupt others more, and are less subject to interruptions themselves. Men also adopt a challenging, sometimes abrasive style, which may elicit responses from other men but silences most women. Tacit collaboration of faculty members permits men to dominate class discussions disproportionately to their numbers. Additionally, men's contributions appear to be taken more seriously than women's. The result, we may hypothesize, is that articulate students become more knowledgeable and silent ones less so. If colleges acknowledged this phenomenon, their catalogues would carry a warning: "The value you receive may well depend on your sex."

HIGHER EDUCATION
IN THE UNITED STATES

Goals of Education

College education in the United States is distinct in its goals and methods: Classes are small compared to European and other overseas university systems, and thus they offer a comparatively high level of individual attention per student. The emphasis on small classes reflects the premise that oral discussion—that is, the ability to speak fluently in the manner of accomplished people—is a fundamental tool for teaching and learning, as well as for later public or professional life. The increasing prevalence of discussion-based teaching in recent years is an indication of educators' renewed attention to discussion skills. For example, the adoption of required first-year seminars and "common core" curricula has entailed emphasizing small classes, discussion formats, and active student involvement in the learning process.

College teachers often say that active participation by all students over the course of a semester is an important teaching objective. Although no student can be expected to talk exactly as much as every other student, approximate equality is a common goal; but many teachers say they are uncertain how to reach it. They hope that students will somehow achieve it by themselves: that no student will dominate, and none will be entirely removed from discussion. This attitude is particularly common among teachers who view discussion as a route to student empowerment. William Welty includes as part of effective teaching the idea that the teacher should sit back to let the students have an equal role in running the class: "Many advocates of discussion method teaching argue that, for true learning to take place, the faculty member must relinquish authority and control so that students . . . learn for themselves." The students pose questions, challenge each other, and use the teacher at best as a resource to facilitate their own self-generated quest for knowledge.

But a problem exists because these two goals—being a facilitative teacher *and* producing full student participation—are actually in conflict unless (and this never happens) all the students are equally motivated, prepared, and skilled in classroom discourse. We might call these goals the "democracy" goal and the "equality" goal. The democratic teacher tends to let discussion flow, but it flows only among a few talkative students; the equality teacher sacrifices spontaneity and student-directed talk in order to ensure that the quiet ones do speak. Put most sharply, giving up one principle (the teacher shouldn't interfere too much) puts at risk another principle (a few students shouldn't dominate). The issue is compounded by predictable patterns that indicate which group of students, on the whole, will be dominant. The issue of democracy versus equality is complicated by gender differences. Various factors in the academic classroom work against equal opportunity in the education of males and females. There is no more striking example than the degree to which females underparticipate in classroom discourse.

Women's Education

There is good reason to believe that female students' education is systematically less rewarding than male students' education, especially in terms of academic preparation for later professional and public life. (See the references at the end of the case.) Although differences appear very early, well before college, they are particularly evident at college—especially at coeducational institutions. For this reason, many feminists have joined traditionalists in advocating gender-segregated college education for women.

All-female colleges, they argue, are less likely to diminish female students' options.

In both the pursuit and course of their careers, female graduates of single-sex institutions do very well in comparison with female graduates of coeducational institutions. The National Center for Educational Statistics reports that women are three times more likely to earn a baccalaureate degree in economics and one and one-half times more likely to earn degrees in life sciences, physical sciences, or mathematics at exclusively female schools as compared to coeducational ones. Moreover, graduates of women's colleges are more than twice as likely to receive doctorates. *Business Week's* 1987 list of the 50 women who are rising stars in corporate America shows that 30 percent received their undergraduate degrees from single-sex colleges (Baum 1987). Considering that, during the period when these women attended, women's college graduates accounted for less than 5 percent of college-educated women, they are overrepresented on this list by a factor of six. Finally, 42 percent (13) of the women presently in the U.S. Congress attended women's colleges.

There is some disagreement, of course, about whether these impressive successes are properly linked to the experience students have in school. Skeptics suggest, for example, that students who choose to attend single-sex schools may enter with strong professional interests. Whatever the evidence, the fact of the matter is that college applicants in recent years have tended to eschew single-sex colleges. Part of the problem relates to marketing. By most measures, the graduates of women's colleges are highly satisfied with their education, but it is a truism that few incoming students select their college *because* it is all-female. Conversion to the cause of women's education usually occurs after their studies begin. How, then, does one convince the next generation of women that they will come to value something they don't presently appreciate? Within the last decade, a large number of women's colleges have either closed or become coeducational. In the latter case, although various factors are cited in each school's decision to admit male students, a common factor is the desire to increase the applicant pool. The president of one formerly single-sex college said: "If you're selling something people don't want, you'd better change your product line."

Given this trend, it is likely—though not inevitable—that single-sex colleges will continue to convert to coeducation. What happens to female students' education when this occurs? Will female students be able to speak their minds without fear of male dominance? A research project at Meadows College provided an opportunity to find out.

THE COEDUCATIONAL CLASSROOM
AT MEADOWS COLLEGE

History

Meadows College was a women's undergraduate liberal arts college for more than 100 years. Because of its strong commitment to women's education, it received a grant in 1980 from the Fund for the Improvement of Post-Secondary Education (FIPSE) to help faculty members integrate materials from the growing scholarship on women into their regular curricula offerings. Within five years, the Balanced Curriculum Project, as it was called, involved over half the faculty in the effort at course transformation. Faculty and students participated together in a series of workshops, seminars, and discussions that heightened their consciousness of women's contributions to—and experience of—the social and intellectual world.

When changing demographic trends and declining interest in single-sex education compelled Meadows College to become coeducational in the late 1980s, the faculty prepared for the arrival of men with concerns for their women students firmly in mind. They were determined to fashion new approaches to coeducation that explicitly attended to both female and male students as "gendered subjects" with different and varying needs, strengths, and capacities for growth. And because a major component of undergraduate education is the classroom and its varieties of discourse, they were determined to create and maintain "gender-sensitive" classrooms in which both male and female participation were equally sought and rewarded.

To plan for coeducation, a series of faculty-staff task forces were set up, one of which focused on the "learning environment." In the words of the Learning Environment Task Force report (adopted later by the Board of Trustees), "previous research has shown that women can be silenced in coeducational classrooms, and that men and women may differ in their learning styles. . . . We believe that if we can be sensitive to these issues, we can keep the classroom climate both welcoming and challenging for all students. . . . We would like to encourage teaching practices that challenge students to question and argue, that encourage multiple points of view, and that value students and their experiences." As a result of this concern, the college set up a Teaching and Learning Project with the dual goals of helping interested faculty expand their teaching repertoires and analyzing the dynamics of classroom discourse through a videotaping project.

The Teaching and Learning Project

All beginning Meadows students are required to take a first-year seminar, an interdisciplinary course on a common topic approached through the lenses of different disciplines. These classes are designed explicitly to foster the skills of discussion, oral presentation, and the writing of college-level essays. During the first semester of coeducation, first-year seminar teachers were asked to volunteer to be videotaped, both to help them improve their teaching and to obtain data to use for the research on classroom dynamics. Four signed up—three females and one male—and the videotapes of their classes were coded for indices of male and female participation rates. The following semester the four teachers were interviewed about their experiences teaching the seminar. In open-ended, semistructured interviews, they were queried about their general teaching goals, the skills and traits they looked for in students, their experience with coeducation, and their experience within the first-year seminar.

These teachers cannot be seen as representative of all (even of all Meadows) college discussion leaders. Their tapes are only arbitrarily selected moments in time and cannot stand for their first-year seminar classes as a whole. It can be suggested, however, that compared to other Meadows faculty, first-year seminar teachers were more attentive to the dynamics of conducting discussions; they had, in fact, all attended several workshops on discussion techniques. Furthermore, within this group, the volunteers were probably among the most committed to the goal of creating fully participatory classrooms. It is fair to say they believed themselves to be prepared for this new experience.

THE RESULTS AND THE INTERVIEWS

Marie Navarre

Marie Navarre is a French teacher whose first-year seminar focused on intellectual and artistic revolutions, with a special concentration on twentieth-century changes in artistic consciousness. The class that was coded dealt with Freud's contribution, and the assignment was the first selection in his *Five Lectures on Psychoanalysis*.

Marie began the class by asking questions that appeared to be far outside her students' knowledge. Within minutes, her problem became clear: In a comical version of the classic teaching nightmare, the college bookstore had ordered a different edition of Freud's writings than the one Marie thought she had requested. When Marie and the class realized this, much to everyone's amusement, she put aside her teaching notes and asked the class to tell her about what they had read. A male student waved his hand enthusiastically, calling out, "I'll tell you all about it." His exposition of the first lecture lasted several minutes.

The class that day was composed of 15 female and two male students. The videotape data covered 32 minutes of discussion. Of that half-hour, Marie spoke for a total of 21 minutes, or two-thirds of the time. Proportionately, one might expect the 15 females to consume the bulk of the remaining ten minutes (an average of 40 seconds each for a total of nine minutes) and for the males to divide up the remaining minutes. In fact, the first student to speak talked a total of six minutes and 21 seconds, while the other male said nothing that day. Five females shared the remaining four minutes, with one student speaking for over half that time (two minutes and 34 seconds). The second most vocal female spoke for 46 seconds, and three others shared the remaining minute. Ten female students were silent that day. In sum, one of the males contributed 12 times the per capita allotment of class time or three times more than the dominant female.

The coders who examined the videotape felt that the atmosphere in Marie's class was relaxed and informal and that she was a teacher who listened eagerly and accepted students' ideas. When she asked the class to teach *her* about the day's assignment the students did not seem surprised: Turning the class over to the students may have been typical of her generally encouraging style. Furthermore, the dominant male was frequently interrupted by students while he was speaking; other students were obviously not intimidated by him. In her interview, Marie observed that

> The presence of males made a very big difference. This year I spoke less and the class talked more. I think this has to do with both of the males—and a few of the women—who were much more verbal than anyone last year. . . . The female freshmen seemed different this year; they were interested in all types of things, not just thinking about a career. . . . What I liked best about the coeducational classroom was the camaraderie between the students. Both of the young men were very friendly. Some of the women were equally friendly; others were shy. There were a couple of women who were put out because the men seemed overly outspoken. . . . Some students, I think, may have felt discouraged by the fact that it was so easy for some to speak up in class discussions. I didn't interfere too much. I let the students argue when they wanted to instead of calling on people to speak. By the end of the semester all the students had contributed in a personal way, but there was certainly not anywhere near equal participation.

Marie's overall impression was illustrated by the coded discussion; there were several very active participants, especially the male who introduced the discussion, and many quiet or silent ones. In describing her goals as a teacher Marie spoke of her ideal students as "those who are really involved and really care . . . who are willing to challenge each other and challenge the teacher." Elaborating on this, she said that when she first came to Meadows College she was disappointed in the lower level of class participation in comparison with her experience at a coeducational college, particularly because some Meadows students who never participated were brilliant writers (implying, to her, that they had a lot to contribute). She said she came to appreciate seeing young women develop over four years in a single-sex atmosphere, "so when the coeducational decision was made I was shocked." Recalling her earlier statement that she was struck by the wider interests of freshmen in the coeducational class, Marie inferred that a coeducational Meadows College included not only males but also a different population of females and that this produced a more varied and lively classroom dialogue than was formerly seen at the college. Class participation seemed to take less work on her part: "I spoke less and the class spoke more, yet I *am* troubled by those pockets of silence." (Marie's was the only one of the first-year seminars studied in which a male student was silent throughout the class.)

Dan Porter

Dan Porter is an English professor whose course was focused on the revolutions in modern literature and especially on women's place in these revolutions. Reading assignments for his class included Henrik Ibsen's *The Doll's House*, Alice Walker's *The Color Purple,* and Virginia Woolf's *To the Lighthouse.* Dan is an authority on Woolf but, perhaps because of this fact, finds her work difficult to teach to first-year students. On the tape that was coded he talked for a relatively large portion of the class. The class discussion lasted 66 minutes and 25 seconds. It was a wide-ranging discussion about various aspects of *To the Lighthouse.* Of this time, Dan spoke for a total of 44 minutes and 30 seconds, or about two-thirds of the time, as had Marie Navarre. But he intervened more often than Marie did. She broke into students' comments six times in 32 minutes; Dan interrupted 48 times in 66 minutes— more than four times as often.

The class included four male and 11 female students. If these 15 students were to divide evenly the remaining 22 minutes of class time, we would expect each one to speak for about a minute and 28 seconds. In fact, the four males spoke for a total of eight minutes and 17 seconds, or an average of two minutes and four seconds apiece. All four spoke, although two predominated. Of the 11 females, eight spoke, dividing up 13 minutes and 28 seconds of class time to average one minute and 46 seconds apiece. The pattern of overall participation in this discussion was thus more even than in Marie's class. The four males spoke, on average, slightly more than two minutes; the eight females who spoke averaged a minute and 46 seconds, only a little less than the males' speaking time. Three students were silent throughout the entire class; they were all females.

Dan commented on the conversational dynamics:

> I had four male students, all from prep schools, and from the very first day they dominated, not only because they were male but also because they had prep school experience. Every time I let the class go, the men seemed to take over so I always had to be there in the conversation. I had to do a lot of calling on people. There wasn't a lot of interaction between the students because of that. The four men seemed to support each other. The women talked less, but occasionally they would engage each other. My portrait of the class is a lot of individuals which I work to draw together.

Viewing the pattern of interchanges one could see that Dan's contributions and interruptions were integral to pushing the discussion forward and involving the majority of students. He acted as an ever-present conversational monitor, and his interruptions supported his purpose of drawing students together. They also served to reduce the number of opportunities for a single student to dominate any portion of the class. Marie's discussion, by contrast, was more spontaneous and student-centered (quite possibly because she had not read the material in advance). But the pattern of participation in Dan's class was the more even of the two.

How did Dan reflect on the experience of teaching in a coeducational context? Dan's ideal student was one "who not only does the work but is open-minded and will argue." Although initially disappointed at the decision to go coed because of the educational program that Meadows had developed for women, he also found the change exhilarating:

> I saw this as a challenge; being a male, I wanted to teach other males the things I had learned. That's exciting and I like challenges. I think we had been very successful in moving most of our students into a feminist view of things, although they were not always aware of it. But we were less successful in making them independently active. I anticipated coeducation, thinking that the atmosphere was going to change as we attracted new students, and it did.

In other words, as with Marie, Dan both expected and experienced coeducation as bringing more active students, male and female, into the classroom. But Dan also found an unexpected challenge in his seminar, the resistance of male students to feminist ideas. He said:

> At first they were very open and very sympathetic to the feminist approach, but then they felt that they were hearing the same thing in all of their classes. . . . I ask myself: If I structure the class for the men to learn more, will I be denying the women the rich education they were prepared to receive?
> There was one day, the day before Thanksgiving, when three of the guys had to leave early for some reason and the fourth was absent. When they left and there were only women in the class, I felt a tremendous relief. I could talk about things more easily.
> I admit I am interested in my own experience of being a male dealing with the resistance, the openness, the complex dynamics of men who were opened up. My role had to change from being a male feminist without giving much thought to my male experience but basically identifying with women, to being a male feminist conscious of my male experience. I think it will be a new kind of growth for me, this looking at gender and relationships.

In this interview one can see Dan struggling with the need to manage the class interactions while remaining open to challenges posed by the male students' response to feminist subject matter. While he welcomed the "activity" male challenges brought to the class, he wanted to move the students toward having conscious feminist sympathies. This complex challenge required him to be a very active manager of the discourse. Perhaps this is one factor accounting for the wide range of student participation.

Sarah Turner

Sarah Turner taught a class on the sixties to 16 females and two males in her first-year seminar. Her teaching proved to be a provocative contrast to the other professors' approaches. She described herself as having "diverse, almost contradictory teaching goals—to help each student develop a 'voice' of his or her own and concurrently to get each to understand my own experience of the 1960s." Of the four coded classes, Sarah's class provided the most nearly equitable distribution of participation between the teacher and her students. She spoke for approximately 13 minutes of the total time of 51 minutes; the remaining time was allotted to students' discussion of texts about the antiwar movement.

Sarah was closely involved with the coeducation project from its inception and was particularly sensitive to the often illusory promises of "coeducation." She was concerned from the outset with the danger that the inclusion of males would leave female students with less than their fair share of opportunities to participate in classroom discourse. And she worried that female students' traditionally strong skills, listening and empathy, might serve as mechanisms for their self-subordination. Believing that "it is important (particularly for female students) to construct their own relationships to the materials," she worked consciously to develop a classroom atmosphere in which each student made the leap from being interested in the texts to being an active participant in the discussion.

Sarah's efforts paid off in the sense that almost all her students said something during the seminar hour. And the class, although fairly tightly structured by her own questions, did break loose at times to allow students to make public the personal relationships they had constructed with the material. Yet most female students contributed only briefly, and Sarah's fears that male students would claim more than their share of conversational space proved well founded. Male students, only two of the group's total of 18, represented one-ninth of the class, but they claimed approximately one-fourth of the total talk time. For each male student this represented about two minutes, while female students, on average, spoke for only 44 seconds.

Each of the male students was talkative compared with any of the female students. This concerned Sarah, particularly because, as she said, "the brief contributors tended to contribute short answers to an 'authority,' meaning myself. . . . This left the more vocal students, those who talked for more than a few seconds, unpracticed in the art of public discourse." For example, there was an incident in which Rachel, the most talkative female student, expressed the opinion that if the North Vietnamese people wished to be communists it should have been their own affair. She was then ridiculed by Andrew, who said that Rachel's feelings were naive and uninformed. Rachel gave way without protest; Andrew continued to hold the floor, proclaiming, "What we really should be discussing about this text is . . . "

This tape raises several key questions associated with the introduction of coeducation. Although the other teachers who watched their own tapes also noticed males dominating classroom discussions, Sarah watched hers with an explicit interest in participation rates. Discussing the tape, she remarked:

> Three questions were of particular concern to me: First, assuming that classroom participation possesses both inherent and vocational value, to what extent should I—or any professor—intervene to provide female (and other conversationally disadvantaged students) with equal access to the conversational floor? Second, to what extent should we act as classroom managers? More generally, should we be in the business of teaching students how to listen and respond to

each other? Finally, to what extent is it possible for college professors to intervene in classroom dynamics and still approach our objective of providing a nonhierarchical social system in which the students develop their own voices?

In Sarah Turner's class the male-female participation rate was more nearly equal than in the other classes, yet the teacher found herself acting, at times, against her notion of ideal teaching. She recognized more "interventionist" moments on the tape than she wished to see—a violation of what she called her democratic and student-centered pedagogical ideals. Yet when she saw the male students clamoring for permission to dominate the class she was pleased with her ability to keep their domination to a minimum.

Dorothy Tacoski

Dorothy Tacoski is a political science professor who eschewed the "interventionist" strategies Dan and Sarah sometimes employed. Describing her ideal students as "the kind that have looked me over, decided they will have some fun with me and that they will take me on," she might lead a listener to conclude that she was following a male model. In responding to the question of whether this was so, Dorothy was noncommittal:

> As I see it, the college exists to help students who show signs of wanting to learn. The most effective and exciting classes happen for me when I respond to people who demonstrate the greatest interest. One of the exciting things about the move to coeducation is having the chance to educate people for the independence that will enable them to make it out there in the real world. Women and men come to college, in part, to gain autonomy.

Dorothy also mentioned that she liked to teach students who have relatively weak skills, a group for which she has to provide the challenge herself. In fact bright students, she said, are harder for her to challenge in class. Thus we would expect her class to be dominated by bright and articulate individuals. What place would the teacher have in such a class?

> The classroom is as good a place as any for students, male or female, to learn the rules of the game. For better or worse I see diversity—a virtue in my book—in student differences. Part of my job is to stay on the margin. I try to promote growth by every means *but* running the conversation.

An examination of her tape showed a very active group of 18 students, four male and 14 female, engaged in a debate on colonialism and African literature, the core topic for her first-year seminar. The most vocal member of the class was a woman who had apparently lived in Africa; her knowledge was wide-ranging, and her pronunciation of multisyllabic African names was self-confident. The students, cumulatively, talked three times as much as their teacher. Unlike the students in Sarah Turner's class, these men and women did not respond directly to the teacher's inquiries; they seemed, instead, to be motivated by the comments of their classmates. Dorothy's position often appeared to be that of an outsider looking for a point of entry in the dense and rapid conversation. When she did gain a place on the conversational floor, she made substantive comments addressed to the topic rather than evaluations of individual contributions. The students responded in kind by listening, by taking notes, and by waiting for an opening that would permit them to continue talking themselves.

Apparently the conversation was too freewheeling for some of the female students; six of them stayed out of the conversation entirely, an option chosen by none of the males. As a consequence, male students dominated the seminar; they constituted one-seventh of the class population but spoke for more than one-third of the time, in spite of the fact that the single most vocal member of the class was a woman. This student spoke for a total of five minutes, 24 seconds; the only other student to approach this talk time was a male student who talked for four minutes and 30 seconds.

Like many faculty members, Dorothy perceived this group of students as generally more energetic and competent than students from the previous year's exclusively female seminar. She recalls that male students led the way in discussion early in the semester; female students started to become somewhat more active around the third week.

Dorothy's interview provided additional insight on male-female differences. Male students, she said, were often eager to talk even if they didn't "get it," whereas the women would talk only when they believed they knew what they were talking about. Moreover, she added, the brightest female students were somewhat tentative in their speech and, unlike assertive males who seemed to encourage each other's contributions, these tentative bright women probably had the effect of discouraging the shyer or less able ones. This version of a role modeling hypothesis may help to explain why six out of 14 females stayed out of the conversation entirely, while none of the males removed himself from the conversational space. Although the issue of occupying (or vacating) conversational "space" often seems metaphorical, Dorothy Tacoski reported a startlingly concrete example of the phenomenon:

> When the students were giving oral presentations, all of the women stayed at their seats. But each of the men got up, walked to the front of the room, used the board, used the map, and moved me out of the way.

In concluding her report Dorothy landed on a key question:

> This videotape project has made me wonder: If we confirm the existence of a more and a less advantaged gender, are we cheating women of opportunities? In a coeducational setting, are we simply giving them a safe place to practice adjusting to a world where they will always, somehow, be a little less central?

REFERENCES

Baum, Laurie. 1987. "Corporate Women: They're About to Break Through to the Top," *Business Week* (June 22), pp. 72–78.

Hall, Roberta M., and Bernice R. Sandler. 1982. "The Classroom Climate: A Chilly One for Women?" (Washington, D.C.: Project on the Status and Education of Women of the Association of American Colleges).

Krupnick, Catherine G. 1985. "Women and Men in the Classroom: Inequality and Its Remedies," *Journal of the Harvard Danforth Center* (May), pp. 18–25.

Lott, B. 1987. "Sexist Discrimination as Distancing Behavior: A Laboratory Demonstration," *Psychology of Women Quarterly* 11, pp. 47–58.

Welty, William. 1989. "Discussion Method Teaching: How to Make It Work," *Change* 21:4 (July-August), pp. 40–49.

Women's College Coalition. 1991. "Fact Sheet About Women's Colleges." (Washington, D.C.).

Zimmerman, D. H., and C. West. 1975. "Sex Roles, Interruptions, and Silences in Conversation," in *Language and Sex: Differences and Dominance*, edited by B. Thorne and N. Henley (Rowley: Newbury House), pp. 105–129.

SECTION C

The Question of Pornography

An Ordinance of the City of Minneapolis
Amending Title 7, Chapter 139 of the
Minneapolis Code of Ordinances relating to Civil Rights:
In General.

The City Council of the City of Minneapolis do ordain as follows:

Section 1. That Section 139.10 of the above-entitled ordinance be amended to read as follows:

139.10 *Findings, declaration of policy and purpose.*

(a) *Findings.* The council finds that discrimination in employment, labor union membership, housing accommodations, property rights, education, public accommodations and public services based on race, color, creed, religion, ancestry, national origin, sex, including sexual harassment AND PORNOGRAPHY, affectional preference, disability, age, marital status, or status with regard to public assistance or in housing accommodations based on familial status adversely affects the health, welfare, peace and safety of the community. Such discriminatory practices degrade individuals, foster intolerance and hate, and create and intensify unemployment, sub-standard housing, under-education, ill health, lawlessness and poverty, thereby injuring the public welfare.

(1) SPECIAL FINDINGS ON PORNOGRAPHY: THE COUNCIL FINDS THAT PORNOGRAPHY IS CENTRAL IN CREATING AND MAINTAINING THE CIVIL INEQUALITY OF THE SEXES. PORNOGRAPHY IS A SYSTEMATIC PRACTICE OF EXPLOITATION AND SUBORDINATION BASED ON SEX WHICH DIFFERENTIALLY HARMS WOMEN. THE BIGOTRY AND CONTEMPT IT PROMOTES, WITH THE ACTS OF AGGRESSION IT FOSTERS, HARM WOMEN'S OPPORTUNITIES FOR EQUALITY OF RIGHTS IN EMPLOYMENT, EDUCATION, PROPERTY RIGHTS, PUBLIC ACCOMMODATIONS AND PUBLIC SERVICES; CREATE PUBLIC HARASSMENT AND PRIVATE DENIGRATION; PROMOTE INJURY AND DEGRADATION SUCH AS RAPE, BATTERY AND PROSTITUTION

AND INHIBIT JUST ENFORCEMENT OF LAWS AGAINST THESE ACTS; CONTRIBUTE SIGNIFICANTLY TO RESTRICTING WOMEN FROM FULL EXERCISE OF CITIZENSHIP AND PARTICIPATION IN PUBLIC LIFE, INCLUDING IN NEIGHBORHOODS; DAMAGE RELATIONS BETWEEN THE SEXES; AND UNDERMINE WOMEN'S EQUAL EXERCISE OF RIGHTS TO SPEECH AND ACTION GUARANTEED TO ALL CITIZENS UNDER THE CONSTITUTIONS AND LAWS OF THE UNITED STATES AND THE STATE OF MINNESOTA.

(b) *Declaration of policy and purpose.* It is the public policy of the City of Minneapolis and the purpose of this title:

(1) To recognize and declare that the opportunity to obtain employment, labor union membership, housing accommodations, property rights, education, public accommodations and public services without discrimination based on race, color, creed, religion, ancestry, national origin, sex, including sexual harassment AND PORNOGRAPHY, affectional preference, disability, age, marital status, or status with regard to public assistance or to obtain housing accommodations without discrimination based on familial status is a civil right;

(2) To prevent and prohibit all discriminatory practices based on race, color, creed, religion, ancestry, national origin, sex, including sexual harassment AND PORNOGRAPHY, affectional preference, disability, age, marital status, or status with regard to public assistance with respect to employment, labor union membership, housing accommodations, property rights, education, public accommodations or public services;

(3) To prevent and prohibit all discriminatory practices based on familial status with respect to housing accommodations;

(4) TO PREVENT AND PROHIBIT ALL DISCRIMINATORY PRACTICES OF SEXUAL SUBORDINATION OR INEQUALITY THROUGH PORNOGRAPHY;

(5) To protect all persons from unfounded charges of discriminatory practices;

(6) To eliminate existing and the development of any ghettos in the community; and

(7) To effectuate the foregoing policy by means of public information and education, mediation and conciliation, and enforcement.

Section 3. That Section 139.20 of the above-entitled ordinance be amended by adding thereto a new subsection (gg) to read as follows:

(gg) *Pornography.* Pornography is a form of discrimination on the basis of sex.

(1) Pornography is the sexually explicit subordination of women, graphically depicted, whether in pictures or in words, that also includes one or more of the following:

(i) women are presented dehumanized as sexual objects, things or commodities; or

(ii) women are presented as sexual objects who enjoy pain or humiliation; or

(iii) women are presented as sexual objects who experience sexual pleasure in being raped; or

(iv) women are presented as sexual objects tied up or cut up or mutilated or bruised or physically hurt; or

(v) women are presented in postures of sexual submission; or

(vi) women's body parts—including but not limited to vaginas, breasts, and buttocks—are exhibited, such that women are reduced to those parts; or

(vii) women are presented as whores by nature; or

(viii) women are presented being penetrated by objects or animals; or

(ix) women are presented in scenarios of degradation, injury, abasement, torture, shown as filthy or inferior, bleeding, bruised, or hurt in a context that makes these conditions sexual.

(2) The use of men, children, or transsexuals in the place of women in (1) (i-ix) above is pornography for purposes of subsections (l) - (p) of this statute.

Section 4. That section 139.40 of the above-mentioned ordinance be amended by adding thereto new subsections (l), (m), (n), (o), (p), (q), (r) and (s) to read as follows:

(l) *Discrimination by trafficking in pornography.* The production, sale, exhibition, or distribution of pornography is discrimination against women by means of trafficking in pornography:

(1) City, state, and federally funded public libraries or private and public university and college libraries in which pornography is available for study, including on open shelves, shall not be construed to be trafficking in pornography but special display presentations of pornography in said places is sex discrimination.

(2) The formation of private clubs or associations for purposes of trafficking in pornography is illegal and shall be considered a conspiracy to violate the civil rights of women.

(3) Any woman has a cause of action hereunder as a woman acting against the subordination of women. Any man or transsexual who alleges injury by pornography in the way women are injured by it shall also have a cause of action.

(m) *Coercion into pornographic performances.* Any person, including transsexual, who is coerced, intimidated, or fraudulently induced (hereafter "coerced") into performing for pornography shall have a cause of action against the maker(s), seller(s), exhibitor(s) or distributor(s) of said pornography for damages and for the elimination of the products of the performance(s) from the public view.

(1) *Limitation of action.* This claim shall not expire before five years have elapsed from the date of the coerced performance(s) or from the last appearance or sale of any product of the performance(s), whichever date is later;

(2) Proof of one or more of the following facts or conditions shall not, without more, negate a finding of coercion;

(i) that the person is a woman; or

(ii) that the person is or has been a prostitute; or

(iii) that the person has attained the age of majority; or

(iv) that the person is connected by blood or marriage to anyone involved in or related to the making of the pornography; or

(v) that the person has previously had, or been thought to have had, sexual relations with anyone, including anyone involved in or related to the making of the pornography; or

(vi) that the person has previously posed for sexually explicit pictures for or with anyone, including anyone involved in or related to the making of the pornography at issue; or

(vii) that anyone else, including a spouse or other relative, has given permission on the person's behalf; or

(viii) that the person actually consented to a use of the performance that is changed into pornography; or

(ix) that the person knew that the purpose of the acts or events in question was to make pornography; or

(x) that the person showed no resistance or appeared to cooperate actively in the photographic sessions or in the sexual events that produced the pornography; or

(xi) that the person signed a contract, or made statements affirming a willingness to cooperate in the production of pornography; or

(xii) that no physical force, threats, or weapons were used in the making of the pornography; or

(xiii) that the person was paid or otherwise compensated.

(n) *Forcing pornography on a person.* Any woman, man, child, or transsexual who has pornography forced on him/her in any place of employment, in education, in a home, or in any public place has a cause of action against the perpetrator and/or institution.

(o) *Assault or physical attack due to pornography.* Any woman, man, child, or transsexual who is assaulted, physically attacked or injured in a way that is directly caused by specific pornography has a claim for damages against the perpetrator, the maker(s), distributor(s), seller(s), and/or exhibitor(s), and for an injunction against the specific pornography's further exhibition, distribution, or sale. No damages shall be assessed (A) against maker(s) for pornography made, (B) against distributor(s) for pornography distributed, (C) against seller(s) for pornography sold, or (D) against exhibitors for pornography exhibited prior to the enforcement date of this act.

(p) *Defenses.* Where the materials which are the subject matter of a cause of action under subsections (l), (m), (n), or (o) of this section are pornography, it shall not be a defense that the defendants did not know or intend that the materials were pornography or sex discrimination.

(q) *Severability.* Should any part(s) of this ordinance be found legally invalid, the remaining part(s) remain valid.

(r) Subsections (l), (m), (n), and (o) of this section are exceptions to the second clause of Section 141.90 of this title.

(s) *Effective date.* Enforcement of this ordinance of December 30, 1983, shall be suspended until July 1, 1984 ("enforcement date") to facilitate training, education, voluntary compliance, and implementation taking into consideration the opinions of the City Attorney and the Civil Rights Commission. No liability shall attach under (l) or as specifically provided in the second sentence of (o) until the enforcement date. Liability under all other sections of this act shall attach as of December 30, 1983.

Amending Title 7, Chapter 141 of the Minneapolis Code of Ordinances relating to Civil Rights: Administration and Enforcement.

The City Council of the City of Minneapolis do ordain as follows:

Section 1. That Section 141.50 (l) of the above-entitled ordinance be amended by adding thereto a new subsection (3) to read as follows:

(3) *Pornography:* The hearing committee or court may order relief, including the removal of violative material, permanent injunction against the sale, exhibition or distribution of violative material, or any other relief deemed just and equitable, including reasonable attorney's fees.

Section 2. That Section 141.60 of the above-entitled ordinance be amended as follows:

141.60 *Civil action, judicial review and enforcement.*

(a) *Civil actions.*

(1) AN INDIVIDUAL ALLEGING A VIOLATION OF THIS ORDINANCE MAY BRING A CIVIL ACTION DIRECTLY IN COURT.

(2) A complainant may bring a civil action at the following times:

(i) Within forty-five (45) days after the director, a review committee or a hearing committee has dismissed a complaint for reasons other than a conciliation agreement to which the complainant is a signator; or

(ii) After forty-five (45) days from the filing of a verified complaint if a hearing has not been held pursuant to Section 141.50 or the department has not entered into a conciliation agreement to which the complainant is a signator. The complainant shall notify the department of his/her intention to bring a civil action, which shall be commenced within ninety (90) days of giving the notice. A complainant bringing a civil action shall mail, by registered or certified mail, a copy of the summons and complaint to the department and upon receipt of same, the director shall terminate all proceedings before the department relating to the complaint and shall dismiss the complaint.

No complaint shall be filed or reinstituted with the department after a civil action relating to the same unfair discriminatory practice has been brought unless the civil action has been dismissed without prejudice.

TO: Minneapolis City Council
FROM: Catharine A. MacKinnon and Andrea Dworkin
RE: Proposed Ordinance on Pornography
DATE: 26 December 1983

Several of you have suggested to us that a short paper addressing some frequently asked questions would be helpful. Here we briefly discuss what this ordinance is trying to do, how it would work, why it is different from past approaches, and we assess supposed obstacles.

1. What this ordinance is trying to do

This ordinance defines pornography for what it is. Its central feature is that it subordinates women through sex. The influence of pornography on men who rule societies, and thus on the development of misogynist social institutions, can be traced back through feudalism, but it is only through relatively recent technology that the social environment has been glutted with pornography so that it hurts women openly, publicly, and with social legitimacy. This same pervasiveness and open availability has also made it possible to understand and document the effects of pornography, hence its place in the institutionalization of second class citizenship for women, for the first time in history.

The use of women in pornography and the impact of pornography on women's status and treatment is the primary focus of this ordinance. Pornography promotes environmental terrorism and private abuse of women and girls and, to a lesser extent, men and boys and transsexuals. Society's efforts toward the civil and sexual equality of women and men are severely hampered—frankly, nearly destroyed—by the success of pornography. Most frequently, the pornography promotes rape, pain, humiliation and inferiority as experiences that are sexually pleasing to all women because we are women. The studies show that it is not atypical for men to believe and act on the pornography. Each time men are sexually aroused by pornography—the sexually explicit subordination of women—they learn to connect women's sexual pleasure to abuse and women's sexual nature to inferiority. They learn this in their bodies, not just their minds, so that it becomes a physical, seemingly natural, response. When real women claim not to want inequality or force, they are not credible compared with the continually sexually available "real women" in pornography. These men are the same normal men who make decisions that control much of women's lives and opportunities at every level of society. Until women achieve equal power with men, such men are in a position to control women's employment, educational advancement, social status and credibility in the media, on paper, on the street, in meetings, in court, in their own homes, and in public office. The fact that some women have successfully fought some of this discrimination does not prove it does not exist; it proves that victories, like the victory this ordinance would be, can be won.

In the hearings, we learned that it takes coercion to make pornography—for instance, *Deep Throat*, the highest grossing film ever. We learned that pornography is forced on women and children and that frequently the women and children are then raped or forced to do what is in the pornography. We learned that pornography is used in sexual assaults and to plan the sexual assaults. We learned that exposure to pornography increases male aggression toward women and leads men to see women as things, less than human, and wanting and liking rape and torture and humiliation. We also learned that pornography has been used to, and has the effect of, terrorizing women in their homes, in their neighborhoods, and in their places of work. We learned that pornography is used in relationships that range from the intimate to the anonymous in ways that give women no choice about seeing the pornography or doing the sex.

The purpose of the ordinance is to make available an effective remedy to those who choose to use it, so that women need no longer be paralyzed or passive or held back by the lack of a legitimate avenue for redress in the face of pornography—the systematic discrimination, the condoned brutality, and the glorified debasement that defines the condition of an entire group of people.

2. How the ordinance would work

Like any other law that prohibits discrimination, this law would make available the administrative apparatus of the Human Rights Commission and the courts to adjudicate complaints. Once the law goes into effect, a person who has been coerced into a pornographic performance, had pornography forced on them, or has been assaulted or physically attacked or injured in a way directly caused by a specific piece of pornography could choose to complain to the Commission or go directly to court. Any woman can also complain against traffickers in pornography. Because the data from the hearings show that pornography increases male aggression against women, the public availability of the pornography, as defined in the ordinance, is in and of itself a violation of women's rights to equal personhood and citizenship. The systematic sexual subordination of the pornography *is* the injury under this section of the act.

The Commission or the court would then see if the pornography complained of meets the definition of pornography in the statute. The definition of pornography in the statute states exactly what pornography is and does. It describes exactly the trafficking in women engaged in by the pornographers, which ranges from dehumanizing women as sexual things and commodities to torturing and maiming women as sexual acts. The dehumanization is fundamental to the subordination and the precondition for the more explicit violence. It is tempting to consider proceeding one step at a time, disallowing the explicit violence while allowing the dehumanization, objectification, and submission. This would leave the *inequality* intact. Such an approach would not go to the heart of this form of subordination. It would also draw a legal line that would take immense resources to adjudicate because it is not a line that can be drawn because it is not a line that is drawn in the pornography.

The definition includes everything that is pornography and does not include anything that is not. It does not include sex education, for instance, or erotica, which is sexually explicit sex premised on equality. Any law can be abused. Cynical attempts to undermine this law may center on attempts to apply it to materials and acts for which it was not intended. The pornographers have a lot of money and power at stake in making this law look bad. We believe that the Commission and the courts are as reliable instruments for distinguishing frivolous abuses from bona fide injuries in these cases as they are in any other kind of discrimination case.

The most legally likely place for issues other than sex discrimination to arise—issues such as the First Amendment—is as a defense. When sued under this ordinance, the pornographers are likely to say that it violates their First Amendment rights. The point here is that customarily people have to have a legal injury before they can sue. They can not customarily sue a law-making body just because it has passed a civil law that they do not like or agree with or think *might* be applied to them. People activate civil claims by alleging that someone else hurt them in a way the law recognizes.

This means that other legal issues, such as the First Amendment, are most likely to be raised as defenses by pornographers against those who complain or sue them for injuries, rather than as a basis for a direct suit against anyone. Once an action commences against a respondent, they can seek to involve the city or the agency and/or to challenge the ordinance on its face. We discuss why we think that such uses of the First Amendment may not prevail in section 4.

3. Why this approach is better than past approaches

The major distinction between the civil rights approach to pornography and past approaches to all the problems of sexual inequality it involves is that this is the first time the legal concept of the injury is the same as the real social injury pornography does. Obscenity laws, besides allowing inconsistent, ill-conceived or politically motivated criminal prosecutions, created a lot of confusion about pornography by misidentifying the harm. Many people mistake obscenity for pornography. Obscenity is a criminal legal term. One possible root meaning of the word "obscene" is the ancient Greek for "off stage"—in effect, that which should not be shown, especially in the theatre for aesthetic reasons. This suggests that the injury of obscenity has to do with what is publicly viewed; the injury of pornography is what is done, whether it is public or private. Another possible and more likely root meaning of the word "obscene" is the Latin for "against filth": Is a given work "filth" and are we, the people, against it. Obscenity is not a synonym for pornography in this meaning either. Obscenity is a social value judgment. Pornography is concrete. Its root meaning is "the graphic depiction of whores." Everybody may have an idea of what is or is not obscene, especially given the myriad inconsistent legal definitions over the last 200 years. Pornography is specific, concrete, and, as we have said, about the sexually explicit subordination of women. In pornography, women are graphically depicted as whores by nature, that is, defined by our status as sexual chattel. Because the definition in the ordinance is concrete, specific, narrow, and describes what is actually there, it is not vague, not overly broad, not about ideas that some people think are good or bad, moral or immoral, normal or abnormal, natural or unnatural, nor does the ordinance suggest, as obscenity law does, that women's bodies are dirty or sex is dirty. A final distinction between obscenity and pornography is crucial. Courts have been hampered in enforcing obscenity laws because there was no evidence of the harm obscenity does to match the scope of the laws enacted. The harm of obscenity could not be documented or measured because it did not exist. Evidence from the hearings provided evidence for the harm of pornography because it identified the harm that pornography actually does: to the status and treatment of women.

The proposed ordinance differs from past approaches by going significantly beyond any existing law that regulates acts committed against women. Now, before this law, people who are coerced into pornography have no effective way to reach the pornography made by coercing them. The profit incentive to coercing more and more women remains. If they complain, they are not believed, in part because pornography in general convinces people that women love doing it and in part because the specific pornography they are forced to make is often convincing in depicting their simulated enjoyment. Now, before this law, when women are sexually assaulted, because the society is saturated by pornography, they are unlikely to be believed in court and are continually asked pornographic questions like, did you like it? Now, before this law, child pornography is a crime in Minnesota but forcing pornography on children is not. Often, adult pornography in which women are infantilized is used. Such pornography continues to target children for sexual assault, even if the models have actually aged one day beyond their minority.

Unlike all other previous approaches to the growing social problem of pornography, including zoning laws which have at times hurt poor and working-class neighborhoods or segregated women out of whole sections of cities, this law stands against the real traffic in real women. It is a civil law *against* pornography, but it is also *for* the equality of the sexes, women's rights, and the integrity and dignity of all persons regardless of sex. And it will *do* something: empower people and call into question the legal immunity of the exploiters for the first time.

4. Assessment of supposed obstacles

Nothing exactly like this law has ever been tried, so it can not be said conclusively that it will or will not work or will or will not be constitutionally upheld. Because it is part of the civil code, not the criminal code, there will be no state ban or police enforcement. Because it is not an obscenity law, nothing ever done under obscenity law strictly controls the interpretation of this law, although prior case law may indicate judicial attitudes toward some of the issues involved. The First Amendment right to speech has never been absolute. In the one case where the Supreme Court has balanced a municipal sex discrimination ordinance prohibiting sex segregation in advertising against the First Amendment, the ordinance won (1973). More recently, the Supreme Court, recognizing child pornography to be a form of child abuse, allowed states to make it a crime. The harm that the child pornography industry did to children allowed something that is speech (not obscenity) to be illegal consistent with the First Amendment. (The ACLU defended child pornography as speech throughout the litigation.) Our hearings show a similar level of harm done to women in adult pornography, as well as the integral role adult pornography plays in child abuse. The pornographers have relied for their impunity upon the indistinguishability of what they push from any other form of expression. This proposed ordinance draws a line that distinguishes them. The pornographers have convinced many that their freedom is everyone's freedom, obscuring what this statute is based on: the freedom of the pornographers enforces the subordination of women.

The First Amendment mainly prohibits state acts that interfere with speech. But there is an affirmative, if less prominent, side to the First Amendment that would allow the silence of women because of discrimination to be taken into the balance. The fairness doctrine in broadcasting, for example, recognizes that government sometimes has an obligation to help make access to speech available on an equal basis. The First Amendment's goals are furthered by restricting the speech of some so that others might have access to it. Pornography directly contributes to a silencing of women that is socially pervasive. The First Amendment is undermined when women are kept from having access to the social preconditions to exercise the rights the First Amendment guarantees from infringement by states. Equal access to the means of speech, which pornography discriminatorily denies to women sexually and socially, is a First Amendment goal that is furthered by this law.

The civil rights approach, unlike morals legislation and police power, is strengthened by the support of legal concepts outside the First Amendment, namely equal protection (the Fourteenth Amendment) and anti-discrimination law. That the systematic relegation of an entire group of people to inferiority because of a condition of birth should be illegal is not a new idea. This ordinance to further the equality of the sexes embodies an interest particularly appropriate for that level of representative government closest to the people.

Violence Against Women

In Week of an Infamous Rape, 28 Other Victims Suffer

Don Terry

From poor women, whose suffering rarely makes headlines, to bankers on the fast track, to little girls in pigtails, vulnerability to rape is shared by all women and girls, experts say.

In the week in which a white investment banker was brutally beaten and raped as she jogged through Central Park, there were 28 other first-degree rapes or attempted rapes reported across New York City, the police said.

First-degree rape involves either the threat or the use of violence.

The attack on the jogger sparked angry cries for vengeance and increased police patrols, partly, some have argued, because those charged in the attack were minority-group teen-agers and the victim was an affluent white woman.

Nearly all the rapes reported during that April week were of black or Hispanic women. Most went unnoticed by the public.

AGES RANGE FROM 8 TO 51

The investment banker was attacked during the late evening of Wednesday, April 19. The other victims that week—April 16–22—were attacked while walking along the street, waiting for a train and visiting a friend.

The victims that week ranged in age from 8 years old to 51. But Linda Fairstein, an assistant Manhattan district attorney who heads the sex-crimes prosecution unit, said she has seen rape victims as young as a few months old and as old as their 90's.

"Sexual violence happens to women of every racial and ethnic and economic background," said Brooklyn District Attorney Elizabeth Holtzman. "And the perpetrators also come from every racial and economic background."

"The Central Park attack was treated as extraordinary," said Francoise

Jacobsohn, president of the New York City Chapter of the National Organization For Women. "It was not extraordinary. Sexual violence is a continuing problem. But we only talk about it when it's on the front pages. It happens all the time."

Less than two weeks after the Central Park case made headlines across the country, a 38-year-old black woman was taken at knife point from a Brooklyn street by two men who forced her up to the roof of a four-story building, raped and beat her. Then they threw her 50 feet to the ground. She suffered two broken ankles, a fractured right leg and abdominal injuries.

In New York City last year, 3,584 rapes and attempted rapes were reported. Those figures include first-, second- and third-degree rape charges. Second- and third-degree rape charges are brought when victims are either too young or not mentally competent to consent to sexual intercourse.

Last year, there were also 1,665 reported cases of sodomy and sexual abuse in the city, bringing the total number of reported sexual assaults to 5,249, a decrease of 60 from 1987.

But the rape statistics may only scratch the surface.

Detective Ellen King, who retired in May after 14 years with the New York City Police Department's sex-crimes unit, said law-enforcement officials across the nation estimate that only 1 or 2 out of every 10 rapes or sexual assaults are reported to the police.

Fear, shame and the victim's fear of being blamed for somehow encouraging the attack keep many women from reporting rapes, say experts and some victims.

"I was afraid he'd kill me," said a 53-year-old woman who was raped by an acquaintance in his 50's. "So I didn't press charges. It's not so easy to do."

Rapists are as varied as their victims—doctors and lawyers, homeless men and teen-age boys. The attackers can be strangers, carrying guns or knives, or acquaintances, armed with the victim's trust.

And every rapist carries the specter of death.

"Rape is a life-threatening situation," Detective King said, "I often talk with women who say, 'I should have kicked, I should have screamed.' I tell them, 'Look, whatever you did was the right thing, because you are alive, because you survived.'"

The 29 first-degree rapes reported from April 16 to April 22, were recorded sketchily in police records as investigations began. Authorities withheld the names of the victims and the specific locations of the crimes.

Rape crisis counselors and authorities point out that attackers and victims are most often of the same race. That was true in nearly all of the rapes that occurred during that April week. Among the victims were 17 blacks, 7 Hispanic women, 3 whites, and 2 Asians.

SUNDAY, APRIL 16

7:30 P.M. A 12-year-old girl was accosted by four boys, ages 11, 12, 13 and 15, in an apartment building in Harlem. They pulled her into a hallway, where they each raped her. The youngest boys were arrested. The 15-year-old has not yet been charged.

10 P.M. An 18-year-old woman was in her home in Port Richmond, Staten Island, when she was raped by an acquaintance at 10 P.M. A 22-year-old man was arrested and charged the next day.

MONDAY, APRIL 17

4:30 A.M. A woman, 22, was visiting a male friend in Brooklyn when he forced her into a bedroom, took her money and raped her. No arrest was made. The police said the location of the crime was unknown because the victim refused to cooperate.

9:50 A.M. A woman, 51, was alone in a small store in the Bushwick section of Brooklyn when a man walked in, carrying a gun. He took $200 and pushed her into the back room, where he ordered her to disrobe, but he fled before raping her.

3:30 P.M. As she walked through the northern reaches of Central Park on the East Side, a woman, 26, was hit in the face, robbed and raped. The suspect escaped.

4 P.M. A 14-year-old girl was walking along Prospect Place in the Crown Heights section of Brooklyn when a 22-year-old man approached her and placed an object to her neck. He forced her to a nearby apartment where he raped her.

11:35 P.M. A woman, 18, walking down a street in Jamaica, Queens, was grabbed from behind by a man with a knife. He dragged her to a roof and raped her. The attacker escaped.

TUESDAY, APRIL 18

6:40 A.M. Two brothers and two other men accosted a 20-year-old woman on the street in Brooklyn Heights and forced her to a rooftop where each man raped her. The brothers, 24 and 29 years old, were arrested and charged with first-degree rape. Their accomplices were being sought.

2:15 P.M. A 15-year-old girl in East Harlem was taken from an elevator by a man with a knife. He pushed her into an apartment, robbed and raped her. The man was later arrested and charged in several similar rapes in the area.

6 P.M. A woman, 22, was forced into a vacant office in a building in Midtown Manhattan, where she was raped. Her suspected attacker was arrested a week later.

8:30 P.M. A woman, 24, was walking along East 138th Street in the Melrose section of the Bronx when she was grabbed from behind. The attacker blindfolded her and drove her to an unknown location, where he raped her.

9:30 P.M. On a sidewalk in Far Rockaway, Queens, a woman, 28, was approached by a man who asked her if she would have sex with him. She refused. The man, 21, then dragged her to a beach, beat her about the face with his fists and raped her. He was arrested nine days later.

11 P.M. A 25-year-old woman was assaulted by an acquaintance who invited the woman to his home in the Crown Heights section of Brooklyn. The man forced the woman to undress and then raped her.

WEDNESDAY, APRIL 19

12:30 P.M. As she walked in the Canarsie section of Brooklyn, a 14-year-old girl was grabbed by two teen-agers. One of the boys had a gun. They forced her to an apartment, where they raped her. Before letting her go, the boy with the gun fired a shot into a wall.

2 P.M. A 15-year-old girl walked into an apartment building in the Coney Island section of Brooklyn, where she was confronted by a man who pulled a pistol and told her to follow him. He took her to an apartment, where two other men were waiting. Each man then raped her.

10:05 P.M. A 28-year-old investment banker, jogging through Central Park, was attacked by a group of teen-agers. They kicked and beat her, smashed her in the head with a pipe and raped her. The teen-agers, who were from East Harlem, were quickly arrested.

THURSDAY, APRIL 20

2 A.M. A 15-year-old girl was raped by a 36-year-old acquaintance in the Bronx.

3 A.M. A woman, 20, was sitting with a male acquaintance in the Bronx. He forced her to smoke crack, then demanded sex. When she refused, he punched and choked her. Then he raped her.

4:30 A.M. A woman, 34, was going to meet a friend when she stopped to talk with two male acquaintances in the Bathgate section of the Bronx. When she asked if a mutual friend still lived in the area, the men offered to take her to the friend. Instead, they led her to a building on Southern Boulevard, where they raped her.

10 A.M. A 27-year-old woman accompanied an 18-year-old man she had just met on a walk through Central Park. Once in the park, he raped her.

4 P.M. In the Melrose section of the Bronx, an 8-year-old girl was raped by an acquaintance, a 50-year-old man.

11 P.M. An 18-year-old woman and a 25-year-old acquaintance had been socializing when the man demanded sex and raped the woman in an apartment in midtown Manhattan.

FRIDAY, APRIL 21

2:30 A.M. A 42-year-old woman was visiting a 20-year-old acquaintance in his home in Far Rockaway, Queens. At some point, the visit turned ugly, and the man raped her.

6 P.M. In an apartment building in the East Flatbush section of Brooklyn, a 13-year-old girl was riding an elevator when a 15-year-old boy grabbed her and forced her to go to the roof, where he raped her.

SATURDAY, APRIL 22

3:05 A.M. On a Long Island Rail Road platform in Woodside, Queens, a 27-year-old woman was confronted by a man who said he had a gun. He ordered her to undress and attempted to rape her. He could not perform sexually, a common occurrence during rape, experts say, and fled after robbing her. Four days later, a man, 28, was arrested and charged with attempted rape and robbery.

5:45 A.M. A man with a gun approached a woman, 27, from behind in Woodhaven, Queens. He marched her to an abandoned truck and raped her. Two days later, a man, 35, from Brooklyn was arrested in the assault.

6 A.M. Two men, one of them armed with a stick, confronted a 23-year-old woman on a street in the Brownsville section of Brooklyn. They beat and raped her on the street.

6:30 A.M. A woman, 20, was alone on a street in the Bedford-Stuyvesant section of Brooklyn when a man grabbed her from behind, forced her into an abandoned car and raped her.

10 P.M. Two men, one holding a gun, forced a woman, 26, beneath the Williamsburg Bridge in Brooklyn and raped her.

According to F.B.I. statistics, a forcible rape is committed in this country every six minutes.

COMMENTS AND
RECOMMENDED READINGS

The most prominent explanatory accounts of gender maximalism are biological, psychoanalytic, or sociological. The biological (or sociobiological) view is most fully elaborated by Edward O. Wilson in the context of a comprehensive review of animal sociality in *Sociobiology: The New Synthesis* (Cambridge: Harvard Univ. Press, 1975). Wilson develops the human story in *On Human Nature* (Cambridge: Harvard Univ. Press, 1978). See also Donald Symons, *The Evolution of Human Sexuality* (New York: Oxford Univ. Press, 1979). Wilson's maximalism is effectively criticized, without abandoning sociobiology, by Sarah Blaffer Hrdy in *The Woman That Never Evolved* (Cambridge: Harvard Univ. Press, 1981). See also Bettyann Kevles, *Female of the Species: Sex and Survival in the Animal Kingdom* (Cambridge: Harvard Univ. Press, 1986). For general critiques of sociobiology, see Peter Singer, *The Expanding Circle: Ethics and Sociobiology* (New York: Farrar, Straus & Giroux, 1981) and Philip Kitcher, *Vaulting Ambition: Sociobiology and the Quest for Human Nature* (Cambridge: MIT Press, 1985).

The psychoanalytic account of gendered perspectives, stressing women's role as primary parents, is elaborated by Dorothy Dinnerstein in *The Mermaid and the Minotaur: Sexual Arrangements and Human Malaise* (New York: Harper & Row, 1976). Nancy Chodorow combines psychoanalytic and sociological perspectives in *The Reproduction of Mothering: Psychoanalysis and the Sociology of Gender* (Berkeley: Univ. of California Press, 1978). For critical reflections on psychoanalytic frameworks and gender identity, see Judith Butler, "Gender Trouble, Feminist Theory, and Psychoanalytic Discourse," in *Feminism/Postmodernism* (New York: Routledge, 1990), edited by Linda J. Nicholson.

Essays on sociobiological, psychoanalytic, and other approaches to gender are collected in *Theoretical Perspectives on Sexual Difference* (New Haven: Yale Univ. Press, 1990), edited by Deborah L. Rhode.

The debate on gender maximalism and gender minimalism is reflected in the literature on feminist ethics, which encompasses three distinct, though sometimes overlapping, genres. The first identifies feminist with feminine and stresses points of divergence between masculine and feminine perspectives. Much of this literature focuses specifically on education. See, for example, Nel Noddings, *Caring: A Feminine Approach to Ethics and Moral Education* (Berkeley: Univ. of California Press, 1984); Mary Field Belenky, et al., *Women's Ways of Knowing: The Development of Self, Voice, and Mind* (New York: Basic Books, 1986); and *Who Cares? Theory, Research, and Educational*

Implications of the Ethic of Care, edited by Mary M. Brabeck (New York: Praeger, 1989). On the broader question of connections between education and culture, see the essays in *Changing Education: Women as Radicals and Conservators*, edited by Joyce Antler and Sari Knopp Biklen (Albany: State Univ. of New York, 1990).

The second genre takes the issue of equality between the sexes as its principal focus and regards the emphasis on differences as problematic—or at least as generating conundrums that need resolution. See especially Martha Minow, *Making All the Difference: Inclusion, Exclusion and American Law* (Ithaca: Cornell Univ. Press, 1990). Also helpful is Jean Grimshaw, *Philosophy and Feminist Thinking* (Minneapolis: Univ. of Minnesota Press, 1986), especially Chapter 7, "The Idea of a Female Ethic." On gratuitous gendering and its significance for political theorizing, see Jane J. Mansbridge, "Feminism and Democratic Community" in *Democratic Community*, edited by John W. Chapman and Ian Shapiro (New York: New York Univ. Press, forthcoming). For a general set of essays, see *Feminist Ethics* (Lawrence: Univ. Press of Kansas, 1991), edited by Claudia Card.

The third genre focuses on questions of power. Its themes are domination and oppression, degradation and silence. In its positive aspect, it aims to produce a literature of liberation. See especially the work of Catharine A. MacKinnon, *Feminism Unmodified: Discourses on Life and Law* (Cambridge: Harvard Univ. Press, 1987) and *Toward a Feminist Theory of the State* (Cambridge: Harvard Univ. Press, 1989). Carole Pateman's essays on diverse topics in democratic theory are gathered in *The Disorder of Women* (Stanford: Stanford Univ. Press, 1989). For a survey of the variety of feminisms, see Rosemarie Tong, *Feminist Thought: A Comprehensive Introduction* (Boulder: Westview Press, 1989).

The most authoritative review of empirical research on the effects of pornography is *The Question of Pornography: Research Findings and Policy Implications* (New York: Free Press, 1987), by Edward Donnerstein, et al. This study indicates that antisocial effects are produced by depictions of sexual violence, often without any explicit sex, whereas depictions of explicit nonviolent sex have slight or nonexistent negative effects. It seems therefore that, if we wish to reduce the incidence of rape and other crimes of sexual violence, public policies should be directed at prohibiting materials with explicit violence (and only implicit sex), such as R-rated "slasher" films. However, this implication is not decisive if the harm of pornography is inherent in its mere existence rather than its antisocial effects. This view is defended by Andrea Dworkin and Catharine MacKinnon, the authors of the Minneapolis ordinance, in *Pornography and Civil Rights: A New Day for Women's Equality* (Minneapolis: Organizing Against Pornography, 1988). For an assessment of this view, as well as an account of the history of the Minneapolis ordinance and other similar efforts, see Donald Downs, *The New Politics of Pornography* (Chicago: Univ. of Chicago Press, 1989). A principal question to consider regarding Dworkin's and MacKinnon's view is: If the harm to be eliminated is depictions of the systematic subordination of women, shouldn't our efforts be directed to commercial advertisements, soap operas, music videos, and the like, which have a much more pervasive influence than pornography? Of course, this implication, among others, raises concerns about censorship. See the essays in *Women Against Censorship* (Vancouver: Douglas and McIntyre, 1985), edited by Varda Burstyn.

Whatever one's assessment of the effects of pornography, there is little disagreement regarding the systematic failure of the criminal justice system to respect the plight of victims of sexual violence. For an account of the way the process of handling rape complaints compounds the victimization—as well as proposals for reform—see Susan Estrich, *Real Rape* (Cambridge: Harvard Univ. Press, 1987).

PART IV

AT WORK

INTRODUCTION

In *Muller v. Oregon*[1] the U.S. Supreme Court upheld the right of states to limit the number of hours women could be required to work. Just three years earlier the Court had rejected a similar claim on behalf of men, arguing that states could not interfere with freedom of contract between employers and employees, unless the work was unusually hazardous (e.g., in mines and smelters). In *Muller*, however, it discerned a crucial difference "to the effect that long hours of labor are dangerous to women, primarily because of their special physical organization."[2] Further, women's maternal functions, the Court said, place them at a disadvantage in economic competition. So, for these reasons, states may enact protective legislation for women, even if the laws restrict employers' liberty of contract.

The validation of protective legislation sufficed to make the *Muller* decision famous. In addition, the state of Oregon was represented by the Boston lawyer (later Supreme Court Justice) Louis Brandeis, who made legal history by filing a brief containing few references to previous Court decisions but copious historical and sociological materials documenting the detrimental effects of women's working conditions on their health and safety. (This type of legal argument came to be known as "a Brandeis brief.") It is not widely known that, in composing this brief, Brandeis was aided considerably by Florence Kelley and Josephine Goldmark (his sister-in-law), both activists for women's rights. Also, the Justice who wrote the Supreme Court's opinion, David Brewer, had himself been an advocate for women's causes before joining the Court. It is ironic that a decision supported by some of the most progressive voices of the time is regarded, some 85 years later, as a classic example of sexual stereotyping.

Yet *Muller* stands for three propositions that do not rest on traditional stereotypes and may still guide our thinking about gender issues in the workplace: (1) liberty of contract between employer and employee is not absolute; (2) the well-being of children, as it is affected in the workplace, is a legitimate public concern; and, most controversially, (3) different treatment of women and men is sometimes necessary, as the Court put it, "to secure a real equality of right."[3]

An obvious constraint on liberty of contract is the principle of nondiscrimination. Abstractly, the principle is easily formulated: Employers cannot exclude anyone from available opportunities or benefits on grounds irrelevant to the work. However, the specific meaning of this principle is a matter of dispute, as several of the cases in this part reveal.

Two interpretations in particular compete for our allegiance. According to the first, nondiscrimination consists in equal treatment: Any opportunity or benefit offered to some—whether it is wages or schedule of advancement or weeks of paid leave—must be offered to all who are similarly situated, regardless of gender. This interpretation secures equal right of access to economic positions for those able and willing to pursue them. It treats persons as individuals, not as members of a group. Applicable rules and classifications are gender-neutral. Further, by eliminating gratuitous assumptions about women's physical capacities, dependency, and judgment, it helps to dissolve the legacy of separate spheres (both at home and at work) and facilitates women's participation in business, professional, and civic life.

At the same time, because women are relatively new entrants in many workplaces designed originally without them in mind, equal treatment lends itself in practice to women's assimilation to already existing categories. For example, to preserve gender-neutrality in job-protected leave policies, pregnancy is regarded as a form of disability. In this way, all "temporarily disabled" employees, whatever the source of disability, are treated the same. Some people argue, however, that assimilation obscures asymmetries, deeply rooted in biology or culture, between women and men. Because of these asymmetries, equal access does not ensure equal prospects of success. Therefore, policies failing to take account of gender differences are flawed. For example, in a workplace that lacks a disability-leave policy, the issue of job protection during pregnancy does not go away.

The alternative interpretation of nondiscrimination substitutes for equal treatment what we may call equal consideration. This interpretation is contextual; it looks not only to the benefit being distributed but also to the situation of the recipient. It takes account of the reality of asymmetry—namely, that at this historical moment pregnancy, motherhood, and child rearing are special concerns of women. Accordingly, in order to treat women with equal consideration, the workplace must accommodate these multiple commitments.

The development of fetal protection policy illustrates how these alternative interpretations may play themselves out. In the Supreme Court case included in Section C, Johnson Controls had barred women with childbearing capacity from jobs involving high lead exposure, such as making batteries. Justice Blackmun argued for the Supreme Court that this policy was discriminatory because women are as capable of doing the job as men. The job, he said, is "making batteries," and childbearing capacity is irrelevant because a person with the capacity to become pregnant is able to make batteries as well as anyone. Thus, Blackmun selected a gender-neutral job description, implicitly affirming the equal treatment interpretation of nondiscrimination. However, Blackmun's selection begged the question because the correct job description was part of what was in dispute. Johnson Controls claimed that its responsibilities as a company included making batteries, to be sure, but in a way consistent with its concern for future offspring: hence, the relevance of childbearing capacity. Was it illegitimate for the company to have such a concern?

Blackmun's choice of job description rested on an assumption about responsibility for children. To support the gender-neutral classification, he had to argue that the well-being of children was a matter for their parents and not the parents' employers. Thus, even if parents made mistakes—even if they ran unwarranted risks with their future children's lives by taking jobs that exposed them to chemicals at dangerous levels—it was not for the company to determine that they should do otherwise. In this way, Blackmun asserts that parents do not need special protective policies. Yet he would presumably concede that the public takes a great interest in the welfare of children. For example, laws against child neglect or abuse permit state intervention, including, most drastically, removal of children from the home, if parents fail to meet a basic duty of care. Nor is the public interest confined to children already born. Blackmun's own opinion in *Roe v. Wade*[4] recognizes a public interest in "potential life" during the third trimester of pregnancy. Why should this interest not show itself in the workplace?

Blackmun seems to be worried about the following line of argument: *If* the safety of employees and their future offspring is a legitimate concern of business, and *if* scientific studies demonstrate that some workplace substances have a more deleterious effect on women (before and during pregnancy) than on men, *then* childbearing capacity is a valid basis of discrimination. This conclusion follows, however, only if nondiscrimination consists in equal treatment, not if it consists in equal consideration. The latter requires that firms accommodate women's multiple commitments—and do so without exposing them to special risks or otherwise disadvantaging them. Of course a possible consequence of such an approach is that female employees may cost firms more than male employees. In general, higher costs could arise from higher medical insurance costs (because of pregnancy), or from parental leave policies (which, though aimed at both parents, are likely to be utilized mostly by women), or even from the prospect of tort suits brought by or on behalf of newborns affected by lead. Equal consideration means that such higher costs are not a legitimate basis of distinction. (It is important to bear in mind that the question of costs for women's entry into the workforce would not arise—or at least not have the force it appears to have—if women were compensated for child care and other domestic work.)

Equal consideration rests on the idea that a person's prospects of success should not be hindered by factors whose "natural" distribution is arbitrary from a moral point of view. Because both men and women want children but only women have childbearing capacity, the work of reproduction is arbitrary in just this way. Hence, we should expect business firms to accommodate themselves to this fact. To paraphrase John Dewey, they should be as much interested in constructing workplaces favorable to participation by women as in the removal of obstacles and abuses.[5] Thus, it is not that women are less capable than men in the workplace; it is that they can reasonably be expected to be on the job only if the workplace respects their multiple commitments. If this means that women cost firms more than men, it is only to achieve a real equality of right.

NOTES

1. *Muller v. Oregon,* 208 U.S. 412 (1908).
2. At 420n.
3. At 422.
4. *Roe v. Wade,* 410 U.S. 113, 163 (1973).
5. John Dewey, "The Future of Liberalism," in *Problems of Men* (New York: Philosophical Library, 1946), p. 136.

Discrimination

Women's History Goes to Trial:
EEOC v. Sears, Roebuck and Company

INTRODUCTION TO THE DOCUMENTS
Sandi E. Cooper

The new scholarship on women has been discovered by the American legal system in a courtroom battle over working women employed at Sears, Roebuck and Company.[1] Empowered by Title VII of the 1964 Civil Rights Act, the United States Equal Employment Opportunity Commission (EEOC) initiated investigations of a number of American corporations in the 1970s, urging the adoption of affirmative action plans. Most companies complied, establishing programs to recruit and train female and nonwhite male employees in nontraditional jobs.[2] Sears announced an affirmative action program in 1968, and by 1973 had set up a more elaborate plan including goals. Six years later, EEOC investigations concluded that the Sears plan had made little difference in the salaries and status of women employees. They remained, according to the EEOC, underrepresented in better-paying commission sales jobs and managerial posts, and moreover, women managers were paid lower wages than men. In response to EEOC pressure, Sears went to court to challenge the federal government's authority to propose and enforce hiring guidelines. In May 1979 the government won its case in federal court, where its right to establish affirmative action plans was upheld.[3]

The EEOC then filed a discrimination suit against the giant retailer, charging discrimination in two main categories of employment: commission sales—the selling of items with high ticket prices that netted high commissions and, thus, better pay than ordinary wages; and wage differences between men and women in managerial and administrative jobs.[4] Sears countered that women were reluctant to compete with men to sell traditionally male products (such as plumbing or automotive supplies) to male buyers. Overall, argued Sears, women preferred to work in departments selling items that were familiar or nonthreatening.[5] In response, the EEOC pre-

173

sented an array of statistics to describe women who applied for jobs, women who were hired, and what type of jobs the latter were given—in an effort to demonstrate *patterns* of discrimination against women.[6] Sears, however, maintained that the government's statistics did not prove discrimination and Sears disputed the EEOC's "a priori assumptions of male/female sameness with respect to preferences, interests, and qualifications."[7]

In fighting the government's charges, Sears argued that its hiring policies reflected American values about men and women. Since it was a national company, its work force mirrored national social patterns.[8] To bolster its argument, the defense counsel consulted pollsters on American public opinion, as well as economists and social scientists whose work supported the view that women preferred nurturing and supportive ideals over competitive values.

Feminist scholarship in women's history became a participant in this confrontation on July 2, 1984, with the formal, pretrial deposition of Rosalind Rosenberg on behalf of Sears.[9] The trial itself began in September in Chicago (United States District Court, Northern District of Illinois, Eastern Division) with Judge John Nordberg presiding.

Professor Rosenberg, Associate Professor of History, Barnard College, was among many expert witnesses called to support Sears's position. She took the stand on March 11, 1985.[10] Her court testimony was based on an "Offer of Proof" drawn up prior to her appearance. This document summarizes the positions that a witness intends to argue. It serves as written testimony and provides a basis for testimony and cross-examination. The "Offer of Proof concerning the Testimony of Dr. Rosalind Rosenberg" interprets the new scholarship on American women in a way that sustained Sears's defense against discrimination charges.[11]

Lawyers for the government consulted Dr. Alice Kessler-Harris, Professor of History, Hofstra University, in their effort to challenge Sears's historical expert.[12] The second document printed here, "Written Testimony of Alice Kessler-Harris," was prepared in spring 1985 and served as the basis of her oral testimony and cross-examination in June. It summarizes an opposing interpretation of the history of American working women.[13]

On February 3, 1986, Judge Nordberg ruled that the EEOC had not proven its charges against Sears, Roebuck and Company. Copies of the trial documents . . . —briefs, depositions, offers of proof, and transcripts of examination and cross-examination involving the two women historians—are available at the Schlesinger Library, Radcliffe College, Cambridge, Massachusetts.[14]

NOTES

1. For a discussion of the use of the expert witnesses, see the classic article by Lawrence Rosen, "The Anthropologist as Expert Witness," *American Anthropologist* 79, no. 3 (September 1977): 555–78. See also S. Charles Bolton, "The Historian as Expert Witness: Creationism in Arkansas," and Carl M. Becker, "Professor for the Plaintiff: Classroom to Courtroom," in *Public Historian* 4, no. 3 (Summer 1982): 59–77.

2. Those in compliance included General Electric, General Motors, and American Telephone and Telegraph.

3. Judge June L. Green ruled against Sears on May 15, 1979, in Washington. See Edward Cowan, "Sears Loses Its Suit over Job Bias Rules," *New York Times* (May 16, 1979). See also Phyllis Segal, "Right War, Wrong Tactics," *National NOW Times* (March 1979), 1, 3.

4. EEOC v. Sears, Roebuck and Co., no. 79-C-4373, Plaintiff's Pretrial Brief—Commission Sales Issues (Revised, November 19, 1984), pp. 1–2; Plaintiff's Pretrial Brief, Checklist Compensation Issue, pp. 1–3. Here the government noted that disparate salary rates for men and women were continued even after 1976 when the company altered its system for compensating executive personnel.

5. EEOC v. Sears, Roebuck and Co., Trial Brief of Sears, Roebuck and Co. (September–October 1984), pp. 8–15 passim. Quoting from the case of Malloch v. J. C. Penney, Sears argued: "Plaintiffs have failed to take into account . . . the fact that many women preferred the noncommission areas. Either by training or prior experience or just as a matter of likes and dislikes, many women preferred working with the fashion side of the store rather than in areas such as appliances, stereos, or carpets" (p. 19). In the summation of the case, Sears maintained "Sears managers continually tried to persuade reluctant women—even those only marginally qualified—to consider commission selling as well as other nontraditional jobs. . . . Many managers reported that they had interviewed every woman in the store and found not one who was willing to sell big ticket merchandise" (Post Trial Brief of Sears, Roebuck and Co., June 26, 1985), p. 9.

6. Plaintiff's Pretrial Brief—Commission Sales Issues (Revised November 19, 1984), pp. 24–27, 38–71 (for tables).

7. Trial Brief of Sears, p. 21. Arguments discrediting statistical evidence as a source of discrimination were made in the Trial Brief of Sears, Roebuck and Co., pp. 5, 16–18, 25–26, 50–54, 74–77. For instance: "Sears will offer evidence to prove in many cases, it is not the most appropriate analytical method for use in this compensation case. Instead, cohort analyses of females and males entering Sears at the same time and traced year to year provide a clear picture" (p. 54). See also reference to the issue in Juan William, "Despite Doubts, U.S. Presses to Resolve Sears Bias Case," *Washington Post* (July 9, 1985).

8. Trial Brief of Sears, Roebuck and Co., pp. 22–27 passim. The most succinct statement of this point was made by Rosalind Rosenberg in the "Offer of Proof," no. 24, reprinted below.

9. The "Deposition of Rosalind Rosenberg" was made in the New York District Office of the EEOC, July 2 and 3, 1984, pt. 1 (55 pp.) and pt. 2 (156 pp.). The opposing deposition, that of Alice Kessler-Harris, was made on April 12 and 15, 1985, in a New York City law office.

10. Rosalind Rosenberg's major publication is *Beyond Separate Spheres: The Intellectual Roots of Modern Feminism* (New Haven, Conn.: Yale University Press, 1982), a book that examines a group of American women social scientists who challenged Victorian presumptions about women's behavior based on biology.

11. Minor changes in punctuation and spelling have been made. Otherwise both documents stand as they were presented to the court.

12. Alice Kessler-Harris is the author of *Out to Work: A History of Wage-earning Women in the United States* (New York: Oxford University Press, 1982), and *Women Have Always Worked* (New York: Feminist Press, 1981).

13. Alice Kessler-Harris's "Written Testimony" served as the basis of her oral testimony in court on June 6 and 7, 1985, found in the Trial Transcript, pp. 16493–

613. The rules of the court permitted Sears to return Rosalind Rosenberg to the stand to rebut Kessler-Harris's testimony. (See "Trial Testimony of Dr. Rosalind Rosenberg," June 22, 1985, pp. 18140–18306). For this appearance, she submitted a second written document (not included here) entitled "Written Rebuttal Testimony of Dr. Rosalind Rosenberg," 20 pp. plus an appendix of 12 pp. Summation of arguments concluded June 26–28, 1985.

14. For a more detailed analysis of this case, see Ruth Milkman, "Women's History and the Sears Case," *Feminist Studies* 12, no. 2 (Summer 1986): 375–400.

UNITED STATES DISTRICT COURT
FOR THE NORTHERN DISTRICT OF ILLINOIS
EASTERN DIVISION

EQUAL EMPLOYMENT OPPORTUNITY COMMISSION,
    Plaintiff,

v.   No. 79-C-4373

SEARS, ROEBUCK AND CO.,   JOHN A. NORDBERG
    Defendant   District Judge

OFFER OF PROOF CONCERNING THE
TESTIMONY OF DR. ROSALIND ROSENBERG

. . .

1. The EEOC assumption that women and men have identical interests and aspirations regarding work is incorrect. Historically, men and women have had different interests, goals, and aspirations regarding work. These differences in interests and attitudes, though in many instances diminishing, have persisted into the present.[1]

2. The Equal Employment Opportunity Commission (EEOC) fails to place workers in their social and historical settings and ignores the fact that many workers, especially women, have goals and values other than realizing maximum economic gain. The labor force contains millions of workers whose lives and values were shaped in earlier eras, a fact of particular significance because of the rapid changes that occurred in American society during the 1970s. For example, it was not until the 1976 edition that Dr. Benjamin Spock's influential book on child care gave its approval to mothers working outside the home (earlier editions discussed the working mother in a section on "Special Problems").[2]

3. The distinction between male and female serves as a basic organizing principle for every human culture. Although societies differ in the specific tasks they assign to the two sexes, all societies allocate adult roles on the basis of sex. Historically, these allocations have been reinforced externally through social pressures and governmental action and internally through the internalization of social norms.[3]

4. Throughout American history there has been a consensus, shared by women, that, for women, working outside the home is subordinate to family needs. This consensus has been so strong that traditionally a stigma attached to married women working outside the home unless their work was essential to family support. Historically, the states have reinforced the traditional division of labor in marriage by requiring husbands to support their wives and making nonsupport a ground for divorce.[4]

5. Even the semisubsistence farming families in seventeenth-century America divided work according to sex. Women cared for the children, prepared the food, nursed the sick, made the clothes, and tended the garden. Men worked the fields, cared for the livestock, and represented the family in the outside world. Many of the jobs that men and women perform in the labor force today are the modern equivalents of traditional male and female tasks. For women these modern equivalents are simply added on to traditional tasks, especially if the woman is a wife and mother.[5]

6. As America began to commercialize toward the end of the eighteenth century and work that had formerly been done at home was transferred to offices and factories, those who took the newly created jobs tended to be those who had formerly done the same kind of work at home. Thus, the early textile workers were the unmarried daughters of New England farmers, and the early clerks were the sons who, being males, historically had been responsible for representing the family in the marketplace.[6]

7.† Before the twentieth century, the double burden of fulfilling woman's historic role and being a member of the labor force was so great that wives and mothers rarely attempted to do both. In 1900, only thirteen percent of all women workers were married. The rest were young women, working for a few years as domestic servants, factory workers, and department store clerks until they too married. Given the demands of housewifery and motherhood on the one hand and the long hours demanded of wage labor on the other, few married women wanted to or could work outside the home.[7]

8. The depression of the 1930s sharpened society's disapproval of married women working. According to a 1936 poll, eighty-two percent of the respondents felt that wives should not work if their husbands were working. The Federal Economy Act, passed in 1932, precluded employment in government service of two members of the same family. The impact of that law fell overwhelmingly upon married women. Legislation was introduced in many states to restrict employment of married women. At the local level,

---

† *Editor's note.*—The following paragraph was changed in court on May 10, 1985, to read as follows: "Before the twentieth century, the double burden of fulfilling woman's role inside the home and contributing to the labor force outside the home was so great that few married women attempted to do both, unless financial pressures, divorce, or widowhood drove them to it. In 1900 most women workers were young and unmarried. Most were working as domestic servants, factory workers, and department store clerks until they too married. Given the demands of housewifery and motherhood on the one hand and the long hours demanded of wage labor outside the home on the other, few married women wanted to or could work outside the home."

many school systems refused to hire married women as teachers and dismissed women teachers who subsequently married; across the country,
many businesses refused to hire married women.[8]

9. The expanding post–World War II economy, the popularity of birth
control, the modernization of housekeeping, the reduction of the work
week, and the growing availability of part-time work all have made it easier
for wives and mothers to enter the work force in the twentieth century.
Inflation has made it necessary. Between 1940 and 1980, the labor force participation of married women (husbands present) more than tripled, increasing from 14.7 percent to 50.2 percent. By 1980, 62 percent of the mothers of
school-age children were in the labor force.[9]

10. Even as they have entered the labor force in increasing numbers,
women have retained their historic commitment to the home.

(a) As illustrated by the World War II experience, American individualism has stood in the way of government policies that would make it easier
for married women and women with small children to work. During World
War II, when the country desperately needed women workers in its war
industries, the federal government failed to meet child care needs, even
though America's English allies provided extensive child care facilities during the war. As soon as the war was over, child care was abandoned altogether by the American government.

(b) Men perceive paid employment as their primary contribution to
family life, a contribution that exempts them from the responsibility of par-
ticipating in housework or child care to the same extent as women. Husbands' contributions to household labor largely are unaffected by wives'
hours at work. Employed wives divide their work hours almost equally between home and job, while husbands devote eighty percent of their work
time to job and twenty percent to home. In studies done in the 1960s, full-
time employed wives averaged almost 70 hours per week in paid and unpaid
work, while their husbands spent closer to fifty-five hours per week. In the
1960s, women did eighty percent of the housework; in 1975, they were still
doing seventy-five percent of it.[10]

11. Because housework and child care continue to affect women's labor
force participation even today, many women choose jobs that complement
their family obligation over jobs that might increase and enhance their earning potential.[11]

12. Even if women wanted to realize maximum incomes, the time required for housework and child care limits their choices in the marketplace.
Many women must choose jobs with flexible hours to meet what they perceive to be their responsibilities at home. Jobs that require fulltime work,
irregular hours, or weekend work present greater difficulties for wives and
mothers than they do for husbands and fathers.[12]

13. Retailing has long been especially attractive to women because the
conditions of work there facilitate many women's efforts to balance home-
making with breadwinning. Women seeking part-time work in the 1970s
were four times as likely to choose retail sales positions as any other
occupation.[13]

14. Women, anticipating that their labor force participation will be interrupted by child rearing and home responsibilities, are less likely to make the same educational investments as men. Historically, few women have pursued professional degrees, including business degrees, although the number of women entering professional schools rose dramatically in the 1970s. Although the number of women attending college has almost doubled since the 1950s, men and women continue to choose different areas of study, choices that affect earning power and career advancement.[14]

15. The different attitudes, goals, and expectations toward work that have characterized men and women throughout American history have been reflected and reinforced by government laws and policies. Many of these laws and policies, such as state protective laws, were regarded as beneficient and liberal when adopted. Education policies and grants have channeled men and women into traditional jobs. Women to this day are excluded from the draft. Military policies have reinforced traditional male/ female differences through training and leadership opportunities. Service-related policies such as the GI Bill, housing subsidies, and preferences for veterans in hiring have provided enormous advantages to men. Other government policies and programs in areas such as tax policy, housing, social security, and transportation also have had the purpose or effect of reinforcing traditional family patterns.[15]

16. Women's role in American society and in the American family unit has fostered the development of "feminine" values that have been internalized by women themselves and reinforced by society, through its customs, its culture, and its laws. This message is also reinforced by language usage. For example, only in the past decade has the United States Census abandoned the term "salesmen" in favor of the term "sales workers."[16]

17. Historically, the emphasis on independence and competition among men and on dependence and cooperation among women has been especially marked in American society. The rapid expansion of capitalism in America led to a heavy emphasis on such qualities as political liberty, economic mobility, and competitive individualism for men. Women, on the other hand, were exhorted to be nurturant and selfless, to serve as a stabilizing force in an otherwise unstable society.[17]

18. Throughout American history women have been trained from earliest childhood to develop the humane and nurturing values expected of the American mother. Thus trained, women have assumed primary responsibility for maintaining family relationships. Early sex role messages have been and continue to be contained in books, toys, advertisements, television, movies, and print media. They are explicitly and implicitly reinforced by parents, teachers, and peers.[18]

19. Women's participation in the labor force is affected by the values they have internalized. For example:

a) Women tend to be more relationship-centered and men tend to be more work-centered. Although both men and women find satisfaction and a sense of self-worth in their jobs, men are more likely than women to derive their self-image from their work. Most employed women continue to derive their self-image from their role as wife and mother. Women tend to be more interested than men in the cooperative, social aspects of the work situation.[19a]

b) Women are trained from earliest childhood to develop different expectations from men about what aspirations are socially acceptable. Women who challenge those expectations by choosing jobs typically pursued by men often experience doubts about their ability to do well. A 1984 study of 628 graduate women in science, engineering, and medicine at Stanford University concludes that "women feel less self-confident and assertive than their male counterparts, less sure of their ability, less trusting of their own judgment, and more fearful of making mistakes."[19b]

c) Women are seen by themselves and by society as less competitive than men and more concerned with protecting personal relationships.[19c]

d) Men's more extensive experience in competitive sports prepares them for the competitiveness, aggressiveness, teamwork, and leadership required for many jobs. The prohibition of sex discrimination in athletic programs encompassed by Title IX of the Education Amendments of 1972 was based on a recognition of the handicap women's absence from sports places upon them. Despite Title IX, men still participate in the more aggressive competitive sports much more than do women.[19d]

20. These differences in female and male self-perception present difficulties for women in traditionally masculine occupations.

(a) Louise Kapp Howe, who interviewed women in a variety of "pink collar" occupations in the early 1970s, discovered difficulties especially with respect to commission sales. One woman union organizer whom she interviewed had brought sales women together in "consciousness raising" sessions to discuss their fears concerning advancement and taking a chance at the high-commission sales jobs. The sales women worried about being too competitive and alienating men if they acted too aggressively. Other women complained that working for a commission made them feel that they had to push people to purchase or use things that they did not need.

(b) While studying a department store that had an affirmative action plan, Howe asked a woman working in the personnel office why men were in the big-ticket commission departments and women were not. The woman responded:

> We're trying to equalize that. . . . But certain departments—heavy stock departments, for example, like major appliances, are mostly requested by men, and certain jobs, like cashiers, tend to be female. Even though I try to spread things out. See, men don't ask for cashier jobs, and I try to put people in places they want to be. And women almost always ask for soft goods, for sportswear or dresses, nine out of ten times, so I don't have too much chance to do what I'd like, do I?[20]

21. While a wife and family have been perceived as aids to a man's quest for success, the roles of wife and mother have required that a woman's life

be subordinated to the needs of her family. Because women tend to place family commitments ahead of career aspirations, they are more likely than men to interrupt their careers to care for their children, and less willing than men to move to take advantage of new opportunities.[21]

22. The emphasis placed on "consciousness raising" by the feminist movement during the late 1960s and early 1970s was based on a recognition that men and women have internalized different personality traits and different attitudes toward labor force participation.[22]

23. Despite rapid changes in lifestyles and attitudes occurring over the last decade, traditional values still persist. Insofar as there has been any shift toward egalitarian marriages that would free women from the primary obligation of the home, that shift has taken place more often among college-educated Americans. For the majority of American couples who have never attended college, the traditional values within the family and without continues to be the ideal.[23]

24. As the historical evidence shows, it is not surprising that men and women differ in their expectations concerning work, in their interests as to the types of jobs they prefer or the types of products they prefer to sell, and in the continuity of their participation in the labor force. It is naive to believe that the natural effect of these differences is evidence of discrimination by Sears.

. . .

NOTES

1. Alice Kessler-Harris, "American Women and the American Character: A Feminist Perspective," in John Hague, ed., *American Character and Culture* (Westport: Greenwood Press, 1979), p. 232—Even after women were "sucked into the competitive maelstrom, . . . they continued to rationalize their activities in terms of familiar humane and nurturing values." These values, which were suited to family succor, tended to foster "inappropriate behavior patterns for participation in a competitive world"; Nancy Cott, *The Bonds of Womanhood: "Woman's Sphere" in New England, 1780–1835* (New Haven: Yale University Press, 1977), 200–201; Carl Degler, *At Odds: Women and the Family in America from the Revolution to the Present* (New York: Oxford University Press, 1980), pp. 26–28; Alice Kessler-Harris, *Out to Work: A History of Wage-Earning Women in the United States* (New York: Oxford University Press 1982), pp. 50–51, 105, 128, 312; U.S. Department of Labor, Employment and Training Administration, R&D Monograph 24, *Years of Decision*, vol. 4, A Longitudinal Study of the Educational and Labor Market Experience of Young Women, pp. 115, 136–37, found that when young women were asked in 1968 what they wanted to be at the age of thirty-five, only fourteen percent of the white and ten percent of the black non-college-educated women expected to work in occupations that were not "typical" for females. A similar study conducted five years later, in 1973, showed only a slightly increased interest among young women in atypical occupations (nineteen percent of the white and thirteen percent of the black non-college-educated women). College women demonstrated a slightly greater interest in nontraditional jobs than did less educated women, but even among college women traditional aspirations dominated. Only twenty-two percent of black and twenty-five percent of white col-

lege-educated women declared an interest in masculine jobs. Furthermore, the presence or expectation of children was found to decrease the likelihood that college women would expect to be in a male occupation.

2. Ronald Schatz, *The Electrical Workers: A History of Labor at General Electric and Westinghouse, 1923–60* (Urbana: University of Illinois Press, 1983), p. 42—Schatz shows that both men and women at GE opposed incentive pay system between the wars because they believed it would be a source of discord among workers; p. 125—Schatz shows that in the 1940s women union leaders were reluctant to encourage women to compete for men's jobs, "a man has to make money in order to keep his family"; Lillian Rubin, *Worlds of Pain: Life in the Working Class Family* (New York: Basic Books, 1976), pp. 130–131—Rubin shows that although working class women believe in equal pay for equal work, they persist in their reluctance to compete for better-paying jobs. As one woman says, "If a man with a wife and kids needs a job, no woman ought to be able to take it away from him," and another woman adds, "I don't like women who want to be men."

3. Sandra Bem, "Gender Schema Theory: A Cognitive Account of Sex Typing," *Psychological Review* 88 (1981): 354; Michelle Rosaldo and Louise Lamphere, *Woman, Culture, and Society* (Stanford: Stanford University Press, 1974), pp. 1–42; Jane M. Atkinson, Review of Anthropology, *Signs* 8 (Winter 1982): 238–58.

4. Kessler-Harris, *Out to Work*, p. 49—in the nineteenth century, "the domestic code . . . held that the home required woman's moral and spiritual presence far more than her wage labor;" p. 51—"For his wife to be earning income meant that the husband had failed;" p. 105—in 1869 one observer said that "some people think women are unfitted for the discharge of home duties by staying in stores and factories a few years;" p. 303—by 1953 there were shortages of stenographers, typists, nurses, teachers, and social workers due to "low depression birth rates and high postwar marriage rates"; p. 312—by 1970, "still caught in the belief that the home came first, about one-third of the married women who earned wages took part-time jobs, and many took jobs for which their education and skills overqualified them. They chose to work for the convenience of being close to home or for hours that suited children's schedules." Alice Kessler-Harris, "Rosie the Riveter: Who Was She?" *Labor History* (1983): 252—even though industries recruited women during World War II as never before, "most women with children chose not to engage in this war." Leo Kanowitz, *Women and the Law* (Albuquerque: University of New Mexico Press, 1969), p. 96.

5. Laurel Thatcher Ulrich, *Goodwives: Image and Reality in Lives of Women in Northern New England, 1650–1750* (New York: Knopf, 1982), pp. 13–34; Julie Matthaei, *An Economic History of Women in America* (New York: Schocken, 1982), pp. 195–215.

6. Nancy Cott, *The Bonds of Womanhood*, pp. 19–62; Thomas Dublin, *Women at Work: The Transformation of Work and Community in Lowell, Massachusetts, 1826–1860* (New York: Columbia University Press, 1979), pp. 1–13.

7. Kessler-Harris, *Out to Work*, p. 153.

8. The 1936 poll was conducted by George Gallup; Ruth Shallcross, "Should Married Women Work?" *Public Affairs Pamphlets* (November 1940): pp. 1–31—This study of popular reactions to married women's working found that some businesses were much more likely to exclude married women than others (eighty-four percent of insurance companies compared with eleven percent of mercantile concerns); Winifred Wandersee, *Women's Work and Family Values, 1920–1940* (Cambridge: Harvard University Press, 1981), p. 100—shows that sales work was an area that attracted an unusually high number of married women (in 1940, 42 percent of saleswomen were

married, compared with 35.5 percent of female labor force overall); William Chafe, *The American Woman: Her Changing Social, Economic, and Political Roles, 1920–1970* (New York: Oxford University Press, 1972), pp. 108–11.

9. Chafe, *The American Woman*, pp. 190–91; Carl Degler, *At Odds: Women and the Family in America from the Revolution to the Present* (New York: Oxford, 1980), pp. 418–35; Eileen Appelbaum, *Back to Work: Determinants of Women's Successful Reentry* (Boston: Auburn House, 1981), pp. 1–35. (Appelbaum appears to think that inflation did not occur until 1973.)

10. (a) Chafe, *The American Woman*, pp. 159–72, 186–87; Leila Rupp, *Mobilizing Women for War: German and American Propaganda, 1939–1945* (Princeton: Princeton University Press, 1978), pp. 179–81.

(b) Laura Lein, "Male Participation in Home Life: Impact of Social Supports and Breadwinner Responsibility on the Allocation of Tasks," *The Family Coordinator* 28 (October 1979): 489; Karen D. Fox and Sharon Y. Nichols, "The Time Crunch: Wife's Employment and Family Work," *Journal of Family Issues* 4 (March 1983): 61–79. See also Elise Boulding, "Familial Constraints on Women's Work Roles," *Signs* 1 (Spring 1976): 95–117.

11. Kessler-Harris, *Out to Work*, p. 312.

12. Appelbaum, *Back to Work*, pp. 97–98—"Currently, about 34% of all employed women in the United States work part of the week, and most of these women work only part of the year as well. . . . Among white women . . . 84% of those who work less than 35 hours a week do so by choice. Moreover, there has been a rapid increase in voluntary part-time employment." There are more women seeking part-time jobs than there are part-time jobs for them. "Adult women have frequently sought part-time employment as a means of meeting home and child care responsibilities while contributing to family income."

13. Susan Porter Benson, "Women in Retail Sales Work: The Continuing Dilemma of Service," in Karen Brodkin Sacks and Dorothy Remy, eds., *My Troubles Are Going to Have Trouble With Me* (New Brunswick: Rutgers University Press, 1984), p. 118—"Part-time work opportunities are important to many women, as are the relatively attractive and nonhazardous work surroundings. In some ways, the department store is a familiar and nonthreatening work environment; every woman was a customer before she became a saleswoman. Paid vacations are still more common in retailing than in factory work, and the prospect of a long summer layoff can be attractive to women with school-age children." Appelbaum, *Back to Work*, p. 106.

14. Rosalind Rosenberg, *Beyond Separate Spheres: Intellectual Roots of Modern Feminism* (New Haven: Yale University Press, 1982), pp. 36–51; See exhibits 9–13.

15. Judith Baer, *The Chains of Protection: The Judicial Response to Women's Labor Legislation* (Westport, Conn.: Greenwood Press, 1978), pp. 14–42; U.S. Department of Labor Women's Bureau, Pamphlet 15, "State Labor Laws in Transition: From Protection to Equal Status for Women," 1976, pp. 3–20; Sally Hilsman Baker, "Women in Blue-Collar and Service Occupations," in Ann Stromberg and Shirley Harkness, eds., *Women Working: Theories and Facts in Perspective* (Palo Alto, Calif.: Mayfield, 1978), pp. 356–57. "More often than not, high schools accept and reinforce these young women's aspirations, self-images, and beliefs that employment will be only 'temporary'"; Ruth Schulzinger and Lisa Syron, *Inch by Inch: A Report on Equal Opportunity for Young Women in New York City's Vocational High Schools* (Center of Public Advocacy Research, November 1984), p. 45, "New York City continues to maintain a sex-segregated vocational high school system . . . seven of the ten predominantly male schools remain 90% sex-segregated." Task Force on Sex Discrimination, Civil

Rights Division, U.S. Department of Justice, *Interim Report to the President* (October 3, 1978), pp. v, 43, 74, 281; Civil Rights Division, U.S. Department of Justice, *The First Quarterly Report of the Attorney General to the President and the Cabinet Council on Legal Policy as Required by Executive Order 12336* (June 28, 1982), pp. 25–31 (on continuing discrimination in social security); Julia A. Eriksen, "An Analysis of the Journey to Work for Women," *Social Problems* 24 (April 1977): 428–35; Dolores Hayden, *Redesigning the American Dream: The Future of Housing, Work, and Family Life* (New York: Norton, 1984), pp. 7, 152–53.

16. Jeanne Block, "Conceptions of Sex Role: Some Cross-Cultural and Longitudinal Perspectives," *American Psychologist* 23 (June 1973): 512–26; Sandra Bem, "The Measurement of Psychological Androgyny," *Journal of Consulting and Clinical Psychology* 42 (1974): 155–62; Compare Census for 1970 with Census for 1980.

17. Barbara Welter, "The Cult of True Womanhood: 1820–1860," *American Quarterly* 18 (Spring 1966): 151; Kathryn Kish Sklar, *Catherine Beecher: A Study in American Domesticity* (New Haven: Yale University Press, 1974), passim; Jane Addams, *Twenty Years at Hull House* (1910). The fact that men still tend to define themselves in terms of "agency" and that women still tend to define themselves in terms of "communion" is stressed in the work of Block (see above) and Gilligan (see below).

18. Jeffrey Rubin, et al., "The Eye of the Beholder: Parents' Views on Sex of Newborns," *American Journal of Orthopsychiatry* 44 (July 1974): 512–19—found that parents attribute different qualities to girls and boys from birth; Jane Bergman, "Are Little Girls Being Harmed by Sesame Street?" in J. Stacey et al., *And Jill Came Tumbling After: Sexism in American Education* (New York: Dell, 1974), pp. 111–115; Patricia Mamay and Richard Simpson, "Three Female Roles in Television Commercials," *Sex Roles* 7 (1981): 1223–32; Dick and Jane Slide Show.

19a. Philip Blumstein and Pepper Schwartz, *American Couples: Money, Work, and Sex* (New York: William Morrow, 1983), pp. 325–26—this is a study of 12,000 couples from different social and economic backgrounds. Pp. 325–26—On men's and women's attitudes toward work and relationships: "Work is an important part of a man's self-image. For most married couples, it is still the man's work that remains sacrosanct. His superior earning power means it is in the couple's best interest to make choices that will support his presence in the work world. It is interesting that even when the couple shares the provider responsibility, the husband's career will probably continue to be put first. . . . Women in their relationships with men increasingly see employment as part of their self-image, although this does not yet include taking on the provider role. We believe that this role is still foreign to most of them. They wish to work, but not as the primary support of the family. Further, while some women in our study are 'work-centered,' it remains a minority. We think that most employed women continue to value their role as companion and caretaker. Women in the study seem to want respect for both roles and are seeking a way to perform them both successfully. They also want to preserve part of men's traditional commitment to the world of work: They still want their partners to achieve. Women want to look up to, or at least directly across at, their male partner if they are to respect him." P. 167—"All women, both heterosexual and homosexual, are more likely to put their relationships before their work." Husbands: thirty-nine percent describe themselves as relationship-centered. Wives: fifty-nine percent describe themselves as relationship-centered. Carol Gilligan, *In A Different Voice: Psychological Theory and Women's Development* (Cambridge: Harvard University Press, 1982), pp. 24–63; Nancy Chodorow, *The Reproduction of Mothering: Psychoanalysis and the Sociology of Gender* (Berkeley: University of California Press, 1978), pp. 173–210.

19b. Elizabeth Kirchner and Sarah Vondracek, "What Do You Want To Be When You Grow Up? Vocational Choice in Children 3–6" (paper presented to the meeting of the Society for Research in Child Development, Philadelphia, March 1973) (ERIC document ED 076 244)—shows that, even as preschoolers, girls choose fewer occupations than boys do and are more likely to project themselves into a parent role; Helen Astin, "Stability and Change in the Plans of Ninth Grade Girls," *Personnel and Guidance Journal* 46 (June 1968): 961–66—shows decline in desire to pursue careers in sciences and the professions from sixteen percent in the ninth grade to five percent four years later; U.S. Department of Labor, *Years of Decision*, pp. 115, 136–37 (see note 1)—shows that only fourteen to twenty-five percent of all young women expect to have nontraditional careers; A. Regula Herzog, "Paid Work, Child Care, and Housework: A National Survey of High School Seniors," *Sex Roles* 9 (1983): 132, "most seniors do not consider it desirable that the mother of preschool children work even half time"; Carolyn J. Breedlove and Victor G. Cicirelli, "Women's Fear of Success in Relation to Personal Characteristics and Type of Occupation," *The Journal of Psychology* 86 (1974): 181–90, shows that women lack confidence about their ability to do well in "masculine" fields; Diana Diamond, "High Test Scores Don't Bring Confidence, Automatic Success," *Stanford Observor*, November 1984—women lack confidence in themselves despite the fact that their academic background and graduate entrance examination scores are better than those of men.

19c. Block, "Conceptions of Sex Role," 512–26; Sandra Bem, "The Measurement of Psychological Androgyny," *Journal of Consulting and Clinical Psychology* 42 (1974): 155–62; Gilligan, *In a Different Voice*, pp. 24–63.

19d. Jeana Wittenberg, et al., "Sex Equity in American Education," *Educational Leadership* (January 1981): 311–19, "Although women are now 1/3 of all athletes their athletic programs do not have comparable athletic budgets." Sheryl Sklorman, "Girl Athletes, Citizen Activists, Title IX: The Three Point Play," *The High School Journal* (May 1981): 326–30—"sport prepares one for assuming an instrumental social role, a role calling for active, assertive, and self-assured social behavior."

20. Louise Kapp Howe, *Pink Collar Workers*, pp. 87–88, 47.

21. Julie Matthaei, *An Economic History of Women in America*, p. 298; Margaret Hennig and Ann Jardim, *The Managerial Woman* (Garden City, NY: Anchor Press, 1977), pp. 42–43; Margaret Poloma, et al., "Reconsidering the Dual-Career Marriage: A Longitudinal Approach," in Joan Aldous, ed., *Two Paychecks: Life in Dual Earner Families* (Beverly Hills: Sage, 1982), pp. 176–79 (researchers found that though a little over half the couples originally gave nearly equal weight to both careers, "in no case was a move made that enhanced the wife's career opportunities").

22. "Consciousness Raising," in Anne Koedt, ed., *Radical Feminism* (Quadrangle, 1973), pp. 280–81, "The consciousness raising process is one in which personal experiences, when shared, are recognized as a result not of an individual's idiosyncratic history and behavior, but of the system of sex-role stereotyping"; Carol Williams Payne, "Consciousness Raising: A Dead End," *Ibid*, p. 282—"The group was formed . . . to talk about problems women have in working and wondering whether self-doubts and lack of confidence were related to their being women."

23. Arland Thornton and Deborah Freedman, "Changes in the Sex Role Attitudes of Women, 1962–1977: Evidence From a Panel Study," *American Sociological Review* 44 (October 1979): 831–42; Mirra Komarovsky, *Blue Collar Marriage* (New York: Vintage, 1962), p. 60; Constantina Safillios-Rothschild, "Women and Work: Policy Implications and Prospects for the Future," in Stromberg and Harkness, *Women Working*, pp. 421–22; Rubin, *Worlds of Pain*, p. 131.

WRITTEN TESTIMONY
OF ALICE KESSLER-HARRIS

1. Sears' experts have argued that women's occupations in the labor force are the product of women's choice, that women do not want better-paying jobs, and cannot handle stress, competition, or risk. History does not support these contentions, and instead places Sears' witnesses' statements squarely within a long tradition of employer excuses for, and manipulations of, women's work force experience.

2. History does not sustain the notion that women have, in the past, chosen not to take nontraditional jobs. The development of social history in the last fifteen years has moved historians in new directions in exploring the history of wage-earning women. Among its major achievements is the recovery of information previously ignored or forgotten about working women: information that has revealed how much of the past was lost, and altered our interpretations of what in fact has happened. Two areas have had special importance: the knowledge that women have functioned in virtually every capacity now assumed to be male, and the rich information that has emerged about women's diverse lives and aspirations. Sensitivity to these issues and new knowledge about the goals and aspirations of working people have opened questions about the ways in which the values and attitudes that are reflected by social institutions may differ from those of ordinary people. The result is to sharpen our understanding of the relationship between individual needs and their expression, and those of a larger society.

a. This new historical information calls into question the idea that women can "choose" not to work in certain areas, and insists that choice can be understood only within the framework of available opportunity. It flatly contradicts the notion that biology, culture, or socialization enables us to make statements about "all" women or about women generally. In particular, it provides the basis for refuting testimony that attributes to most women, and especially to those women who did work for wages, perceptions and attitudes that influenced the lives of relatively few.[1]

b. A more accurate interpretation of the history of women's work in the U.S. would take the following form. The structure of the labor force is the product of a complex interaction between labor force needs and a socialization process that reinforces desirable roles. Women's "interests" as well as their expectations are thus a consequence of life experiences that are reinforced or discouraged by the larger society. In an industrial society, a major part of the cycle of reinforcement is played by employers whose hiring policies significantly influence women's self-perception, their assessment of reasonable aspirations, and their announced goals. What appear to be women's choices, and what are characterized as women's "interests" are, in fact, heavily influenced by the opportunities for work made available to them. In the past, opportunities offered to women have been conditioned by society's perceptions of women and assumptions about them. Thus, women have been hired into limited numbers of jobs, and discriminated against in the work force generally. The resulting profile of "women's work" has been then perceived to be what the women "chose."

3. Although a rough sexual division of labor has existed in the U.S., as elsewhere, the nature of that division varies from place to place, and its outlines have never been rigid.[2]

a. Whatever the sexual division of labor in a particular society at a particular time, economists and anthropologists who have studied the transition to industrialism agree that people renegotiate their relationships in response to changing economic need.[3] It cannot be said that in the U.S. the sexual division of labor has remained the same from the colonial period to the present. By 1820, women were employed in at least seventy-five kinds of manufacturing establishments, and by 1850 in nearly 175 different industries. These ranged from typesetting and bookbinding to brushmaking, shoebinding, whipmaking, the manufacture of gunpowder, saddles, and clocks.[4]

b. Historically, women's participation in nontraditional jobs has been a function of whether or not there was sufficient male labor available at the right price. Men and women have frequently done the same jobs in different places or regions depending on this male availability. For example, both spinning and weaving processes in the textile mills of the north were typically done by women in the first half of the nineteenth century, because men, with other options, refused these jobs. As the mills moved South, in the late 1800s, the task of weaving was frequently transferred to men because men were available to perform the work, as they had not been in New England.[5] Similarly, women held jobs as printers and publishers in colonial America and in the new republic. As the nation urbanized, and printing moved to cities where more male labor was available, men came increasingly to predominate in the industry. Cigar rolling, a male occupation in New York and Philadelphia, was a female job in Detroit.[6]

c. Men and women have sometimes engaged in the same tasks in the same places at different times. The textile mills again provide an example. As Irish immigration rose dramatically in the 1840s and 1850s, Irish men took over jobs that Yankee women had performed.[7] Women replaced men at telephone switchboards in the 1880s and as bank tellers after 1940. Men replaced women as healers and midwives in the early nineteenth century, and as librarians and social workers in the 1930s.[8]

d. Men and women have not infrequently worked side by side at the same tasks when labor needs so dictated. During the colonial period, and much later in the West and in the South, women and men worked the fields alongside each other, stripped tobacco together and shared responsibility for household finances. Together, they have been tavern keepers and brewmasters in the nineteenth century, street car conductors and mail deliverers in World War I; and taxi drivers in World War II.

4. The idea of the sexual division of labor is a malleable concept, subject to particular societal needs which frequently change. Employers have used the notion that women's roles are in the home from the period of early in-

dustrialization to the present to regulate female work force participation, offering the argument that women possess certain characteristics that are not conducive to success in the labor force. These characteristics have always been used selectively, in ways that suit labor force conditions, indicating that they are not so much characteristics of women, as convenient tools for structuring the labor force.

a. For example, in 1917, the banking community, faced with a shortage of labor, attracted women into clerical and lower-level managerial jobs by arguing that "women are exceptionally fitted for work of this character— their neatness, deft handling of money and papers, tact and a certain intuitive judgment all being qualifications that count in their favor." In the early 1930s, when men became available for work due to the depression, the industry changed its mind and argued that it could not hire women, even as tellers, because they were poor at figures, and because the public would not accept the notion of handing over their money to women. Between 1941 and 1944, faced again with male labor shortages, banks relented and began to hire women as tellers. Industry journals then argued that women would make ideal tellers because they were good at dealing with the public.*[9]

b. Insurance and real estate, both highly competitive, announced themselves in the 1920s to be fields where women could earn high salaries and where age and lack of prior experience were not disadvantages. The insurance industry justified its recruitment of women with the argument that women were performing a service to the American family. Women responded. But by the 1930s, these fields were again seen as unseemly for women, and remained closed to them until the 1960s.[9a] The industries had redefined the jobs as too difficult for women's mathematical capabilities.

c. These varying characterizations of women as unsuited in different ways have frequently been adopted without regard to women's interest or availability, and in the face of the evident need of millions of women to engage in wage work. Since such characterizations have been influential in structuring the labor force into its present shape, it is crucial in looking at working women to examine not what employers say women can or cannot do, but what women *actually* do under conditions where they are either seeking jobs or working at them.

d. In the late-nineteenth-century West, for example, where men and women claimed allegiance to the values of domesticity,[10] women in fact plowed, fought, wrestled steers, and so on, leading one historian to conclude that western women "entered the previously male-dominated business world, and they did so successfully." In so doing, they "tended to ignore, or at least not slavishly strive toward, Eastern dictated models of femininity or the ideal of true womanhood."[11] Black women and immigrant women, under historical circumstances that have consistently demanded

---

* In 1940, bank tellers were 80% male; in 1944, they were 65% female, a shift in sexual composition that increased after the war. Tellers are 80% female today.

wage work, have sought and accepted jobs that contradicted attitudes about family lives that they themselves professed to hold. Many Irish immigrant women, for example, while declaring themselves attached to families, nevertheless remained single, saved money for themselves, and aided nieces and other female relatives in the search for upward mobility.[12]

5. These examples are by no means exceptions. Although many women who have not needed to engage in wage work have conformed to notions of domesticity, rapid and frequent shifts in women's participation in new areas of work when they were there admitted, as well as the eagerness with which women have taken new jobs, suggest that ideas about women's traditional roles are neither deeply rooted in women's psyche nor do they form a barrier that inhibits women's work force participation.

a. During the Civil War, for example, as a result of budget-cutting by the Treasurer of the U.S., Francis Elias Spinner, women for the first time entered office jobs in the Treasury Department. There were virulent objections by those who argued that such jobs would unsex women.[13] This affected neither the women who were recruited nor the Department, which justified its action on economic grounds. Thereafter, the women became permanent members of the staff.

b. In World War I, with a male labor shortage, women in several cities were hired as street car conductors despite the protests of those who argued that it was unseemly for women to work outdoors, and that contact with the public might be conducive to immorality. The women conductors, in contrast, argued that working on streetcars was far healthier than their former jobs. As one worker put it, "the wages are good, it's outdoor work, and a million times easier than washing."[14]

c. Between 1910 and 1930, during and after the suffrage struggle, women vocally pressed for opportunity. The real estate and life insurance industries were expanding greatly during this period and responded by including women among their increasing ranks. The proportion of women selling life insurance multiplied sixfold; the proportion selling real estate multiplied tenfold. When the depression diminished opportunity, the proportion of women in both jobs declined.[15]

d. During both world wars, women quickly accepted training to become welders, shipfitters, and crane operators. They worked in every variety of wartime and civilian production. Nor can this be said to be merely a product of wartime fervor, for most of these women left other, more traditional jobs in order to earn better pay. In the words of one woman who took a job cleaning street car tracks, the "almighty dollar" made the work worth the physical effort.[16]

e. Independently of national need, women rapidly filled such nontraditional jobs as that of telephone company lineman in 1973 once AT&T was induced through legal action to allow them entry, and they entered business, law, and professional schools beginning in the late 1960s as soon as those institutions opened their doors, in response to already existent social trends.

6. In the twentieth century, the key to whether women have conformed to notions of domesticity or not resides in the presence of economic opportunity. Where opportunity has existed, women have never failed to take the jobs offered. When opportunities have been closed to them, women have rationalized their inability to participate fully in the world of work with notions of domesticity.

a. The example of female physicians is instructive. In the late nineteenth century, despite the strenuous objections of male physicians and their virtual exclusion from male medical schools and hospitals, women managed to create their own medical schools and to acquire training in medicine. By 1894, twenty-three percent of students in Boston's medical colleges were women. But, after that date, female medical colleges allowed themselves to be merged with those run by men; the male-dominated schools set quotas on the numbers of women they would admit, and the female proportion of physicians plummeted. In 1910, the female percentage of physicians in the U.S. was higher than it was in 1960. Not until the strong social pressures of the 1960s began was medicine reopened to women.[17]

b. Numerous other examples of this phenomenon exist.Women made themselves available in large numbers for jobs not only in banking, in the 1920s, but as well as for work in the electronics industry, and on automobile assembly lines when jobs that had formerly been closed to them were opened.[18] That they did not move into other areas suggests that they were not offered opportunities there, not that they would not have taken them.

c. Moreover, there is little evidence that expressions of belief in traditional roles have any bearing on the labor market behavior of women who need to work. Catharine Beecher, Lydia Sigourney and Sara Josepha Hale all offer examples of nineteenth-century women who preached domesticity while earning their livings as ambitious, aspiring, professional women. More recently, the behavior of women towards paid work has contrasted sharply with attitudes recorded by survey researchers, as well as with those that have received public sanction.

d. Despite efforts to keep married women out of the work force in the depression of the 1930s, and despite the statements of many women that they disapproved of paid work for married women, married women increased their work force participation rate in that decade by fifty percent, the fastest rate of increase to that date.[19] This suggests that neither public pressure nor women's willingness to make public statements that conform to their expected roles reflect what women do, or how they actually function at work.

e. Nor do such surveys speak to the diversity of women's lives. Margaret Hagood, who interviewed southern farm women in the 1930s, reported that "seven eighths of these women prefer field work to housework and are prouder of their prowess in the field and in the tobacco shed than in the kitchen."[20]

f. During World War II, women who had always earned wages resisted efforts to channel them into less lucrative traditional employment, choosing instead to take advantage of higher-income jobs opened by the absence of men, regardless of the kind of job. The work experience itself seems to have been more important than social approval or disapproval in shaping the desire to remain at work. While eighty-five percent of the women who took jobs in 1941 said that they wanted to work only for the duration, fully seventy-five percent of all new workers wanted to keep their jobs in 1945.[21] Most of these were eased out. In seeking employment and in resisting termination after the war, women gave evidence that the search for higher income and the resultant security it afforded were far more important to them than any conception of traditional roles.

g. In the 1950s, women again paid lip service to the notion that a woman's role was in the home, yet the absolute numbers of women in the work force increased dramatically, as did the proportions of married women and of women with children under age eighteen.[22] This evidence suggests that how women feel about their family lives can and should be separated from their work force expectations and aspirations. A 1960s study confirms this conclusion. It reported that the proportion of women endorsing equal rights in the labor market "was higher than the proportion endorsing equality in the home."[23]

7. Historical evidence as well as some recent studies indicate that, as among men, orientations to paid work among women differ for different people; but for both groups income is, and has been, the primary incentive to paid work.

a. Contrary to most myths about women's work, every historical study of wage-earning women has indicated that women do not work for "pin money." Early twentieth-century studies record that families could not survive on the income of one wage-earner, and that wives contributed upwards of twenty-five percent of the family income. One historian reports that during World War I women took full advantage of expanding economic options to improve their status.[24] This trend continued until the 1960s.

b. By 1962, married women employed full-time contributed nearly forty percent of family income, and clerical and sales workers contributed a higher proportion than any other occupational category except unskilled workers. These data demonstrate that married female sales workers were more likely to be major contributors to their household income than women working in most other occupations. It suggests that women sales workers have husbands who themselves do not have high-paying jobs. One statistician at the Bureau of Labor Statistics (BLS) concluded that families did not consider this income as "transitory" no matter how intermittently it was received[25] (Transitory income is defined by BLS as that which is available for increasing a family's standard of living or adding to savings).

8. Work choices are influenced for men and for women by many circumstances. Just as many have forgotten that income has always been very important to women, so too one may lose sight of the fact that work choices of men have not been conditioned by income alone. Among Italian immigrants, family values have dictated that both men and women sacrifice

higher income if it comes at the cost of family life. Recent studies suggest that men stick to jobs in which they have no interest because their real interest is in their family and leisure lives, and at least one study suggests that job security is more important than income, and that men will sacrifice income if they perceive that there is risk involved.[26]

9. While protective labor legislation was said to reflect widespread opinion, and to benefit some working women, many other women, including printers, taxi drivers, mail carriers, professional women, and telegram deliverers objected to it on the grounds that it restricted their freedom to work at some jobs and limited their hours in others. While some employers sought this legislation in order to neutralize competition, others opposed it. They managed to release, among others, waitresses, cannery workers, nurses and hatcheck girls from the restrictive laws, on the grounds that such laws unduly restricted the employers' capacity to conduct their businesses.[27]

a. New York's female printers, arguing that their schedules were necessary to obtain the child care provided by husbands or other working family members, successfully petitioned the N.Y. legislature for exemption from the prohibition on night work. Other groups were not successful.

b. Female textile mill operatives in Massachusetts complained that the net result of such legislation was a loss of wages, and struck to restore wages lost when their hours were cut. Waitresses and female typesetters objected when night work laws threatened to deprive them of the most lucrative shifts. Streetcar conductors objected to removal from their jobs because they liked the freedom that split shifts gave them to run errands, pick up children at school and the like.

c. The struggle over protective labor legislation indicates that notions of traditional roles did not influence the kinds of jobs women would take if given the opportunity. The women who worked odd hours in canneries or in nursing, for example, and sought the flexibility that night work provided in making provision for child care, make it clear women wanted and needed "nontraditional" employment.

10. There also is little evidence that women have avoided reasonable risks in employment.

a. In World War I, women took dangerous jobs in glass factories in preference to washing clothes because they paid more.[28a]

b. One study of eleven Western States in 1943 indicates that women tended to look for jobs that promised higher income in preference to more secure jobs with lower incomes.[28b]

c. Historically, it was not uncommon in retail sales to pay women on a salary-plus-commission basis. Sometimes the salary could be as little as $2 per week, necessitating success in obtaining commission income just to survive. Women took these jobs as well as those without commission, knowing that whether or not a commission was involved, they would be fired if they did not "produce"; for historically retail sales was far from an easygoing social haven for unassertive women.[29]

11. The argument that women are only interested in certain kinds of

work reflects women's perceptions of opportunities available to them which are themselves products of employers' assumptions and prejudices about women's roles. It constitutes evidence that discrimination in fact exists in the work force.

a. The National Manpower Commission, for example, argued in its 1957 volume, *Womanpower*,[30] that traditional attitudes frequently govern employers' hiring patterns. In particular, the Commission stated that

> The distinctions between "men's" and "women's" jobs appear to be particularly sharp in certain manufacturing fields; and in professional service, and sales work, jobs are often closed to women because it is taken for granted that they should be held by men.

b. Given these patterns, sociologist Valerie Kincade Oppenheimer concludes that employer expectations are confusing to women who are then discouraged from applying for jobs. Oppenheimer goes on to argue that employers tend to believe that women have lower career aspirations.[31]

c. This combination of employer expectation and discouragement was most clearly demonstrated in a 1973 experiment on advertising. When jobs were described in male terms and/or placed under male headings, few women applied for them. But when the same jobs were described in sex-neutral language or in language that suggested both women's suitability and an employer's amenability to hiring women for the job, many more women applied.[32]

12. An argument that women's interests and viewpoints did not shift until the early 1970s can only be based on ignorance of the recent as well as the distant past.

a. Long-term trends show the increasing work force participation of all women dates back to the 1890s. Since then there has been a steady increase in the numbers of married and single women seeking wage work. The 1930s witnessed the first big leap in the labor force participation of married women, a trend that was continued in the 1940s and which has persisted ever since. The decade from 1940 to 1950 witnessed a reversal of the proportion of married and single wage earners among women. In the 1940 labor force, thirty-one percent of women workers were married, and forty-eight percent were single. By 1950, forty-seven percent of working women were married, and thirty-two percent were single. Sociologist Valerie Kincade Oppenheimer said of these changes that "while the 1940 to 1960 increases for women of all marital statuses combined have been sizable, the increases for married women with husbands present have been truly enormous."[33] By 1950, one third of all women with children under age eighteen were in the labor force; by 1960 nearly forty percent of such women were earning wages.[34]

b. Women have consistently fought against discrimination in attempts to remove or limit their participation in the labor force. The first movement for women's rights in the United States originated in 1848, primarily around economic issues. Since then, there is abundant evidence that women have repeatedly protested such discriminatory behavior as the failure of employers to allow women jobs and the absence of equal pay. In the 1920s such protests were frequently articulated, including the objections of women whose employers failed to promote them. The Bureau of Vocational Information deplored the fact that even women with college degrees tended to be placed, against their wishes, in dead-end jobs. Women resisted attempts to eliminate married women workers in the 1930s, and fought against removal from their jobs in the post-war 1940s. By the 1950s women began to articulate the object of their protest not as just particular employers but rather as society at large. The Women's Bureau of the Department of Labor received dozens of letters in the early 1950s protesting the contradictions inherent in a society that styled itself as one of individual freedom while denying women equal access to jobs.

c. Women's complaints had some effect before 1970. During the 1960s women's presence in those male occupations most difficult to break into had already begun to increase. The population of female blacksmiths, cabinet makers, carpet installers, electricians, and plumbers all increased substantially during the sixties.[35]

d. In 1961, President John F. Kennedy officially acknowledged the existence of discrimination in the federal government, and set up a commission to investigate the condition of women in the country as a whole. The Executive Order that created the President's Commission on the Status of Women stated that "prejudices and outmoded customs" could act as "barriers to the full realization of women's basic rights."[36] Simultaneously, President Kennedy urged the Civil Service Commission to eliminate discriminatory practices, a directive that the CSC chairman, John Macy, asserted had immediate impact.

e. Among other analyses offered, the report of the Commission on the Status of Women, issued in 1963, asserted that employers' tendencies to rely on "conventional assumptions" rather than on "actualities" was responsible for much discrimination against women.[37]

f. The Commission urged that Congress act on sex discrimination, which it did with the passage of the Equal Pay Act. The subsequent amendment by President Johnson of Executive Order 11246 to include in its strictures discrimination against women also represents action by the federal government specifically and exclusively devoted to elimination of sex discrimination and the improvement of women's work opportunities.

g. These laws, and the prohibitions on sex discrimination in the Civil Rights Act of 1964, resulted in large measure from the pressure put on the government by women, led by Esther Peterson, head of the Women's Bureau of the Department of Labor, to provide means for the eradication of sex discrimination.

h. The new laws were also in part a result of the potential political pressure of the already substantial numbers of women who by the 1960s had moved into the work force. Consciousness of discrimination among these women is evidenced by the fact that in the EEOC's first year of operation, 1966, to everyone's amazement, forty percent of the complaints submitted to the agency concerned sex discrimination.[38]

i. That the discontent of women regarding their treatment in the labor force preceded the 1970s is further substantiated by the founding of the National Organization for Women in 1966, and a scholarly study that demonstrates that changes in women's attitudes toward work and the family had been in place since at least 1964. Moreover, these changes were not limited to well-educated women, but were prevalent among women with work experience of any kind.[39]

13. History's evidence clearly indicates that substantial numbers of women have been available for jobs at good pay in whatever field those jobs are offered, and no matter what the hours. Failure to find women in so-called nontraditional jobs can thus only be interpreted as a consequence of employers' unexamined attitudes or preferences, which phenomenon is the essence of discrimination.

NOTES

1. Specifically, the testimony of Rosalind Rosenberg omits information, the possession of which alters the interpretation of the data she provides. Her testimony deduces the behavior of working women from literature and studies that purport to reflect their behavior and values but in fact rarely do. These errors in interpretation arise from the fact that her expertise does not lie in the history of wage earning women, but comes rather from the experience and ideology that dominate the lives of upper-income, professional women and those who did not work for wages. The result of these errors is to assume that women were not traditionally engaged in earning income, and to ignore the enormous diversity of motivation and experience that has characterized the experience of wage earning women throughout United States history.

2. As anthropologist Michelle Zimbalist Rosaldo notes, "there are societies in which women trade or garden, and those in which men do; societies in which women are queens and those in which they must always defer to a man" ("A Theoretical Overview," in Rosaldo and Louise Lamphere [eds.], *Woman, Culture, and Society*, at 18 [1974]).

3. Esther Boserup, *Woman's Role in Economic Development* at 5 (1970).

4. Helen Sumner, *History of Women in Industry in the United States*, Vol. IX of the Report on Condition of Women and Child Wage Earners in the United States, Senate Document #645, 61st Congress, 2d Session at 17 (1910); Edith Abbott, *Women in Industry: A Study in Economic History*, 68–69, 80 (1969).

5. Thomas Dublin, *Women at Work: The Transformation of Work and Community in Lowell, Massachusetts, 1826–1860*, ch. 8, 9 (1979); Abbott, *supra*, n. 4, at ch. 6.

6. For transitions in these industries, see Abbott, *supra*, n. 4, at ch. 9, 11; Ava Baron, "Women and the Making of the American Working Class: A Study of the Proletarianization of Printers," 14 *Review of Radical Political Economics*, 23–42 (Fall 1982); Patricia Cooper, "The Transformation of the Cigar Industry in the 19th Century" (unpublished manuscript).

7. Dublin, *supra*, n. 5, ch. 9; Maurine Wiener Greenwald, *Women, War, and Work:*

The Impact of World War I on Women Workers in the United States, 190 (1980); Marc McCulloch, *White Collar Labor in Transition,* ch. 2 (1980).

8. Barbara Ehrenreich and Deirdre English, *For Her Own Good: 150 Years of the Experts' Advice to Women,* ch. 2, 3 (1978); Alice Kessler-Harris, *Out to Work: A History of Wage Earning Women in the U.S.,* ch. 9 (1982).

9. "Banking and Business Training for Women," *The Bankers Magazine* at 1 (August 1917), reprinted by the Financial Center for Women; McCulloch, *supra,* n. 7 at 81–82. For a similar process as regards secretaries, see Margery Davies, *Women's Place Is at the Typewriter: Office Work and Office Workers, 1870–1930,* ch. 5 (1982).

9a. Kessler-Harris, *supra,* n. 8, ch. 8.

10. Domesticity is here defined as an ideology developed in the nineteenth century and continuing in altered form thereafter, which assigns the sphere of the household to women, as their proper and ordinary place. In its early incarnation, as defined by historian Barbara Welter, the ideal domestic woman was to be pious, pure, and submissive as well as devoting her life's energies to the harmonious functioning of the home. Increasingly as the nineteenth century progressed, these ideas became less a description of what women actually did and more a way of structuring their home and work lives.

11. Sandra Myres, *Westering Women and the Frontier Experience,* at 269 (1982).

12. Jacquelyn Jones, *Labor of Love, Labor of Sorrow: Black Women, Work, and the Family from Slavery to the Present,* pp. 134–35, 158, 259–60 (1985); Hasia Diner, *Erin's Daughters in America: Irish Immigrant Women in the Nineteenth Century,* ch. 2, 4 (1983); Sara Eisenstein, *Give Us Bread but Give Us Roses: Working Women's Consciousness in the United States, 1890 to the First World War,* ch. 5 (1983).

13. Ross Baker, "Entry of Women into Federal Job World—At a Price," 8 *Smithsonian,* 83–85 (July 1977).

14. Greenwald *supra,* n. 7, at 155.

15. Janet Hooks, *Women's Occupations through Seven Decades,* Women's Bureau Bulletin No. 218, 88–89 (1947).

16. Greenwald *supra,* n. 7, at p. 32, ch. 1, 4; Karen Anderson, *Wartime Women: Sex Roles, Family Relations and the Status of Women During World War II,* ch. 2 (1981); Chester W. Gregory, *Women in Defense Work During World War II: An Analysis of the Labor Problem and Women's Rights,* ch. 6–9, (1979).

17. Mary Roth Walsh, *Doctors Wanted: No Women Need Apply. Sexual Barriers in the Medical Profession, 1835–1975,* at 183, 185 (1977).

18. The 1920 Census of Occupations counted 15,000 women working in auto plants. This figure includes laborers and semi-skilled operatives employed as buffers, polishers, and sanders, among other occupations. That this was not simply a holdover from the war is indicated by the fact that the Michigan Department of Labor and Industry recorded 17,250 women in the industry in 1925. Shortly thereafter, a slump in the auto industry raised the numbers even higher, when first General Motors and then Ford replaced well-paid male assembly line workers with lower-paid women. No difficulty was encountered in finding women, for whom even these lower wages represented an economic incentive over their still lower wages in traditionally female occupations. When the depression struck, however, the auto industry was able to obtain men for these lower wages. The women lost their jobs. Robert Dunn, *Labor and Automobiles* (1929).

19. Susan Ware, *Holding Their Own: American Women in the 1930s,* at 29 (1982); Kessler-Harris, *supra,* n. 8, at 258–65; Ruth Milkman, "Women's Work and the Economic Crisis: Some Lessons from the Great Depression," 8 *Review of Radical Political Economics* 73–97 (Spring 1976).

20. Margaret Hagood, *Mothers of the South: Portraiture of the White Tenant Farm Woman*, p. vi. (1977).

21. Anderson, *supra*, n. 16, pp. 162–63; Maureen Honey, *Creating Rosie the Riveter: Class, Gender and Propaganda During World War II*, p. 11 (1984); Ruth Milkman, "Redefining 'Women's Work': The Sexual Division of Labor in the Auto Industry During World War II," 8 *Feminist Studies* 338–72 (Summer 1982); Alan Clive, "Women Workers in World War II: Michigan as a Test Case," 20 *Labor History* 44–72 (Winter 1979). All of these sources document the obstinacy with which employers hung onto their sexual stereotypes, despite the war emergency.

22. Howard Hayghe, "Families and the Rise of Working Wives: An Overview," *Monthly Labor Review* at 13 (May, 1976); Women's Bureau, U.S. Department of Labor, Bulletin No. 297, *1975 Handbook on Women Workers* at 15–16, 27 (1975).

23. Karen Oppenheim Mason, et al., "Change in Women's Sex Role Attitudes, 1964–1974," 41 *American Sociological Review* 593 (August 1976).

24. Margaret Byington, *Homestead: The Households of a Mill Town*, [1910] ch. 3 (1974); Greenwald *supra*, n. 7, at 20–21.

25. Margaret S. Carroll, "The Working Wife and Her Family's Economic Position," 85 *Monthly Labor Review* 373 (April 1962). The wife's importance in income earning had already been noted in 1954, when the *Monthly Labor Review* at 1209 (November) reported that the tendency of women to work reflected a search for income rather than a response to an emergency.

26. Abraham Bluestone, "Major Studies of Workers' Reasons for Job Choice," *Monthly Labor Review* at 306 (March 1955). Bluestone also points out, at 301, that workers may not divulge to an interviewer their underlying motives for job choice. "Instead, they may be rationalizing in terms of socially accepted criteria." Willingness to take risks, like attitudes toward the job itself, may in fact be a function of the differing places of men and women in the organizational structure, as Rosabeth Moss Kanter suggests. See "The Impact of Hierarchical Structures on the Work Behavior of Women and Men," 23 *Social Problems* 415–30 (April 1976).

27. Protective labor legislation has often been divided into two types: restrictive and regulatory. The first of these denied women the right to work for more than a given number of hours per day, at certain times, and so on. The second regulated sanitary, lighting and other health-related conditions in the workplace. It was around the first, restrictive legislation, that the battle raged in the first part of the twentieth century. For a fuller description of its impact and illustrations, see Kessler-Harris, *Out to Work* ch. 7; and Judith Baer, *The Chains of Protection: The Judicial Response to Women's Labor Legislation* (1978).

28a. Greenwald *supra*, n. 7, at p. 30.

28b. D'Ann Campbell, "Was the West Different? Values and Attitudes of Young Women in 1943," 47 *Pacific Historical Review* 458 (August 1978).

29. Elizabeth Butler, *Saleswomen in Mercantile Stores: Baltimore 1909*, pp. 11–113 (1912); Annie McLean, "Two Weeks in Department Stores," 4 *American Journal of Sociology* 724 (May 1899); Frances Donovan, *The Saleslady*, pp. 67–68, 198–99 (1929).

30. *Womanpower: A Statement by the National Manpower Council*, pp. 88–89 (1957).

31. Valerie Kincade Oppenheimer, "The Sex-Labelling of Jobs," 7 *Industrial Relations* 229, 233 (May 1968).

32. Sandra L. Bem and Daryl J. Bem, "Does Sex-biased Job Advertising 'Aid and Abet' Sex Discrimination?" 3 *Journal of Applied Social Psychology* pp. 6–18 (1973). When advertisements for the jobs of telephone linemen and framemen were written for men, only five percent of the women in this experimental study applied for the jobs; when they were written for women, forty-five percent of the women applied for the jobs.

33. Oppenheimer, *The Female Labor Force in the United States: Demographic and Economic Factors Governing its Growth and Changing Composition*, p. 10 (1970).

34. Bureau of Labor Statistics, U.S. Department of Labor, *U.S. Working Women: A Databook*, p. 22 (1977).

35. Kessler-Harris *supra*, n. 8, pp. 308–309; Janice Hedges and Stephen Bemis, "Sex Stereotyping, Its Decline in Skilled Trades," 97 *Monthly Labor Review* at 16 (May 1974).

36. Patricia Zelman, *Women, Work and National Policy: The Kennedy-Johnson Years*, p. 27 (1980).

37. President's Commission on the Status of Women, *American Women*, p. 30 (1963).

38. Bem and Bem *supra*, n. 32, at 6.

39. Mason, et al., *supra*, n. 23, at 589.

SECTION B

Comparable Worth

Feminists, Union Leaders, and Democrats: The Passage of Comparable Worth Laws

Sara M. Evans and Barbara J. Nelson

Wages are a reflection of relative power in our society.

—Nina Rothchild,
Minnesota Commissioner of Employee Relations

Minnesota was the first state to establish a comparable worth wage policy for state employees, fund it, and completely distribute the raises. From legislation to completed implementation took only five years, and during this time the state legislature also passed a law—the first in the nation—requiring that each local jurisdiction in Minnesota establish a comparable worth wage policy for its employees. In Minnesota the policy has always been called "pay equity" to emphasize its goal and encourage widespread support. "Other places may have comparable worth," said chief legislative author Senator Linda Berglin to the mostly skeptical members of the Association of Minnesota Counties, "but Minnesota has pay equity." Passage of both pay equity laws was the product of fortuitous timing, skillful and committed legislators, an established women's policy community that had both a governmental and a grassroots base, and the vision of the state's largest public union, AFSCME. As is the case in most legislation, the problems of implementation were rarely considered, and when considered, were judged acceptable.

In this chapter we analyze the passage of both Minnesota pay equity laws and put Minnesota's efforts in national context. The experience in Minnesota is both typical and atypical of activism on this issue. Far more than has been currently recognized, Minnesota has been similar to most of the states that have moved quickly on comparable worth. Like them, Minnesota had legislation permitting collective bargaining in the public sector, had Democratic control of the House, Senate, and governorship during most of the period when the policy was adopted, and had an active Women's Commission to develop policy over the long run. But Minnesota was also one of the first states to act, enjoying the uncharacteristic luxury of considering comparable worth at a time when opposition forces were not as well organized as they would come to be. . . .

STATE EFFORTS IN
NATIONAL PERSPECTIVE

The movement for comparable worth for public employees has progressed steadily since women's groups and unions in Washington began to press the policy in 1973. Considering the opposition of the Reagan administration, the record is quite impressive. By August 1987, forty-two states had engaged in research or data collection on comparable worth, thirty-six had appointed task forces or commissions, twenty-eight had participated in a job evaluation study, and twenty had provided some sort of comparable worth payments to at least a portion of state employees.

The twenty states that have put money into some workers' paychecks form the basis of our comparisons with the Minnesota experience. Most of these states share both the structural conditions that promote progressive action and the specific political arrangements that act as the midwives to change. The cultural and economic structures these states share are frequently found in states that readily accept "liberal" economic policy. Thirteen of the active states have political cultures that at least partially support community-mindedness, a way of doing the state's business that has been described as moralistic in contrast to individualist or traditional. In addition, the twenty most active states are more likely to have healthy, diversified economies; relatively high average personal incomes; more progressive (in the technical sense) taxation policies; and somewhat higher state and local tax burdens.

Specific political arrangements helped to translate the readiness for equity policy into equity action. Politicians and activists were most successful *when three political conditions coincided:* public sector collective bargaining, Democratic control of the state, and energetic Commissions on the Status of Women. Thirteen of the twenty most active states on this issue, Minnesota included, met all of these political conditions, and four of the most active states met at least two of them. The states that have met three of these conditions but have not implemented any portion of comparable worth pay raises (Alaska, Hawaii, Maine, Maryland, and Missouri) are the structurally most likely places for the next comparable worth successes. In fact, all five of these states have proceeded with comparable worth up to the point of making salary adjustments. But the next move is the most difficult and depends on very idiosyncratic combinations of political opportunity and political leadership. Missouri, a Phyllis Schlafly stronghold, offers the biggest challenge to organizers. One Missouri legislator who spoke with us reported that she had asked her priest if comparable worth was related to abortion, and only on hearing "no" had she settled into serious activism in favor of the issue. If these are the problems in states with supportive political conditions, states without at least two of the facilitative political characteristics are likely to be late adopters, if indeed they ever consider state-wide action for comparable worth. The intersection between state and national action will be very important for the states without the structural or political forces promoting change. Without the example of national legislation for federal workers, or the more remote but more effective option of mandated change through congressional legislation, many states will remain inhospitable to the theory and political activism of comparable worth.

Each of the three political conditions supporting comparable worth deserves more attention because each elucidates a milieu conducive to success in policy innovation. Laws permitting collective bargaining in the public sector were perhaps the most important factors promoting comparable worth activism because they signalled the legitimacy and stability of worker organizations and facilitated the creation of coalitions of feminist and union activists typical of most early state action. There were exceptions, of course. Washington, the first state to embark on comparable worth, does not permit collective bargaining in the public sector, and neither does Oklahoma, though in Washington AFSCME was nevertheless a powerful actor in initiating comparable worth. But all of the other states making comparable worth adjustments to date allow public employees to unionize.

Comparable worth was more successful in states where Democrats exercised substantial (though by no means complete) control of the House, Senate, and governorship during the first four legislative biennia of the 1980s. While many individual Republican politicians support comparable worth, the issue increasingly became associated with the Democrats and their constituencies, as the differences in the 1984 presidential platforms showed. Seventeen of twenty states giving comparable worth raises had substantial Democratic control during adoption or implementation. It is noteworthy that Democrats controlled forty-two states during this period. It was not Democratic control alone that promoted comparable worth, however, but Democratic control in conjunction with supportive labor laws and successful women's commissions. The existence of Democratic political power clearly supported public union activity even when the location of activity was the negotiation table and not the floor of the legislature.

The activism of commissions or task forces on the status of women provided the arena where policy was developed and where interest could be maintained as the political seasons changed. Public commissions on the status of women existed in sixteen of the states providing comparable worth raises, but in some other states more informal arrangements provided the continuity to act over a long period of time. In Minnesota, Oregon, California, and Connecticut, for example, the policy development efforts for comparable worth came from institutionalized women's groups like commissions on the status of women, which were in turn aided and supported by grass-roots feminist organizations, public unions (most frequently AFSCME or SEIU), and interested legislators.

These official women's groups were especially important because the states that acted most extensively on comparable worth tended to have highly professionalized legislatures, with relatively weaker interest-group power over the lawmaking process. The structure of legislative decision-making made internal staff allies, like the legislatively housed Minnesota Commission on the Economic Status of Women, very important. The advantages that accrued to issues with inside support tended to make state legislative efforts for comparable worth more elite than grass-roots-dominated. Local efforts outside of Minnesota showed much greater variation of grass-roots and elite predominance in the issue. . . .

The content of comparable worth policies differs notably from state to state. Indeed, state variability of similarly labelled policies is one of the least-discussed aspects of the diffusion of innovation literature. The National Committee on Pay Equity reports a variety of approaches to the equal value question as comparable worth policy. Some states such as Washington, Minnesota, and New York base their policies on job evaluation and the comparison of equally valued jobs. Other states such as New Jersey and New Mexico have raised wages for the lowest-paid state workers before doing a job evaluation, which may or may not ever be completed. The states in this second group have established what in Europe, especially Sweden, would be called a wage solidarity policy, although the policymakers using this approach in the United States do not use that language. With wage solidarity, the lower-paid workers in a firm or sector (depending on the level at which bargaining is conducted) routinely get a higher-percentage raise than better-paid workers do. In this way, lower-paid and lower-skilled workers continue to make a living wage and the wage-spread between the lowest- and highest-paid workers is kept in check. This policy also allows more productive sectors to have higher wages. In this country, states that adopted an implicit wage-solidarity approach to comparable worth did so mostly for political reasons, either wanting to get raises to low-paid, mostly female and minority workers before a job evaluation could be done, or not wanting to undertake a job evaluation and be bound by the findings about job values.

In practice there are three operational definitions of achieving equal pay for equal value, two associated with the job evaluation approach and a third associated with the wage solidarity approach. Among those states with a comparable worth policy based on job evaluation, only Minnesota currently uses the pay in male-dominated jobs as the standard against which jobs with a preponderance of women are compared. (New York began its analysis by using the values of white and male jobs as the standard against which other jobs would be compared, but technical and political actions by the state altered this approach.) In most other states, comparable worth means pay for points, where each increase in job evaluation points added a specified sum to wages. In practice, however, many states modified pay for points, bringing each job classification below the all-jobs pay practices line up to, or near, it. In wage solidarity states a certain percentage-raise or dollar increase in base pay, usually implemented as a one-time permanent change in wage rates, constitutes a pay equity policy.

The conflicts surrounding agenda setting for comparable worth were remarkably similar in most of the active states, in large part because the issue came to be understood in similar ways by the policymakers and the publics in those states. With the exception of Wisconsin, where the Association of Manufacturers and Commerce waged a vitriolic campaign against comparable worth based on accusations of employee inefficiency and high wages in the public sector, the politics of comparable worth were conducted in the language of increased wages for historically underpaid female- and minority-dominated jobs. Within this setting two types of conflicts arose. The first concerned job evaluation. Did the state already use job evaluation and, if so, did it use one or more than one system? A 1986 report by the U.S. Government Accounting Office showed that 46 of 48 states responding to a GAO survey used job evaluation, and 34 of the 46 used a single system. But many states redid their job evaluation systems when they decided to initiate comparable worth. In that case other questions arose. To what extent did management control job evaluation? Did the interest of management in job evaluation go beyond examining jobs for equal value to encompass a possible reclassification of the personnel system or redefinition of existing job classifications? The extent to which management controlled evaluation and classification was defined by each state's labor laws and practices and the policies developed to implement comparable worth. In Oregon the attempt to reconfigure the entire classification system contributed to the failure of the pay equity efforts of 1985–86. The prior existence of a job evaluation system used in Minnesota's comparable worth implementation greatly facilitated the process.

The second conflict concerned financing. Would comparable worth primarily be an add-on to the wage bill, or would it redistribute existing wages or wage increases? If the political choice was to make comparable worth an add-on, many of the conflicts that arose focused around financing. If the choice was to emphasize restraining the pressure on the wage bill, many of the conflicts were over sharing the pain of slower wage growth or possible wage freezes, as well as sharing the gain in higher salaries for undervalued and underpaid classes. The first situation, in which Minnesota and Iowa fell, meant that advocates had to win the support of the people who controlled the state's revenue and appropriation politics. The second situation, in which Oregon fell, meant that advocates had to win the support of the other labor groups, many of which saw comparable worth as a loss. The real world can of course pose both types of problems for advocates, although the tendency so far has been for one or the other type of financial, and thus political, situation to dominate.

STATE EMPLOYEES PAY EQUITY ACT

Structurally and politically, Minnesota was well positioned to take the lead in comparable worth. In particular, the political culture of Minnesota created an atmosphere supportive of this issue. In his classic study *Cities of the Prai-*

rie, Daniel J. Elazar describes the moralistic political culture of Minnesota with emphasis on its traditions of community-mindedness: "[T]he political order is conceived to be a commonwealth—a state in which the whole people have an undivided interest." These traditions are part of the territorial legacy of Minnesota, a product first of English settlers of Puritan stock and then of German and Scandinavian settlers who brought their traditions of community participation. Political arrangements helped as well. Minnesota had a long and successful populist tradition and sustained its socialist experiments longer than did most states and cities on the eastern seaboard.

The political institutions and processes in Minnesota continue to reflect this legacy. Traditionally, the two major political parties define themselves as more liberal than their national counterparts. The Democratic-Farmer-Labor (DFL) party was formed in 1944 as a merger of the then-dominant Farmer-Labor party and the struggling Democratic party. Until quite recently the Independent Republican (IR) party, a name adopted in 1975 in response to national trends away from partisanship, had traditionally portrayed itself as more sympathetic with the reform climate of Minnesota than with the increasingly powerful conservative wing of the national Republican party. The progressive nature of both parties on women's issues can be seen by the fact that both have feminist (not women's) caucuses. Partisanship was eschewed in the legislature, however, where elections were nonpartisan between 1913 and 1973.

Both the public and the private sectors are highly unionized in Minnesota. In 1981, 43.5% of the public-sector workers and 20.7% of private-sector workers belonged to unions or professional associations that bargained for them. The labor history of the state was not without violence, however. In 1934 the famous teamsters' strike in Minneapolis pitted hundreds of workers against police and armed guards hired by the business owners. Four people died in the strike, and the union was finally recognized by employers. Modern labor relations have generally been calmer. Public-sector employees were given the right to unionize in 1971, and the existing labor organizations of public workers, some of which had been in existence since the 1930s, quickly took on their new roles.

AFSCME first raised the issue of comparable worth in 1974. Council 6 of AFSCME (which represents state employees) wanted the state to investigate possible discrimination in the pay practices and promotions of women. This move paralleled the efforts that AFSCME had underway in Washington State at that time. Paul Goldberg, the executive director of Council 6, expressed the union's concern when he told the press that "Salary rates for experienced, responsible clerical positions often requiring post high school business education are $10 to $150 less than the pay for inexperienced janitors, whose duties may be extremely limited." The next year Council 6 successfully bargained for the study, but it was never funded or conducted.

By the late 1970s, however, a key set of state leaders capable of pursuing comparable worth coalesced around the Council on the Economic Status of Women. The legislature established the Council in 1976 with a budget of

$95,000 and a requirement to report back by the end of 1977 on the "laws and practices constituting barriers to the full participation of women in the economy." DFL Representative Linda Berglin, who chaired the Council, hired Nina Rothchild, a suburban school-board member and political activist, to serve as the Council's senior staff. Together they stood at the center of a network that reached out into grass-roots women's organizations, AFSCME, and the Coalition of Labor Union Women (CLUW), feminist caucuses in both major political parties, and members of the Minnesota legislature sympathetic to women's issues.

Two powerful women with complementary talents, Berglin and Rothchild oversaw a stream of research and publications on women in the Minnesota economy. Defining "economic status" broadly, the Council examined and made legislative recommendations on issues such as sex discrimination in insurance, inheritance taxes, and housing; minimum wage and tip credits; tax credits for child care; age discrimination; and family planning. In avoiding divisive issues like abortion (which the Council declined to define as an economic issue) and by lobbying only *for* its own bills and not *against* bills of which it disapproved, the Council compiled a remarkably successful record in its first two and a half years, winning passage of 21 of 32 recommended bills. Legislators who agreed to sponsor Council legislation received copies of suggested wording for the bill, background information packets, and suggestions for persons who could be called upon to testify.

The Council maintained a special interest in the status of women who worked for the state, holding hearings in 1976 on women as state employees and publishing a report on the same topic in 1977. The analysis noted the low wages of women and their concentration in jobs held primarily by women. By documenting wage disparities and the gender segregation of the state's labor forces, the Council contributed to a growing recognition that the 1963 Equal Pay Act and Title VII of the 1964 Civil Rights Act did not raise women's wages because women and men so rarely held the same jobs.

In 1978 and 1979, in moves distinct from the research of the Council, the state undertook an examination of its personnel system that would later have profound ramifications on the course of comparable worth policy making. Faithful to its traditions, Minnesota was a national leader in civil service reform. Its interest in personnel reform and rationalization predated similar actions on the part of the federal government. The Minnesota Legislative Audit Commission completed an evaluation of the state's personnel system in 1978, and in 1979 the Department of Finance published its "Public Employment Study" which included the findings of a Hay Associates study of salary and benefit policies. These reports provided the data necessary to compare equally valued jobs. The crucial information was contained in the job evaluation Hay undertook of 762 multi-incumbent job classes. Hay Associates did not plan for its data to be used in a comparable worth analysis. In fact it reported that "'in general there appears to be a slight tendency to pay male-dominated occupations at a higher level than female-dominated classes. However . . . this includes an extremely small percentage of positions.'"

In the fall of 1981, the Council on the Economic Status of Women appointed a Pay Equity Task Force to reanalyze the Hay Associates data by comparing male- and female-dominated job classes having the same point values. The Council had undergone a good many changes in the two-year period between the publication of the Hay Associates report and the formation of the Task Force. In 1981 the DFL-controlled legislature granted permanent status to the Council with an amendment that prohibited it from advocating abortion in any way. Newly elected IR Governor Al Quie appointed several conservatives to be public members of the Council, including some who had worked to abolish it. During the summer, AFSCME, the Council's long-time ally in economic issues concerning women, was involved in a strike against the state.

With the AFSCME strike resolved and interest in comparable worth growing everywhere, the Council astutely appointed the members of the Pay Equity Task Force with an eye for future legislation. The Council called on the services of six legislators representing both parties who were sensitive to women's issues and well-placed in the legislature. The Task Force also included representatives of important constituencies, most notably AFSCME. In using the term "pay equity" to name the Task Force, the Council chose to emphasize the issue of fairness and build its political constituency.

Council staff member Bonnie Watkins compiled the list of comparable jobs after the Council pried the Hay data out of a reluctant Department of Employee Relations. Her first task was to sort out male- and female-dominated job classes, defining these as jobs which were 80% or more male and 70% or more female. Her second task was to compare the pay scales of equally valued positions for gender differences.

The results were striking; it was found that women's jobs routinely paid around 20% less than men's jobs at the same Hay-point level. In 1981, the highest monthly pay of the Delivery Van Driver position, a male-dominated class receiving 117 Hay points, was $1,382. The highest monthly salary for the Clerk Typist 2 position, a female-dominated class with 117 Hay points, was $1,115. At the highest end of the pay range, the Delivery Van Driver position made $267 (23.9%) more per month than the Clerk Typist position. The findings repeated themselves at every level of Hay points. Grain Inspector 2, at 173 Hay points, earned a monthly maximum of $1,693 while Human Services Specialist, at 177 Hay points, earned a monthly maximum of $1,343, a 26.1% difference. The highest salary for the Pharmacist position, 353 Hay points, was $2,297, which compared to $1,911 (or 20.2% less) for the Registered Nurse 3 position having the same number of points.

Once the tabular analysis was completed, Watkins plotted each class on a graph whose axes were Hay points and income (highest point of the pay range for that job). The resulting now-familiar scattergram demonstrated the dramatic differences in pay between comparable male and female jobs. Not a single female-dominated job class reached the pay line established by the male classes.

The Task Force report based on Watkins' analysis was released in Janu-

ary 1982. It made public the disparities between male- and female-dominated job classes receiving equal points under the Hay system. The report
formed the basis of the State Employees Pay Equity Act introduced by Council Chair Linda Berglin, who had moved to the state Senate in 1980. The bill
was shepherded through the legislature by Berglin and DFL Representative
Wayne Simoneau with a minimum of fanfare. The bill established the principle of pay equity as the *primary* basis of remuneration in state employment, spelled out a process by which it could be achieved, but did not carry
an appropriation. The state was in the midst of a deep recession in 1982 and
the specter of a possible budget deficit made a new personnel appropriation
a difficult if not impossible option. In hearings, scattergrams graphically depicted the Task Force's findings while lobbyists quietly assured legislators
that funding for the bill could wait another year. Rick Scott, the chief lob-
byist for AFSCME, later indicated that the decision to separate the law and
the appropriation was the most critical step in establishing the policy. The
final vote on the measure was 63 for and 0 against in the Senate, and 82 for
and 3 against in the House. Governor Al Quie signed the bill with no delay.

The press remained silent, in large part because the bill's sponsors chose
a low-keyed approach to passage, and there was no opposition from the
business community. In March the *Minneapolis Star and Tribune* barely noted
passage of the bill. Buried in a longer article on the sixth page of the second
section were a series of photographs under "Other bills signed by the Governor were. . . ." The second of five read: "Establish a state policy of comparable worth in state employment, aimed at ensuring that so-called 'wom-
en's' jobs carry salaries equal to comparable jobs usually reserved for
men." . . .

SECTION C

Fetal Protection

INTERNATIONAL UNION, UNITED AUTOMOBILE, AEROSPACE
AND AGRICULTURAL IMPLEMENT WORKERS OF AMERICA,
UAW, et al.,
Plaintiffs-Appellants,
and
Local 322, Allied Industrial Workers of America, AFL-CIO,
Intervening Plaintiff Appellant,

v.

JOHNSON CONTROLS, INC.,
Defendant-Appellee
No. 88-1308

United States Court of Appeals, Seventh Circuit.
Argued Sept. 15, 1988.
Reargued En Banc June 15, 1989.
Decided Sept. 26, 1989.

COFFEY, Circuit Judge.

Since 1982 Johnson Controls, Inc. (hereinafter "Johnson Controls" or "Johnson") has maintained a fetal protection policy designed to prevent unborn children and their mothers from suffering the adverse effects of lead exposure. International Union, United Automobile, Aerospace and Agricultural Implement Workers of America, UAW (hereinafter "UAW"), several UAW local unions and a group of individual employees brought suit alleging that this policy violated Title VII, 42 U.S.C. § 2000e, et seq. The district court granted summary judgment in favor of Johnson Controls and the plaintiffs appealed. . . . [F]ollowing rehearing en banc, a majority of the court voted to affirm the decision of the district court.

Editors' note: The opinions that follow have been abridged, and most citations have been deleted.

I

The Battery Division of Johnson Controls, Inc., was created upon Johnson Controls' 1978 purchase of Globe Union, Inc. (hereinafter "Globe" or "Globe Union"). Globe Union was formed through the consolidation of two battery companies and had been in the battery business for almost fifty years before Johnson's purchase. Globe Union and Johnson Controls have maintained ongoing efforts to improve industrial safety through measures designed to minimize the risk lead poses to those directly involved in the manufacturing of batteries.

The steps that Globe Union and Johnson Controls have taken to regulate lead exposure have not been focused merely on complying with governmental safety regulations, but originate from their longstanding corporate concern for the danger lead poses to the health and welfare of their employees, their employees' families and the general public. During the period of the 1970's when OSHA's regulation of employee exposure to lead was virtually non-existent, Johnson Controls' predecessor, Globe Union, initiated a large number of innovative programs in an attempt to control and regulate industrial lead exposure. For example, in 1969, Dr. Charles Fishburn, M.D., who later became one of the primary proponents of Johnson Controls' fetal protection policy, instituted programs for monitoring employee blood lead levels. In an attempt to manage lead exposure, other safety programs were initiated at Globe and Johnson including a lead hygiene program, respirator program, biological monitoring program, medical surveillance program and a program regulating the type, use and disposal of employee work clothing and footwear to minimize lead exposure. Globe Union also transferred employees out of high lead environments whenever a physician's medical evaluation report established that the individual had a high blood lead level. In the case of such transfers, medical removal benefits were provided to the employee before OSHA required such compensation. Globe Union and Johnson Controls have continued to address their serious concern for industrial safety through efforts to design and regulate lead manufacturing areas to reduce employee lead exposure. . . .

Globe Union, Johnson Controls' predecessor, established its first policy regarding fetal protection from lead exposure in 1977 as part of its comprehensive efforts to protect its employees from exposure to lead. Globe Union's announcement of the policy in a memorandum to battery plant and personnel managers stated:

> "This change [the announced policy] has come about slowly as more and more medical opinion and evidence is persuasive of the risk to the unborn, developing child.
>
> We have stopped short of excluding women capable of bearing children from lead exposure, but do feel strongly that those women who are working in lead exposure . . . and those women who wish to be considered for employment be advised that there is risk, that we recommend *not* working in lead if they are considering a family, and further that we ask them to sign a statement that they have been advised of this risk." . . .

Johnson adopted its current fetal protection program in 1982 following its determination, based upon scientific research, that it was medically necessary to bar women from working in high lead exposure positions in the battery manufacturing division. The fetal protection policy applies to work environments in which any current employee has recorded a blood lead level exceeding 30 μg/dl during the preceding year or in which the work site has yielded an air sample during the past year containing a lead level in excess of 30 μg per cubic meter.[1] The policy recites that women with childbearing capacity will neither be hired nor allowed to transfer into those jobs in which lead levels are defined as excessive.[2] A grandfather clause in Johnson's fetal protection policy permits fertile women who were assigned to high lead exposure positions at the time of the adoption of this policy to remain in those job assignments if they are able to maintain blood lead levels below 30 μg/dl. Those employees who are removed from positions because of excessive lead levels are transferred to another job in Johnson's employ without suffering either a loss of pay or benefits.

The major reason Johnson adopted its current fetal protection policy was the inability of the previous voluntary policy to achieve the desired purpose: protecting pregnant women and their unborn children from dangerous blood lead levels. Between 1979 and 1983, at least six Johnson Control employees in high lead exposure positions became pregnant while maintaining blood lead levels in excess of 30 micrograms. In addition, at least one of the babies born to this group of employees later recorded an elevated blood lead level. . . .

In announcing its new, more defined policy, Johnson Controls emphasized its continuing interest in the protection of employees and their families from occupational health hazards and was responding to the increased understanding of the risk of lead exposure that had developed in the five years since it established its former voluntary policy. . . .

. . . Medical research also shows that a risk to the unborn child's health is present at a much lower blood lead level than an adult. The ill effects to the unborn child can occur during the early stage of pregnancy, before the mother is aware that she is pregnant, and can continue throughout the pregnancy. . . .

Prior to adopting its updated fetal protection policy, Johnson seriously considered alternatives to the exclusion of women with childbearing capacity from high lead exposure positions, but after research and consultation with medical and scientific experts found itself unable to structure and implement any alternatives which would adequately protect the unborn child from the risks associated with excessive lead exposure. Johnson's experience demonstrated that the voluntary exclusion program was ineffective. To date neither Johnson nor any other battery manufacturer has been able to produce a lead free battery, or to utilize engineering research and technology to implement a system or procedure capable of reducing the lead exposure of its employees to acceptable levels for fertile women. Limitation of the fetal protection policy to women actually pregnant was found ineffective because there is the very definite possibility that lead exposure will occur between conception and the time the woman discovers her pregnancy. Such a limitation is further inadequate because reduction of blood lead levels following removal from a lead exposure area requires a significant length of time that frequently extends well into the pregnancy term. Limitation of the policy to women planning pregnancy also was not found to be a suitable alternative because of one of the exigencies of life, the frequency of unplanned or undetected pregnancies. Permitting fertile female employees to attempt to maintain a blood lead level below 30 μg/dl or utilizing the mean or median blood lead levels of current workers as a measure of whether a woman should be permitted in a position would also not effectively protect the unborn child. The reason these actions would be inadequate is that an employee's risk of high lead levels is usually greatest immediately after commencement of work in a high lead environment. . . .

II

Proper analysis of the Title VII issues this case presents requires a thorough understanding of the following fundamental question: Does lead pose a health risk to the offspring of Johnson's female employees? . . .

The record very clearly establishes that once lead is deposited in the mother's blood, it crosses the placenta and affects her unborn child. Because the fetus' blood system is nourished by the mother, the unborn child possesses approximately the same blood lead level as the mother. It is similarly undisputed that the unborn child "is medically judged to be at least as sensitive, and, indeed, is probably even more sensitive to lead than the young child. . . . "

The chief reason why an unborn child's lead exposure is of such great concern is that it has been medically established that lead attacks the fetus' central nervous system and retards cognitive development. . . .

Unlike physical birth defects, such as those associated with thalidomide, lead's sometimes subtle damaging effects may not fully manifest themselves until the child is diagnosed as having learning problems in a school setting some five to six years after birth. . . .

Probably the worst aspect of lead's influence upon an unborn child's future intellectual development is that its effects have frequently been found to be irreversible. Further, the most recent research suggests that the unborn child may be affected at lead levels previously believed safe. . . .

Lead exposure can also pose other physical threats to the unborn child such as reduction of the infant's birth weight, premature delivery, and stillbirth. . . . Lead may also affect the other vital fetal organs including, but not limited to, the liver and kidneys.

The danger resulting from lead exposure cannot simply be avoided through removing a pregnant woman from lead exposure promptly after the discovery of pregnancy. Dr. Chisholm, a recognized expert in the research field of treatment and prevention of lead poisoning in young children, observed that "excluding only women who are actually pregnant from work areas where there are elevated blood lead levels would not sufficiently protect the health and safety of the unborn child." . . . This is true because *lead continues to exert an effect upon the mother and her unborn child for a significant period of time after she has been removed from lead exposure.*

III

. . . We are convinced that the components of the business necessity defense the courts of appeals and the EEOC have utilized in fetal protection cases balance the interests of the employer, the employee and the unborn child in a manner consistent with Title VII. The requirement of a substantial health risk to the unborn child effectively distinguishes between the legitimate risk of harm to health and safety which Title VII permits employers to consider and the "[m]yths or purely habitual assumptions" that employers sometimes attempt to impermissibly utilize to support the exclusion of women from employment opportunities. Likewise, the requirement that the risk of harm to offspring be substantially confined to female employees means that a fetal protection policy applying only to women recognizes the basic physical fact of human reproduction, that only women are capable of bearing children. Finally, the employee's option of presenting less discriminatory alternatives to a fetal protection policy assures that these policies are only as restrictive as necessary to prevent the serious risk of harm to the unborn child. Accordingly, we agree with the Fourth Circuit, Eleventh Circuit and EEOC that the business necessity defense can be appropriately applied to fetal protection policy cases under Title VII. We now proceed to determine whether this defense can be utilized to sustain Johnson Controls' fetal protection policy.

IV

In *Wards Cove Packing Co. v. Atonio,* 109 S.Ct. 2115, 2125–26 (1989), the Supreme Court recently described the general policies underlying the business necessity defense that we utilize in considering Johnson Controls' fetal protection policy:

> "Though we have phrased the query differently in different cases, it is generally well-established that at the justification stage of . . . a disparate impact case, the dispositive issue is whether a challenged practice serves, in a significant way, the legitimate employment goals of the employer. The touchstone of this inquiry is a reasoned review of the employer's justification for his use of the challenged practice. A mere insubstantial justification in this regard will not suffice, because such a low standard of review would permit discrimination to be practiced through the use of spurious, seemingly neutral employment practices. At the same time, though, there is no requirement that the challenged practice be 'essential' or 'indispensable' to the employer's business for it to pass muster: this

degree of scrutiny would be almost impossible for most employers to meet, and would result in a host of evils. . . . "

*   *   *

A. Substantial Risk of Harm to the Unborn Child

Both the UAW and Johnson Controls agree on appeal that the significant evidence of risks to the health of the fetus contained in the record establishes a *substantial* health risk to the unborn child. The UAW in its brief admits that "it is clear that . . . substantial risk of harm to the fetus . . . has been established." UAW Brief at 33. Similarly, Johnson states that "[t]he evidence in the record on [substantial risk of harm to the fetus] is overwhelming." Johnson Controls Brief at 22. In light of the parties' agreement on the question of substantial risk of harm to the unborn child, this issue is not before this court on appeal.

Although the parties do not contest this question on appeal, the evidence in the record that we recounted in Section II, *supra*, conclusively supports the accepted medical and scientific finding that lead creates a substantial risk of harm to unborn children. In order to present the risk of harm necessary to sustain a fetal protection policy "it is not necessary to prove the existence of a general consensus on the [question of risk of harm to the unborn child] within the qualified scientific community. It suffices to show that within that community there is so considerable a body of opinion that significant risk exists . . . that an informed employer could not responsibly fail to act on the assumption that this opinion might be the accurate one." *Olin*, 697 F.2d at 1191. The overwhelming medical and scientific research data demonstrating a substantial risk to the unborn child from lead exposure, found in the record and set forth in Section II, *supra*, approaches a "general consensus within the qualified scientific community," and certainly "suffices to show that within that community there is [a] considerable body of opinion that significant risk exists." Accordingly, we are convinced that there is no genuine issue of material fact with respect to this component of Johnson Controls' business necessity defense.

B. Exposure Through a Single Sex

The UAW's efforts in this case have primarily been devoted toward negating the second element of Johnson's business necessity defense, that the risk of transmission of potentially harmful lead exposure to unborn children is substantially confined to fertile female employees. On this issue, as with the question of substantial risk of harm to the unborn child, "it is not necessary to prove the existence of a general consensus on the [issue] within the qualified scientific community." *Olin*, 697 F.2d at 1191.

In this case Johnson Controls' experts, without exception, testified that a male worker's exposure to lead at levels within the 50 $\mu g/dl$ maximum set forth in OSHA's current (1978) lead exposure guidelines did not pose a substantial risk of genetically transmitted harm from the male to the unborn child. Moreover, Johnson's experts took the position that because the data dealt exclusively with animals, the results of these studies were not scientifically established as being applicable to humans. In contrast, the UAW witnesses posited that animal studies had demonstrated that there was a possible risk of genetic damage to human offspring as a result of male lead exposure. The UAW witnesses attempt to bridge the wide chasm between the results of animal studies and a conclusion of genetic harm allegedly transmitted through the male human being with human studies merely establishing a correlation between male lead exposure and changes in sperm shape. It is interesting to note that the UAW has not presented any medical evidence in the record of any human study scientifically documenting genetic defects in human beings resulting from male lead exposure. It is this lack of convincing scientific data that the plaintiffs attempt to gloss over and cast aside in ignoring the differences between the effect of lead on the human and animal reproductive systems. . . .

This recognition of the physical differences between the human sexes creates a distinction between men and women that accords with our previous recognition that Title VII permits distinctions based upon the real sex-based differences between men and women, especially those related to child birth. As we observed in *Torres v. Wisconsin Dept. of Health and Human Social Services*, 859 F.2d 1523, 1527–28 (7th Cir.1988) (en banc):

> "'Myths and purely habitual assumptions about a woman's [or a man's] inability to perform certain kinds of work are no longer acceptable reasons for refusing to employ qualified individuals, or for paying them less.' *City of Los Angeles Department of Water and Power v. Manhart*, 435 U.S. 702, 707 (1978). On the other hand, there are real as well as fictional differences between men and women. *Id. For instance, the Supreme Court has never hesitated to recognize sex-based differences involving physiology, marriage, childbirth, or sexuality. See Michael M. v. Superior Court of Sonoma County*, 450 U.S. 464, 469 (1981) ('[T]his Court has consistently upheld statutes where the gender classification is not invidious, but rather realistically reflects the fact that the sexes are not similarly situated in certain circumstances.'); *id.* at 481 [101 S.Ct. at 1210] (Blackmun, J., concurring) ('The Constitution surely does not require a State to pretend that demonstrable differences between men and women do not really exist.')" . . .

C. Adequate But Less Discriminatory Alternatives

We are cognizant of the fact that Johnson's fetal protection policy might very well not have been sustainable had the UAW presented facts and reasoning sufficient for the trier of fact to conclude that "there are 'acceptable alternative policies or practices which would better accomplish the business purpose . . . [of protecting against the risk of harm], or accomplish equally well with a lesser differential . . . impact [between women and men workers].'" *Olin*, 697 F.2d at 1191 (quoting *Robinson v. Lorillard Corp.*, 444 F.2d 791, 798 (4th Cir.), *cert. dismissed*, 404 U.S. 1006 (1971)). . . . The UAW's failure to specifically articulate a less discriminatory alternative argument in the manner required in Federal Rules of Appellate Procedure 28 (a) (4) means that it has failed to adequately present this issue to this court.

Even were we to conclude that the UAW had presented this issue for appeal, we would be constrained to hold that the UAW failed to present facts sufficient for a trier of fact to conclude that less discriminatory alternatives would equally effectively achieve an employer's legitimate purpose of protecting unborn children from the substantial risk of harm lead exposure creates.

The above passage from *Wards Cove* makes clear (1) that the UAW bears the burden of presenting specific economically and technologically feasible alternatives to Johnson Controls' fetal protection policy; (2) that if the UAW presents such alternatives, the UAW also bears the burden of demonstrating that its proposed alternative policy is *"equally* effective [as Johnson Controls' fetal protection policy] in achieving [Johnson's] legitimate employment goals," *Wards Cove*, 109 S.Ct. at 2127 (emphasis added); and (3) that this inquiry is to be undertaken with the recognition that "'[f]actors such as the cost or other burdens of proposed alternative selection devices are relevant in determining whether they would be equally as effective as the challenged practices in serving the employer's legitimate business goals,'" *Id.* at 2127 (quoting *Watson v. Fort Worth Bank & Trust*, 108 S.Ct. 2777, 2790 (1988) (O'Connor, J.)), and that "'[c]ourts are generally less competent than employers to restructure business practices'. . . . "*Id.* (quoting *Furnco Construction Corp.*, 438 U.S. at 578). In our case the inquiry is terminated at the first stage. The UAW, in its briefs and argument, has failed to present even one specific alternative to Johnson's fetal protection policy, much less a demonstration of how any particular economically and technologically feasible alternative would effectively achieve Johnson's purpose of preventing the risk of fetal harm associated with the exposure to lead of fertile female employees. . . .

V

There is a reasonable basis in fact, grounded in medical and scientific research data, for concluding that Johnson Controls has met its burden of establishing that the fetal protection policy is reasonably necessary to industrial safety. Thus, the fetal protection policy should be recognized as establishing a bona fide occupational qualification protecting the policy against claims of sex discrimination. . . .

NOTES

1. These lead levels coincided with the Centers for Disease Control's standard in effect at that time which concluded that blood lead levels in excess of 30 μg/dl were excessive for children. (As will be noted later in this opinion, the Centers for Disease Control have since revised downward the acceptable blood lead levels for children). We note that, because of Johnson's concern for the mother and the unborn baby, the

lead levels Johnson established in its fetal protection policy are below the 50 μg/m3 airborne lead levels and 50 μg/100g blood lead levels permitted under OSHA's lead exposure regulations for all employees. 29 C.F.R. § 1910.1025 (c) (1) and (k) (1) (i) (D). While OSHA blood lead regulations utilized the measure of μg per 100 grams and Johnson Controls' standard uses the measure of μg per deciliter, the parties have treated these measures as equivalent and we shall also treat them in this manner.

2. The fetal protection policy defines women of childbearing capacity as: "All women except those whose inability to bear children is medically documented."

INTERNATIONAL UNION, UNITED AUTOMOBILE, AEROSPACE
AND AGRICULTURAL IMPLEMENT WORKERS OF AMERICA,
UAW, et al.,
Petitioners

v.

JOHNSON CONTROLS, INC.
No. 89–1215

SUPREME COURT OF THE UNITED STATES
Argued October 10, 1990
Decided March 20, 1991

ON WRIT OF CERTIORARI TO THE UNITED STATES
COURT OF APPEALS
FOR THE SEVENTH CIRCUIT

JUSTICE BLACKMUN delivered the opinion of the Court.

In this case we are concerned with an employer's gender-based fetal-protection policy. May an employer exclude a fertile female employee from certain jobs because of its concern for the health of the fetus the woman might conceive?

I

Respondent Johnson Controls, Inc., manufactures batteries. In the manufacturing process, the element lead is a primary ingredient. Occupational exposure to lead entails health risks, including the risk of harm to any fetus carried by a female employee.

Before the Civil Rights Act of 1964 became law, Johnson Controls did not employ any woman in a battery-manufacturing job. In June 1977, however, it announced its first official policy concerning its employment of women in lead-exposure work:

"[P]rotection of the health of the unborn child is the immediate and direct responsibility of the prospective parents. While the medical profession and the company can support them in the exercise of this responsibility, it cannot assume it for them without simultaneously infringing their rights as persons.

*   *   *

". . . since not all women who can become mothers wish to become mothers (or will become mothers), it would appear to be illegal discrimination to treat all who are capable of pregnancy as though they will become pregnant."

Consistent with that view, Johnson Controls "stopped short of excluding women capable of bearing children from lead exposure," but emphasized that a woman who expected to have a child should not choose a job in which she would have such exposure. The company also required a woman who wished to be considered for employment to sign a statement that she had been advised of the risk of having a child while she was exposed to lead. The statement informed the woman that although there was evidence "that women exposed to lead have a higher rate of abortion," this evidence was "not as clear . . . as the relationship between cigarette smoking and cancer," but that it was, "medically speaking, just good sense not to run that risk if you want children and do not want to expose the unborn child to risk, however small. . . . "

Five years later, in 1982, Johnson Controls shifted from a policy of warning to a policy of exclusion. Between 1979 and 1983, eight employees became pregnant while maintaining blood lead levels in excess of 30 micrograms per deciliter. This appeared to be the critical level noted by the Occupational Health and Safety Administration (OSHA) for a worker who was planning to have a family. The company responded by announcing a broad exclusion of women from jobs that exposed them to lead:

" . . . [I]t is [Johnson Controls'] policy that women who are pregnant or who are capable of bearing children will not be placed into jobs involving lead exposure or which could expose them to lead through the exercise of job bidding, bumping, transfer or promotion rights."

The policy defined "women . . . capable of bearing children" as "[a]ll women except those whose inability to bear children is medically documented." It further stated that an unacceptable work station was one where, "over the past year," an employee had recorded a blood lead level of more than 30 micrograms per deciliter or the work site had yielded an air sample containing a lead level in excess of 30 micrograms per cubic meter.

II

In April 1984, petitioners filed in the United States District Court for the Eastern District of Wisconsin a class action challenging Johnson Controls' fetal-protection policy as sex discrimination that violated Title VII of the Civil Rights Act of 1964, as amended. Among the individual plaintiffs were petitioners Mary Craig, who had chosen to be sterilized in order to avoid losing her job, Elsie Nason, a 50-year-old divorcee, who had suffered a loss in compensation when she was transferred out of a job where she was exposed to lead, and Donald Penney, who had been denied a request for a leave of absence for the purpose of lowering his lead level because he intended to become a father. Upon stipulation of the parties, the District Court certified a class consisting of "all past, present and future production and maintenance employees" in United Auto Workers bargaining units at nine of Johnson Controls' plants "who have been and continue to be affected by [the employer's] Fetal Protection Policy implemented in 1982."

The District Court granted summary judgment for defendant-respondent Johnson Controls. Applying a three-part business necessity defense derived from fetal-protection cases in the Courts of Appeals for the Fourth and Eleventh Circuits, the District Court concluded that while "there is a disagreement among the experts regarding the effect of lead on the fetus," the hazard to the fetus through exposure to lead was established by "a considerable body of opinion"; that although "[e]xpert opinion has been provided which holds that lead also affects the reproductive abilities of men and women . . . [and] that these effects are as great as the effects of exposure of the fetus . . . a great body of experts are of the opinion that the fetus is more vulnerable to levels of lead that would not affect adults"; and that petitioners had "failed to establish that there is an acceptable alternative policy which would protect the fetus." The court stated that, in view of this disposition of the business necessity defense, it did not "have to undertake a bona fide occupational qualification's (BFOQ) analysis."

The Court of Appeals for the Seventh Circuit, sitting en banc, affirmed the summary judgment by a 7-to-4 vote. The majority held that the proper standard for evaluating the fetal-protection policy was the defense of business necessity; that Johnson Controls was entitled to summary judgment under that defense; and that even if the proper standard was a BFOQ, Johnson Controls still was entitled to summary judgment.

The Court of Appeals first reviewed fetal-protection opinions from the Eleventh and Fourth Circuits. Those opinions established the three-step business necessity inquiry: whether there is a substantial health risk to the fetus; whether transmission of the hazard to the fetus occurs only through women; and whether there is a less discriminatory alternative equally capable of preventing the health hazard to the fetus. The Court of Appeals agreed with the Eleventh and Fourth Circuits that "the components of the business necessity defense the courts of appeals and the EEOC have utilized in fetal protection cases balance the interests of the employer, the employee and the unborn child in a manner consistent with Title VII." The court further noted that the burden of persuasion remained on the plaintiff in challenging a business necessity defense, and—unlike the Fourth and Eleventh Circuits—it thus imposed the burden on the plaintiffs for all three steps.

Applying this business necessity defense, the Court of Appeals ruled that Johnson Controls should prevail. Specifically, the court concluded that there was no genuine issue of material fact about the substantial health-risk factor because the parties agreed that there was a substantial risk to a fetus from lead exposure. The Court of Appeals also concluded that, unlike the evidence of risk to the fetus from the mother's exposure, the evidence of risk from the father's exposure, which petitioners presented, "is, at best, speculative and unconvincing." Finally, the court found that petitioners had waived the issue of less discriminatory alternatives by not adequately presenting it. It said that, in any event, petitioners had not produced evidence of less discriminatory alternatives in the District Court.

Having concluded that the business necessity defense was the appropriate framework and that Johnson Controls satisfied that standard, the court proceeded to discuss the BFOQ defense and concluded that Johnson Controls met that test, too. The en banc majority ruled that industrial safety is part of the essence of respondent's business, and that the fetal-protection policy is reasonably necessary to further that concern. The majority emphasized that, in view of the goal of protecting the unborn, "more is at stake" than simply an individual woman's decision to weigh and accept the risks of employment.

With its ruling, the Seventh Circuit became the first Court of Appeals to hold that a fetal-protection policy directed exclusively at women could qualify as a BFOQ. We granted certiorari to resolve the obvious conflict between the Fourth, Seventh, and Eleventh Circuits on this issue, and to address the important and difficult question whether an employer, seeking to protect potential fetuses, may discriminate against women just because of their ability to become pregnant.

III

The bias in Johnson Controls' policy is obvious. Fertile men, but not fertile women, are given a choice as to whether they wish to risk their reproductive health for a particular job. The Civil Rights Act of 1964, as amended, prohibits sex-based classifications in terms and conditions of employment, in hiring and discharging decisions, and in other employment decisions that adversely affect an employee's status. Respondent's fetal-protection policy explicitly discriminates against women on the basis of their sex. The policy excludes women with childbearing capacity from lead-exposed jobs and so creates a facial classification based on gender. Respondent assumes as much in its brief before this Court.

Nevertheless, the Court of Appeals assumed, as did the two appellate courts who already had confronted the issue, that sex-specific fetal-protection policies do not involve facial discrimination. These courts analyzed the policies as though they were facially neutral, and had only a discriminatory effect upon the employment of women. Consequently, the courts looked to see if each employer in question had established that its policy was justified as a business necessity. The business necessity standard is more lenient for the employer than the statutory BFOQ defense. The Court of Appeals here went one step further and invoked the burden-shifting framework set forth in Wards Cove Packing Co. v. Atonio, thus requiring petitioners to bear the burden of persuasion on all questions. The court assumed that because the asserted reason for the sex-based exclusion (protecting women's unconceived offspring) was ostensibly benign, the policy was not sex-based discrimination. That assumption, however, was incorrect.

First, Johnson Controls' policy classifies on the basis of gender and childbearing capacity, rather than fertility alone. Respondent does not seek to protect the unconceived children of all its employees. Despite evidence in the record about the debilitating effect of lead exposure on the male reproductive system, Johnson Controls is concerned only with the harms that may befall the unborn offspring of its female employees. Johnson Controls' policy is facially discriminatory because it requires only a female employee to produce proof that she is not capable of reproducing.

Our conclusion is bolstered by the Pregnancy Discrimination Act of 1978 (PDA), in which Congress explicitly provided that, for purposes of Title VII, discrimination "on the basis of sex" includes discrimination "because of or on the basis of pregnancy, childbirth, or related medical conditions." "The Pregnancy Discrimination Act has now made clear that, for all Title VII purposes, discrimination based on a woman's pregnancy is, on its face, discrimination because of her sex." In its use of the words "capable of bearing children" in the 1982 policy statement as the criterion for exclusion, Johnson Controls explicitly classifies on the basis of potential for pregnancy. Under the PDA, such a classification must be regarded, for Title VII purposes, in the same light as explicit sex discrimination. Respondent has chosen to treat all its female employees as potentially pregnant; that choice evinces discrimination on the basis of sex.

We conclude that Johnson Controls' policy is not neutral because it does not apply to the reproductive capacity of the company's male employees in the same way as it applies to that of the females. Moreover, the absence of a malevolent motive does not convert a facially discriminatory policy into a neutral policy with a discriminatory effect. Whether an employment practice involves disparate treatment through explicit facial discrimination does not depend on why the employer discriminates but rather on the explicit terms of the discrimination. The beneficence of an employer's purpose does not undermine the conclusion that an explicit gender-based policy is sex discrimination and thus may be defended only as a BFOQ.

IV

Under S 703(e) (1) of Title VII, an employer may discriminate on the basis of "religion, sex, or national origin in those certain instances where religion, sex, or national origin is a bona fide occupational qualification reasonably necessary to the normal operation of that particular business or enterprise." We therefore turn to the question whether Johnson Controls' fetal-protection policy is one of those "certain instances" that come within the BFOQ exception.

The BFOQ defense is written narrowly, and this Court has read it narrowly. Our emphasis on the restrictive scope of the BFOQ defense is grounded on both the language and the legislative history of S 703.

The wording of the BFOQ defense contains several terms of restriction that indicate that the exception reaches only special situations. The statute thus limits the situations in which discrimination is permissible to "certain instances" where sex discrimination is "reasonably necessary" to the "normal operation" of the "particular" business. Each one of these terms— certain, normal, particular—prevents the use of general subjective standards and favors an objective, verifiable requirement. But the most telling term is "occupational"; this indicates that these objective, verifiable requirements must concern job-related skills and aptitudes.

The concurrence defines "occupational" as meaning related to a job. According to the concurrence, any discriminatory requirement imposed by an employer is "job-related" simply because the employer has chosen to make the requirement a condition of employment. In effect, the concurrence argues that sterility may be an occupational qualification for women because Johnson Controls has chosen to require it. This reading of "occupational" renders the word mere surplusage. "Qualification" by itself would encompass an employer's idiosyncratic requirements. By modifying "qualification" with "occupational," Congress narrowed the term to qualifications that affect an employee's ability to do the job.

Johnson Controls argues that its fetal-protection policy falls within the so-called safety exception to the BFOQ. Our cases have stressed that discrimination on the basis of sex because of safety concerns is allowed only in narrow circumstances. In Dothard v. Rawlinson, this Court indicated that danger to a woman herself does not justify discrimination. We there allowed the employer to hire only male guards in contact areas of maximum-security male penitentiaries only because more was at stake than the "individual woman's decision to weigh and accept the risks of employment." We found sex to be a BFOQ inasmuch as the employment of a female guard would create real risks of safety to others if violence broke out because the guard was a woman. Sex discrimination was tolerated because sex was related to the guard's ability to do the job—maintaining prison security. We also required in Dothard a high correlation between sex and ability to perform job functions and refused to allow employers to use sex as a proxy for strength although it might be a fairly accurate one.

Similarly, some courts have approved airlines' layoffs of pregnant flight attendants at different points during the first five months of pregnancy on the ground that the employer's policy was necessary to ensure the safety of passengers. In two of these cases, the courts pointedly indicated that fetal, as opposed to passenger, safety was best left to the mother.

We stressed that in order to qualify as BFOQ, a job qualification must relate to the "essence" or to the "central mission of the employer's business."

The concurrence ignores the "essence of the business" test and so concludes that "the safety to fetuses in carrying out the duties of battery manufacturing is as much a legitimate concern as is safety to third parties in guarding prisons (Dothard) or flying airplanes (Criswell)." By limiting its discussion to cost and safety concerns and rejecting the "essence of the business" test that our case law has established, the concurrence seeks to expand what is now the narrow BFOQ defense. Third-party safety considerations properly entered into the BFOQ analysis in Dothard and Criswell because they went to the core of the employee's job performance. Moreover, that performance involved the central purpose of the enterprise. See Dothard ("The essence of a correctional counselor's job is to maintain prison security") and Criswell (the central mission of the airline's business is the safe transportation of its passengers). The concurrence attempts to transform this case into one of customer safety. The unconceived fetuses of Johnson Controls' female employees, however, are neither customers nor third parties whose safety is essential to the business of battery manufacturing. No one can disregard the possibility of injury to future children; the BFOQ, however, is not so broad that it transforms this deep social concern into an essential aspect of battery making.

Our case law, therefore, makes clear that the safety exception is limited to instances in which sex or pregnancy actually interferes with the employee's ability to perform the job. . . .

In other words, women as capable of doing their jobs as their male counterparts may not be forced to choose between having a child and having a job.

We conclude that the language of both the BFOQ provision and the PDA which amended it, as well as the legislative history and the case law, prohibit an employer from discriminating against a woman because of her capacity to become pregnant unless her reproductive potential prevents her from performing the duties of her job. We reiterate our holdings in Criswell and Dothard that an employer must direct its concerns about a woman's ability to perform her job safely and efficiently to those aspects of the woman's job-related activities that fall within the "essence" of the particular business.

V

We have no difficulty concluding that Johnson Controls cannot establish a BFOQ. Fertile women, as far as appears in the record, participate in the manufacture of batteries as efficiently as anyone else. Johnson Controls' professed moral and ethical concerns about the welfare of the next generation do not suffice to establish a BFOQ of female sterility. Decisions about the welfare of future children must be left to the parents who conceive, bear, support, and raise them rather than to the employers who hire those parents. Congress has mandated this choice through Title VII, as amended by the Pregnancy Discrimination Act. Johnson Controls has attempted to exclude women because of their reproductive capacity. Title VII and the PDA simply do not allow a woman's dismissal because of her failure to submit to sterilization. Nor can concerns about the welfare of the next generation be considered a part of the "essence" of Johnson Controls' business. Judge Easterbrook in this case pertinently observed: "It is word play to say that 'the job' at Johnson [Controls] is to make batteries without risk to fetuses in the same way 'the job' at Western Air Lines is to fly planes without crashing."

Even on this sparse record, it is apparent that Johnson Controls is concerned about only a small minority of women. Of the eight pregnancies reported among the female employees, it has not been shown that any of the babies have birth defects or other abnormalities. The record does not reveal the birth rate for Johnson Controls' female workers but national statistics show that approximately nine percent of all fertile women become pregnant each year. The birthrate drops to two percent for blue collar workers over age 30. Johnson Controls' fear of prenatal injury, no matter how sincere, does not begin to show that substantially all of its fertile women employees are incapable of doing their jobs.

VI

A word about tort liability and the increased cost of fertile women in the workplace is perhaps necessary. One of the dissenting judges in this case expressed concern about an employer's tort liability and concluded that liability for a potential injury to a fetus is a social cost that Title VII does not require a company to ignore. It is correct to say that Title VII does not prevent the employer from having a conscience. The statute, however, does prevent sex-specific fetal-protection policies. These two aspects of Title VII do not conflict.

More than 40 States currently recognize a right to recover for a prenatal injury based either on negligence or wrongful death. According to Johnson Controls, however, the company complies with the lead standard developed by OSHA and warns its female employees about the damaging effects of lead. It is worth noting that OSHA gave the problem of lead lengthy consideration and concluded that "there is no basis whatsoever for the claim that women of childbearing age should be excluded from the workplace in order to protect the fetus or the course of pregnancy." Instead, OSHA established a series of mandatory protections which, taken together, "should effectively minimize any risk to the fetus and newborn child." Without negligence, it would be difficult for a court to find liability on the part of the employer. If, under general tort principles, Title VII bans sex-specific fetal-protection policies, the employer fully informs the woman of the risk, and the employer has not acted negligently, the basis for holding an employer liable seems remote at best.

The tort-liability argument reduces to two equally unpersuasive propositions. First, Johnson Controls attempts to solve the problem of reproductive health hazards by resorting to exclusionary policy. Title VII plainly forbids illegal sex discrimination as a method of diverting attention from an employer's obligation to police the workplace. Second, the spectre of an award or damages reflects a fear that hiring fertile women will cost more. The extra cost of employing members of one sex, however, does not provide an affirmative Title VII defense for a discriminatory refusal to hire members of that gender. Indeed, in passing the PDA, Congress considered at length the considerable cost of providing equal treatment of pregnancy and related conditions, but made the "decision to forbid special treatment of pregnancy despite the social costs associated therewith."

We, of course, are not presented with, nor do we decide, a case in which costs would be so prohibitive as to threaten the survival of the employer's business. We merely reiterate our prior holdings that the incremental cost of hiring women cannot justify discriminating against them.

VII

Our holding today that Title VII, as so amended, forbids sex-specific fetal-protection policies is neither remarkable nor unprecedented. Concern for a woman's existing or potential offspring historically has been the excuse for denying women equal employment opportunities. See, e.g., Muller v. Oregon, 208 U.S. 412 (1908). Congress in the PDA prohibited discrimination on the basis of a woman's ability to become pregnant. We do no more than hold that the Pregnancy Discrimination Act means what it says.

It is no more appropriate for the courts than it is for individual employers to decide whether a woman's reproductive role is more important to herself and her family than her economic role. Congress has left this choice to the woman as hers to make.

The judgment of the Court of Appeals is reversed and the case is remanded for further proceedings consistent with this opinion.

It is so ordered.

*   *   *

JUSTICE WHITE, with whom THE CHIEF JUSTICE and JUSTICE KENNEDY join, concurring in part and concurring in the judgment.

The Court properly holds that Johnson Controls' fetal protection policy overtly discriminates against women and thus is prohibited by Title VII unless it falls within the bona fide occupational qualification (BFOQ) exception, set forth at 42 U.S.C. S 2000e-2(e). The Court erroneously holds, however, that the BFOQ defense is so narrow that it could never justify a sex-specific fetal protection policy. I nevertheless concur in the judgment of reversal because on the record before us summary judgment in favor of Johnson Controls was improperly entered by the District Court and affirmed by the Court of Appeals.

I

In evaluating the scope of the BFOQ defense, the proper starting point is the language of the statute. Title VII forbids discrimination on the basis of sex, except "in those certain instances where . . . sex . . . is a bona fide occupational qualification reasonably necessary to the normal operation of that particular business or enterprise." For the fetal protection policy involved in this case to be a BFOQ, therefore, the policy must be "reasonably necessary" to the "normal operation" of making batteries, which is Johnson Controls' "particular business." Although that is a difficult standard to satisfy, nothing in the statute's language indicates that it could never support a sex-specific fetal protection policy.

On the contrary, a fetal protection policy would be justified under the terms of the statute if, for example, an employer could show that exclusion of women from certain jobs was reasonably necessary to avoid substantial tort liability. Common sense tells us that it is part of the normal operation of business concerns to avoid causing injury to third parties, as well as to employees, if for no other reason than to avoid tort liability and its substantial costs. This possibility of tort liability is not hypothetical; every State currently allows children born alive to recover in tort for prenatal injuries caused by third parties, and an increasing number of courts have recognized a right to recover even for prenatal injuries caused by torts committed prior to conception.

The Court dismisses the possibility of tort liability by no more than speculating that if "Title VII bans sex-specific fetal-protection policies, the employer fully informs the woman of the risk, and the employer has not acted negligently, the basis for holding an employer liable seems remote at best." Such speculation will be small comfort to employers. First, it is far from clear that compliance with Title VII will pre-empt state tort liability, and the Court offers no support for that proposition. Second, although warnings may preclude claims by injured employees, they will not preclude claims by injured children because the general rule is that parents cannot waive causes of action on behalf of their children, and the parents' negligence will not be imputed to the children. Finally, although state tort liability for prenatal injuries generally requires negligence, it will be difficult for employers to determine in advance what will constitute negligence. Compliance with OSHA standards, for example, has been held not to be a defense to state tort or criminal liability. Moreover, it is possible that employers will be held strictly liable, if, for example, their manufacturing process is considered "abnormally dangerous."

Relying on Los Angeles Dept. of Water and Power v. Manhart, 435 U.S. 702 (1978), the Court contends that tort liability cannot justify a fetal protection policy because the extra costs of hiring women is not a defense under Title VII. This contention misrepresents our decision in Manhart. There, we held that a requirement that female employees contribute more than male employees to a pension fund, in order to reflect the greater longevity of women, constituted discrimination against women under Title VII because it treated them as a class rather than as individuals. We did not in that case address in any detail the nature of the BFOQ defense, and we certainly did not hold that cost was irrelevant to the BFOQ analysis. Rather, we merely stated in a footnote that "there has been no showing that sex distinctions are reasonably necessary to the normal operation of the Department's retirement plan." We further noted that although Title VII does not contain a "cost-justification defense comparable to the affirmative defense available in a price discrimination suit," "no defense based on the total cost of employing men and women was attempted in this case."

Prior decisions construing the BFOQ defense confirm that the defense is broad enough to include considerations of cost and safety of the sort that could form the basis for an employer's adoption of a fetal protection policy. In Dothard v. Rawlinson, 433 U.S. 321 (1977), the Court held that being male was a BFOQ for "contact" guard positions in Alabama's maximum-security male penitentiaries. The Court first took note of the actual conditions of the prison environment: "In a prison system where violence is the order of the day, where inmate access to guards is facilitated by dormitory living arrangements, where every institution is understaffed, and where a substantial portion of the inmate population is composed of sex offenders mixed at random with other prisoners, there are few visible deterrents to inmate assaults on women custodians." The Court also stressed that "[m]ore [was] at stake" than a risk to individual female employees: "The likelihood that inmates would assault a woman because she was a woman would pose a real threat not only to the victim of the assault but also to the basic control of the penitentiary and protection of its inmates and other security personnel." Under those circumstances, the Court observed that "it would be an oversimplification to characterize [the exclusion of women] as an exercise in 'romantic paternalism.'"

We revisited the BFOQ defense in Western Air Lines, Inc. v. Criswell, 472 U.S. 400 (1985), this time in the context of the Age Discrimination in Employment Act of 1967 (ADEA). There, we endorsed the two-part inquiry for evaluating a BFOQ defense used by the Fifth Circuit Court of Appeals in Usery v. Tamiami Trail Tours, Inc., 531 F. 2d 224 (1976). First, the job qualification must not be "so peripheral to the central mission of the employer's business" that no discrimination could be "reasonably necessary to the normal operation of the particular business." Although safety is not such a peripheral concern, the inquiry "adjusts to the safety factor . . . [t]he greater the safety factor, measured by the likelihood of harm and the probable severity of that harm in case of an accident, the more stringent may be the job qualifications. . . . " Second, the employer must show either that all or substantially all persons excluded "would be unable to perform safely and efficiently the duties of the job involved," or that it is "impossible or highly impractical" to deal with them on an individual basis. We further observed that this inquiry properly takes into account an employer's interest in safety—"[w]hen an employer establishes that a job qualification has been carefully formulated to respond to documented concerns for public safety, it will not be overly burdensome to persuade a trier of fact that the qualification is 'reasonably necessary' to safe operation of the business."

Dothard and Criswell make clear that avoidance of the substantial safety risks to third parties is inherently part of both an employee's ability to perform a job and an employer's "normal operation" of its business. Indeed, in both cases, the Court approved the statement that an employer could establish a BFOQ defense by showing that "all or substantially all women would be unable to perform safely and efficiently the duties of the job involved." The Court's statement in this case that "the safety exception is limited to instances in which sex or pregnancy actually interferes with the employee's ability to perform the job," therefore adds no support to its conclusion that a fetal protection policy could never be justified as a BFOQ. On the facts of this case, for example, protecting fetal safety while carrying out the duties of battery manufacturing is as much a legitimate concern as is safety to third parties in guarding prisons (Dothard) or flying airplanes (Criswell).

Dothard and Criswell also confirm that costs are relevant in determining whether a discriminatory policy is reasonably necessary for the normal operation of a business. In Dothard, the safety problem that justified exclusion of women from the prison guard positions was largely a result of inadequate staff and facilities. If the cost of employing women could not be considered, the employer there should have been required to hire more staff and restructure the prison environment rather than exclude women. Similarly, in Criswell the airline could have been required to hire more pilots and install expensive monitoring devices rather than discriminate against older employees. The BFOQ statute, however, reflects "Congress' unwillingness to require employers to change the very nature of their operations."

In enacting the BFOQ standard, "Congress did not ignore the public interest in safety." The Court's narrow interpretation of the BFOQ defense in this case, however, means that an employer cannot exclude even pregnant women from an environment highly toxic to their fetuses. It is foolish to think that Congress intended such a result, and neither the language of the BFOQ exception nor our cases requires it. . . .

SECTION D

Parental Leave

The Family and Medical Leave Act of 1987:
Pro and Con

STATEMENT BY
HON. PATRICIA SCHROEDER
(D-Colo.)

I am pleased to be here today to open this oversight hearing on parental leave. I would like to thank the Chairman for extending an invitation to me to speak to the growing need for a national family policy that offers families flexible solutions to the growing problems they face when balancing work and family responsibilities.

I speak today not only as a sponsor of The Family and Medical Leave Act, but also as someone with personal experience: I practice what I preach. I have 18 staff employees, nine in Denver and nine in Washington. Over the last two years I have had one senior staffer on parental leave, one on an extended medical leave, and have granted leave for two separate adoptions. All four leaves were for staff in my D.C. office alone.

Pregnancy, serious illness, and adoption are a workplace reality that all employers face today. Thirty years ago men comprised 70 percent of the labor force. Not so today. Women make up 44 percent of the labor force and are the fastest growing segment of American workers. Between 1947 and 1985, the number of women in the labor force increased by 178 percent, while for men, the number rose only 47 percent. By the 21st Century, women are expected to make up almost one-half of the work force.

Editors' note: This section contains testimony presented before various committees of Congress by proponents and critics of the Family and Medical Leave Act of 1987. Although the act has been revised slightly since 1987, the arguments for and against it have not changed. President Bush vetoed this legislation several times, most recently in September 1992, in the midst of a reelection campaign focusing on "family values."

The real news isn't that women are working; it is that they continue to do so in record numbers after they have children. Sixty percent of mothers with school-age children or younger are in the work force.

America has become a society in which everyone is expected to work—including women with young children. In the 1960s and 70s a paid job became an important symbol of self-worth and personal independence. In the 1980s, work continues to be the way most adults identify themselves; for most of us, work is the central organizing principle of our lives. But the truth is that most women work for economic reasons. Millions of families depend on women's earnings. Over two-thirds of working women are either heads of households or have a spouse earning under $15,000 annually.

The dramatic demographic changes that have transformed the workplace have also had a profound effect on the American family. In the 1950s, the so-called "golden age of the family," 2 out of 3 families fit the "classic" model of a father as breadwinner, and a mother at home as homemaker. Today less than 10 percent of families fit this description.

Unfortunately, many of society's institutions and policies are out of sync with today's reality. Personnel policies were designed during an era when over 70 percent of the work force was male. As a result, the revolutionary demographic changes of the last thirty years have placed a tremendous strain on families.

Here are just a few statistics that demonstrate this gap:

- Sixty percent of America's working women today receive no maternity related benefits during or after pregnancy; current law requires only that maternity-related medical leave be treated in the same way as other temporary disability leave.
- Only one-half of large employers offer unpaid job-protected parental leave for women after childbirth.
- And, paternity leave for fathers is generally limited to a few days.

No wonder families have called upon the federal government to help close the gap between outdated employment practices and the needs of today's new diverse workforce.

The question is: How long will corporate leaders and business owners ignore the new realities of the American work force and the American family? In particular, how much longer will they undermine their own productivity by expecting today's workers to fit yesterday's personnel policies?

You will undoubtedly hear today from those in the business community who oppose legislative efforts to close the gap between reality and practice. They have already established a substantial legislative record in numerous hearings over the past two years. Representative Clay has graciously included business representatives at every hearing before his Subcommittee on Labor-Management Relations, even those like the National Federation of Independent Businesses whose membership is almost 90 percent exempt from our bill.

At every turn, their testimony shows them to be the scions of gloom and doom predictions that a federal parental leave law will shut down American business, reduce our competitiveness, price small business out of existence, and restrict an employer's right to flexibility.

I would like to respond to a few of these concerns.

First, let me say that the business community is as diverse today as it ever has been. Many businesses have led the way on parental leave. U.S. West from my own District not only testified in favor of the "concept" of parental leave, but has also endorsed Rep. Clay's and my bill. I have also received letters from small business owners in my District who are behind me 100 percent. The thing that I hear from these business owners, and others, is that parental leave works. Parental leave policies save employers the cost of hiring and training new employees. Most of all these policies help attract the best and the brightest and retain a valued and trusted work force.

- One survey of large business found that 87 percent of employers reroute work rather than hire new employees or use temporaries.
- Another found that small business offered parental leave after a period of medical leave at about the same rate as large employers.

Second, the U.S. Chamber of Commerce cost figures on parental leave would leave any CEO to wonder. After revising their $16.2 billion cost figure downward to a mere $2.6 billion, the GAO took a look at these new numbers and found them to be exaggerated. Testifying before the Senate, the GAO called the economic assumptions faulty:

- not everyone who was entitled to take leave would;
- most employees would not take the full amount of time available to them;
- men were less likely to take any leave;
- and many employers would reroute work, rather than hire a temporary replacement.

Third, many in the business community seem to ignore that parental leave is not without a cost to those who take it. Employees go on UNPAID leave and must manage with less at a time when expenses are particularly high.

Fourth, business has always managed to live with labor standards, standards that many like the Chamber of Commerce and others have fought since the 19th Century: child labor laws, minimum wage, maximum hours and overtime pay, equal pay, Social Security, Medicare and the Pregnancy Discrimination Act, many of which they now support!

Fifth, employers call for the flexibility to offer employees what they want through cafeteria-style benefit packages. But the best estimates seem to indicate that less than 7 percent of all employers offer their employees such plans.

And finally, America is alone among advanced industrialized countries in not offering its workers parental leave. Over 100 countries, including the industrialized nations, guarantee workers some form of job-protected, partially-paid maternity related benefits. By 1986, nine western European Community countries provided paid parental leave to both men and women.

These countries are our competitors. Surely we can match them in protecting our families.

In closing, there is one final area of opposition I would like to lay to rest. Parental leave is neither a beltway issue nor a yuppie bill.

Public opinion polls from the *Wall St. Journal* to the *Houston Post* reflect the majority view among Americans: families and parents should be able to take unpaid leave to care for newborn or adopted children, or to care for a seriously ill child or parent. The Princeton-based Opinion Research Poll found that the majority of the public—regardless of sex, age, or employment status—supports parental leave legislation.

- Three-fourths of the public and *more than eight working women in ten say they favor the Family and Medical Leave Act of 1987.*

The reason: legislation is necessary to help provide families with stability and economic security.

If polls don't persuade you, then the efforts in almost 30 states across the country to pass some form of parental leave legislation should. Four states (MN, RI, OR, and CT) in the past few months have already passed and signed into law, bills to provide parents time-off to care for their families.

At least twelve states already guarantee maternity-related leaves. State economies have not fallen apart; moreover, there appears to be no greater burden to employers to comply with these laws than any others.

Yet while state efforts to pass new parental leave legislation grow, and demonstrate a national consensus for helping families harmonize their work and family responsibilities, a variety of state bills would, nevertheless, lead to a patchwork policy that would be cumbersome for business large and small alike.

It is time for a sound, well-thought out federal response to the needs of today's family. We need legislation that provides families with flexibility—and encourages a pro-family work place that demonstrates American respect for its work force. To do so, we must establish a minimum amount of protection for all American families irrespective of where they live. Setting such basic new standards is a fitting and proper role for government.

Families have done enough coping. They have proved—beyond any doubt—their strength to weather change. But when a family crisis threatens its economic security, then the government must work to bring public policy in line with the family's needs. The continued health of today's family depends on the family's ability to provide for its own well-being. This isn't government intervention; it's common sense.

STATEMENT BY
ELEANOR HOLMES NORTON

Professor of Law, Georgetown University
Formerly Chair of the Equal Employment Opportunity Commission

I am pleased to be here to testify in favor of H.R. 925.

Today I am representing a broad range of women's and civil rights groups and trade unions, 31 in number, a list of which is appended to my statement.

To the organizations in whose behalf I appear, the FMLA is a major priority because it would give a much needed, concrete benefit to working women and men, including federal workers, and through them to hard-pressed American families.

This is historic legislation. In a country in which most legislation aids individuals, H.R. 925 is notable for the way it strengthens the support system of the family.

Because working women continue to bear disproportionate responsibility for the nuts and bolts of family life, H.R. 925 may be viewed as feminist legislation. It is that and it is much more.

It is perhaps the first piece of overtly family legislation.

It is difficult to think of legislation passed in the last 30 years to benefit women that has had a greater impact on the wellbeing of the American family than Title VII of the 1964 Civil Rights Act, which it was my great privilege to administer, and other legislation guaranteeing equal employment opportunity to women. Yet none of that legislation was as explicitly for the benefit of the family as the FMLA.

This legislation, as much as any you have had before you, makes clear the inescapable link between benefits for working women and benefits for the entire family.

The disarray in much of family life in the United States today has proceeded from the economy's demand that women work, coupled with the society's failure to accommodate its institutions to this economic reality.

As women's labor force participation skyrocketed, other societies moved quickly to provide support systems for families with two working parents. Several European countries, including France, Italy and Britain, instituted some form of national maternity insurance for working women prior to World War I. They and many other countries have maintained and expanded these policies through the economic vicissitudes of this century.

Today, 75 countries have enacted laws providing for maternity benefits, including paid leave before and after childbirth, and free health and medical care for pregnancy and childbirth. Many have explicit family policies that go far beyond maternity leave and encompass child care provision, housing and health services to support families.

The pervasiveness of such legislation throughout the world makes all the more remarkable this country's failure to acknowledge, through legislation, the necessity to accommodate work and family needs.

Working parents are lucky if they can find safe, healthy, affordable care for their children while they are at work. Working parents are lucky if they do not lose their jobs when they are unable to work because of their own serious medical conditions, and luckier still if during such absences they receive any sort of wage replacement with which to put food on the table.

They are lucky if they do not lose their jobs when they want to take time off from work to be with a newborn or a newly adopted child, or to care for their parents or other adult relatives who are seriously ill. And very few are lucky enough to receive any sort of wages during such family leave.

None of this should be a matter of luck in an advanced 20th century democracy that claims to care about family life. . . .

As a general matter, without structures in place to help American families deal with the need for both parents to be breadwinners, the burden has been absorbed disproportionately by working women.

According to a Department of Health and Human Services estimate, 2.2 million people, predominantly women, cared for 1.2 million frail elderly people in 1982. Approximately one million of them were employed for some time during the care-giving experience. And this, of course, is in addition to the more familiar figures for mothers with children who are young.

Reliance on healthier family members is often the most cost-efficient and desirable way to care for the elderly. But this care cannot be rendered with mirrors. If no accommodation to this need is made on the job, the result will almost surely be an increasing shift of care to high cost, professional institutions, much of it at taxpayers' expense.

We note here a major deficiency of H.R. 925, its failure to provide leave for employees to care for elderly spouses or close family members, other than parents. Even the OPM guidelines define family member more broadly than does H.R. 925, although their limitation to dependents is also troublesome.

We urge the subcommittee to expand the definition of family leave to rectify this omission.

The most immediate cost, the greatest hardship of the legislative vacuum is that working women and men not infrequently lose their jobs when they need to take family or medical leave.

For the single parent, usually a woman, losing her job when she is unable to work during a time of serious health condition, or because one of her children is seriously ill, can often mean borrowing beyond prudence, going on welfare, or destitution for herself and her family.

Indeed, it is hard to understand how single parents, who have no choice but to work to support their families, have survived under the present system.

For this highly vulnerable group, whose numbers have exploded, a job guarantee for periods when they or their children have serious health conditions is urgently necessary. The high rates of single parenthood among minority families and of labor force participation by minority single mothers make job-guaranteed leave especially critical for minorities.

Even for the two parent family, job-guaranteed leave is essential to continued family and financial stability. In these families, too, most women work.

If it is serious if the mother loses her job, it is catastrophic if the father loses his job. They both work because they cannot live on the father's full-time income alone. How, then, are they to live only on the mother's full time salary, which is on the average about 63 percent of the man's salary, or worse, on her part time salary?

At the very least, if the father in such families is temporarily unable to work, his job too should be restored after he recovers.

Beyond such immediate costs, the long range costs of our society's failure to accommodate work and family responsibilities are of such scope that we can only guess at their magnitude.

We know of the awesome physical and emotional drain placed on working parents who must balance work and family responsibilities without any societal help. The experts speak eloquently to that, especially of the impact on new mothers who must worry about their job security and about having time to bond with their infants and guide them as they grow.

But we do not yet know what the consequences of this stress will be on our children's emotional and physical health, and on society-at-large in the next generation.

We know that people lose their jobs and suffer major economic hardship when their employers refuse to provide family or medical leave. But we do not know what the long term effect of this will be on the structure of unemployment or on the Social Security system.

We know of the high incidence of single parenthood and of poverty, especially among blacks and other minority groups, and of a new generation of children growing up poor, often perpetuating a generational cycle of poor health, reduced opportunities, dependency and despair. But the consequences for the country's economic and social stability can only be feared.

The Family and Medical Leave Act takes only the most modest step toward mitigating hardships on families when work, family and health priorities conflict temporarily.

H.R. 925 protects against only the most egregious financial disaster that families may suffer at times of medical or family need, job loss. The law would mandate no salary replacement.

When the proposed act is compared to the national family and medical leave policies in place in many industrialized and Third World countries, we must blush at just how modest it truly is.

In most of these countries, paid maternity leave is routine. Some countries are moving toward maternity leave and to grant paid paternity leave, as well.

In urging passage of this legislation, we are not seeking the 38 weeks of

90 percent paid leave, with up to 12 more unpaid weeks, that new mothers get in Sweden, or the 20 weeks of maternity leave at 80 percent of earnings available in Italy, or the 16 weeks at 60 percent of earnings available in Japan, or the fully paid 45 days available in the Philippines.

We are seeking for American families the bare minimum, and it is simply not arguable that they deserve and need at least that.

Our chief regret about this legislation is that fiscal and political realities have forced us to accept a step that is in this way decades behind comparable countries and the needs of American families.

For this reason, we strongly support the bill's establishment of a Commission on Paid Family and Medical Leave to make recommendations about means of funding paid leaves, perhaps through some form of insurance.

We can only express our amazement that even the bare-bones requirements of this legislation have provoked opposition, when there is no evidence that, with zero population growth, temporary leaves will increase the incidence of people taking family or medical leaves, and when the legislation has already been compromised to exempt those small companies which might claim hardship.

Allegations of loss in productivity or other financial hardship are not only unsupported, the opposite may well be the case. As large companies which offer even paid leaves have already found, these leaves would preserve employer investment in experienced workers who return after temporary leaves.

In the past, business has never hesitated to come forward with concrete evidence of hardship. It has offered no credible evidence of hardship as to this legislation because it incorporates a virtually no cost minimum labor standard.

Employers either will give the work to co-workers for the brief time that will usually be involved, or obtain temporary workers from the highly qualified pool of temps that are available today.

One of the fastest growing industries are companies providing high quality temporaries. For their own purposes, of course, businesses have used such temporaries for years, when they need workers to perform contracts they have won to do additional work, for example, or when someone leaves and cannot immediately be replaced.

This legislation would require no changes in business-as-usual. . . .

STATEMENT BY JOHN J. SWEENEY
International President,
Service Employees International Union, AFL-CIO

It's a national shame that the richest country in the world still has workers who must confront an impossible choice—the choice between their jobs or care for their newborns or sick family members. For many workers who fall ill there is no choice at all.

I fully support H.R. 925, which provides up to 18 weeks of unpaid parental leave and up to 26 weeks for a personal illness. It's an important step forward in legislative efforts to strengthen and nurture the family. Over the long haul, a wider range of support structures for the American family will be needed. While our report called for more time off, H.R. 925 seeks to strike a balance between the public interest and legitimate business concerns.

There is a large grassroots constituency who need and will support this bill. The policies of many employers, particularly those in the large service sector, have simply not kept up with the vastly changing workforce.

An unpaid family leave policy is a minimum standard, a right not a "benefit." It will not stifle employers' efforts to provide other family benefits.

Unpaid parental leave will not bankrupt American businesses. To the contrary, H.R. 925 is good business and good for business.

Today's family is in crisis. The heart of the crisis for working families, I believe, is contained in one incredible fact—a shocking fact.

The fact is that even as the number of wage earners per family has gone up over the past 10 years, family income has gone down. Today's family needs at least two paychecks just to maintain yesterday's standard of living. According to the joint economic committee, real family income would have declined 18 percent since 1973 without the influx of mothers into the workforce. In short, parents work because they must.

As a result, the "typical" American family of the past has virtually disappeared. Only one in 10 families consists of a husband who is the sole breadwinner and a stay-at-home wife who tends exclusively to the home and kids.

The new norm is the dual-earner family in which both the husband and wife, father and mother, work outside of the home. At the same time, the number of single-parent families has skyrocketed—now 16 percent of all families.

To support the family, women are in the paid workforce in record numbers. Over half of all women work outside the home, accounting for 44 percent of the workforce. In 10 years, working women will outnumber working men. An even more startling trend is the influx of mothers with young children into the labor force. In 1985, 54 percent of the women with children under six were working—four times the 1950 level. And half of all mothers with infants are in the workforce.

A majority of women in the labor market means working parents—men and women—need support structures for coping with the dual demands of work and family.

We've heard a lot of talk that employers are already meeting this need in the workplace; that this legislation is redundant. The facts say otherwise. For example:

Only 40 percent of working women in small and medium size firms are covered by disability plans that deal with the time of childbirth and recovery; compared to 95 percent of large businesses.

A recent study by the U.S. Chamber of Commerce found that only 50 percent of 700 firms surveyed had either a parental or disability leave plan. Of these, only 31 percent routinely granted eight weeks or more leave.

Among the firms granting unpaid leave in the survey, a majority (57 percent) required employees to pay (at the group rate) for continuation of their health benefits at this critical time.

And only 33 percent of the total firms surveyed keep workers' jobs open, throwing into question whether these are genuine leave policies to start with.

My members also tell me that there's an overwhelming need out there not being met. The sad reality is that many businesses are lagging far behind the changing times.

Let's look at private industry where we represent nearly half a million people in predominantly low-wage jobs—clericals, healthcare workers in hospitals and nursing homes, custodial workers and others. Their experience is that the needs of working parents are too often ignored.

Nearly all of our members working in private industry get some disability leave, averaging three-to-four months, so they are doing better than the national statistics. However, there is much variation—down to as little as 15 days. Only about half of the contracts call for continued benefits. Worse, only about 40 percent guarantee a return to the same job.

For these highly vulnerable workers, many of whom earn under $20,000 a year, a job-protected leave for new parents and for personal illness would help to relieve the emotional and financial strains put on these workers.

Many of these people face the fear of losing their job when they decide to have children or become ill.

A minimum parental leave standard is one of the basic guarantees on which every worker and their family should be able to count.

There has been a lot of discussion about how a family leave policy fits in with other family-oriented workplace policies. Let me tell you how our union has approached this set of needs as we bargain for ways to better the lives of working families.

We've found a natural progression in the working family benefits won at the bargaining table. Some form of pregnancy leave is always first, that's because it's a minimum standard, not a benefit, and it's important to make a distinction. As a next step, locals try to bargain for sick leave to cover family emergencies.

Next, we bargain for flexible scheduling or reduced hours to allow workers to tailor their hours to conform with the demands of family life.

So far, we have been talking about relatively low cost items—unpaid leaves and flexible hours.

Our members, like many working parents, cite the high expense, inaccessibility and low quality of child care in survey after survey. Day care costs between $1,500 and $12,000 a year. But its cost makes it perhaps the most difficult item to address at the bargaining table.

An unpaid family and disability leave policy—the most basic standard—does not hamper employers' flexibility to provide other working family benefits. Still, business groups persist in claiming that it will stifle the trend towards flexible benefit plans, which they view as the answer to the dual-earner family.

As these "flexible" plans become more prevalent, several points should be kept in mind.

First, we've not run into unpaid family leave as one of the benefit options. It's really the most fundamental protection for working families and it's not costly. No one should have to choose between being a breadwinner and being a caring family member.

Second, health cost control, not the family, is the main rationale for flexible plans. In their first year, 43 percent of the plans included higher health insurance deductibles, 26 percent higher worker contributions for family care, and 16 percent higher premium co-pays for employee coverage. That kind of cost-shifting is not "flexibility" and it's anti-family.

Third, flexible benefit plans are not often found in the service sector which employs the "new workforce" in large numbers.

And finally, the most frequent working family option in these plans is a wage reduction plan (found in 66 percent of flexible plans). Simply put, employees are allowed to put some of their pre-tax wages into an individual account to pay for childcare. This benefit doesn't cost the employer anything, except a small administrative fee.

Low income workers may not benefit at all. Prior to the 1986 tax reforms, workers earning less than $20,000 in adjusted gross income fared better by taking the Federal childcare tax credit. Working families need more than salary reduction plans; they need employer contributions to make the benefit real.

By flexibility, businesses could also be referring to their ability to replace full-time workers who leave with permanent "contingent" workers who work fewer hours at lower pay and no benefits. A marginal workforce, while cutting costs in the short-run, undermines productivity in the long run. Efforts should be made to improve the benefits of part-timers and not to make these workers more "disposable." That's why I'm happy to see that this bill covers these workers.

In short, this bill will not stifle business flexibility. It doesn't hamper business efforts to design flexible benefit plans. But they are not a panacea for the working family; employers must be willing to spend money, and they are not a substitute for a job-protected family leave policy.

Neither the Service Employees International Union nor other proponents of H.R. 925 have ever argued that unpaid family leave is cost-free. However, we strongly challenge business predictions of an imminent financial calamity.

Companies already go to great lengths to reduce job turnover—which currently averages about 15 percent in non-manufacturing. In the healthcare industry with its predominantly female workforce, turnover runs closer to 20 percent. For nursing homes, it averages 40 percent or more. A family leave policy could serve to lower these excessive turnover rates.

High turnover of women employees is also a short-sighted labor market policy.

In general, juggling work and babies takes a toll on productivity. Fortune's recent survey of 400 working parents found that nearly 70 percent of mothers suffer from stress. Some 41 percent of parents lose an average one day's work in three months and 10 percent lose five days or more to tend to a sick child or other family matters. The survey found that childcare is the single strongest predictor of absenteeism and workers' job performance.

This suggests that a better avenue for employers to use to improve their "competitiveness" in the world economy is to design family-oriented benefits. The rewards can be substantial. Flexitime has been shown to raise productivity by as much as 50 percent; and on-site childcare centers to cut absenteeism in half or more.

You might wonder why employers have been slow to adopt family benefits which both strengthen the family and enhance efficiency. Perhaps employers don't understand yet how family-oriented policies fit in with the bottom-line. The other explanation is that companies still haven't learned to measure productivity.

In short, H.R. 925 is an important step forward in legislative efforts to strengthen and nurture families. It's time to end the risk of job loss for all the 34 million employed women of prime child-bearing age if they want some time to care for their newborns. This national family leave policy will benefit workers and also the U.S. economy by contributing to high productivity. At the same time, the cost to employers will be negligible. For these reasons, we urge prompt passage of H.R. 925. . . .

STATEMENT BY PHYLLIS SCHLAFLY
President, Eagle Forum

The proposed Family and Medical Leave bill, popularly known as the Mandated Parental Leave Bill, doesn't have anything to do with maternity or with the disability connected with childbirth. We already have a Pregnancy Anti-Discrimination Law. Two-thirds of U.S. companies grant maternity leave and, in most companies, maternity medical costs are included in the health and medical benefits plan.

The proposed Mandated Parental Leave bill is a proposal to force employers to skew their employees' benefit package in favor of one narrow group of workers at the expense of others. The proposed bill is highly discriminatory in favor of highly-paid, two-earner yuppie couples who, as a practical matter, would be the only ones able to benefit.

The proposed bill is highly discriminatory against every other type of employee: the men whose wives are fulltime homemakers and mothers, the single parents and all low-income workers who could not afford to take off unpaid time, women over child-bearing age, all singles, self-employed persons, women who work at home, and all temporary workers including the one who replaces the one who receives the parental leave.

The proposed bill is highly discriminatory in the burden it imposes on some types of employers. Its costly mandate would fall more heavily on businesses which employ a majority of women since, as a practical matter, more women would receive the benefits.

The proposed bill would discriminate against small businesses because the costs and loss of productivity that result from training and substituting a temporary worker are more costly when a small business has only one person in a given job category rather than a pool of workers who can be transferred.

Other costs of the bill include carrying double health and medical benefits during the period of the leave, for both the employee on leave and the temporary worker who takes her place, and the cost of the unemployment insurance for the temporary worker who will be dismissed when the employee on leave returns to work.

The 13 million new jobs in the private sector in the last five years have been created by small businesses. Yet many small companies are struggling at the margin to stay in business and to meet foreign competition. Any newly-mandated cost will have to come at the expense of something else.

The proposed bill is a foolish approach to the problem of job security. In today's world, competitiveness is the name of the game, and a business that is not competitive simply cannot provide jobs for anyone. The most important job benefit anyone can have is a job that pays a wage.

The advocates of the proposed Mandated Parental Leave bill try to shame us by saying that other countries in the world have mandated parental leave. That's right, many other countries have made the mistake of mandating costly benefits, and they have mandated their citizens right out of jobs. Europe has had a net loss of a million jobs in the last couple of years, and unemployment is much higher than in the United States.

The proposed mandated parental leave bill would be the wrong way to go even if it didn't cost anything. The whole trend of employee benefits in the country today is toward a "cafeteria" system of benefits.

Since employee benefits add an additional 33 to 40 percent of "goodies" over and above wages, it makes a real difference to workers which benefits they get. People's lifestyles and needs differ. The cafeteria approach allows each employee to choose the benefits that best suit his or her needs. To mandate a particular benefit desired by only one small group is unfair to others.

There isn't even any evidence that the unpaid parental leave mandated in this bill is the specific benefit that every working mother would choose. Mothers of small children might prefer other benefits, such as a more inclusive health and medical plan, a pension plan, more paid vacation or holidays, a work day that is one hour shorter, a four-day work week, flexible time schedules, job sharing, or child-care facilities or vouchers.

The tremendous array of other employee benefits in the American economy has grown up voluntarily, either from employers' decisions or collective bargaining. These include paid holidays and vacations, health and medical plans, and pension plans. There is no evidence that the job benefits available in America would be as high as they are today if government had straitjacketed business by mandating the benefits chosen by the posturing politicians.

The advocates of the mandated parental leave bill complain that we have no national child care policy. On the contrary, we do. Our successful policy is to let employers and employees work out their own solutions. That's the system that works the best and fairest for all.

Do we believe that the Federal Government should be concerned about the financial bind that Americans are in today when it comes to the costs of having and raising children? You bet we do. We believe that Congress has an obligation, first of all, to eliminate the current discrimination that exists against some kinds of children and their mothers and in favor of other kinds of children and their mothers.

While de facto discrimination against various groups still exists in practice, in some areas and against some minorities, de jure discrimination (specified in the law) has been pretty much eliminated. When challenged, legal discrimination on the basis of race, creed, color, or sex can hardly ever stand up in court, and it's hard to find a lawmaker at the Congressional or State level who has the temerity to propose a discriminatory bill.

There is one class of Americans, however, that still is openly and massively discriminated against. This class of Americans is made up of the 16 million fulltime homemakers. The discrimination is most blatant in the income tax law. Nobody really defends the discriminatory provisions. Public officials and media spokesmen just evade the issue by not talking about it.

The income tax law discriminates against the mothers who take care of their own children, and in favor of the mothers who pay someone else to take care of their children. It's so outrageous that one wonders how the lawmakers had the nerve to pass something so unfair.

Mandated parental leave, the current trendy issue promoted by the feminists, is a plan to give one more preferential benefit to the employed mother which, as a practical matter, cannot be used by the fulltime mother.

Mandated parental leave is another discriminatory benefit that would force the traditional family, which provides its own child care on a lower average income, to subsidize the two-earner couples who have a higher average income. Mandated parental leave should be rejected first of all because it is a new discrimination against a class of mothers already savagely discriminated against.

STATEMENT BY VIRGINIA B. LAMP
Labor Relations Attorney,
United States Chamber of Commerce

The American business community today faces new challenges of achieving a balance between work and family life, between increasing our productivity and meeting the human resource needs of any particular work force and between enhancing our international competitiveness in world markets and placing new social responsibilities and financial burdens on employers by government at all levels. Flexibility is the key for businesses facing pressure from international competition. Employers simply cannot afford to pass new costs on to consumers to absorb increased costs of doing business.

The business community faces serious competitive challenges—both internationally and domestically. One of the most serious—and disturbing—comes from the Congress. In the 100th Congress, there are numerous proposals that would mandate employers to provide new benefits. "Let's simply require the employer to provide this benefit" seems to be the commonly accepted approach to any real or perceived social need. Unfortunately, this approach undermines a successful, voluntary, private-sector employee benefit system that is already responsive and flexible toward the needs and capabilities of both employers and employees.

Our concern with federally mandated benefits generally, and this legislation specifically, is not the worthiness of the benefit, but rather the inflexible, costly and perhaps counterproductive Federal mandate.

On its surface, mandating unpaid, job-protected leave for disability or the care of a child or parent appears to be a simple way to guarantee equal treatment, while according special priority to family responsibilities. However, the American business community views such an approach as simplistic, when one stops to consider the complexity and diversity of work-family problems.

If parental "bonding" or nurturing after the birth or adoption of a child is the desired goal, it will not result from government coercion. Federal legislation simply cannot make us "bond" with our children. Legislation will not create responsible, caring parents. Ultimately, family responsibility is individual responsibility. Balancing a family and career is a challenge each of us confronts at the most personal level. One working parent may desire time off to bond after birth or adoption; another parent may prefer dental benefits for teenagers, or more flexible work schedules to avoid having a "latch key" child, or vouchers for day-care or sick-child services, or increased pay, or a host of other "family" benefits. Each of us knows of parents who spend a great deal of time with their children, but yet, appear to do a poor job of parenting. Many hard-working people, on the other hand, have become successful parents without generous leave periods.

Any single mandated benefit is likely to lead to a reduction in other—sometimes more preferred—employee benefits. A mandated benefit, regardless of how worthy, does not increase the employee benefits "pie." It merely divides it in a manner dictated by a powerful special interest group or a number of special interest groups. If one employee benefit is required, then another benefit—perhaps one more desired by the employees of a particular company—must be eliminated or reduced so as to offset the costs associated with the new mandated benefit. On the average, employers spend nearly 40 percent of their payroll on employee benefits.

Parental leave (even unpaid leave) imposes a substantial cost on employers. As a result, other benefits or compensation must be reduced necessarily in order to absorb the cost.

A growing, healthy economy has led over the years to an extensive system of employer-sponsored employee benefits. These benefits not only include the obvious—vacation time, sick leave, Social Security, workers' compensation and unemployment insurance—but also benefits ranging from group health care and life insurance coverage (both of which are provided to 99 percent of the workers in large and medium-size firms) to the pensions and retirement plans offered to 75 percent of that work force. Of course, the rate of coverage among smaller firms is less extensive, often because of their inability to afford to provide even these core benefits. The adverse impact of H.R. 925 on small business must be considered by Congress.

Not every employer can afford to give the benefits that a large company gives to its employees. For large businesses, this legislation is redundant since studies indicate that 95 percent of the Fortune 1,500 companies already provide parental and disability leave. However, the dynamic, growing sector of our economy is dominated by small businesses struggling to survive. These small businesses will be the prime targets of H.R. 925. During 1981 and 1982, large companies laid off one million workers; small businesses hired 2.6 million. In 1983 and 1984, large companies created about 1.5 million new jobs; small businesses created nearly four million. It would be ironic if the mandated parental leave legislation winds up destroying the very jobs that have helped to assimilate second-income wage earners into the labor force—the very jobs that the sponsors of H.R. 925 seek to protect. The small business impact of such a law is what led more than 1,800 small business delegates to petition the "1986 White House Conference on Small Business" to make opposition to this legislation a priority issue. It is noteworthy that over 600 of those delegates were women business owners. Opposition to this legislation became the Number Two priority (second only to the liability crisis) of the Conference.

The most "pro-family" policy is one that encourages job creation, not one that discourages it. In addition, advocates of a new Federal intervention in employee benefits have ignored employers' efforts to accommodate employees with conflicting family responsibilities.

Firms cited multiple reasons for offering parental leave programs. "Recruitment and retention" was the single most cited reason, and "union negotiation" was the least cited factor.

Furthermore, private employers increasingly are changing their policies and environments to meet the needs of working parents. A range of solutions exists for the needs of working parents in any one workplace. Any one solution is not necessarily the best solution. Employers and employees can assess their needs and their capability of providing particular benefits. Then the appropriate, affordable employer response can be instituted. The policies that best address the family needs could include such benefits or programs as: parental leave, day-care centers, sick-child vouchers, information and referral programs, "flex time," job sharing, part-time work, home-based work, compressed work schedules, drug and alcohol abuse assistance, flexible benefits, or increased pay. Obviously, employers are going to be restricted by cost considerations in tailoring specific responses.

Maternity leave is frequently a state-granted leave in other industrialized countries. Interestingly enough, those European countries with the most generous maternity leaves are the same nations with the highest rates of unemployment for women of child-bearing age. And, few countries can boast of a higher percentage of women in its work force than the U.S. Younger women, in particular, are making tremendous strides in climbing corporate ladders in this country and entering into fields such as law, medicine, and engineering. In those countries with generous maternity leaves, women are remaining, for the most part, in menial low-skilled jobs or are unemployed. In addition, those women in agriculture or domestic work (the two most prevalent women-dominated professions in the world) are oftentimes outside the scope of coverage for these state benefits.

But, more important, in comparing the U.S. to other nations, is the fact that our free market approach to business has encouraged job creation, economic growth, and entrepreneurial activity—the likes of which are virtually nonexistent in countries where business is over-regulated by government-mandated benefits. Our government and the American people—more than other nations—have recognized the energy, vitality and flexibility of the private sector.

The contention that "unpaid leave" would not cost anything is not true. The costs are substantial.

The cost of H.R. 925 as currently written (excluding eldercare costs), would result in a cost to the economy and to employers of $27.2 billion. This does not include an offset for benefits that currently are being furnished by employers. The largest costs incurred by employers would be the cost of hiring temporary replacements for workers who are on leave and the lower productivity that would result from replacing regular employees with temporary replacements. The $27.2 billion would add 1.4 percent to the nation's employment costs and about 0.7 percent to the general price level of goods and services sold in order to pay for these benefits.

Expansion of the benefits to include full pay for workers on parental leave and short-term disability benefits could raise the cost to employers to $75.6 billion. This would raise the wage bill for the nation by 3.7 percent.

The treatment of the "parental" and the "temporary disability" parts of H.R. 925 as insurable risks—treated the same way as we treat unemployment and using the same tax base as the unemployment insurance tax base—would have resulted in a more than doubling of the unemployment insurance tax on employers in 1984 (from an average rate of 2.8 percent to an average rate of 5.7 percent). The cost of the "child care" provision of H.R. 925 could add as much as 1.7 percent to the tax rate and the cost of the "disability" part of H.R. 925 would add 1.2 percent to the payroll tax. The total cost would be reduced by the cost of temporary disability benefits that currently are being provided by employers.

The Pregnancy Discrimination Act of 1978 already requires all employers to treat pregnancy and childbirth the same as any other temporary medical condition. If an employer permits employees to take leave with or without pay or guarantees the job upon return for any short-term disability (i.e., broken leg or hepatitis), the same type of leave must be available to pregnant employees. Equality of treatment for working women is preferable to mandating special treatment for women with family responsibilities—the latter being what California law and most other nations most often provide. Although technically H.R. 925 applies to men and women, we all realize that women have tended to assume the vast majority of family responsibilities. This stereotype may have an adverse impact on working women if this legislation becomes law.

Mandated benefits stifle the trend toward flexible benefits. "Flexible benefits" or "cafeteria plans" are the current trend that works well for both the employer and the employee. With benefit costs currently near 40 percent of payroll, employers simply cannot afford to keep expanding their employee benefits "pie." Employers initially may hesitate to offer child-care services as a fixed benefit because only a small proportion of employees would use the services each year. But, an employer can add child-care services to a flexible benefit package without concern over its seeming unfairness to those other employees who do not need such a benefit. A variety of benefits may be offered to employees—anywhere from two benefits to several. We encourage employers to provide these benefits, to the extent that the work force desires them and employers can afford them. They may include: childcare services; educational assistance; relocation assistance; physical fitness programs; additional vacation days; health insurance; life insurance; retirement benefits.

The business community is responding to the changing demography of our work force. Flexible benefits and innovative solutions to the demands of working parents are being developed and are preferable to rigid, inflexible, costly, and probably counterproductive Federal mandates.

Ultimately, a healthy economy—fostering job creation and a cooperative labor-management environment—can offer the basic financial and personal support that families must have to survive.

Our bottom line is laws cannot make us good parents, and government involvement may hurt as much as—or more than—it helps in this case.

If Congress is intent on legislating in this area, the Chamber would recommend commissioning extensive studies of other nations' experiences with mandated leave—how often men take such leave, any adverse impact in terms of employment opportunities for women of child-bearing age, any adverse impact on small business activity, and any adverse impact on job creation statistics, as well as on other leading economic indicators.

STATEMENT BY ELIZABETH KEPLEY

Director, Legislative Affairs,
Concerned Women for America

First, we believe that the issue of parental leave is a worthy one and must be addressed. It will affect both married and single women. As more women face the decision of entering the workforce or staying at home, the relationships within the roles of parenting, the family unit as a whole, and the business world will become more closely intertwined. We wish to see viable, creative solutions implemented to meet the needs of both the housewife and the working woman and to strengthen the roles of the parent, the child, and the employer.

Concerned Women for America advocates the strengthening of the family unit, but we believe that responsible parenting can not be federally mandated. It is the personal responsibility of parents to fulfill this duty. The original intent of the proposed legislation was to encourage parents to bond with their newborn infants, but the actual effects of the legislation are quite different. Parent-child bonding occurs at the onset of the infant's life; yet the bill allows parents to take their leave anytime within two years of the birth.

Studies recognize the importance of maternal-child relationships, of bonding and subsequent attachment. However, a child's separation from its parents after only 18 weeks of intimate bonding can actually be a traumatic, counterproductive experience.

The bill will not prevent maternal deprivation nor will it provide the necessary time for the bonding process to occur. Maternal deprivation is a general term used to describe a child living at home who is deprived of his mother's loving care.

Secondly, we are concerned that parental leave legislation will hurt the traditional and the poor family. The latest U.S. Census Bureau statistics reports that the median income for families with the wife at home is $23,562. It is $34,560 for families with both parents in the labor force. The redistributive effects caused by possible passage of this legislation are regressive. Due to mandated benefits, the employee benefit package will favor those families that can afford to take the unpaid leave. It will be detrimental for those families who cannot afford to take the leave. They will pay for a federally mandated benefit that they can not use and lose other more beneficial benefit packages. . . .

Finally, the ramifications of this legislation will hurt the women which it is trying to help—those women, married and single, who wish to progress in the workplace. Although discrimination is against the law in America, we believe that mandated parental leave policies will discourage businesses from hiring women of child-bearing age. Companies know that women are far more likely to take parental leave than men.

How will this mandated policy effect single women? or women who are members of the two-person family unit comprised of a husband and wife? It will result in those women and men who have no need of a parental leave policy paying for the child care of their fellow employees. There is an old adage which says that one must rob from Peter to pay Paul. These employees will have fewer or smaller benefit packages offered to them as employers struggle to cover the cost for parental leave.

In conclusion, businesses must be encouraged in their search for creative solutions to providing parental leave policies that will meet the differing variety of employee needs. Women have achieved so much in our recent history thanks to our vibrant free enterprise system. It would be tragic if passage of mandatory parental leave stunts these advances.

COMMENTS AND
RECOMMENDED READINGS

Much debate about discrimination and affirmative action results from a simple failure to clarify key terms. A useful strategy is to begin by distinguishing the following ideas: (1) *discrimination:* treating individuals differently on the basis of a characteristic that some possess and others do not, typically benefiting the one group or disadvantaging the other; (2) *affirmative action:* enlarging an applicant pool (e.g., in hiring or promotions) so as to include members of groups previously excluded on the basis of a characteristic irrelevant to the available position, without altering the criteria already in place for selecting among applicants; (3) *preferential treatment:* selecting one candidate for a position over another who is otherwise equal, solely because the first candidate is a member of a group previously excluded on irrelevant grounds, while retaining the same criteria of selection; (4) *reverse discrimination:* selecting one candidate over another who is more qualified than the first, as evaluated by the criteria in place, because the first is a member of a previously excluded group; and (5) *revision of standards:* changing the criteria of selection, typically so as to eliminate a bias that benefits members of one group (identified by an irrelevant characteristic) or disadvantages members of another.

After the terms are clarified, the next step is to consider arguments for and against these policies. For example, because affirmative action (as defined) is noncontroversial, one can begin with arguments in favor of affirmative action, such as fairness, increased efficiency, and promotion of diversity. Then one can ask whether these same arguments also support such policies as preferential treatment or reverse discrimination, or which new arguments have to be added, if these policies are to be justified.

The philosophical essays in *Equality and Preferential Treatment,* edited by Marshall Cohen, et al. (Princeton: Princeton Univ. Press, 1977), are especially helpful for sorting out arguments. Also, a lucid, balanced summary of arguments is offered by Robert Fullinwider in *The Reverse Discrimination Controversy* (Totowa: Rowman and Littlefield, 1980). For a historical overview of economic discrimination against women, see Claudia Goldin, *Understanding the Gender Gap: An Economic History of American Women* (New York: Oxford Univ. Press, 1990), and Barbara R. Bergmann, *The Economic Emergence of Women* (New York: Basic Books, 1986). An analysis of the Sears case as an occasion for thinking through "equality versus difference" is presented by Ruth Milkman, "Women's History and the Sears Case," *Feminist Studies* 12:2 (1986), pp. 375–400. See also the comment by Joan Wallach Scott, "The Sears

Case," in *Gender and the Politics of History* (New York: Columbia Univ. Press, 1988). The claim that discrimination is not the most important factor in explaining women's economic inequality is central to Victor R. Fuchs's *Women's Quest for Economic Equality* (Cambridge: Harvard Univ. Press, 1988).

A special twist in the history of sex discrimination is the value placed by many progressive women, such as Florence Kelley, on protective legislation (see discussion in the introduction to Part IV). Indeed, in the first wave of the women's movement, much of the opposition to the Equal Rights Amendment came from progressive women, who saw it as undermining the economic gains women had made in the early part of the twentieth century. This debate continues in new forms today. On the inadequacy of egalitarian arguments for dealing with the inherent differences or asymmetries between women and men, see Elizabeth H. Wolgast, *Equality and the Rights of Women* (Ithaca: Cornell Univ. Press, 1980). For a defense of egalitarianism with a special animus against protectionist thinking, see Wendy Kaminer, *A Fearful Freedom: Women's Flight from Equality* (Reading: Addison-Wesley, 1990).

It is also helpful to begin with clarifications when considering the policy issue of comparable worth. Here the question is: What are comparable worth schemes designed to do? Consider these possibilities: (1) to redress past sex discrimination (specifically, sex segregation in jobs) that is "allowed" by a free market in labor; (2) to correct for market failures (by which many women end up with low wages), so as to achieve the outcomes a well-ordered market would have generated on its own; (3) to ensure that workers are paid what they deserve, where that is determined independently of the market; (4) to increase women's salaries, by redistributing income from men to women; or (5) to decrease the gap between the lowest-paid and the highest-paid workers. These objectives are not necessarily incompatible, but they are very different from one another and all of them appear in the literature on comparable worth. Needless to say, one's assessment of relevant arguments will depend on what one thinks the point is. For a careful, fair-minded review of the arguments on both sides, leading to a rejection of comparable worth schemes, see Ellen Frankel Paul, *Equity and Gender: The Comparable Worth Debate* (New Brunswick: Transaction Publ., 1989). Another clear summary of the arguments is offered by Michael Evan Gold in *A Dialogue on Comparable Worth* (Ithaca: ILR Press, 1983). For the view that comparable worth is likely to have only a slight effect on the discrepancy between male and female earnings, and that affirmative action programs and civil rights litigation are more promising avenues of change, see Henry J. Aaron and Cameran M. Lougy, *The Comparable Worth Controversy* (Washington, D.C.: Brookings Institution, 1986).

To set the debate on fetal protection policies in historical context, see the legal cases on pregnant women in the workplace collected in *The Constitutional Rights of Women: Cases in Law and Social Change*, 2nd edition (Madison: Univ. of Wisconsin Press, 1988) by Leslie Friedman Goldstein. Most of the journal literature on fetal protection is by lawyers. A typical essay is

Martha Field's "Controlling the Woman to Protect the Fetus," *Law, Medicine and Health Care* 17:2 (Summer 1989), pp. 114–129.

It is frequently observed that the United States is the only industrial country in the world lacking a formal policy of parental leave from employment. Sweden, for example, allows both men and women nine months of leave at 90 percent of their earnings and an additional nine months at further reduced pay. Yet it is not sufficient simply to point out that European countries provide such benefits. One has to ask what criteria should be employed in evaluating outcomes. For example, are parental leave policies warranted even if they result in higher unemployment or in lower productivity? For an excellent collection of essays, see Edward F. Zigler and Meryl Frank, eds., *The Parental Leave Crisis* (New Haven: Yale Univ. Press, 1988). See also Janet Shibley Hyde and Marilyn J. Essex, eds., *Parental Leave and Child Care: Setting a Research and Policy Agenda* (Philadelphia: Temple Univ. Press, 1991).

For a comparative perspective on the issues in Part IV, see Hilda Kahne and Janet Giele, *Continuing Struggle: Women's Work and Lives in Modernizing and Industrial Countries* (Boulder: Westview Press, 1992).

PART V

SOCIAL SERVICES

INTRODUCTION

Among the legacies of the modern United States from its nineteenth-century past is the ethic of self-reliance. Alexis de Tocqueville captured the spirit of it when he identified the tendency of Americans to detach themselves from their fellow citizens, draw into their own intimate circle of family and friends, and leave others to fend for themselves. These individualists, as he called them, cultivated a way of life that depended on receiving nothing from anyone else and owing nothing to anyone else. "They acquire the habit of always considering themselves as standing alone, and they are apt to imagine that their whole destiny is in their own hands."[1] Accordingly, a major component of the ethic of self-reliance is the obligation of citizens to avoid being a burden to others. Citizens are expected to support themselves economically, or, if they are dependent, they should depend only upon someone who has voluntarily assumed the obligation of support. Advocates of self-reliance suppose, of course, that each person can readily fashion a life without being involuntarily dependent or indebted to others. Thoreau's retreat into the Concord woods is paradigmatic, though, curiously, he relied on local women to cook his meals and wash his clothes.

Tocqueville regarded individualism as a pathological growth in democratic societies, not only the United States, and he focused his attention on forms of association that could combat its effects. Yet individualism in Tocqueville's sense has enjoyed a resurgence in recent years, as it does periodically in American history, and has generated a concern just the opposite of his. Some worry that the ethic of self-reliance has eroded—or been undermined—in the twentieth century, principally as a consequence of government income-support programs. Those who make this claim usually have welfare entitlements particularly in mind, though if the point is valid it applies also to the array of tax breaks, subsidies, and loan guarantees that have made the survival of various businesses, industries, and professions a matter of government policy. This concern does not prevent Americans from reaching out to those in need, but typically forms of assistance are packaged in such a way as to reaffirm the ethic of self-reliance. The recent bipartisan convergence on "workfare"—illustrated in "California Welfare Reform" (Section A)—is perhaps the most telling case.

251

American ambivalence about dependence is sustained by what many observers regard as a paradox inherent in government support programs. In itself, assisting people in need is a benevolent activity and certainly to be encouraged. The ethic of self-reliance insists only that it should be temporary and should serve the needy in achieving (or recovering) their independence. The paradox is that the benevolent act itself may create or foster dependency. This is partly a matter of individual psychology, partly of institutional dynamics. A standing government program that offers continuing assistance creates incentives for individuals to avoid seeking routes out of dependency. If the program also sets conditions on receipt of benefits—which it does in part to prevent arbitrary decisions by administrators—it forces recipients to conform their conduct to the stipulated conditions. As a result, the exigencies of living engender habits of subordination to petty authorities. In the worst cases, illustrated by "The Hearing of Mrs. G." (Section A), government assistance becomes a rite of humiliation and degradation.

Because the ethic of self-reliance implies that the dominant aim of social services should be to nurture freestanding, autonomous individuals who control their own destiny, it corrodes sympathy for individuals in circumstances of intractable dependency. These may be physical (e.g., in cases of disability or addiction), or financial (e.g., in economic dislocation), or emotional (e.g., in domestic partnerships characterized by violence). The ethic of self-reliance offers little guidance regarding our obligations in these situations. Worse, the very predicaments people are in—for example, a battered woman loving a man who relates only through denigration and abuse, or a drug-dependent pregnant woman wanting to give birth to a healthy child but continuing to ingest cocaine—remain opaque. (See "Cocaine Mothers" in Section B and "Battered Women's Refuges" in Section C.)

The ambivalence and opacity carry over to motivational assumptions underlying policy choices. For example, on the question of how to respond to drug-dependent pregnant women, there is widespread support for a punitive approach. The idea is that threat of criminal sanctions for failure to meet a minimum duty of care to their newborn children will deter women from using drugs during pregnancy. Yet this approach is plausible only on the assumption that addicts act voluntarily and calculate rationally the risks of their habit to themselves and others. At the same time, motivational assumptions of the alternative, therapeutic approach may be equally problematic. Thus it is said that threat of criminal prosecution will only deter drug-dependent women from seeking the prenatal medical care they and their newborns need, placing them at even greater risk. But it may well be that the women would welcome such a "threat" because given the inability to handle their problem on their own, it would provide a ready excuse for placing themselves in the hands of caretakers, especially if they know that the usual sentence is a mandatory drug treatment program followed by probation.

Of course recognizing the limits of self-reliance should not obscure the worth of autonomy as an ideal or the circumstances in which overcoming dependency is the proper goal of public policy. In this regard, the "Dollar-a-Day" program for teenage mothers (Section B) is of special interest. Viewed narrowly, the program is an experiment with incentives for altering sexual behavior. In this context, Planned Parenthood voices concerns about interference with reproductive freedom. But viewed more broadly the program is an exploration of the social conditions for restoring self-esteem and responsible choice: a matter, as the case suggests, that Planned Parenthood had not thought very much about. The other side of reproductive choice is reproductive responsibility. Whether or not women have obligations to others in how they manage their fertility, society has an interest in women deliberating and making responsible choices, as freestanding, autonomous, rational adults. During periods of dependency, therefore, it may be appropriate for society to attempt to influence reproductive decisions—such as delaying pregnancy until maturity is achieved—so that young women may secure the sense of competence necessary to manage their own lives.

NOTES

1. Alexis de Tocqueville, *Democracy in America* (New York: Schocken Books, 1961), Vol. II, Second Book, Chapter III, p. 120.

The Provision of Welfare

Subordination, Rhetorical Survival Skills, and Sunday Shoes: Notes on the Hearing of Mrs. G.
Lucie E. White

THE STORY[78]

Mrs. G. is thirty-five years old, Black, and on her own. She has five girls, ranging in age from four to fourteen. She has never told me anything about their fathers; all I know is that she isn't getting formal child support payments from anyone. She lives on an AFDC[79] grant of just over three hundred dollars a month and a small monthly allotment of Food Stamps. She probably gets a little extra money from occasional jobs as a field hand or a maid, but she doesn't share this information with me and I don't ask. She has a very coveted unit of public housing, so she doesn't have to pay rent. She is taking an adult basic education class at the local community action center, which is in the same building as my own office. I often notice her in the classroom as I pass by.

The first thing that struck me about Mrs. G., when she finally came to my office for help one day, was the way she talked. She brought her two oldest daughters with her. She would get very excited when she spoke, breathing hard and waving her hands and straining, like she was searching for the right words to say what was on her mind. Her daughters would circle her, like two young mothers themselves, keeping the air calm as her hands swept through it. I haven't talked with them much, but they strike me as quite self-possessed for their years.

At the time I met Mrs. G., I was a legal aid lawyer working in a small community in south central North Carolina. I had grown up in the state, but had been away for ten years, and felt like an outsider when I started working there. I worked out of two small rooms in the back of the local community action center. The building was run-down, but it was a store front directly across from the Civil War memorial on the courthouse lawn, so it was easy for poor people to find.

There were two of us in the office, myself and a local woman who had spent a few years in Los Angeles, working as a secretary and feeling free, before coming back to the town to care for her aging parents. Her family had lived in the town for generations. Not too long ago they, and most of the other Black families I worked with, had been the property of our adversaries—the local landowners, businessmen, bureaucrats, and lawyers. Everyone seemed to have a strong sense of family, and of history, in the town.

In the late 1960s, the town had erupted into violence when a local youth who had read some Karl Marx and Malcolm X led some five thousand people down the local highway in an effort to integrate the county swimming pool. He had been charged with kidnapping as a result of the incident and had fled to Cuba, China, and ultimately Detroit. My colleague would talk to me about him in secretive tones. Her father was one of those who sheltered him from justice on the evening of his escape. I think she expected that one day he would come back to take up the project that was abandoned when he fled.

Since World War II, the town had been a real backwater for Black people. People told me that it was a place that was there to be gotten out of, if you could figure out how. Only gradually, in the 1980s, were a few African American families moving back into the area, to take up skilled jobs in chemicals and electronics. But the lives of most Blacks in the county in the early 1980's could be summed up by its two claims to fame. It was the county where the state's arch-conservative senior Senator had grown up. Locals claimed that the Senator's father, the chief of police at one time, was known for the boots he wore and the success he had at keeping Black people in their place. It was also the county where Steven Spielberg filmed *The Color Purple*. By the time Spielberg discovered the county, the dust from the 1960s had long since settled, and the town where I worked had the look of a sleepy Jim Crow village that time had quite entirely passed by.

Mrs. G. and two daughters first appeared at our office one Friday morning at about ten, without an appointment. I was booked for the whole day; the chairs in the tiny waiting room were already filled. But I called her in between two scheduled clients. Mrs. G. looked frightened. She showed me a letter from the welfare office that said she had received an "overpayment" of AFDC benefits. Though she couldn't read very well, she knew that the word "overpayment" meant fraud. Reagan's newly appointed United States attorney, with the enthusiastic backing of Senator Jesse Helms, had just announced plans to prosecute "welfare cheats" to the full extent of the law. Following this lead, a grand jury had indicted several local women on federal charges of welfare fraud. Therefore, Mrs. G. had some reason to believe that "fraud" carried the threat of jail.

The "letter" was actually a standardized notice that I had seen many times before. Whenever the welfare department's computer showed that a client had received an overpayment, it would kick out this form, which stated the amount at issue and advised the client to pay it back. The notice did not say why the agency had concluded that a payment error had been made. Nor did it inform the client that she might contest the county's determination. Rather, the notice assigned the client a time to meet with the county's fraud investigator to sign a repayment contract and warned that if the client chose not to show up at this meeting further action would be taken. Mrs. G.'s meeting with the fraud investigator was set for the following Monday.

At the time, I was negotiating with the county over the routine at these meetings and the wording on the overpayment form. Therefore, I knew what Mrs. G. could expect at the meeting. The fraud worker would scold her and then ask her to sign a statement conceding the overpayment, consenting to a 10 percent reduction of her AFDC benefits until the full amount was paid back, and advising that the government could still press criminal charges against her.

I explained to Mrs. G. that she did not have to go to the meeting on Monday, or to sign any forms. She seemed relieved and asked if I could help her get the overpayment straightened out. I signed her on as a client and, aware of the other people waiting to see me, sped through my canned explanation of how I could help her. Then I called the fraud investigator, canceled Monday's meeting, and told him I was representing her. Thinking that the emergency had been dealt with, I scheduled an appointment for Mrs. G. for the following Tuesday and told her not to sign anything or talk to anyone at the welfare office until I saw her again.

The following Tuesday Mrs. G. arrived at my office looking upset. She said she had gone to her fraud appointment because she had been "afraid not to." She had signed a paper admitting she owed the county about six hundred dollars, and agreeing to have her benefits reduced by thirty dollars a month for the year and a half it would take to repay the amount. She remembered I had told her not to sign anything; she looked like she was waiting for me to yell at her or tell her to leave. I suddenly saw a woman caught between two bullies, both of us ordering her what to do.

I hadn't spent enough time with Mrs. G. the previous Friday. For me, it had been one more emergency—a quick fix, an appointment, out the door. It suddenly seemed pointless to process so many clients, in such haste, without any time to listen, to challenge, to think together. But what to do, with so many people waiting at the door? I mused on these thoughts for a moment, but what I finally said was simpler. I was furious. Why had she gone to the fraud appointment and signed the repayment contract? Why hadn't she done as *we* had agreed? Now it would be so much harder to contest the county's claim: we would have to attack *both* the repayment contract *and* the underlying overpayment claim. Why hadn't she listened to me?

Mrs. G. just looked at me in silence. She finally stammered that she knew she had been "wrong" to go to the meeting when I had told her not to and she was "sorry."

After we both calmed down I mumbled my own apology and turned to the business at hand. She told me that a few months before she had received a cash settlement for injuries she and her oldest daughter had suffered in a minor car accident. After medical bills had been paid and her lawyer had taken his fees, her award came to $592. Before Mrs. G. cashed the insurance check, she took it to her AFDC worker to report it and ask if it was all right for her to spend it. The system had trained her to tell her worker about every change in her life. With a few exceptions, any "income" she reported would be subtracted, dollar for dollar, from her AFDC stipend.

The worker was not sure how to classify the insurance award. After talking to a supervisor, however, she told Mrs. G. that the check would not affect her AFDC budget and she could spend it however she wanted.

Mrs. G. cashed her check that same afternoon and took her five girls on what she described as a "shopping trip." They bought Kotex, which they were always running short on at the end of the month. They also bought shoes, dresses for school, and some frozen food. Then she made two payments on her furniture bill. After a couple of wonderful days, the money was gone.

Two months passed. Mrs. G. received and spent two AFDC checks. Then she got the overpayment notice, asking her to repay to the county an amount equal to her insurance award.

When she got to this point, I could see Mrs. G. getting upset again. She had told her worker everything, but nobody had explained to her what she was supposed to do. She hadn't meant to do anything wrong. I said I thought the welfare office had done something wrong in this case, not Mrs. G. I thought we could get the mess straightened out, but we'd need more information. I asked if she could put together a list of all the things she had bought with the insurance money. If she still had any of the receipts, she should bring them to me. I would look at her case file at the welfare office and see her again in a couple of days.

The file had a note from the caseworker confirming that Mrs. G. had reported the insurance payment when she received it. The note also showed that the worker did not include the amount in calculating her stipend. The "overpayment" got flagged two months later when a supervisor, doing a random "quality control" check on her file, discovered the worker's note. Under AFDC law, the insurance award was considered a "lump sum payment."[80] Aware that the law regarding such payments had recently changed, the supervisor decided to check out the case with the state quality control office.

He learned that the insurance award did count as income for AFDC purposes under the state's regulations;[81] indeed, the county should have cut Mrs. G. off welfare entirely for almost two months on the theory that her family could live for that time off the insurance award. The lump sum rule was a Reagan Administration innovation designed to teach poor people the virtues of saving money and planning for the future.[82] Nothing in the new provision required that clients be warned in advance about the rule change, however.[83] Only in limited circumstances was a state free to waive the rule.[84] Without a waiver, Mrs. G. would have to pay back $592 to the welfare office. If the county didn't try to collect the sum from Mrs. G., it would be sanctioned for an administrative error.[85]

I met again with Mrs. G. the following Friday. When I told her what I had pieced together from her file, she insisted that she had asked her worker's permission before spending the insurance money. Then she seemed to get flustered and repeated what had become a familiar refrain. She didn't want to make any trouble. She hadn't meant to do anything wrong. I told her that it looked to me like it was the welfare office—and not her—who had done something wrong. I said I would try to get the county to drop the matter, but I thought we might have to go to a hearing, finally, to win.

Mrs. G. had been in court a few times to get child support and to defend against evictions, but she had never been to a welfare hearing. She knew that it was not a good idea to get involved in hearings, however, and she understood why. Fair hearings were a hassle and an embarrassment to the county. A hearing meant pulling an eligibility worker and several managers out of work for a few hours, which—given the chronic under-staffing of the welfare office—was more than a minor inconvenience. It also meant exposing the county's administrative problems to state-level scrutiny.

Front-line eligibility workers were especially averse to hearings because the county's easiest way to defend against its own blunders was to point to the worker as the source of the problem. As a result, the workers did all they could to persuade clients that they would lose, in the end, if they insisted on hearings. The prophesy was self-fulfilling, given the subtle and diffuse retaliation that would often follow for the occasional client who disregarded this advice.

I could tell that Mrs. G. felt pressure from me to ask for a hearing, but she also seemed angry at the welfare office for asking her to pay for their mistake. I said that it was her decision, and not mine, whether to ask for the hearing, and reassured her that I would do my best to settle the matter, no matter what she decided. I also told her she could drop the hearing request at any time, for any reason, before or even after the event. When she nervously agreed to file the hearing request, I didn't second-guess her decision.

My negotiations failed. The county took the position that the worker should have suspended Mrs. G.'s AFDC as soon as the client had reported the insurance payment. This mistake was "regrettable," but it didn't shift the blame for the overpayment. Mrs. G.—and not the county—had received more welfare money than she was entitled to. End of discussion. I then appealed to state officials. They asked if the county would concede that the worker told Mrs. G. she was free to spend her insurance award as she pleased. When county officials refused, and the details of this conversation did not show up in the client's case file, the state declined to intervene. Mrs. G. then had to drop the matter or gear up for a hearing. After a lot of hesitation, she decided to go forward.

Mrs. G. brought all five of her girls to my office to prepare for the hearing. Our first task was to decide on a strategy for the argument. I told her that I saw two stories we could tell. The first was the story she had told me. It was the "estoppel"[86] story, the story of the wrong advice she got from her worker about spending the insurance check. The second story was one that

I had come up with from reading the law. The state had laid the groundwork for this story when it opted for the "life necessities" waiver permitted by federal regulations.[87] If a client could show that she[88] had spent the sum to avert a crisis situation, then it would be considered "unavailable" as income, and her AFDC benefits would not be suspended. I didn't like this second story very much, and I wasn't sure that Mrs. G. would want to go along with it. How could I ask her to distinguish "life necessities" from mere luxuries, when she was keeping five children alive on three hundred dollars a month, and when she had been given no voice in the calculus that had determined her "needs."

Yet I felt that the necessities story might work at the hearing, while "estoppel" would unite the county and state against us. According to legal aid's welfare specialist in the state capital, state officials didn't like the lump sum rule. It made more paper work for the counties. And, by knocking families off the federally financed AFDC program, the rule increased the pressure on state and county-funded relief programs. But the only way the state could get around the rule without being subject to federal sanctions was through the necessities exception. Behind the scenes, state officials were saying to our welfare specialist that they intended to interpret the exception broadly. In addition to this inside information that state officials would prefer the necessities tale, I knew from experience that they would feel comfortable with the role that story gave to Mrs. G. It would place her on her knees, asking for pity as she described how hard she was struggling to make ends meet.[89]

The estoppel story would be entirely different. In it, Mrs. G. would be pointing a finger, turning the county itself into the object of scrutiny. She would accuse welfare officials of wrong, and claim that they had caused her injury. She would demand that the county bend its own rules, absorb the overpayment out of its own funds, and run the risk of sanction from the state for its error.

As I thought about the choices, I felt myself in a bind. The estoppel story would feel good in the telling, but at the likely cost of losing the hearing, and provoking the county's ire. The hearing officer—though charged to be neutral—would surely identify with the county in this challenge to the government's power to evade the costs of its own mistakes. The necessities story would force Mrs. G. to grovel, but it would give both county and state what they wanted to hear—another "yes sir" welfare recipient.

This bind was familiar to me as a poverty lawyer. I felt it most strongly in disability hearings, when I would counsel clients to describe themselves as totally helpless in order to convince the court that they met the statutory definition of disability.[90] But I had faced it in AFDC work as well, when I taught women to present themselves as abandoned, depleted of resources, and encumbered by children to qualify for relief.[91] I taught them to say yes to the degrading terms of "income security," as it was called—invasions of sexual privacy, disruptions of kin-ties, the forced choice of one sibling's welfare over another's.[92] Lawyers had tried to challenge these conditions, but for the most part the courts had confirmed that the system could take such license with its women. After all, poor women were free to say no to welfare if they weren't pleased with its terms.[93]

As I contemplated my role as an advocate, I felt again the familiar sense that I had been taken. Here I was, asking Mrs. G. to trust me, talking with her about our conspiring together to beat the system and strategizing together to change it. Here I was, thinking that what I was doing was educative and empowering or at least supportive of those agendas, when all my efforts worked, in the end, only to teach her to submit to the system in all of the complex ways that it demanded.

In the moment it took for these old thoughts to flit through my mind, Mrs. G. and her children sat patiently in front of me, fidgeting, waiting for me to speak. My focus returned to them and the immediate crisis they faced if their AFDC benefits were cut. What story should we tell at the hearing, I wondered out loud. How should we decide? Mechanically at first, I began to describe to her our "options."

When I explained the necessities story, Mrs. G. said she might get confused trying to remember what all she had bought with the money. Why did they need to know those things anyway? I could tell she was getting angry. I wondered if two months of benefits—six hundred dollars—was worth it. Maybe paying it back made more sense. I reminded her that we didn't have to tell this story at the hearing, and in fact, we didn't have to go to the hearing at all. Although I was trying to choose my words carefully, I felt myself saying too much. Why had I even raised the question of which story to tell? It was a tactical decision—not the kind of issue that clients were supposed to decide.[94] Why hadn't I just told her to answer the questions that I chose to ask?

Mrs. G. asked me what to do. I said I wanted to see the welfare office admit their mistake, but I was concerned that if we tried to make them, we would lose. Mrs. G. said she still felt like she'd been treated unfairly but—in the next breath—"I didn't mean to do anything wrong." Why couldn't we tell both stories? With this simple question, I lost all pretense of strategic subtlety or control. I said sure.

I asked for the list she had promised to make of all the things she bought with the insurance money. Kotex, I thought, would speak for itself, but why, I asked, had she needed to get the girls new shoes? She explained that the girls' old shoes were pretty much torn up, so bad that the other kids would make fun of them at school. Could she bring in the old shoes? She said she could.

We rehearsed her testimony, first about her conversation with her worker regarding the insurance award and then about the Kotex and the shoes. Maybe the hearing wouldn't be too bad for Mrs. G., especially if I could help her see it all as strategy, rather than the kind of talking she could do with people she could trust. She had to distance herself at the hearing. She shouldn't expect them to go away from it understanding why she was angry, or what she needed, or what her life was like. The hearing was their territory. The most she could hope for was to take it over for a moment, leading them to act out her agenda. Conspiracy was the theme she must keep repeating as she dutifully played her role.

We spent the next half hour rehearsing the hearing. By the end, she seemed reasonably comfortable with her part. Then we practiced the cross-examination, the ugly questions that—even though everyone conceded to be irrelevant—still always seemed to get asked . . . questions about her children, their fathers, how long she had been on welfare, why she wasn't working instead. This was the part of these sessions that I disliked the most. We practiced me objecting and her staying quiet and trying to stay composed. By the end of our meeting, the whole thing was holding together, more or less.

The hearing itself was in a small conference room at the welfare office. Mrs. G. arrived with her two oldest daughters and five boxes of shoes. When we got there the state hearing officer and the county AFDC director were already seated at the hearing table in lively conversation. The AFDC director was a youngish man with sandy hair and a beard. He didn't seem like a bureaucrat until he started talking. I knew most of the hearing officers who came to the county, but this one, a pale, greying man who slouched in his chair, was new to me. I started feeling uneasy as I rehearsed how I would plead this troubling case to a stranger.

We took our seats across the table from the AFDC director. The hearing officer set up a portable tape recorder and got out his bible. Mrs. G.'s AFDC worker, an African American woman about her age, entered through a side door and took a seat next to her boss. The hearing officer turned on the recorder, read his obligatory opening remarks, and asked all the witnesses to rise and repeat before god that they intended to tell the truth. Mrs. G. and her worker complied.

The officer then turned the matter over to me. I gave a brief account of the background events and then began to question Mrs. G. First I asked her about the insurance proceeds. She explained how she had received an insurance check of about six hundred dollars following a car accident in which she and her oldest daughter had been slightly injured. She said that the insurance company had already paid the medical bills and the lawyer; the last six hundred dollars was for her and her daughter to spend however they wanted. I asked her if she had shown the check to her AFDC worker before she cashed it. She stammered. I repeated the question. She said she may have taken the check to the welfare office before she cashed it, but she couldn't remember for sure. She didn't know if she had gotten a chance to talk to anyone about it. Her worker was always real busy.

Armed with the worker's own sketchy notation of the conversation in the case file, I began to cross-examine my client, coaxing her memory about the event we had discussed so many times before. I asked if she remembered her worker telling her anything about how she could spend the money. Mrs. G. seemed to be getting more uncomfortable. It was quite a predicament for her, after all. If she "remembered" what her worker had told her, would her story expose mismanagement in the welfare office, or merely scapegoat another Black woman, who was not too much better off than herself?

When she repeated that she couldn't remember, I decided to leave the estoppel story for the moment. Maybe I could think of a way to return to it later. I moved on to the life necessities issue. I asked Mrs. G. to recount, as best she could, exactly how she had spent the insurance money. She showed me the receipts she had kept for the furniture payments and I put them into evidence. She explained that she was buying a couple of big mattresses for the kids and a new kitchen table. She said she had also bought some food—some frozen meat and several boxes of Kotex for all the girls. The others in the room shifted uneasily in their chairs. Then she said she had also bought her daughters some clothes and some shoes. She had the cash register receipt for the purchase.

Choosing my words carefully, I asked why she had needed to buy the new shoes. She looked at me for a moment with an expression that I couldn't read. Then she stated, quite emphatically, that they were Sunday shoes that she had bought with the money. The girls already had everyday shoes to wear to school, but she had wanted them to have nice shoes for church too. She said no more than two or three sentences, but her voice sounded different—stronger, more composed—than I had known from her before. When she finished speaking the room was silent, except for the incessant hum of the tape machine on the table and the fluorescent lights overhead. In that moment, I felt the boundaries of our "conspiracy" shift. Suddenly I was on the outside, with the folks on the other side of the table, the welfare director and the hearing officer. The only person I could not locate in this new alignment was Mrs. G.'s welfare worker.

I didn't ask Mrs. G. to pull out the children's old shoes, as we'd rehearsed. Nor did I make my "life necessities" argument. My lawyer's language couldn't add anything to what she had said. They would have to figure out for themselves why buying Sunday shoes for her children—and saying it—was indeed a "life necessity" for this woman. After the hearing, Mrs. G. seemed elated. She asked me how she had done at the hearing and I told her that I thought she was great. I warned her, though, that we could never be sure, in this game, who was winning, or even what side anyone was on.

We lost the hearing and immediately petitioned for review by the chief hearing officer. I wasn't sure of the theory we'd argue, but I wanted to keep the case open until I figured out what we could do.

Three days after the appeal was filed, the county welfare director called me unexpectedly, to tell me that the county had decided to withdraw its overpayment claim against Mrs. G. He explained that on a careful review of its own records, the county had decided that it wouldn't be "fair" to make Mrs. G. pay the money back. I said I was relieved to hear that they had decided, finally, to come to a sensible result in the case. I was sorry they hadn't done so earlier. I then said something about how confusing the lump sum rule was and how Mrs. G's worker had checked with her supervisor before telling Mrs. G. it was all right to spend the insurance money. I said I was sure that the screw up was not anyone's fault. He mumbled a bureaucratic pleasantry and we hung up.

When I told Mrs. G. that she had won, she said she had just wanted to "do the right thing," and that she hoped they understood that she'd never meant to do anything wrong. I repeated that they were the ones who had made the mistake. Though I wasn't sure exactly what was going on inside the welfare office, at least this crisis was over.

NOTES

78. This story is based upon my work as a legal aid lawyer in North Carolina from 1982 to 1986. Certain details have been changed to avoid compromising client confidentiality.

79. Aid to Families with Dependent Children, 42 U.S.C. §§ 601, 615 (1982).

80. *See* 42 U.S.C. § 602(a)(17)(Supp. III 1982 ed.) and 45 C.F.R. 233.20(a) (3)(ii)(F)(1988). The implementing regulation states that "[w]hen the AFDC assistance unit's income . . . exceeds the State need standard for the family because of receipt of nonrecurring earned or unearned lump sum income (including . . . personal injury . . . awards, to the extent it is not earmarked and used for the purpose for which it is paid, i.e., monies for back medical bills resulting from accidents or injury . . .), the family will be ineligible for aid for the full number of months derived by dividing the sum of the lump sum income and other income by the monthly need standard for a family of that size."

81. In contrast to other federal statutes, such as the Internal Revenue Code, which exclude insurance settlements for personal injury from income, *see, e.g.*, I.R.C. § 104 (1982), the AFDC statute has been interpreted to authorize states to include personal injury awards in the income definition to which the lump sum rule applies. The federal regulations implementing the lump sum rule went farther than the statutory authorization, by affirmatively *requiring* the states to classify all non-recurring lump sum payments, including insurance awards, as income. *See supra* note 80. The statute's inclusion of personal injury awards in its definition of "income" was unsuccessfully challenged by poverty advocates in Lukhard v. Reed, 481 U.S. 368 (1987)(AFDC statute permits states to define personal injury awards as "income" for AFDC purposes, even though common usage and other federal statutory schemes do not do so).

82. The provision was added to the AFDC statute by § 2304 of the Omnibus Budget Reconciliation Act of 1981 (OBRA), 95 STAT. 845, *as amended*, 42 U.S.C. § 602(a)(17)(Supp. III 1982). *See* S. REP. No. 35, 97th Cong., 1st Sess. 436, *reprinted in* 1981 U.S. CODE CONG. & ADMIN. NEWS 396, 702; Bell v. Massinga, 721 F.2d 131 (4th Cir. 1983).

83. *See* Gardebring v. Jenkins, 485 U.S. 415 (1988)(Federal AFDC regulations do not require that each recipient be given advance notification of the lump sum provision before the provision can be enforced).

84. *See* 45 C.F.R. § 233.20(a)(3)(ii)(F)("A State may shorten the period of ineligibility when: . . . the lump sum income or a portion thereof becomes unavailable to the family for a reason beyond the control of the family . . . "). In its explanation of this regulation, the Department of Health and Human Services stated that "a State may shorten the period of ineligibility where it finds a life-threatening circumstance exists, and the non-recurring income causing the period of ineligibility has been or

will be expended in connection with the life-threatening circumstance." *See* 47 Fed. Reg. 5654 (Feb. 5, 1982).

85. The federal government monitors the state welfare agencies which administer the AFDC program for erroneous overpayments, but not erroneous underpayments. If a state's "error rate" is deemed too great, the federal government sanctions the state by reducing its AFDC funding. *See* Casey & Mannix, *Quality Control in Public Assistance: Victimizing the Poor through One-sided Accountability*, 22 Clearinghouse Rev. 1381 (1989). This policy was reviewed and critiqued in a study commissioned by Congress and performed by the National Academy of Sciences in 1988. *See* Panel on Quality Control of Family Assistance Programs, Committee on National Statistics, Commission on Behavioral and Social Sciences and Education, From Quality Control to Quality Improvement in AFDC and Medicaid (F. Kramer ed. 1988).

86. In public benefit cases, the courts have generally held that the doctrine of estoppel cannot be used against the government when a government agent's misinformation results in a claimant's loss of benefits. *See* Schweiker v. Hansen, 450 U. S. 785 (1981). The *Hansen* opinion states in dicta that estoppel may be justified in some circumstances, but the court did not specify what those circumstances might be. *Id.* at 788. Lower court cases have allowed estoppel against the government when an official gives a claimant erroneous factual information which the claimant was not in a position to identify and avoid, and when compensating the claimant will neither undermine important federal interests or deplete the public treasury. *See, e.g.*, Scime v. Secretary of H.H.S., 647 F. Supp. 89, 93 (W.D.N.Y. 1986), *rev'd*, 822 F.2d 7; McDonald v. Schweiker, 537 F. Supp. 47, 50 (N.D.Ind. 1981).

87. *See supra* note 84. The state implemented the exception for "life threatening circumstances" through D.S.S. Administrative Letter No. IPA-8-84 (DSS-3430)("Lump Sum Payments")(March, 1982). The regulation illustrates "Life-threatening situations" by a list of six specific events, such as "serious health hazard to a member of the assistance unit, such as but not limited to a situation where the recipient's house is uninhabitable and the recipient must use the lump sum for essential repairs or necessary utilities." The seventh item on the list authorizes the "county director or his designee" to determine other life-threatening situations on a case by case basis. *See id.* § C-1-g.

88. I use "she" because virtually all of my clients who received AFDC benefits were single mothers. Although single fathers with custody of their children are technically eligible to receive AFDC, they account for an insubstantial percentage of the recipient pool: in my four years of welfare advocacy, I did not encounter any single fathers on AFDC.

89. The costs of this posture have been eloquently described by Patricia Williams in *Alchemical Notes, supra* note 24, at 419–20 (1987): "I got through law school, quietly driven by the false idol of the white-man-within-me, and I absorbed a whole lot of the knowledge and the values, which had enslaved me and my foremothers. . . . I learned to undo images of power with images of powerlessness; to clothe the victims of excessive power in utter, bereft naivete; to cast them as defenseless supplicants raising—*pleading*—defenses of duress, undue influence and fraud. I learned that the best way to give voice to those whose voice had been suppressed was to argue that they had no voice."

90. To be eligible for disability payments under the Social Security Act, one must be unable to engage in substantial gainful activity because of a medically determinable physical or mental impairment that is expected to result in death or to continue for at least 12 months. *See* 42 U.S.C. 423(d)(1982).

91. Under current law, in order to receive AFDC benefits, a family must meet

the categorical requirement of "deprivation"—the absence of two able-bodied parents in the home—as well as a means test. *See* 42 U.S.C. 606(a)(1982). This requirement has been widely criticized for its exclusion of two-earner families living in poverty, and for the consequent pressure it places upon poor couples to live apart in order to receive benefits. *See, e.g.,* R. SIDEL, WOMEN AND CHILDREN LAST: THE PLIGHT OF POOR WOMEN IN AFFLUENT AMERICA (1986); Simon, *Rights and Redistribution in the Welfare System,* 38 STAN. L. REV. 1431 (1988).

92. To receive AFDC, women—with narrowly drawn exemptions for cause—must cooperate with the state in prosecuting paternity and child support actions, and in assigning child support payments to the state to repay AFDC benefits. *See* 42 U.S.C. 602(a)(26)(B)(1982). In Roe v. Norton, 422 U.S. 391 (1975), the Supreme Court found these conditions to be constitutional. *See* Sugarman, *Roe v. Norton: Coerced Maternal Cooperation,* in IN THE INTEREST OF CHILDREN: ADVOCACY, LAW REFORM, AND PUBLIC POLICY 365 (R. Mnookin ed. 1985). In addition, a mother must apply for AFDC benefits for all of her children living in the household, even those who have an independent source of income such as child support or Social Security benefits. That income is then deemed available to the other children, and justifies a cut in the family's AFDC grant. *See* 42 U.S.C. 602(a)(38)(Supp. III 1982). This provision was found constitutional in Bowen v. Gilliard, 483 U.S. 587 (1987). *See* Hirsch, *Income Deeming in the AFDC Program: Using Dual Track Family Law to Make Poor Women Poorer,* 16 N.Y.U. REV. L. & SOC. CHANGE 713 (1987–88). For a history of oppressive conditions of AFDC participation on the state level, *see* W. Bell, AID TO DEPENDENT CHILDREN (1965).

93. *See* Bowen v. Gilliard, 483 U.S. at 608. The majority responded to the record of harms caused by the sibling-deeming requirement by stating that "[t]he law does not require any custodial parent to apply for AFDC benefits." The dissent responded that "[t]he court has thus assumed that participation in a benefit program reflects a decision by the recipient that he or she is better off by meeting whatever conditions are attached to participation than not receiving benefits." *Id.*

94. *See* MODEL RULES OF PROFESSIONAL CONDUCT RULE 1.2 Comment (1983)("In questions of means, the lawyer should assume responsibility for technical and legal tactical issues . . . . "). Whether this provision intends for lawyers unilaterally to select the basic legal theories they will advance in a case is, however, a subject of debate.

California Welfare Reform
David M. Kennedy

INTRODUCTION

In California, 1984 was a year of deep concern about welfare. Conservative Republican Governor George Deukmejian and the Democratic state legislature both felt an urgent need to do something about the spiraling size and cost of the state's Aid to Families with Dependent Children (AFDC) program, which paid cash benefits to eligible poor families. California's AFDC benefits, indexed to inflation in the early 1970s, had reached $555 a month for a family of three, the highest of the country's ten largest states. With 11 percent of the nation's population, the state had 15 percent of the entire national caseload, and its annual expenditures accounted for fully 21 percent of the national total. By the end of 1985, the caseload was expected to rise 14 percent over 1977–78 levels to better than 1.6 million. The caseload expansion and cost-of-living grant increases meant that total AFDC expenditures would increase 94 percent—$1.7 billion—over the same period, to more than $3.5 billion. As elsewhere in the country, eligibility for welfare also conferred access to Medicaid health benefits, which in California were unusually comprehensive and correspondingly expensive.

Governor Deukmejian, first elected in 1982, had come to Sacramento determined to do something about California's AFDC burden. His solution was high-profile "workfare" legislation which would have forced all California welfare recipients to look for jobs under state supervision and, if unsuccessful, to work off their benefits in public service jobs. Deukmejian's bill was carried in the legislature by very conservative members; it was violently opposed by liberal Democrats and welfare rights activists who painted the measure as "slavefare." But by late 1984, the Democrats were themselves feeling pressure to act. An initiative on the ballot that year called for the state's welfare benefits to be cut roughly in half to the average of all other states. Opponents of the measure mounted a campaign focusing on the ill effects passage would have on the very young and very old poor, and it was defeated, but Democrats in Sacramento began to have real fears about facing "soft on welfare" charges in upcoming elections.

It was in this highly charged atmosphere that David Swoap, the conservative secretary of the California Health and Welfare Agency (HWA), and Art Agnos, a liberal assemblyman from San Francisco, began to discuss work and job training programs that might shrink California's welfare rolls and help recipients to self-sufficiency. Swoap and Agnos had strong and opposing views about the nature of welfare recipients and welfare dependency, but they both wanted to break the political deadlock over welfare reform and both felt open, at least potentially, to new ideas.

Agnos and Swoap looked carefully at studies of welfare dynamics and the effectiveness of different work and training programs, and ultimately sat down early in 1985 to design a program for California. As the political significance of Agnos' and Swoap's collaboration became clear, other legislators and welfare rights advocates hastened to join in. The poles of the debate were clear. On the presumption that they would otherwise do little to help themselves, should able-bodied welfare recipients simply be made to work, for the state if necessary? Or, on the presumption that most recipients would work if only they could, should they be eased off welfare with the help of job training programs, child care, and similar support?

ATTITUDES

David Swoap, who as head of HWA was responsible both for administering California's welfare operations and for developing and pushing Governor

Deukmejian's legislation, first sought out Art Agnos, chairman of the Health and Welfare Subcommittee of the Assembly's Ways and Means Committee, in August 1984, after the administration's workfare legislation had died in the legislature for the second time. Agnos was inclined to listen; he was well aware of the political danger welfare was beginning to pose to his party, and he'd dealt with Swoap before on other matters and had found the HWA chief trustworthy and likable.

Still, the two men were almost complete ideological opposites. In an early meeting, Agnos scrawled a few lines on a scrap of paper defining their positions. Swoap and his fellow conservatives, he wrote, believed that "people do not want to work unless intimidated or threatened with sanctions or some forced undesirable alternative." Agnos and his fellow liberals, in contrast, said that "people want to work . . . and will, given opportunity, choice, and training/education." It was a crisp summary of the two-year political deadlock between the administration and the legislature. Liberals had been entirely unwilling to countenance threats and force, and the administration had shown no interest in providing job training or other services.

Swoap had a long history in conservative circles, having held welfare positions under Ronald Reagan both in California and in Washington, as Undersecretary of Health and Human Services, before taking the HWA job in the Deukmejian administration. Swoap believed strongly that it was too easy to get on and stay on welfare, and that it was good for recipients, and just for society, to require them to work. California was still struggling with public services cuts due to a 1978 tax cap, and "particularly in times of fiscal stringency," Swoap said, "there's no reason not to ask able-bodied people to do something in exchange for the support society is giving them." The Deukmejian administration was also convinced that many recipients were working illegally in the underground economy and collecting benefits at the same time, and if forced to report or work elsewhere during the day would simply give up their benefits and continue their illegal work.

Agnos could hardly have agreed less. His responsibilities for welfare at Ways and Means ran more to fiscal matters than to policy, but as a former social worker he tended to believe that most welfare recipients were on the rolls only because they weren't well educated or trained, couldn't afford transportation or day care or manage without Medicaid, or because there was no local work for them to compete for. Workfare, he believed, was little more than punishment for the victims.

Agnos looked instead to a pioneering program in Massachusetts called Employment and Training Choices, which had been brought to his attention by staunch workfare opponent Senator Diane Watson, chair of the Senate Health and Human Services Committee, who represented a very poor Los Angeles district. Participants in the voluntary program were offered a choice of job training programs, given child care and transportation allowances while training, helped to find jobs afterward, and guaranteed an extension of Medicaid benefits if they worked their way off welfare. Mass ET, as the program was invariably called, hadn't been around for very long, but there were early indications that it was both popular and successful.

Agnos' early talks with Swoap simply served to confirm the gulf between them. "On the Democratic side, we were looking at trying to do
something for the bulk of people, who will benefit from a positive opportunity if offered education, training, childcare," Agnos recalled later. "There
was an obsession on the Republican side with the negative possibilities of
every opportunity we talked about. 'They'll cheat here, they'll cheat there.'
They wanted simple workfare, where you might end up cleaning bottles or
picking up paper in exchange for your welfare check. And that was the pro-
grammatic and philosophical impasse that we found ourselves in."

Agnos offered up a new idea. "I said to Swoap, let's do it differently this
time," he said later.

> Let's get out of Sacramento, and you take me anyplace in America where you
> think what you want to do is working. And I'll take you to a place in America
> where I think what we want to do is working, meaning Massachusetts, because
> I knew what was going on there. He thought that was a good idea, and I said
> after the session is over, in a month and a half or so, we'll get together and we'll
> plan a trip.

As it happened, Swoap threw his back out and the trip was delayed
until early 1985. The political situation in Sacramento didn't change to speak
of in the interim. The general intellectual climate around welfare reform to
some extent did, however. "The debate until 1984, I'd say, was mostly ideological," said Julia Lopez, Agnos' key welfare aide. "You had very strongly
held beliefs on both sides, without much solid information to rely on." More
or less coincidentally, solid information became a little easier to come by just
as Agnos and Swoap began their discussions.

THE SAN DIEGO EXPERIMENT

One source was a preliminary evaluation based on the first nine months of
a San Diego County pilot workfare program. San Diego had passed a local
referendum calling for straight work-for-benefits workfare in 1982. The plan
needed state approval, and while the legislature had been skeptical it ultimately gave in to the local sentiment. The resulting "San Diego Job Search
and Work Experience Program" got underway in 1983.

The San Diego experiment was an unusual opportunity to take a close
empirical look at the kind of program elements often contained in workfare
proposals. San Diego's original scheme was simply to make recipients work
in public or private sector nonprofit jobs in exchange for their benefits, but
the legislature had insisted, as a price for approving the program, that the
county help recipients look for regular jobs before putting them into workfare slots. The experiment as it was finally instituted thus began with a
three-week job search workshop in which recipients were instructed in how
to prepare a resume, dress for interviews, and the like, and then supplied
with job listings, yellow pages, and telephones with which to look for work.
The next step was an "Experimental Work Experience Program": three

months of workfare in a public or private nonprofit agency. This basic pattern, job search followed by workfare, in fact mirrored Deukmejian's statewide welfare reform bill.

The impact the governor's proposal would have if it passed had been hotly debated in Sacramento, with relatively little information to go on. San Diego's experiment was quite consciously intended to help answer such questions. It was designed in conjunction with the Manpower Demonstration Research Corporation (MDRC), a New York City-based firm specializing in social science analyses of welfare work experiments, so that the employment and income effects of the job search workshop and of the workshop/workfare combination could be evaluated separately.

In the experimental design that MDRC developed, all new welfare recipients in San Diego were assigned, on pain of denial of benefits, to one of two experimental groups or to a control group (those already on the rolls in San Diego when the program began did not participate in the experiment). Both experimental groups began with the three-week job search workshop. Recipients in one group weren't required to do anything more if they finished the workshop without a job, but still-unemployed recipients in the other moved on to a workfare stint.

Earnings and Employment: Men and Women

Probably the most significant of MDRC's findings was that the San Diego program had quite different effects on men and women. AFDC in California was in fact made up of two program elements: AFDC-Family Group (AFDC-FG) supported single mothers and their children (families headed by single men were also eligible, but AFDC-FG was for all practical purposes a single-mother program), while AFDC-Unemployed Parent (AFDC-U)—a much smaller program—for the most part supported families by paying benefits to recently unemployed fathers.

According to MDRC's analysis, AFDC-FG participants, who were almost all women, showed persistent and statistically significant increases in earnings—as much as $213.00 over three months—and employment—as much as 10 percent—relative to the control group. Women who went through just the job search component rather than the job search/work experience component seemed to fare somewhat better. AFDC-U participants, almost all men, gained relative to the control group in the short term, in both employment and earnings, from participating in both the job search and the job search/work experience components. Neither of the gains was statistically significant, however, and both declined over the period of the study as the performance of the control group improved.

The California legislative analyst's office had a straightforward interpretation of these findings. "The characteristics of the individuals in each group are very different," it said in a review of the MDRC report.

> In general, services provided to AFDC-U recipients do not translate into increased income and employment because these recipients possess the skills needed to find a job *before they enter the programs*. As a result, the employment

services provided by the job search and job search/work experience programs do not significantly increase their chances of finding and keeping a job. On the other hand, AFDC-FG recipients benefit greatly from these services because the services help them increase their chances of finding and keeping a job.

Participation and Sanctions

San Diego County had wondered just how successful a workfare program could be at compelling participation. The MDRC's answer was positive, with some qualifications. Half of the recipients assigned to the job search and job search/work experience components actually participated in the job search exercises, compared to perhaps 10–20 percent for "mandatory" programs that had been tried elsewhere (the MDRC defined "participation" as showing up at a workshop for at least one day). Twenty-seven percent of the recipients in the job search/work experience track ended the workshop unemployed and were assigned to work experience jobs; some 17 percent of those assigned actually did such work (meaning, by MDRC standards, that they spent at least an hour in an assigned job).

The report was somewhat unclear about what happened to the majority of nonparticipants who didn't have good cause for their absence. California law governing job search programs required that recipients had to demonstrate a "pattern of noncompliance," and that welfare administrators undertake a "conciliation" process to try to resolve any differences, before penalties ("sanctions," in welfare jargon) could be imposed. Nearly three percent of the recipients who went through the job search workshops were ultimately sanctioned for noncompliance, compared to 0.5 percent in the control group. No such law applied to the special San Diego work experience component, and 17 percent of the recipients in that component were sanctioned.

Sanctions and Savings

San Diego had hoped that its experiment would move people off welfare, save it money, or both, but when the MDRC's report came out little success was evident on either front, and what there was came not through increased employment but through penalties imposed on recipients. For the most part, participants in the experiment simply weren't working their way out of poverty. Even those women whose earnings increased generally didn't make enough money to go off welfare. Nor did women's earnings and employment increases lead to statistically significant welfare payment reductions, since AFDC-FG recipients were allowed to make a number of employment-related deductions (for child care, for instance) which generally kept earnings-related cuts in benefits to a minimum.

Men who went only through the job search component generally didn't have their benefits reduced either. Those who went through the full job search/work experience component did, but not, for the most part, because their earnings went up substantially. Instead, some who went off the rolls into even part-time jobs lost their benefits because of a federal law which forbade AFDC-U recipients from working more than 100 hours a month. Others lost their benefits for noncompliance. These benefit reductions represented the only verifiable savings from the program.

Reaction

Nobody interested in welfare in Sacramento could afford to ignore the San Diego findings; they were, after all, germane, empirical, and local. None of the parties to the debate shifted very far, however. "People looked at the San Diego data and made anything they wanted out of it," said Joyce Iseri, chief welfare aide to Senate Health and Human Services head Watson. Swoap was especially struck that at least some job search participants had found jobs that weren't advertised or listed with state employment agencies. It reinforced his feeling that it was proper to require recipients to take action for themselves, that there was more work available than his critics would credit. He and those of like mind also saw an AFDC-U sanction rate matching their suspicions about the underground economy. Agnos, Watson, and their allies, on the other hand, saw a program that "hadn't saved a lot of money, put a lot of people in jobs, or cut San Diego's rolls way back," as Iseri put it. The debate continued.

BANE AND ELLWOOD

If the San Diego results seemed to be politically equivocal, Mary Jo Bane and David Ellwood's *The Dynamics of Dependence*, a report released in June 1983, scored unmistakable points for Sacramento's liberals. "It came in very handy in this discussion, because it emphasized that being on AFDC didn't mean that you were handicapped or maimed or somehow not a part of mainstream society," Julia Lopez, Agnos' aide, said.

Bane and Ellwood were both Harvard University welfare and public policy specialists; their study, which was based on an extensive analysis of a large income-history data base at the University of Michigan's Survey Research Center, broke new ground in its careful empirical examination of how long recipients stay on welfare and why they move on and off the rolls. They asked three main questions. How long do female heads of households with children tend to stay on AFDC? What are the characteristics of those who receive welfare income for relatively long periods of time? How do women escape welfare?

They looked at the data in terms of "spells," or the periods individual women spent on welfare. Their main finding was that, examined this way, the welfare population did not appear homogenous. "The AFDC program seems to serve two purposes for two different groups: short term relief and long term income maintenance," they wrote. According to their analysis half of the women who went on AFDC were off within two years or less, and two-thirds within four years; only 17 percent stayed eight years or more.

"Most of the people [AFDC] serves are short-term clients, for whom [long term welfare] dependence is simply not an issue," they argued (although they also reported that a third of all women who ended a spell on welfare returned to the rolls at some time). However, more than half of the people on AFDC at any given time were long-term recipients: the short-term recipients—a majority of those who passed through the program—came and went, while the relatively few long-term recipients accumulated on the rolls. The long-term 17 percent thus ended up receiving over half of all welfare expenditures.

Bane and Ellwood also found that three-fourths of all AFDC spells began with what they called a "relationship change." Nearly half began when a wife became a female head of household, another 30 percent when an unmarried woman "acquired" a child (the authors pointed out that not all single women on AFDC were caring for their own children). Only 12 percent began because the recipient had suffered a fall in income, suggesting, the authors wrote, that "it is not typically the case that a female household head goes on AFDC because she has lost her job, reduced her hours, or experienced a drop in wages." Nearly a third of the women who went *off* welfare did so because their earnings went up, however. A roughly equal proportion went off because they married or rejoined their husbands, and about 14 percent went off because their children turned 18 or left the household (other, including unexplained, reasons accounted for the other twenty-odd percent).

The Dynamics of Dependence served to confirm some of the Sacramento liberals' most basic feelings about welfare and welfare recipients. Art Agnos had in fact held, over the previous several years, a series of hearings around the state to make the point that California's welfare population no longer fit, if it ever had, common stereotypes. "There was a new profile in California of recipients different from the traditional image of low-income women who maybe had been born on welfare, maybe had had a child or two on welfare," Agnos said.

> This was what I call the middle-class divorced poor woman: mostly white with a few kids who was there basically as a result of divorce. Very often she'd dropped out of college to put a husband through school or something like that, but there was no need to threaten or start all over with her.

Bane and Ellwood, as far as he was concerned, more than proved that point. "Their study came out and basically said that folks go in and out of the system," said Julia Lopez. "You have a hard core that stays a long time, but it's a system that's very fluid." The study also underscored the liberals' general disagreement with the Deukmejian administration. "They wanted to build a system for the minority, that would prevent them from doing any work in the underground economy," Lopez said. "And we were saying, 'Why develop a system for the few when we really need to help the majority of folks who aren't working for a number of other reasons?'"

LOSING GROUND

Charles Murray's *Losing Ground*, published in 1984, did for conservatives what Bane and Ellwood had done for liberals. A biting critique subtitled *American Social Policy 1950–1980*, the book argued that the last few decades' government policies toward the poor, however well-intentioned, had been dangerously counterproductive. Murray focused particularly on welfare policy, his thesis in essence being that welfare caused poverty. Welfare made it easier to avoid working at entry-level jobs, sometimes, he argued, even more profitable not to take such jobs; the result was that the poor never began to move up the job ladder. Welfare made it easier to survive as a single mother, especially as a young single mother; the result was that more such families were formed. Welfare cut away at the causal connection between striving and economic performance; the result was that poor people faced, and responded to, morally perverse incentives.

Murray backed up his arguments with reams of statistics showing deterioration, beginning with the Great Society's federal antipoverty programs, in indicators of poverty, illegitimacy, labor force participation and the like. "We tried to provide more for the poor and produced more poor instead," he wrote. "We tried to remove the barriers to escape from poverty, and inadvertently built a trap."

Job programs, Murray argued, were no antidote; they simply didn't work. He relied on published studies to make his case. An evaluation of the multibillion dollar Manpower Development and Training Act, a Great Society job training program, found initial earnings increases of $150–500 annually for men, declining to half that, for the same men, as time passed; women did a little better at $300–600. A study of vocational training programs found wage increases attributable to the training of but 1.5 percent. There were other, similar examples. The programs, Murray argued, were thus failures on their own terms: they did not lift participants out of poverty.

Faced with such dismal results, Murray said, liberal advocates historically had turned to two devices to justify job training programs. A cost-effectiveness case could be made as long as the benefits from training surpassed—eventually—its costs, a condition that usually held if one looked far enough into the trainees' future. "[I]t was to this type of calculation to which the sponsors were reduced," Murray wrote scornfully. "'The average effect [on earnings] for all enrollees is quite large,' we find in one evaluation of the Job Corps, then read on to the next sentence, where it is revealed that the 'quite large' effect amounted to $3.30 per week. It was a statistically significant gain."

The other device was the upbeat anecdote: "John Jones, an ex-con who had never held a job in his life, became employed because of program X and is saving money to send his child to college. Such anecdotes, filmed for the evening news, were much more interesting than economic analyses. They were also useful in hearings before congressional appropriations committees." The implication, Murray argued, was that the story was typical, but the fact, he also argued, was that they were rare, "and that depressingly often John Jones would be out of his job and back in jail in a few months after his moment in the spotlight. . . ."

Murray confirmed and elaborated many of the beliefs senior Deukmejian administration officials already had about welfare, just as Bane and Ellwood had for the administration's opponents. "Everyone seemed to agree with Murray's basic thesis, that there is a serious welfare crisis that is exacerbated by the presence of welfare," said Bruce Wagstaff, a senior HWA analyst.

> That's an underlying assumption of a mandatory work program, that the availability of welfare acts as a disincentive to work, and that you must compel people through the threat of terminating their welfare to engage in work. That otherwise they wouldn't, because they're too accustomed to just accepting welfare, and they'll continue this long term or generational dependency.

Murray's points about job training programs rang just as true in the administration. "Carl [Williams, Swoap's deputy] gives examples of his previous experiences with these programs, where you'd have a lot—I shouldn't even say a lot, you'd have some—people receiving training, receiving nice certificates, but the training was not directed toward labor market opportunities, so they had these nice certificates but no jobs," Wagstaff said. In fact, it rang true in what might have seemed unexpected quarters as well. Senator Bill Greene, whose district in Los Angeles adjoined Diane Watson's, and who had long advocated training programs for his constituents, had by this time "gotten to the point where he could not support any of this stuff anymore," according to his aide, Allen Davenport.

> People were tired of seeing the programs come and go. It really bugged him that some program would come down the pike from Washington or Sacramento and make all these promises and then would go away and nothing had changed. The only successes in the programs had been their administrators; SRI [the Stanford Research Institute] did a great study on that, showing that the careers that were most enhanced by poverty programs were the careers of poverty program administrators.

THE TRIP

Nobody involved in the California welfare debate, as it turned out, was shifted very fundamentally by any of this analysis; the studies mostly confirmed various participants' original beliefs rather than creating some new common ground. The personal and political inclination to reach some accord remained, however. In March 1985, Agnos, Swoap, and several other legislators and HWA officials embarked for a week's tour of state work and job training programs. Swoap had chosen West Virginia and Pennsylvania, which were running what were to his mind model work-for-benefits workfare programs, essentially the San Diego model without the job search component. Agnos had selected Massachusetts, with its ET program.

Much of the subsequent impact of the trip, the participants later agreed, came simply from the fact that they had taken it together. "It's rare in government for everybody to work from a common basis of experience," Swoap said.

> We'd been talking around this issue in Sacramento for years, and everybody involved knew a lot, but we all had different backgrounds, and often we ended up just talking past each other. The trip was remarkable in that we saw the same things—some very instructive things—talked to the same people, sat up late nights discussing what had happened that day, and while we didn't necessarily agree afterward on what it meant, we *were* all beginning in the same place, which was a very important step forward.

Agnos felt exactly the same way. "The overall thing I learned from this is to get the hell out of the committee and caucus rooms and go into the field," he said.

> Not only is the field a living laboratory where you can put your hands, very often, on the problems that personify one point of view or the other, but when you're done you have the same set of anecdotes to draw on, which is very, very important.

Both sides did, indeed, see things that made lasting impressions. "West Virginia, frankly—now remember that this was sort of the Republican showpiece for workfare—was a disaster," Agnos said. "Or if not a disaster, at least not a great success." While West Virginia's program was for the most part intended simply to ensure that welfare recipients worked, on what amounted to moral grounds, some attention was paid to slotting recipients into jobs that would do them some good in the long run, and recipients were supposed to be reviewed every six months to make sure that they hadn't hit some kind of unforeseen dead end. The California delegation in fact saw some positive results, as in several recipients who seemed well on their way to learning a trade in the state printing plant. Even this seemed a little sour to Agnos, since the recipients had had no voice in their assignments. "No-one had asked them if they wanted to be printers, it just happened bang, a random kind of thing," he said.

The major lesson, however, came from a visit the Californian's hosts had arranged to a state water treatment facility, where an Appalachian woman named Velda Jenkins—in her mid-thirties, with three children, on welfare because her husband was in prison—was being trained through her workfare job to be a water quality tester. The West Virginian program managers were particularly proud that they were preparing an essentially unskilled woman for such a sophisticated position. In fact, the treatment plant's budget for janitors had been cut and Jenkins had spent her nearly two years on workfare mopping floors. She'd complained politely at her six month reviews, but nothing had changed. "This was our showcase," Agnos said. The delegation, Swoap included, was particularly disturbed that Jenkins had had no effective recourse once she'd been sidelined; the California party started to refer to this as the "Velda factor," something any system for California would absolutely have to address. "We wanted to empower people without the necessity of having a lawyer every time," Agnos said. "We wanted people to be in charge of their own lives."

The group heard some rather unexpectedly positive messages at the same time. "We got a consistent sense from recipients in these jobs, even in jobs that at first glance weren't very interesting, that they were glad to be out doing something," Swoap said. "We saw that repeated all through West Virginia," Agnos said. "People doing things that they didn't necessarily like, saying 'if they hadn't made me do it I wouldn't have done it, but it's better than doing nothing at home.' That was when my feelings of opposition to the mandatory feature started to change."

The party moved on to Pennsylvania, which had a workfare program much like West Virginia's. The main lesson of that visit came in a National Guard Armory. Agnos had always been inclined to respect California unions' concerns that workfare might cause public sector displacement, while Swoap, according to Sacramento observers, had been inclined to dismiss it, believing that workfare jobs in budget-capped California would at best supplement, rather than supplant, regular workers.

Pennsylvania, according to both men, proved Agnos' case. "This general in the armory," said Agnos,

> just blew our minds by saying, "Well, I went up to see the governor to get six more janitors because the place was dirty and he said, 'we don't have the money for it, but have you ever heard of workfare? Get some welfare recipients to do it for you.'" Just coldbloodedly said it. I said to Dave, we don't want to do that; we want to pay for legitimate work like that out of the budget, not end up replacing state workers that we don't want to pay for.

Thus ended the conservatives' portion of the tour. In Massachusetts, as expected, the delegation found a strikingly different approach. The differences began with the state's ambitions for its Employment and Training Choices program. Where West Virginia and Pennsylvania had aimed, at best, to save some money, move some recipients into private sector jobs, and get a return for their welfare dollars, Massachusetts claimed that it was making a large improvement in the lives of significant numbers of the poor. "In Massachusetts," said Welfare Commissioner Charles M. Atkins, "we have found a way out of poverty."

As its name implied, choice—exercised by recipients—was central to ET. Recipients chose, first, whether to participate in the program. ET was technically mandatory, but in fact AFDC recipients only had to register for the program, and those not actively interested in pursuing it were placed in an "unassigned pool" with essentially no further obligations. To encourage recipients to enter the program and perhaps ultimately to give up welfare, Massachusetts offered day care and transportation allowances while in ET and if necessary extended the child care allowance and Medicaid benefits for a year after recipients started working.

Participants in ET had four basic options to choose from. They could look for work through a San Diego-style job club, with state assistance in learning job search skills and finding openings. They could undertake "assessment and career counseling," in which state social workers helped recipients figure out what they might want to do, and what education and skills they might need to do it. They could select "education and skills training," to learn English as a second language, get a high school equivalent degree, take up to two community college courses, and/or learn a skill. They could choose "supported work," in which recipients' grants were funneled through a private employer who agreed to provide on-the-job training.

They could, finally, put these different options together in almost any order: education and training followed by supported work, for instance, or job search—if unsuccessful—followed by assessment followed by a training or supported work stint. Participants' first step in the program was to meet with an ET worker and work out career goals and a plan to meet them, but if they failed to find jobs—or jobs they wanted to stay in—they were, at least in theory, free to cycle through the program indefinitely. They were also free to drop out of the program if they wanted; there were no sanctions for nonparticipation as there were in San Diego, West Virginia, and Pennsylvania.

Mass ET had only gotten off the ground in October 1983, so it had a limited track record when the California delegation came to look it over. The state was nonetheless extremely proud of what it had accomplished. Out of the states' 85,000 AFDC families, 44,000 people had signed up (20,000 of these were on a waiting list; these and the following figures date from May 1985). Fifteen thousand AFDC recipients had been placed in private sector jobs at an average wage of $5.00 an hour, which worked out to annual earnings of $9,700, against the state's typical welfare grant of $6,800 annually. There was no MDRC-style evaluation of Mass ET in the offing, however; Commissioner Atkins had forbidden any scheme involving a control group on the grounds that he would not deny the program to any ambitious recipient.

Swoap, Agnos et al were struck by several things as they spoke with ET administrators and participants and toured several branch offices. Swoap was impressed that a totally voluntary program was able to generate such participation, and by the "palpable" excitement he sensed among both recipients and caseworkers. He wondered, however, whether ET was simply placing the most motivated and job-ready recipients—those most likely to volunteer—thus making the program's performance unrepresentative of what a similar but mandatory scheme might accomplish. He also found Massachusetts' use of an unassigned pool obnoxious: people unwilling to help themselves, he still felt, should be made to do so.

Agnos was enormously taken with the opportunity ET seemed to offer recipients. "In effect it gave a second chance at what many people get earlier in their lives, in high school or in college; it gave them an opportunity to make a choice—with some serious help—about what they wanted to do with the rest of their lives," Agnos said.

> Here are people with a couple of kids, on welfare, and ET was stopping the train for them, letting them get off, and saying here's another crack at it. When you're 30 years old or 40 years old with kids from five to 15, how do you stop the train of life and retrain for something that you want to do, now that you're older, a little wiser, a little more mature? ET did that, and that's something you normally don't get.

Somewhat ironically, even though Massachusetts made much of its program being voluntary *and* successful, ET put another dent into Agnos' resistance to mandatory programs. "People had all kinds of options, and it was working for the people they did it with," he said. "I began to wonder, if we believe in a program like that, why shouldn't everybody get the benefit of it?"

THE NEGOTIATIONS

The Californians found their whirlwind tour immensely provocative, but it didn't actually resolve anything about how California might go about a program of its own. "What we accomplished on the trip was simply acquiring a set of common experiences," Agnos said. "Everything substantive was still up in the air when we came back."

Something more was required if there was to be political movement. In April 1985, Agnos convened a series of meetings in an Assembly conference room that was to last, off and on, for almost eight months. Agnos and Julia Lopez attended; Swoap and his top staff attended; Joyce Iseri, Dion Aroner, and Allen Davenport—aides respectively to Senator Watson, Assemblyman Tom Bates (Watson's Assembly counterpart), and Senator Greene—attended, as did several other legislators. Agnos and Lopez represented themselves, and Swoap and his deputies represented the administration, but the legislative aides were there on the strict understanding that they did *not* represent their members. Agnos had invited them believing that their welfare expertise would be useful and that any product they contributed to would be more likely to satisfy their influential legislators, but there was no implication that Bates, Watson, and Greene were in any way committed.

Agnos insisted from the outset that participants put aside, insofar as they could, any preconceptions about what might in fact be politically or fiscally possible and simply think out loud together about what an ideal program might look like. "We sat there and Art said, 'Let's start talking about creating a system, all the different parts of a system, as we would if we had our druthers,'" Dion Aroner said, "'How would you do it?'"

Agnos was simply trying to set a tone: none of the participants felt, or felt their fellows to be, perfectly openminded, or that a real program would not have to address fiscal and political realities. Agnos had in fact carried back from the trip a one-page handwritten summary, drafted while on a bus in Massachusetts, of the state of play between himself and Swoap.

They were agreed, in principle, that welfare recipients should work, although they still came to that conclusion from different philosophical directions. They disagreed about what components should actually be in a good program—an ET-style menu, for instance, against simple work-for-benefits—about what incentives recipients should be offered to participate, and about what safeguards should be included to placate unions and guard against the "Velda factor." Those issues, Agnos thought, were negotiable. Some issues were not. Swoap clearly would not support a program unless it was mandatory and backed by significant sanctions. Agnos clearly would not support a program unless it offered recipients real choices. And even if Agnos and Swoap could somehow come to terms, there was no guarantee that other influential parties—like Diane Watson and Tom Bates—would go along.

LOBBYING FROM THE LEFT

Agnos made sure that Sacramento's welfare advocates, with whom he generally had old and close ties, knew about the negotiations, though he swore them to secrecy and told them essentially nothing about the details of the group's discussions. Nonetheless, activists like Casey McKeever, a lawyer at the Western Center on Law and Poverty, and Candace Blase, who worked for the Friends Committee on Legislation of California, knew more than enough about welfare issues and programs to know that they had had a rather different interpretation of the available information.

McKeever and Blase both felt that focusing on recipients and whether a particular program could get them into jobs was a fundamental mistake (although the political appeal in Sacramento of some kind of work legislation was clear enough that they didn't try too hard to change legislative minds on the point). The problem, they thought, was that full-time entry-level jobs often simply didn't pay wages a family could live on. "Look at the San Diego data," McKeever said. "Those who went through both job search and workfare had statistically significant improvements."

> But they still weren't getting off welfare; the jobs they were working weren't paying enough to get them off welfare. You can go through the best of programs like that and it's just going to have very marginal impacts. They don't really improve the lot of the participants. So from our perspective, the approach Agnos seemed to be taking just kind of missed the point. You could put all kinds of money in, and require people to do all sorts of things, but you really weren't going to be in any different place than when you started off. It was just making people in Sacramento feel better, like they were doing something, but they weren't addressing what we felt the real problem was.

McKeever and Blase supported higher minimum wages and a program of job creation. "Otherwise," said Blase, all you're doing with workfare and training programs is increasing the supply of labor in a segment of the labor market which is already underpaid and facing too few jobs. It worsens the condition of those people who are already working in that market, and it doesn't give much bargaining power to the people who are going into it. If you don't deal with the labor market end of it, then you can't improve the condition of large groups you're trying to move into that market.

They also pointed out that in many places around California there didn't seem to be anything like sufficient entry-level jobs anyway. What were the 40 percent of the state's recipients who lived in Los Angeles going to do?

Nonetheless, something, it seemed clear, was going to come out of the continuing—though still largely secret—negotiations. Most of their energies therefore went into supporting the ideas behind Mass ET over those behind San Diego or West Virginia. "We were promoting Massachusetts as the alternative," Blase said. "At that time they were saying they had a certain number of placements and jobs, Agnos was raving about it, everyone was happy with it," McKeever said. "There wasn't much bad to say about it at that point."

BAD NEWS

Such news was not long in coming. As the negotiations continued, Blase received a preliminary analysis of the ET program written by Jean Kluver, a Boston economist, for the New England regional office of the American Friends Service Committee. "The office had been getting a lot of questions from Friends around the country, asking about ET," Kluver said. "'Is this a good program? Is this what we should be pushing for in our states as an alternative to these regressive workfare schemes?'"

The centerpiece of Kluver's analysis was that Commissioner Atkins was wrong, that ET did not in fact represent the way out of poverty. ET graduates in full-time jobs were averaging $5.00 an hour, according to the state. At that wage, Kluver argued, a mother with two children—the most common AFDC family—would lose money moving from welfare to work. The family's AFDC and food stamp benefits would add up to $555 a month. That was less than the gross monthly income from a $5.00 an hour job—$806.00— but taxes, at $120.00 a month, "work expenses" (clothing, transportation, etc.), at $100.00 a month, and child care, at $105.00 a month, even including the ET subsidy, brought her disposable income down to $546.00. If, after the first year of employment, a working mother had to pay the full cost of medical insurance and child care, the picture was even worse: Kluver's figures suggested that her disposable income could drop as low as $51.00 a month. Moreover, Kluver's information suggested that actual average wages for female ET placements were closer to $4.50. "Thus," she said, "while it is true that the gross income of ET graduates is about 180 percent of their previous AFDC grant, these jobs do not pay enough to provide long-term self-sufficiency for most AFDC families."

Kluver herself was cautious in drawing political implications from her analysis; ET was, in her view, much the best of likely work-program alternatives, and she was more interested in improving it—and perhaps shifting the focus of the debate to wages and job creation—than in killing it. Mc-Keever and Blase, in California, were in fact only slightly disheartened by Kluver's analysis, since they felt generally positive about the voluntary program; they didn't even try to press the report on the negotiators. "We weren't relying on social science data or anything like that," McKeever said, in supporting something like ET in California.

> We are saying that this program makes sense and it's better for recipients because of the way it works. We can see it's better for our people to have a lot of child care, to have the choice of programs, not to have workfare and sanctions.

THE DECISION

Agnos and his colleagues continued to meet regularly, trying to make sense of all they had learned, analytically and impressionistically, about welfare, workfare, and job training. The political desire to come up with a program of some kind remained very strong, but the group was still struggling with some basic questions. Did a program have to be mandatory to be effective? Did voluntary programs misdirect resources to people who would help themselves in any case? How important was it to help participants with child care, transportation, and insurance? Was workfare punishment, or useful preparation for a normal working life? Should recipients be slotted immediately into minimum-wage jobs, or should California try to educate and train recipients for a better life? "We were working with the political view that everybody in California wanted welfare recipients to go to work," said Allen Davenport. "So we were working along on the data and ideas that we all had. What would a good and effective program look like?"

SECTION B

Interventions Relating to Pregnancy

Buying Time: The Dollar-a-Day Program
Nancy Kates

On a typical Thursday afternoon at La Mariposa Public Health Station in West Denver, Colorado, a group of 15 Hispanic teenagers sit around the clinic's second floor conference table, drinking pop, eating Doritos, and talking. It doesn't look terribly organized—more of a coffee klatch than a peer support program—but the scene is, in fact, a meeting of Mariposa's Dollar-a-Day group, a program to prevent second pregnancies among low-income teenagers. Almost everyone present is female; more than half have brought their babies with them. Their children range in age from a four-month-old to several who are approaching three. Girls drift in and out, gossiping about friends, boyfriends, school and work. As each girl arrives, counselor Diane Medina quietly hands her seven one dollar bills, and checks her name off a list. Without this one unobtrusive action, the meeting would appear to be entirely social; the conversation does not dwell on pregnancy or motherhood. After receiving her money, one girl launches into an amusing story of an accident with some hair dye, pointing to a large blond patch in her otherwise auburn hair, itself several shades lighter than natural. Several members of the group give her advice about the problem: let it grow out, they say, or dye it again. Another mentions a former group member, who has just gotten married. Some of those absent are at the mall, confesses another girl. "They're shopping," she says. "They just got their checks," referring to government welfare payments sent to a few members of the group.

Dollar-a-Day represents an experimental approach to the problem of teenage pregnancy in the Denver metropolitan area. The theory is deceptively simple: pay teenage girls a dollar a day not to get pregnant. In practice, the program is far more sophisticated. Designed to prevent second pregnancies among teenagers who have already been pregnant before the age of 16, the Rocky Mountain Planned Parenthood program uses money to entice girls to attend a weekly meeting led by professional counselors. After five years of operation, Dollar-a-Day is considered a success: of the 56 young women who completed the program, nine girls—or 17 percent—have become pregnant, a significant improvement over repeat pregnancy rates of 37 to 50 percent or higher among similarly disadvantaged teenagers; by one estimate, it has also saved the State of Colorado in excess of a quarter of a million dollars in welfare and Medicaid payments.[1]

In its first year, however, Dollar-a-Day wreaked havoc for Rocky Mountain Planned Parenthood (RMPP), the local affiliate sponsoring the program. Six months after its inception, the tiny Denver initiative created so much controversy at the national Planned Parenthood Federation (PPFA) in New York, that the national leadership tried to force Denver to stop the program. PPFA President Faye Wattleton and a majority of the 54-member national board of directors denounced the program as coercive; paying teenagers not to get pregnant, they felt, went against the organization's longstanding and deeply held policies advocating reproductive choice and individual rights.

THE CRISIS OF TEENAGE PREGNANCY

Dollar-a-Day began in response to the problem of teenage pregnancy, which by the 1980s, had reached epidemic proportions among the inner city poor. Members of the local Rocky Mountain Planned Parenthood board hoped to do something to break the cycle of "babies having babies." They were particularly concerned about second pregnancies among disadvantaged teens, who, in Denver, were largely black and Hispanic. Statistics showed that teenaged mothers with one child had difficulty getting off welfare and establishing financial independence, but those with two babies would be unlikely to break the cycle of poverty for the rest of their lives. Inner city teenagers at high risk for first or second pregnancies tended to be poor, emotionally needy and deprived young women, who most likely grew up in single parent homes, and were themselves the products of teen pregnancies. These young women had looked to childbearing as a solution to their problems, only to discover too late that motherhood involved even greater responsibility and an entirely new set of difficulties. According to Dr. Jeffrey Dolgan, the architect of the Dollar-a-Day program, this target group was also at high risk for a number of other problems, including drug abuse and domestic violence. Many of the girls in the target population had been physically or sexually abused by their mothers' boyfriends; even those who were not the victims of abuse exuded a sense of hopelessness and a profound lack of self-confidence. For some, having a child gave them something to look forward to. Many dropped out of school to have their babies; those without children had already resigned themselves to living on welfare or working at a Burger King-type job. Dr. Peggy LaTourrette, director of La Mariposa Health Station and a former RMPP board member, comments:

> These women are so needy for love, they'll get it in any place they can find it. If someone says "I love you, let's go have a baby," they take it at face value. Many

of the girls have babies because they think [the baby] will be someone to love them. Instead, they find out that the baby needs all of their love and attention.

Young Hispanic women also grew up in a culture that reinforced early childbearing. "Our 30-year-old mothers end up grandmothers," comments LaTourrette. "Some [grandmothers] get really upset that their girls are pregnant, because this is what they went through at a young age. There are others, though, who look at it as if 'these are my new babies.'" The cycle of single motherhood repeated itself, generation after generation, in certain inner city neighborhoods; like the section of West Denver where 75 percent of the pupils in one elementary school lived in single-parent homes. Most important, perhaps, was the typical attitude of the sexual partners of so-called "high risk" girls. Boyfriends, says Dolgan, liked to prove their machismo by fathering as many children as possible. "They get bad press [among their peers] if they haven't fathered by 16," he comments. "A lot of times they get pregnant because the boy wants them to get pregnant," adds LaTourrette. "Then, after they get pregnant, the boy splits." Although many of these young single mothers had regular boyfriends, few had stayed with the fathers of their babies.

THE DOLLAR-A-DAY CONCEPT

In response to these problems, Denver psychologist Dr. Jeff Dolgan, then director of the Denver Children's Home, proposed a monetary incentive program that would pay high-risk teenaged girls a dollar a day not to get pregnant. Working with teenagers at the Children's Home, he says, he saw very young girls getting pregnant, and recognized that few seemed interested in avoiding pregnancy. He then asked the girls what would get them to come to a voluntary program. Their answer? "Money." With that in mind, Dolgan wrote a proposal in 1984 for a support group for very young teens who had already had their first pregnancy. They would receive a dollar for every day they avoided getting pregnant a second time; the monetary payment would be a lure to get the girls to come to a weekly meeting. The only real model for the program, he says, was businessman/philanthropist Eugene Lang's 1981 offer to a group of Harlem sixth graders: he would pay their college costs if they made it all the way through high school without dropping out. Dollar-a-Day was initially targeted at high-risk teens under the age of 15, but the cutoff age was raised to 16 due to a paucity of applicants.

Dolgan had clear ideas about how the meetings would be structured, and what the kids would get out of them. By recruiting young women who had grown up in the same neighborhood, he hoped to foster a sense of camaraderie that would help group members build confidence, giving them positive peer pressure to avoid pregnancy. Professional adult counselors would offer guidance and direction for the group, but avoid preachy or educational presentations. "It's not a forum for Planned Parenthood," comments Rocky Mountain board member Ellen Anderman, who notes that, unlike other programs sponsored by the organization, this one would *not* dispense contraceptives (unless they were requested). "It was a very strongly held concept that unless the girls brought something up, it wouldn't be discussed." "You have to really understand that the last person the adolescent wants to get information from is an adult," adds fellow board member Sandra Goodman, an educational consultant by training. In fact, Dolgan did not even require girls to stay for the full hour-long meeting; he expected some would come in, get their money, and leave.

Dolgan theorized that small details would have important symbolic meaning for the Dollar-a-Day group. For example, he thought it was essential that refreshments be served at every meeting, as the program handbook he co-authored notes: "Given the depth of neediness and deprivation among low-income, high risk adolescents, refreshments are a crucial variable to the program's success. These children must *in many ways* be fed" (emphasis in original). Similarly, Dolgan thought it essential that each girl receive seven one-dollar bills at each meeting:

> Groups have ritualized interactions. Doling out the dollars becomes a ritual. It recognizes that this is a day-by-day effort. If you hand out a five and two ones, it loses the symbolic import. It's like the A.A. [Alcoholics Anonymous] model, where they count the total days of sobriety—we count the number of meetings they've attended. It has to do with pride and self-esteem.

He thought that such rituals would help girls build identity with the group, which would in turn reinforce the goal of avoiding pregnancy. Dolgan expected that group members would take pride in not missing a meeting, in part because gossip would quickly start about someone who did not show up ("oh, she must have gotten pregnant!"). Girls would mark their progress toward "graduation," which would occur after they attended 100 meetings or reached their 18th birthday. Group members would receive an extra seven dollars on their birthdays. Like the symbolism of the one dollar bills, Dolgan hoped special milestones—like birthdays—would demonstrate each girl's progress.

Dolgan and others involved in Dollar-a-Day had no illusions that they could solve the teenage pregnancy problem, even in Denver. Instead, they saw it as a way to delay motherhood for those too young to handle its responsibilities; participants would be expected to attend the group for two years, or until their 18th birthday. "By helping delay additional pregnancies, the Dollar-a-Day program is 'buying time' for high-risk teens," reads the program manual, "allowing them to mature emotionally and to finish or return to school. It is hoped that participants will discover parenthood is not a solution to their problems." Dolgan employed the "buying time" pun quite literally; while he rejected the notion that the seven dollars was any sort of bribe, he also referred to the entrepreneurial plan as "uniquely American." In fact, Dolgan believed it would be the group—not the money—that really helped girls avoid second pregnancies. "The pay turns out to be a metaphor for adult approval," he comments. "I used dollars because I knew that the program target population was very, very poor and would get more value from money." Yet positive peer pressure from other group members seemed to hold as much weight as approval from adult counselors. "The philosophy is deceptively simple," comments Dolgan. "They have to have some face-saving way for modifying behavior. Peer pressure is a strong motivation."

Dolgan's proposal generated serious debate among the members of the RMPP educational endowment committee, which had sent out a request for proposals from the community addressing the problem of teenage pregnancy. Most of the other proposals received by the committee involved day-long educational workshops on contraception for teens, and other school-linked educational efforts. Many committee members liked the idea of trying something new and innovative, since other types of programs aimed at preventing teen pregnancy had not proven to be effective. But others wondered how the program would be perceived, and asked themselves if Rocky Mountain should get involved in a project linked to financial incentives. Board member Sandra Goodman, who was instrumental in getting the grant application approved, says Dolgan's philosophy was more easily understood and accepted by professionals in the field than by lay persons; both groups were represented on the committee. "Most professionals said 'go for it,'" recalls Goodman, "while the average person [expressing concern about using financial incentives] said 'you want to do *what?*'" "It was perceived as an experiment—we didn't know if it would work," adds another board member. Nevertheless, Dolgan's proposal was attractive for two reasons: it was innovative, and could be done for very little money. He planned to staff the program with volunteer counselors from the Children's Home; the $2,500 budget for the first year would be spent almost exclusively on payments to participants and refreshments. After several months of earnest debate on the program, Dolgan's request was approved by the committee.

The program got underway in the winter of 1985 with 18 girls[2] referred to Jeff Dolgan by Dr. Peggy LaTourrette, director of La Mariposa Health Station. LaTourrette recruited teenagers who had used the clinic in the past, and also donated a conference room in which to hold the meetings. Dolgan and LaTourrette hoped that by holding the meetings at the public health clinic, it would encourage the members of the group to use the public health care system for themselves and their babies. The program was perceived to be in the nature of a tentative experiment; it had been designed as a two-year program, but the initial grant covered only one year. No one knew what to expect.

MAELSTROM IN NEW YORK

It turned out that Dollar-a-Day had been in operation for less than six months when a major controversy erupted—not in Denver, but in the offices of the national Planned Parenthood Federation of America (PPFA) in

New York. Nationally, Planned Parenthood was a loose federation of 174 largely autonomous local affiliates around the country; the national board and staff members spearheaded lobbying on federal policy issues, developed national policies for all affiliates, and reviewed programs, policies and budgets from local organizations. Dollar-a-Day began at a time when relations between the local Rocky Mountain Planned Parenthood and the national office were already tense. Sheri Tepper, the innovative and strong-willed executive director of RMPP, did not see eye to eye with the national office on several policy issues. She had stepped on a number of toes during more than 20 years as director. Tepper took an entrepreneurial approach to Planned Parenthood: she believed clinics should charge for services and be economically self-sufficient. She ran the Denver clinics on the entrepreneurial model, then spread her ideas of economic self-sufficiency to other parts of the country; when a far-flung chapter was about to go out of business due to management problems or lack of funds, Tepper would sometimes bring it under the Rocky Mountain umbrella. Consequently, by 1985, when the Dollar-a-Day controversy began, the Rocky Mountain chapter included clinics in West Virginia, Florida and Missouri, as well as the regional area of Colorado, Wyoming and New Mexico. Rocky Mountain was also one of the nation's largest in terms of clients served, providing family planning services to some 55,000 patients in 1985, and educational outreach to an additional 21,000 people. Although all Planned Parenthood affiliates were strong local entities—many predated the creation of the national Planned Parenthood organization—Tepper's geographical conquests and strong leadership style had strained relations with the New York national office.

When the New York PPFA first read of Dollar-a-Day in a Rocky Mountain report, no staff person or board committee wanted to take responsibility for its review. There had never before been an incentive program funded by Planned Parenthood, to the best of anyone's knowledge, and there was no clear consensus on how to respond. Privately, many staffers and board members expressed uneasiness about the program. Yet given Planned Parenthood's decentralized structure, the national organization had no real authority—beyond the power of persuasion—to change programs that seemed to be out of keeping with the mission and policy of the organization. In extreme cases, local affiliates could be kicked out of the federation and banned from using the Planned Parenthood name, but such a step would likely be perceived as excessive by other local affiliates, particularly in the case of a program serving only 12 girls. Dollar-a-Day became an institutional hot potato at the national offices, thrown from one committee or department to another.

The first group to grapple with Dollar-a-Day was the National Medical Committee, whose members had become concerned that the program might be violating PPFA regulations. The Denver program, which had been called "experimental" by the Denver board in its report, did not seem to be following any of the national organization's protocols for either medical or social science research. Nationally, Planned Parenthood maintained strict protocols for experiments using human subjects; violation of these written regulations was considered grounds for rescinding an affiliate's status as a Planned Parenthood organization. Specifically, the Dollar-a-Day group members were not being compared to a specific, identifiable control group, which would have allowed Planned Parenthood to measure the efficacy of the program.

There were more philosophical questions raised by the program, however. These concerns centered around three primary issues:

- Did offering financial incentives violate longstanding Planned Parenthood policies, goals and objectives advocating freedom of reproductive choice?
- Was it discriminatory, in that it seemed to be targeted to minority women?
- By offering financial incentives to poor women, was the program coercive? By stigmatizing pregnancy, was it encouraging abortion?

Eventually, these questions about Dollar-a-Day were debated in Planned Parenthood's individual rights committee, which ultimately brought its concerns about the program to the attention of the full board. The major issue framed in the committee's debate was whether the Denver program was in keeping with the Planned Parenthood mission statement, which read, in part:

> Planned Parenthood believes in the fundamental right of each individual, throughout the world, to manage his or her fertility, regardless of the individual's income, marital status, age, national origin, or residence. We believe that reproductive self-determination must be voluntary and preserve the individual's right to privacy.

"It really struck a chord in some of us," recalls Jane Johnson, vice president for affiliate development and the staff liaison to the affiliate committee. "That abhorrence that we have of anything that smacks of coercion. It was important because it's about where we live, the very soul of the organization. We are about choice and protecting people's reproductive choices." Vice President for Legal Services Eve Paul, who served as staff liaison to the individual rights committee, argued that it might be hypocritical for Planned Parenthood to support such a program, given its response to federal legislation limiting public funding of abortion. "The US government," she says,

> has taken the view that it is wrong to pay for abortions [with public funds]. A poor woman has a strong incentive to take her pregnancy to term, because the government will pay for delivery but not abortion. We think that's wrong—that the government should influence someone's choice by financial incentive. We feel women have to be free to make those decisions.

Others involved in the discussion objected to Dollar-a-Day on the grounds that it was really a stop-gap measure for a few kids. The program might help a few teenagers, they said, but it did not address needs for education, job-training and other services that would help individuals escape the cycle of poverty. "It attacks one of the symptoms," comments Paul.

> It doesn't go to the heart of the problem. It's a quick fix, it tends to distract people's attention. Maybe it does postpone their getting pregnant for a year or two, but it doesn't really address the problems in their lives.

Another staff member criticized the Denver program, calling it questionable public policy, and asked, "What if someone really needed the money, became pregnant, self-aborted and died?"

Building on the conversation within the individual rights committee, the full board of directors continued the debate on Dollar-a-Day at its June 1985 meeting. Dr. Allan Rosenfield, dean of the School of Public Health at Columbia University and then chairman of the board of Planned Parenthood, stepped down temporarily as chair of the meeting to speak out against the program. "A lot of us reacted quite negatively to it because of the ethical questions," remembers Rosenfield, who had extensive experience with family planning and public health issues in developing countries. "My immediate reaction to it was that the concept of paying low income people to do something was potentially coercive." Planned Parenthood President Faye Wattleton and other board members also expressed their concerns. Then board member Richard Stoops, who was also a member of the Rocky Mountain board, got up to defend the Denver program. He argued that Dollar-a-Day was a positive and creative approach to the problem of teen pregnancy, not an attempt to coerce young women. Furthermore, he said, the money was a way of getting kids to come to a *voluntary* support group meeting, rather than a bribe to prevent pregnancy. Stoops also noted that the program was targeted at poor teenagers, not minorities, and that it should not be perceived as discriminatory. Nevertheless, the majority of the board remained uneasy about the program, and sent the matter back to its affiliate development committee, which was asked to gather more information and begin a dialogue with the Rocky Mountain board.

Soon after the June 1985 PPFA board meeting, letters from New York concerning Dollar-a-Day began flooding the Denver office. Faye Wattleton and Board Chairman Allan Rosenfield each wrote letters; separate letters were also sent by the medical, affiliate development and individual rights committees. "All hell broke loose in the spring of 1985," recalls Ruth Hopfenbeck, then the chair of the RMPP board. She recalls responding to one of the board letters, writing "I think there is far more alarm than cause for alarm." Most Denver board members were surprised by the vehemence of the reaction in New York, and all were puzzled by the involvement of the medical committee, which clearly seemed to have misinterpreted the program. Nor could the Rocky Mountain board understand the national board's

charges of coercion, which seemed to the trustees a further misinterpretation of Dollar-a-Day. Despite assertions to the contrary, the national board
seemed to believe the program was targeted at minority groups, and felt
that an incentive program that focused on a particular ethnic or racial group
was coercive. PPFA board members who themselves were members of minority groups were particularly vocal in airing their concerns over the coercion issue. "Well, Faye Wattleton is black and a woman, and Allan Rosenfield is Jewish," comments one RMPP member. "The two of them just *saw*
coercion." Eventually, Rosenfield, accompanied by two other national board
members, flew to Denver on a Dollar-a-Day fact-finding mission. They also
brought messages from the various committees, including one from the
medical committee promising disciplinary action if the program were not
halted immediately. "Allan Rosenfield talked to Sandy Goodman, and he
said, 'No, you will *not* continue,'" recalls Hopfenbeck. "She's a quiet, soft-
spoken person, but she said to him, 'Yes, we *are* going to continue.'" In the
end, Goodman's seemingly defiant attitude prevailed among her fellow
RMPP board members. "We were surprised that they were unhappy," comments Ellen Anderman, but "it was honestly debated at the [RMPP] board
level. In the end we decided to go forward with it."

Short of revoking Rocky Mountain's legal permission to use the Planned
Parenthood name, there was little the national board could do once Denver
had voted to continue. Almost as abruptly as it began, the whole controversy ended, by the end of the summer. Back in New York, the national
board adopted a "lose the battle, but win the war" strategy, hoping that a
strong policy on incentives could prevent future programs from starting in
the first place, and, at the same time, give the board clear authority to halt
existing programs.

A POLICY ON INCENTIVES

As the storm of controversy with Denver subsided, the individual rights
committee set about developing a policy on incentives, which would then
be sent to the voting membership of the organization—the board and two
representatives from each affiliate—for approval. Given the full agenda of
the individual rights committee, however, and the extensive, soul-searching
debate within the committee on how to draft such a policy, the individual
rights committee did not report back to the membership with a proposed
incentive policy until shortly before the November 1987 membership meeting. Tim Lannan, director of board affairs, notes that the long delay between
the initial controversy with Denver and the emergence of a draft policy was
not unusual for Planned Parenthood. "We process a lot," says Lannan.
"We're a very process-oriented organization."

In the early stages of the discussion, two members of the committee
proposed a policy on incentives that would create a set of criteria under
which such programs could be evaluated in the future. Yet committee members could not agree on the definition of an incentive, and found it difficult

to formulate a uniform set of criteria for all incentive programs. After some discussion, the committee decided against the criteria-based policy in favor of a more general policy on incentive programs.

At that point, the international committee also got involved in the debate. According to Dan Weintraub, vice president for international programs, the concept of an incentive program raised special issues for Planned Parenthood in an international context. PPFA had long been a staunch and outspoken critic of coercive population control efforts used in certain Third World countries, particularly China's forced abortion policies. In its discussion of the proposed incentive policy, the international committee asked Weintraub whether Planned Parenthood would ever allow a Dollar-a-Day-type incentive program in any of its international operations. "I said 'absolutely not!'" recalls Weintraub (he adds that such a program would not be cost effective in the international context, where PPFA spent about six dollars, annually, on each individual served). The real issue for the two committees, however, was "when does an incentive become unacceptable?" Weintraub points out that he does not oppose all incentives, and that in fact Planned Parenthood affiliates *did* offer certain kinds of incentives, such as evening hours or babysitting, to make their services more attractive to consumers. He argues, however, than an incentive designed to *facilitate* the use of family planning services was not coercive, since no individual would make use of unwanted family planning services simply because he/she could get free babysitting while doing so. In developing countries, by contrast, women have been offered gifts such as saris or radios in exchange for being sterilized. Such incentives, says Weintraub, do interfere with an individual's freedom of choice:

> My argument is that the incentive becomes unacceptable when the people are doing it not because they didn't want to become pregnant, but because they wanted the money. The sari or the radio means nothing to you or me, but the question we had to ask ourselves is, if someone offers you a million dollars to be sterilized, would you take it? For some of these women, a sari or a radio is like a million dollars. And while the batteries will go dead and the sari will wear out, the tubes remain tied. My position is that it is a subtle form of coercion.

These distinctions between types of incentives became an integral part of the draft policy eventually produced by the individual rights committee (with input from the international committee). The proposal was approved by the committee and sent to the full board for review. The board made a few minor changes, and sent the draft policy to the membership for voting. It read, in part,

> Planned Parenthood recognizes that . . . many programs of governments and of private agencies may . . . operate as "incentives" for choosing parenthood or non-parenthood. It is the policy of Planned Parenthood Federation of America to evaluate such programs on a case by case basis to determine whether they

enhance freedom of choice (for example, a tax exemption for each child . . . or the provision of free voluntary family planning services to the poor) or restrict freedom of choice (for example, an offer of money or goods to a needy person if that person agrees to accept contraception or sterilization). Planned Parenthood's policy is to favor those programs which in actual operation . . . regardless of the asserted reason for the program, enhance or facilitate freedom of choice, and to oppose those which restrict freedom of choice.

Prior to the actual vote on the incentive policy, however, the PPFA minority caucus objected to the wording of the draft proposal, stating that it "lacked clarity and did not meet the purpose for which it was designed." Due to the concerns of the minority caucus, no vote was taken on the issue. Instead, the individual rights committee was asked to redraft the incentive policy and present it at the following membership meeting, in February 1987. Things proceeded no further, however: the individual rights committee did not pursue rewriting the incentive policy, and the matter was dropped, as far as the national board was concerned.

DOLLAR-A-DAY TO DATE

Locally, the program weathered the storm of controversy from New York and continued, maintaining a core group of girls who joined Dollar-a-Day for a two-year period. In 1987, when the program had been up and running for several years, Dollar-a-Day caused some internal consternation on the RMPP board, when several board members realized that, unlike other Planned Parenthood programs, handing out contraceptives and educating young women about birth control were *not* the primary aims of the group (although contraception information was readily available if the participants *asked* for it). There remain one or two Dollar-a-Day skeptics within the Denver organization, including a radical feminist who points out that the program was designed by a man, and calls it "prostitution in reverse," or "paying for non-performance." The group itself has changed somewhat over the years; a 1984 state constitutional amendment prohibiting public funding for abortion has meant a drastic increase in the number of live births among teenage girls. In the early years of Dollar-a-Day, many of the girls had been pregnant but had had an abortion; today, the first pregnancy has usually been carried to term, and there are more children at the meetings.

Those involved with the program say they can see tangible results in individual participants as well as the larger community. There have been 56 "graduates" of Dollar-a-Day, who have achieved an 83 percent rate of success in avoiding second pregnancies. Approximately 20 more girls have been involved for less than the required two years. The 1989–90 group appears to be on its way to even better results, achieving a 90 + percent success rate.[3] For Jeff Dolgan, it has been heartening to see his theories put into practice, particularly since they seem to be achieving results. Recalls Dolgan:

One day a kid told me she could have become pregnant the night before. But, she thought, "Well, if I get pregnant I can't keep coming to the group." "I'm not going to get paid," was the way she put it. She attached value to the group [in making her decision]. "What did you say to your boyfriend?" I asked her. "I told him to stop," she said. That was new behavior for her—she has no assertive female role models.

Girls are nevertheless still shy about admitting they cared about the group. When asked why she attended, one participant says, "It's something to do on Thursday afternoons," but her casual response contrasts with an impeccable attendance record. While not a huge sum, the money allows girls to buy themselves a special treat once in a while; Dollar-a-Day counselors urge members to spend the money on themselves, rather than their babies. Another group member comments:

> The reason I was interested and started coming to this group is because there are people here that really care and help us out. The money I receive goes for diapers, milk . . . stuff teenage mothers just don't have sometimes.

Similarly, board members such as Ruth Hopfenbeck emphasize that Dollar-a-Day provides support that was otherwise lacking in the lives of these young women:

> If you can just get them [to avoid pregnancy] until they are 18 or 19 you've gone a long way. They are getting care and attention they've never had before. It's a different kind of attention than the kind they would get from a boyfriend.

Dollar-a-Day has also had an impact on the national reproductive health community. There are now spin-off programs operated by six other Planned Parenthood affiliates, aided by a Dollar-a-Day guidebook written by Jeff Dolgan and Sandra Goodman providing "how-to" information for organizations hoping to start a group. One federally funded spin-off was attempted in Denver, by a private non-profit, but was not successful; critics of the federal program say that, unlike the original Dollar-a-Day program, the federal spin-off imposed too many rules and regulations on its participants. The latest offshoot project is being set up by Rocky Mountain itself, targeting high-risk rural teenagers in efforts to prevent *primary* pregnancies. Those involved are uncertain if the concept will work, given the differences between the new program and the model. Dollar-a-Day has also generated national publicity, the result of a local newspaper article that was picked up by television talk shows, other newspapers, and magazines. Rocky Mountain Planned Parenthood board members and staffers have welcomed the publicity, which aids in fundraising and helps publicize the program's vision and goals.

NOTES

1. The $250,000 figure is based on 1988 projections from the Colorado Initiative on Teenage Pregnancy and the Colorado Department of Social Services. Studies from

the two groups estimated the cost to the state of a teenage pregnancy for an individual on welfare was between $13,000 and $18,700 (for the first year of the baby's life). Colorado AFDC payments for a single mother under the age of 18 are $280 per month with one child ($3360 annually) and $360 per month for a teenage mother with two children ($4320 annually), plus Medicaid and Food Stamps. Rocky Mountain Planned Parenthood changed its name to Planned Parenthood of the Rocky Mountains in 1987.

2. Eighteen signed up for the program the first year; about 12 members attended regularly.

3. There were nine pregnancies among the 56 graduates; the 1989–1990 group has had only one pregnancy as of this writing, giving it a success rate over 90 percent. Estimates of the repeat pregnancy rate among high-risk teens vary considerably, but the respected Alan Guttmacher Institute estimated that 37–50 percent of teenage girls in a high-risk group who had been pregnant as young teenagers would become pregnant again before they were 20. Pregnancy rates for teenage girls enrolled in prevention programs were still as high as 50 percent, which bolstered charges that such programs do not work. National estimates from 1979—which include young women in low-risk categories—predicted that 31 percent of teenagers who have had a premarital pregnancy will become pregnant again within two years. (Statistics courtesy of the Alan Guttmacher Institute.) See *Risking the Future: Adolescent Sexuality, Pregnancy and Childbearing*, D. Hayes, ed., Panel on Adolescent Pregnancy and Childbearing, National Research Council (Washington: National Academy Press, 1987).

Cocaine Mothers
José A. Gomez-Ibañez

In February 1989 the Florida state attorney's office for Broward County charged Ms. Gethers, a young 22-year-old, with child abuse after she gave birth to a second baby with signs of cocaine dependency. She had ignored repeated warnings during her second pregnancy about the damage cocaine use might have on her unborn child. The state attorney argued that the woman could be charged despite the fact that Florida law does not recognize a fetus as an individual because, although the abuse began as a fetus, the injuries continued after birth. (See Exhibit 1.)

The Florida case was one of the latest of several across the country dealing with drug abuse during pregnancy.[1] In one early case in 1986, a Los Angeles woman was prosecuted for contributing to the death of her infant son who was born with severe brain damage and died six weeks after birth. Prosecutors argued that she contributed to her son's death by taking amphetamines and marijuana and engaging in other risky behavior against her doctor's orders during pregnancy. The Los Angeles case was eventually dismissed when a judged ruled that the California legislature never intended the child abuse law to apply to a pregnant woman's conduct. The judge noted in his ruling, however, that there seemed to be no constitutional con-

EXHIBIT 1

Broward mother charged in birth of 'cocaine baby'

By JAMES F. McCARTY
And DIEDTRA HENDERSON
Herald Staff Writers

Casandra Denise Gethers' first cocaine-dependent child was a tragedy. The birth of her second cocaine baby, nine months later, was worse—it was criminal, said the Broward state attorney's office, which charged Gethers with child abuse Wednesday.

Gethers, 22, an unemployed cashier from Hollywood and among the thousands of South Florida women who give birth each year to cocaine-dependent babies, is the first in South Florida to be charged with child abuse.

Legal and medical authorities say charges have been filed in Florida against two other mothers of cocaine babies, in Orlando and in North Florida. Other cases are pending across the country. None has ended in the conviction of the mother.

Assistant state attorney Dennis Bailey said he decided to charge Gethers because she gave birth to a second cocaine baby and because she disregarded numerous warnings about the damage she was doing to her unborn child by her cocaine addiction.

Babies born to mothers addicted to cocaine usually are born premature, sickly, shaking and underweight.

Bailey explained that although the alleged child abuse began with a fetus—which is not a human being in the eyes of Florida law—the injuries continued after birth. That fits the description of child abuse, he said.

The prosecutor said the decision to charge Gethers came after much soul-searching.

"Putting her in jail isn't going to solve her problems one iota," Bailey said. "But, at the same time, I can't turn my back on the fact that through her criminal acts she is injuring innocent people."

In an interview, a tearful Gethers said she has turned her life around, quit using drugs and begun searching for a job. She plans to surrender to Hollywood police today.

"I don't feel I'm a child abuser," Gethers said. "Being in my shoes, you wouldn't look at it like child abuse. I was abusing myself, and something grew inside me."

Gethers said that a year ago she was hooked on crack and didn't realize she was pregnant for several months.

But on Nov. 3, less than two weeks before her daughter Tjavier Rachel was born, she said she quit crack for good.

"Now I'm never going to have the chance to be anybody," she said. "I thought my life was changing, that I was doing good, but it's going to be worse now than ever before."

Gethers' mother, Lenora Sams, 38, said her daughter is a good mother "when she wants to be."

"I'm going to be honest with you, she's hot-tempered," Sams said. "I don't think I have the potential to scare her straight. If the state tells her to straighten out, maybe she'll think about it. . . ."

Gethers is on two years' probation for three previous convictions for possession of cocaine and marijuana. Her son, 1-year-old Antonyo John, is living with Gethers and the boy's great-grandparents. Gethers' 3-month-old daughter is staying in a foster home in Fort Lauderdale.

Hollywood police detective Curtiss Navarro said he learned that Gethers continued her use of crack cocaine during pregnancy even while under court-ordered medical supervision.

In South Florida, the occurrence of cocaine babies is especially acute at Jackson Memorial Hospital, which sees about 1,700

EXHIBIT 1 (*continued*)

cocaine babies a year, and Broward General Medical Center, which sees about 1,400. As many as 30 percent of the newborns at these two hospitals are cocaine babies, said Dr. Brian Udell, a Broward neonatalogist who specializes in the field. "I think criminal prosecution is counterproductive," Udell said. "The ultimate outcome is that my patients end up getting worse care. We really need to attack the social problems, while these legal things are going to be very sticky wickets."

That is the essential problem facing police, prosecutors, doctors and social-service workers: when to push for drug rehabilitation and when to push for criminal convictions.

Pat O'Keefe of the National Association for Perinatal Addiction Research and Education in Chicago, said, "We're in favor of treatment, not criminalization. In most cases, where they've tried to put the mom in jail, in the end it has been struck down."

Source: Miami Herald, February 23, 1989. Reprinted by permission.

straint against the legislature amending the child abuse statute to cover the mother's conduct. In 1988 a District of Columbia judge denied probation to a pregnant woman convicted of second degree theft who tested positive for cocaine and ordered her to serve the remaining three months of her pregnancy in jail on the theory that her fetus needed protection from her drug abuse. Criminal charges of child abuse or child endangerment have been brought against women who used cocaine during pregnancy in Toledo, Ohio and Phoenix, Arizona as well, although the resolution of these cases had not been reported at the time Ms. Gethers was charged.

THE SPREAD OF COCAINE USE

The prosecutions in Florida and elsewhere were motivated in part by growing alarm and frustration among law enforcement agencies, the medical community, and the public at large with the rapid spread of cocaine use in the 1980s. Cocaine acts both as a local anesthetic (by constricting local blood vessels) and as a general stimulant to the cardiovascular and central nervous systems. Its anesthetic properties were discovered during the Civil War era and it was soon prescribed for nose and throat surgery and marketed as a toothache remedy.[2] The popularity of cocaine increased as its stimulant and psychotropic properties were recognized. Cocaine for inhalation was available at the corner drugstore in the 1880s and by the turn of the century it was regarded as something of a wonder drug, useful not only as a local anesthetic but as a general cure-all that made the patient feel good too. With more widespread use, the highly addictive nature of cocaine became apparent and reports surfaced of adverse psychotic reactions, convulsions, and even sudden death. Medical research soon revealed cocaine's dangers and its sale and use were severely restricted by the Harrison Anti-Narcotic Act of 1914.

When popular interest in cocaine reemerged in the mid-1970s many of the lessons of the previous century had been forgotten. In some affluent and professional circles the classification of cocaine as a narcotic sixty years earlier came to be regarded as a mistake. Cocaine was thought to be not physically addictive, but at worst psychologically addictive to the weak willed. The stimulant properties of cocaine were believed to enhance social and professional performance and its expense and mystique soon made snorting cocaine trendy and chic in some upper socioeconomic circles.

As the supply of cocaine expanded to meet increasing demand, the price of cocaine dropped and its use spread to all socioeconomic levels of society. By 1985, one survey estimated that 20 million Americans had used cocaine at least once and 5 million used it regularly. A National Institute on Drug Abuse study shows that US high school students now favor cocaine second only to marijuana among illegal drugs.[3]

The high rates of cocaine use, particularly among young men and women, have led to increasing numbers of infants born of mothers who used cocaine during pregnancy. The 1985 survey suggested that 1.1 million women of childbearing age were regular cocaine users. In Jackson Memorial Hospital in Miami, for example, one in ten of the babies born in 1988 tested positive for cocaine.[4] In a sample of the predominantly young and low-income mothers who gave birth in Boston City Hospital from mid-1984 to mid-1987, 18 percent used cocaine during pregnancy (determined either by their own admissions or by a urine test) and 27 percent used marijuana.[5]

Cocaine addiction has proven extremely difficult to combat. Cocaine is highly addictive whether injected intravenously or snorted. "Crack," a cocaine derivative that is now particularly popular, is thought to be particularly addictive and is often available for as little as $5 a dose. Law enforcement efforts to stop cocaine from entering the United States or to catch distributors and sellers have been generally unsuccessful; as soon as police attention is directed to one port of entry or route another develops, and arrested dealers and distributors are soon replaced. Criminal sanctions also appear to have little effect on chronic users.

Drug treatment programs have proven only moderately successful in reducing use.[6] Long-term follow-up studies of heroin addicts show that about one-third of those entering treatment report nonuse (the results are similar whether the patients enter a therapeutic community, a drug free outpatient program, or methadone maintenance). Cocaine treatment has less of a track record as yet, and it is still unclear whether new treatment methods will have to be devised for cocaine dependence. There is a strong suspicion, moreover, that the drug treatment programs skim the cream off the drug-using population. Heroin treatment works best for patients with a stable background and few psychological problems, for example, but appears to have little effect on patients with high levels of criminality and psychopathology. Some drug experts recommend mandatory treatment for convicted criminals who have positive urine tests, but such programs may offer limited hope of reducing drug use and may be sensible primarily because the alternative of incarceration is also so expensive. Perhaps because of doubts about their effectiveness, government funding for drug treatment programs has not kept pace with the population seeking treatment, and there are long waiting lists for treatment in most cities.

Drug prevention and education programs also offer some hope, but perhaps only in the long term.[7] Prevention programs are aimed at persons who use a drug occasionally or might be tempted to do so, while treatment programs are aimed at persons who have become chronic users. Some sociologists and psychologists believe that there are cycles in the use of any particular drug that are conditioned by changing social values and attitudes. As was the case with cocaine in the previous century, use of any particular drug declines only after the drug's novelty wears off, its harmful effects become more widely appreciated, and social norms and peer pressure change to discourage the recruitment of new users. How educational or other programs might accelerate the change in values and peer pressure is poorly understood, however. The few school drug education programs that have been carefully evaluated generally show favorable results, but the students involved are typically from stable middle-class backgrounds and the results may not be generalizable. There is also some fragmentary evidence to support the fear that poorly designed education campaigns may actually increase drug familiarity and abuse among the young.

EFFECTS OF PRENATAL COCAINE EXPOSURE

Medical researchers are only beginning to study the physical and developmental effects of cocaine exposure during pregnancy, but the preliminary results are alarming. The placenta was once thought to be a barrier that protects the fetus from toxic substances during pregnancy, but it is now known that many drugs, including cocaine and heroin, freely cross the placenta into fetal circulation. The fetus may be exposed to the drugs longer than the mother, moreover, because they are not metabolized as rapidly by the immature fetal liver and kidney.[8]

Research has shown that fetal exposure to cocaine, marijuana, and other drugs is associated with reduced birth weight and size. (Low birth weight is a sign of prematurity, which is associated with a higher risk of respiratory distress syndrome, brain hemorrhages, chronic lung disease, and neurodevelopmental problems.) The most exhaustive study of cocaine use on fetal growth to date is based on 1226 infants born in Boston City Hospital during the mid 1980s. The Boston City Hospital researchers estimate that when other risk factors are controlled for (such as the mother's age, amount of weight gain during pregnancy, cigarette smoking, etc.) mothers who had positive urine tests for cocaine use gave birth to babies that weighed 93 grams less, were 0.7 cm. shorter, and had a 0.43 cm. smaller head circumference than infants of non-users. A positive urine test for marijuana was associated with similar reductions in birth weight (29 grams less) and length (0.5 cm. shorter). Women who reported cocaine or marijuana use during pregnancy but did not have positive urine tests, did not have infants with significantly decreased birth weight, length, or head circumference; the researchers speculate that self-reporting mothers were less frequent cocaine or marijuana users than mothers testing positive in urine analyses.[9]

Cocaine is thought to directly reduce fetal growth because the drug constricts the blood supply to the fetus by increasing the maternal heart rate and blood pressure and inducing uterine vasoconstriction. Boston City Hospital researchers also speculate that cocaine may have a second and indirect effect on fetal growth because the drug is known to suppress appetite. The Boston study found that cocaine-using mothers weighed significantly less before pregnancy and gained less weight during pregnancy than non-users. If the lower maternal weight is also attributed to cocaine use, the researchers estimate that cocaine reduces birth weight by an additional 50 percent (137 instead of 93 grams).

Cocaine also appears to interact with other factors that contribute to reduced fetal growth, such as smoking or drinking during pregnancy. The same Boston City Hospital researchers estimate that women who smoke one pack of cigarettes per day, gain only 4.5 kg. (10 lbs.) during pregnancy, and have positive urine assays for marijuana and cocaine could be expected to deliver infants that weigh 416 grams less than the infants of mothers who do not smoke cigarettes, gain 10.5 kg. (23 lbs.) during pregnancy, and do not have positive urine tests for cocaine or marijuana.[10]

Cocaine use during pregnancy is also associated with other serious physiological and behavioral problems, although these problems are less well documented, in part because they are harder to measure than reduced birth weight and size. Researchers have long suspected that cocaine use during pregnancy increases the risk of birth defects, based largely on the fact that cocaine-using women have higher rates of miscarriage. These suspicions were recently confirmed in a study by the Federal Center for Disease Control (CDC) of 5000 mothers of children born with birth defects between 1968 and 1980. The CDC study found that the rate of urinary tract birth defects, including seriously malformed kidneys, was 4.8 times higher among women who reported using cocaine during the first trimester of pregnancy. The CDC researchers speculate that the actual rate of birth defects from cocaine use is much higher because the researchers had to rely on admissions of cocaine use by the mothers and did not have access to urine tests or other evidence.[11] The fact that birth defects appeared to be caused by cocaine use in the first trimester but not later is particularly troubling since many women may not realize they are pregnant early enough to stop cocaine use and to prevent the defects.

Equally troubling are the behavioral problems in newborns and infants of drug addicted mothers that have been reported extensively by the Perinatal Addiction Project at Northwestern University Memorial Hospital, a program that has cared for and monitored drug-addicted mothers and their children for over a decade. The Northwestern researchers find that babies born of cocaine-addicted mothers catch up in weight and length with babies born of non-users within nine months, but that their head size still remains smaller at two years of age.[12] The Northwestern researchers confirm the reports of clinicians that babies born of cocaine-addicted mothers suffer from withdrawal symptoms, including irritability, poor feeding patterns, and increased tremulousness and startles (the "shakes"). In addition, they find that cocaine-exposed babies test lower on standard behavioral tests for newborns, especially in their ability to respond to environmental stimuli. Since a cocaine-exposed newborn is easily irritated and fails to respond normally to his or her caregiver, the Northwestern researchers fear that the parents will have difficulty bonding with their child and that feelings of frustration and inadequacy may both discourage the parents from giving their baby the care it needs and predispose the parents to later physical child abuse.[13]

Researchers also wonder whether the behavioral and other physiological problems of cocaine-exposed newborns might extend to more subtle forms of minimal brain dysfunction, such as learning disabilities and hyperactivity, as these children grow up.[14] However, researchers are quick to point out that the long-term prospects for these children are unclear, in part because few babies were exposed to cocaine during pregnancy until recent years.

LEGAL ISSUES [15]

The Florida state attorney's office case against Ms. Gethers had been strengthened by amendments made by the Florida legislature to the state's child abuse and neglect statute two years earlier. Prior to the 1987 amendments, the Florida statute defined a child as "any person under the age of 18 years of age" and the Florida Attorney General had concluded that this language did not cover a child born addicted (since a fetus is not considered a person under most states' laws). The amended statute specifically included "physical dependency of a newborn infant upon any drug" among the harms that constitute child abuse or neglect for the purposes of civil proceedings (such as taking the child away from the parents). The prosecution for abuse [could be based] solely on the basis of a newborn's drug dependency.[16] Presumably, Ms. Gethers' previous record and ignored warnings made her liable to criminal prosecution.

Courts have long held that states have a legitimate interest in preventing child abuse and neglect. State actions to remove children from the home, criminally prosecute the parents, or undertake other [acts] conflicting [with] family and privacy rights [are permitted] as long as the state statutes are carefully crafted. Generally, the statutes must protect the parent's due process and privacy rights by insuring that there is a thorough investigation and that parents have an opportunity to respond before a long-term remedy is ordered. The statutes must also limit state intervention to circumstances where there is no alternative to protect the child.[17]

Legal experts and others point out that the constitutional and ethical issues of extending child abuse and neglect laws to cover prenatal conduct are fundamentally different from those governing abortion. In the case of abortion one can argue that the mother's and fetus' interests are in conflict. In the case of prenatal neglect or abuse, however, the conflict is less strong since the mother presumably has a strong stake in delivering a healthy baby when she decides to carry the pregnancy to term.[18] From a constitutional perspective the issue is not whether the woman has a right to terminate her pregnancy and the state has a right to protect potential life, but rather whether the woman can be ordered not to engage in certain conduct during her pregnancy (e.g. drug abuse) that is likely to interfere with the state's interest in protecting the future quality of life of her child.[19]

Legal experts also believe that it is not necessary for state law to declare a fetus a person (with all the other attendant constitutional rights and implications) in order to extend neglect and abuse laws to prenatal conduct. In Roe v. Wade, the 1973 Supreme Court ruling that struck down state statutes banning abortion, the Court specifically stated that the word "person" in the 14th amendment did not include a fetus. The Court nonetheless held that the state had an interest in protecting human life and could prohibit abortions in the third trimester of pregnancy, after the fetus was viable.[20] Thus even in a Supreme Court ruling that was hailed by abortion rights advocates, the Court recognized that the state had a compelling interest in the health of a fetus in the last trimester of pregnancy.

The courts' willingness to protect the unborn is also reflected in the fact that in the last forty years courts in all fifty states have recognized prenatal injuries as a legitimate ground for civil damage suits, at least as long as the child was born alive. Courts have allowed children (or their parents) to sue third parties, such as malpracticing doctors, for injuries sustained during pregnancy on the grounds that a child has a "right to begin life with a sound mind and body."[21] Courts have even allowed children to sue their mothers for damages due to prenatal conduct, such as negligence in operating a motor vehicle (which resulted in an accident that injured the fetus) to in one case taking tetracycline during pregnancy (which discolored the child's teeth).[22] If the fetus is not born alive, however, state courts are split on whether negligent parties can be sued for damages under wrongful death statutes or criminally prosecuted under homicide statutes. Some courts don't allow wrongful death suits or homicide prosecutions for unborn fetuses at all, for example, while others allow them if the fetus was viable at the time of injury, and a few allow them whether or not the fetus was viable.[23]

Only two other states besides Florida have amended their child abuse and neglect statutes to specifically cover prenatal drug abuse. One state, New Jersey, has enacted an extraordinarily broad statute that holds that all the provisions of the child endangerment statute shall apply to the unborn. While the New Jersey statute has not been tested in court yet, some legal observers believe that it will be found unconstitutional because it is so broad and vague that it could conceivably cover all kinds of maternal conduct, including exercise, diet, or smoking. The other state, Massachusetts, passed a narrower statute which, like Florida's, is likely to survive constitutional review because it lists drug abuse as the only neglectful form of prenatal conduct.[24]

In states where the legislature has not explicitly extended their child abuse laws to cover prenatal conduct, the courts have a mixed record in allowing such extensions. Sometimes the courts of a single state offer conflicting rulings. On the one hand, for example, New York courts have held in several cases that a drug dependent newborn is a prima facie case of a neglected baby, and in one case a New York court argued that a mother's abuse of alcohol during pregnancy was sufficient to establish neglect.[25] On the other hand, New York City's Human Resources Administration will not take legal action against pregnant women whose actions may be endangering their unborn children for fear of constitutional challenge,[26] and one New York court refused to find actual neglect based on the mother's drug and alcohol addiction when a baby was born with withdrawal symptoms because of the broad implications of such a finding:

> Since it is clear that a child in utero may be endangered or actually harmed by a broad range of conduct on the part of a pregnant woman, it would appear necessary to limit any application of the neglect statute to prenatal maternal conduct to a narrow and clearly defined class of cases. It may be possible to identify some cases in which it is common knowledge that the maternal conduct in question creates an unreasonable risk of harm to the fetus. However, even a "knew or should have known" standard may prove difficult to administer.[27]

NOTES

1. This review of legal cases is drawn from Walter B. Connolly, Jr., and Alison B. Marshall, "Drug Addiction, AIDS and Childbirth: The Legal Issues for the Medical and Social Services Communities," photocopied paper, Miller, Canfield, Paddock and Stone, Detroit, MI.

2. This history of cocaine use is based on Charles V. Wetli, "The Medical Risks of Cocaine," *The Journal of Western Medicine*, 1988, and David Musto, "Lessons of the First Cocaine Epidemic," *The Wall Street Journal*, June 11, 1986.

3. As reported in Ira Chasnoff, "Perinatal Effects of Cocaine," *Contemporary Ob/Gyn* [May 1987].

4. Personal communication from Charles V. Wetli, M.D., Deputy Medical Examiner, Metro Dade County, Florida.

5. Barry Zuckerman et al., "Effects of Maternal Marijuana and Cocaine Use on Fetal Growth," *New England Journal of Medicine*, March 23, 1989, p. 764.

6. This summary of treatment programs is drawn from Francis X. Hartmann and Saul N. Weingart, "Strategies for Demand Side: Prevention, Early Intervention, and Treatment," Program in Criminal Justice Policy and Management, Kennedy School of Government, Harvard University, 1987, working paper no. 87-01-02, pp. 40–46.

7. Hartmann and Weingart, *op. cit.*

8. Jane W. Schneider and Ira J. Chasnoff, "Cocaine Abuse During Pregnancy: Its Effects on Infant Motor Development," *Topics in Acute Care and Trauma Rehabilitation*, 1987, 2(1):58.

9. Zuckerman, *et. al.*, p. 765.

10. Zuckerman, *et. al.*, p. 767.

11. The normal risk of urinary tract defect is 1.5 per 1000 births and the CDC study found 7.2 defects per 1000 births [among women] who reported use of cocaine in the first trimester. Previous studies had reported higher rates of genital defects but these were not confirmed by the CDC researchers. "Defects Reported in Babies of Cocaine Users," *New York Times*, August 13, 1989.

12. Ira J. Chasnoff, et. al., "Prenatal Drug Exposure: Effects on Neonatal and Infant Growth and Development," *Neurobehavioral Toxicology and Tetrology* 8 (1986): 357–362.

13. Schneider and Chasnoff, *op. cit.*, p. 60.

14. E.g., Schneider and Chasnoff, *op. cit.*

15. This section of the case draws heavily from and paraphrases in part Connolloy and Marshall, *op. cit.*

16. Connolly and Marshall, *op cit.*, pp. 38 and 49.

17. Connolly and Marshall, *op cit.*, pp. 13–14.

18. Dawn Johnson, "A New Threat to Pregnant Women's Authority," Hastings Center Report, August 1987, pp. 35–36.

19. Connolly and Marshall, *op cit.*, p. 5.

20. Connolly and Marshall, *op cit.*, p. 4.

21. Connolly and Marshall, *op cit.*, p. 22.

22. Connolly and Marshall, *op cit.*, pp. 25–27.

23. Connolly and Marshall, *op cit.*, pp. 24–25 and 29.

24. Connolly and Marshall, *op cit.*, pp. 36–38.

25. Connolly and Marshall, *op cit.*, pp. 33–35.

26. Connolly and Marshall, *op cit.*, p. 44.

27. Court ruling as quoted by Connolly and Marshall, *op. cit.*, p. 34.

SECTION C

Domestic Violence

Battered Women's Refuges

Lois Ahrens

Refuges for battered women, like rape crisis centers, seem to be undergoing a transformation throughout the United States from feminist, nonhierarchical, community-based organizations to institutionalized social service agencies. The shelter in Austin, Texas provides a typical example of this transformation. As someone who witnessed this process as part of the original Coalition on Battered Women which formed in Austin, Texas in November 1976, and later as one of the shelter's two staff people first hired in May 1977, I have had a long association with the Center, from planning to implementation stages. This experience may help feminists working with battered women avoid the pitfalls we faced.

When we began in November 1976, we were a coalition of twenty women who represented a feminist counseling collective, a women and alcoholism task force, a Chicano group, nurses, social workers, grant writers, a women's center, the local mental health agency, and women who had themselves been battered or who had come from families where mothers or sisters had been battered. We represented a diversity of agencies, ages, ethnicities, and ideologies. Though our differences were abundant, our common goal kept us striving to have everyone's concerns heard. We spent hundreds of hours talking about what we wanted the goals of the group to be because we felt that process to be crucial to creating a nonbureaucratic organization. Through discussion it appeared that we all believed hierarchical models are oppressive to all people, and have historically been especially so to minorities and to women, in particular, battered women. Because of this conviction we believed that the structure of refuges for women should be models for collective work. Each individual should have her own area of expertise and that work should be done in a collaborative manner. We argued that this method would allow for personal growth for staff members

304

and also serve as a model to women living in the Center by showing that women can work together cooperatively, without bosses.

Further, the group ostensibly agreed that when we create bureaucracies each worker's role in the shelter becomes more specialized and fragmented. Such specialization leads to individual involvement in only one area and creates a familiar syndrome. First, workers begin to feel less responsibility and involvement with the entire program. They begin to view work as a 'job', lacking political purpose. Second, the individual worker feels less empowered and less capable of working as peers with women who come to the refuge. Women are transformed into 'clients' to be routed from one desk or department to another (and nowhere viewed as complex individuals). In this scheme everyone suffers and feminist hopes for new models of support are dashed.

PHASE ONE: THE FORMATIVE STAGE

In the beginning, our group was singly-focused, and functioned in a collective and task-oriented fashion. At the time, there seemed to be general agreement on issues such as the value of a feminist perspective in the shelter, the inclusion of lesbians as visible members of the collective, and the need for workers and residents in the shelter to share in decision-making and leadership. We viewed ourselves as a collective, and a very successful one. Our Center opened in June 1977, funded by county and private mental health funds.

PHASE TWO: SIGNIFICANT CHANGES

Soon after the shelter opened, the twenty coalition members agreed to form a twelve-member Coordinating Committee. The coalition agreed that a smaller number of women was needed to meet more frequently to direct the actual workings of the new Center. They elected twelve of their group according to how much time and energy each could devote to a Coordinating Committee. Three different things began to happen at that point. First, two of the Committee members became paid staff people. Staff was working approximately eighty hours a week and therefore had greater and greater knowledge of the shelter operations. Other Coordinating Committee members began to feel threatened by this shift and started treating the staff as 'paid help.' Simultaneously, many Coordinating Committee members chose not to work directly in the shelter. A division grew between members with day-to-day knowledge of shelter happenings and those who became more divorced from the daily realities faced by paid and nonpaid staff. Secondly, many of the original Coalition members who identified themselves as radical feminists became involved in other projects instead of continuing with the Center. They felt they had worked to establish the shelter, but were not interested in committing time to its daily operation. This created a definite tilt in ideological perspective on the Coordinating Committee and a significant lessening of support for the few remaining radical feminists. Third, the Center for Battered Women began its own process of incorporating as a non-profit, tax-exempt organization.

PHASE THREE: BOARD DEVELOPMENT

Until that point we operated under the tax-exempt status of the Austin Women's Center. Six months after the Austin Center for Battered Women began its own incorporation process, elections were held to choose a board of directors. Unfortunately, the first board was not representative of the community. Ballots were sent to those on the mailing list and to all those who had participated in volunteer training. Individuals who merely "expressed interest in the issue of battered women" composed one part of the electorate. Women volunteered to run for directors. This loose system allowed board members to be selected who had had no previous contact with the Center or whose knowledge of the Center was only through friends of the incumbent board members. Volunteers in the shelter were already working overtime, and most could not be convinced of the necessity of volunteer representation on the board. The majority of volunteers had had little or no previous experience as volunteers or as board members, since they were former battered women who were divorced, working full-time jobs, and caring for their children. Most felt their primary interest was in working directly with battered women in the shelter, not in serving on the board.

This vague and unrepresentative election allowed for board members to be elected who represented no community or group, making them responsible or responsive to no one but themselves. This problem grew when two minority women (both volunteers with a community base), feeling overlooked and misunderstood, resigned from the board. The board, rather than address the issues raised by their resignations or call new elections, replaced them by appointing two personal friends, an Anglo male lawyer and an Anglo woman.

The staff viewed this as a consolidation of power by the board, and challenged the appointment rather than election of new board members. The staff protested a number of issues. First, no attempt was made to fill the vacancies with other Black and Chicano women involved with the shelter. Second, the board was not addressing the issues the two women had raised. Third, there had been no precedent for having men on the board. The staff indicated to the board that it was essential for them to examine their own racism and the Center's credibility in the Black and Chicano communities. Further, we were concerned that the replacement board members had no ties to the daily operation of the shelter. The board responded to our concerns by sending letters to the ex-board members thanking them for their past work. Both women continued to work in the Center.

Further, staff recommendations that all board members participate minimally in the eighteen-hour volunteer training was turned down. Board members were elected and served without prior knowledge of the Coalition's original plan for the working of the shelter. The board/staff division became sharper as fewer board members maintained contact with battered women at the shelter. This division and the fact that the more strongly feminist women had already left the original group and so did not run for the board, helped to solidify the more professional, liberal feminist block on the board. This segregation of board members from the program paved the way for what was to come.

PHASE FOUR:
ADMINISTRATION AND STAFF

During this time the Center was growing in the scope of services and programming it offered women and children. The number of staff began to expand from the original two. In July 1977 we hired the first full-time counselor, and by October five staff people funded by CETA were hired. During the same month the board decided that the Center needed an administrator who would report to and make contact with the funding agencies, keep track of the finances, and oversee the Center's administration. An administrator was hired in November and the staff of eight women was divided into two work groups: those involved in funding, administration, and the running of the house, and those who came into direct contact with the women and children using the services of the Center. The latter came to be known as direct services or program staff. The direct services staff consisted of myself as director, two counselors, a childcare worker, and a lawyer/advocate. It became clear to those of us in services that the administrator's principal concern and involvement was the board. We, on the other hand, were concentrating on providing good services, training large numbers of volunteers, and expanding our funding, and felt that this focus would speak for the validity of the internal structure of the shelter.

The administrator never had been a battered woman, nor had she been through the volunteer training. She had little or no contact with women residing at the Center. In response to her approach, two groups developed. One camp, composed of the direct services staff and a large number of volunteers, was collectivist and feminist; the other, made up of the board and administrator, placed greater value on those with credentials and on a hierarchical structure. Under the influence of the administrator, the board of the Center for Battered Women was beginning to push for one director. The stated rationale for this was that other agencies would be better able to work with an organizational structure similar to their own, and that funding sources would be reluctant to grant funds to any group with an 'alternative' form of organization. This seemed at the least ironic, since all the funding we had received prior to this organizational change had been granted because of our demonstration of the direct relationship between a nonhierarchical structure and the power issues of violence against women. We had argued that the Center should provide a model of cooperative, non-hierarchical work, and that the one-up, one-down model was counterproductive in working to change women's (and especially battered women's) lives. Nonetheless, in February 1978, the board voted to make the administrator the director.

PHASE FIVE: DISINTEGRATION

The first step was to demote and render powerless the staff who had been instrumental in formulating the original program and policies—in this case, the direct services staff. This was accomplished by rewriting job descriptions into jobs containing very specific and fragmented functions. Policy-making power went completely to the director. Staff meetings became little more than lectures by the director, allowing no avenue for staff input. I resigned. Three weeks later the board, with guidance from the director, fired one counselor, the childcare worker, and the lawyer. Two of them were dismissed for 'insubordination'. The Center was left with one counselor, who then resigned, leaving none of the original direct services staff. The task of ridding the Center of the original staff was complete.

There were many reactions to this upheaval. Upon resigning I wrote a letter to all volunteers stating the reasons for my resignation and listing the changes which I thought would be forthcoming. Meetings with staff, a few residents and as many as forty volunteers followed. In these meetings volunteers challenged the right of the board to make the changes. They discussed the composition of the board and the resignations of its two volunteers. Volunteers pressed for more representation on the board. The CETA workers hired lawyers and began to appeal their firing to the City of Austin. Ex-staff and volunteers approached funding sources, warning of changes in policy which would have a detrimental effect on the program. Volunteers and ex-staff began to pressure the Women's Center (which was still the parent group) to exercise its authority over the Center for Battered Women board. Joint Women's Center and CBW board meetings were held, with as many as sixty people attending. However, the Women's Center board finally opted to not exercise its control, stating that it had not entered into the internal workings of the CBW board prior to this, and would not do so now. Funding sources monitored the events, but felt it was not wise to intervene into intraorganizational disputes. Many volunteers withdrew completely, feeling the situation to be hopeless. The fired CETA staff appeals dragged on for more than a year and finally, after many hearings, the staff decided that the issues had been lost and trivialized in the process. 'Winning', they felt, would mean nothing. They dropped their cases. The board emerged stronger than ever. All the opposition staff and volunteers were gone from the Center.

PHASE SIX:
DISCREDITING AND MALIGNING

The next step was to find a way to discredit the program and policies of the original staff. The most expedient way of doing this was to let it be known through the informal social service network that the director and her allies had prevented a lesbian (translated 'man-hating') takeover. This was said despite the fact that among the five staff and forty volunteers who left the Center perhaps not more than five were lesbian. With this one word—lesbian—no other explanation became necessary. The validity of the charge remained unquestioned since none of the original staff or volunteers remained. Other agencies willingly took the shelter into the social service fold.

PHASE SEVEN: THE AFTERMATH

The following is a summary of events in the Center since the transition from a collective to a hierarchical structure. The progression toward developing a model of a 'professionalized' social service institution divorced from the community it was to service is evident.

The new leadership of the Center for Battered Women has said that it is very important to separate the issue of feminism and sexism from that of battered women. With the new federal emphasis on the nuclear family, the Center chooses to look at battered women as a 'family violence problem', but refuses to consider the societal, cultural, and political implications of why women are the ones in the family so often beaten. Soon after the original staff people left the shelter, men began to be trained and to serve as volunteers working directly with the women in the house. In the past, those who felt that men should not work in the house as volunteers compromised with those who felt that positive male role-models are necessary. The result was that men were included in regular volunteer training and received additional training to work with children in the house. Now, however, men are also answering the telephone hot-line and staffing the Center.

In the view of the founders of the Center, it is not a good idea for men to work in a shelter for battered women. Their presence can reinforce old patterns for battered women. Male volunteers and/or staff can easily be cast (or cast themselves) in the role of rescuer, encouraging a dependent role. Just when they need to be developing their own strengths, battered women can focus their attention on a man as the person most likely to solve their problems. This helps to perpetuate a continued cycle of dependence and inequality—two of the causes of battering.

The Center for Battered Women has undergone the transformation to a social service agency by becoming more and more removed from its 'client' population. The feminist ideology brought insights into programming for battered women. This belief demanded that staff and volunteers not make separations between themselves and battered women. We were able to integrate an understanding of the oppression and violence against women with a concern for the individual woman. This same ideology created a shelter based on the opinion that informal worker/resident relationships, self-help and peer-support would be more effective in fulfilling some of the immediate needs of battered women than rigid, bureaucratic structures. For example, women now living at the center must make an appointment to see a counselor days ahead of time. In the past, this type of interaction between the staff and a woman could just as easily have taken place at the kitchen table as in an appointed time in a more formal setting.

There is now a distancing of staff from women who stay at the shelter. Direct service people complement policy and procedures made by an administrator and board which is divorced from the group they are intending to serve. Little room remains for the less formal, more supportive sharing which was an original goal.

PREVENTIVE MEASURES

There are some lessons from our experience which may help insure that feminist-based shelters remain places that are responsive to the needs of battered women:

1. It is essential that women who organize shelters have an identifiable feminist analysis, which encompasses an understanding of the ways in which that analysis affects services to battered women. In addition, it is crucial that this specific analysis be part of all board orientations, volunteer training, and public education. This policy is necessary in order to make all who come in contact with the shelter understand that feminist ideology is not a tangential issue, but basic and essential. It will serve the dual purpose of informing possible shelter participants of the ideological basis of the program, as well as continually placing the issue of battered women in a feminist cultural and political context.

2. The issue of lesbianism has lost none of its volatility in recent years. Lesbians have continually taken part in all aspects of the women's movement, and the battered women's movement is no exception. It is therefore imperative that each group or collective initially acknowledge lesbians as a valuable part of their organization as one way of eliminating lesbianism as a negative issue. This can be accomplished by publicly encouraging the active participation of lesbians as staff, board, and volunteers. Further, position papers outlining the ideological framework of the shelter must include the contribution of lesbians in all aspects of the shelter program.

3. As feminists we realize how vital the inclusion of ex-battered women, working class, minority women, and volunteers are in forming a community-based governing board. Too often, these women have little money, little time, and little children! While their inclusion may not guarantee the development of a feminist analysis, it is a step toward keeping services tied to needs.

4. Those of us who have worked developing refuges for battered women know we cannot exist in a service vacuum. In order for a shelter to be effective, we must initiate and maintain working relationships with the police, courts, hospitals, welfare departments, and mental health services. We must also, however, maintain our own organizational integrity. We can work with the police or welfare, but we also must retain enough freedom to be able to be an effective and strong advocate for women who are beaten. Links are vital, but we must be cautious, and understand the tenuous line

between working with existing agencies and being seduced by the 'respectability' and seeming advantages these law enforcement and social service agencies appear to offer, often at the expense of the battered women. The feminist stance and advocacy role must not be diffused.

5. Feminist shelters must join other feminist services and groups in providing a base of support for one another. The roles and functions of each group may be different, but the shared ideological base is of critical importance. This alliance will provide an alternative to the traditional social service network. It is important in terms of referrals, but even more vital because it provides a constituency which can understand the broader implications of the shelter's work. Indeed, should they be needed, other groups can be political allies as well as friends.

CONCLUSIONS

The lure of building powerful social service fiefdoms is not gender-based. The shelter movement will attract women (and men) who view these services as stepping stones to personal career goals. It is vital for us to recognize that many in local, state or federal agencies will more easily accept that which is already familiar, those who do not threaten their own beliefs. The community support needed to maintain a feminist-based shelter for battered women requires political sophistication. Self-education, our own raised consciousness, and good faith are not enough. Consensus decision-making works only if everybody is playing by and believes in the same rules. Our unhappy experience shows that battered women's shelters committed to the full empowerment of women will remain feminist in content and approach only by constant discussion, analysis, and vigilance.

Gay Foster Parenting

In the Best Interest of the Children
Anita Diamant

Before we begin to address the broader issue of a policy for foster care placements, I want to mention Donald Babets and David Jean, the two men whose lives have unfortunately been turned upside down. I regret that the circumstances surrounding this particular case thrust them into the glare of the media spotlight. What happened in removing the two foster children from their care is in no way a reflection of these men's character or abilities.

—Philip W. Johnston,
Massachusetts Secretary of Human Services

A rabbit—an Easter gift grown up—resides in the neat, fenced yard. A calico cat roams in and out of the kitchen while two well-mannered dogs observe their masters' every move from the worn linoleum floor. Over a dinner of Salisbury steak and green beans, David Jean and Donald Babets joke about being "America's sweetheart couple." The "glare of the media spotlight" into which Jean and Babets were thrust when two foster children were removed from their home on May 9 [1985] illuminated a life probably most remarkable for its all-American ordinariness.

The two men share responsibility for the mortgage of their two-family house in Roxbury's Highland Park. They have made provisions for each other in their wills. Photographs of their extended families line the back hallway. Don Babets teaches a first communion class at his church, while David Jean is the music director at his. Over the piano in the simply furnished living room hang framed Thai papercuts, mementos of Babet's five-year tour of duty as a military intelligence noncommissioned officer in Southeast Asia.

But in some respects Jean and Babets are not at all ordinary. They are two white people living in a part of Roxbury that few white Bostonians ever see. They are also members of that tiny minority of Americans who volunteer to complicate their lives, 24 hours a day, by taking foster children into their homes. And they are homosexuals who are open and at ease with that fact, which has eclipsed the other particulars of who they are and what happened to them and to the two small boys who spent two weeks with them—and found safety and respite from the abuse and neglect of their natural mother's home.

*   *   *

In the spring of 1984, Jean and Babets called for information about becoming licensed as foster parents with the Department of Social Services. Like all applicants, they attended 12 hours of training classes led by two social workers. "They tell you about the kind of children in foster care," says Babets, 36, a senior investigator for the Boston Fair Housing Commission. "Some are abused, some are emotionally traumatized, some are special-needs children. They come with families that have drug addiction, alcoholism, a serious illness. These kids are in bad shape."

"They give you trial situations," adds Jean, 32, the business manager of the Crittendon Hastings House, a multi-service women's health agency. "It's easy to talk about some of this in abstract, but until you're really confronted with something, you don't find out what your limits are. For instance, you might decide that you can't really deal with sexual abuse."

Babets and Jean say they were the only men in their group of 10 applicants, and all but one of the women were single. The two men say that while they never specifically brought up the subject of their relationship, "We never hid it." On the application form they deleted the word "mother" and replaced it with "father." "It was clear we were applying together as a couple," says Babets.

The decision to become foster parents was several years in the making for Babets and Jean, who have been partners for nine years. In some ways, their choice reflects a larger trend among baby-boomers, heterosexual and homosexual, married and single, who are bearing and adopting children. Then again, as older brothers from big families, they had spent years helping care for much younger siblings, and this gave them very personal and particular reasons for wanting to assume the joys and headaches of child care.

David Jean is the quieter, less public of the two men. A native of western Massachusetts, he describes his family as "traditional"; his father worked in a factory while his mother cared for the family's six children. "If I was heterosexual and married," he says, "I probably wouldn't think too much about having kids. I'd probably just go ahead and have them. But if I want to have children now, it's more work. I don't think that's bad. It really made me look at why I want to have children: What are my real motives?

"I felt I had some energy for kids, and that I wanted to pass along some of the good things I've received from my parents to children, or to a child: To instill in them the things I think are important, things like caring for other people, respecting them. The way I feel about the world, about nature. It's hard to explain, and I'm afraid to sound shallow, to leave something out.

"I felt something was missing in my life," Jean continues, "something of the excitement that children just naturally have—everything is new to them. That's sort of romantic, I guess, but going through the process of discovering everything is so exciting. I remember I really loved it when my father took time out to explain electricity to me. I thought it was fascinating, but it was even more important that he spent that time with me. I want to pass that along.

"We live in a disposable world," Jean says. "If you get tired of something, you throw it away. It came to me that some parents treat their children like that. Being foster parents seemed like it would be good for both us and the children. The children are out there—there's a 25 percent shortage of homes."

Don Babets, a Midwesterner and the oldest of five children, says, "I'm from a nontraditional family. My mother was a single parent for a number of years. My stepfather adopted me, so that was some of my motivation in wanting to be a foster parent, because I wanted to pass on that feeling of being wanted." Both men say their families understand and have supported their desire to become foster parents. Says Jean, "My parents think we'd be great ones." Adds Babets, "They saw us with the kids. They know we were great parents."

*   *   *

After the initial training sessions, the Department of Social Services is required to perform a routine police-record check and carry out an in-depth home study that includes home visits and exhaustive interviews. Jean says the social worker "asked about our childhood, about which siblings we did or didn't get along with, and why. She asked us about our relationship, and how we responded to stress. What was our last fight about, and how did we resolve it? How did our parents deal with anger?" Says Babets, "I think they had more complete information on this home than they do on a lot of them."

Following the training and assessment, Jean and Babets began waiting and anticipating. Says Babets, "That was an anxious time, especially around the holidays. We thought, hey, we may have some children around here, so we tried to prepare accordingly. First it was Thanksgiving, then Christmas and Easter. Finally, they came around Mother's Day."

In most cases at that time, foster homes required four levels of approval, from the homefinder's recommendations to the area director's okay. However, in Jean and Babets' case the application was sent to the regional office for further review. "I don't blame them," says Babets. "I would have, too." The regional office forwarded the application to the highest level—the central DSS office—where it was finally approved. Early last winter, Deputy Commissioner Joseph Collins called Jean and Babets to inform them that their home had been approved for placement of a child anywhere from 2 years and 9 months old to 9 years old.

But approval and placement are two different processes. "They try to identify the kids' basic clinical needs and match the kids to experience and

strengths of foster homes," explains Babets. Finally, on April 23, 1985, at
3:45 p.m. Jean and Babets received a call from a social worker asking them
if they would be able to take in a 3 1/2-year-old child. They were also asked
to house his 22-month-old brother overnight, until another placement could
be found for him. Within two hours, the social worker dropped off two
scared, crying boys.

It was a hectic first night, with emergency trips to the store for paper
diapers and rubber sheets. But after the children were calmed down, fed,
bathed, and tucked in, Jean recalls, "We went in to look at them sleeping.
You know how cute kids are when they're asleep. I said to Don, 'I don't
think we can split them up. This is bad enough, getting taken out of their
home. We ought to keep them.'" In the morning they called the social
worker and offered to take both children—an offer that was accepted later
the same day.

Jean and Babets bought another bed for the younger child and alter-
nately took days off from work to get the boys settled. Babets researched
and found a good day-care setting for each child. On their first Saturday
together Babets took the children out for a day of "haircuts and shopping. I
took them downtown to Woolworth's and let them each pick out a toy. [The
older child] picked out a gun. I told him, no, I didn't think that was appropriate, and he agreed to get a truck. At that age they love trucks—and
Batman."

Jean and Babets are careful not to give too many particulars about the
children, which would be a violation of the confidentiality all foster parents
are encouraged to observe. Additionally, the men don't want to jeopardize
their status as approved foster parents, though Babets predicts bitterly,
"DSS isn't going to approve placing kids here again."

Still, they are extremely proud of the progress the children made while
in their care. Jean says that his co-workers, who saw the children right after
their placement and immediately before they were removed, marveled at the
difference in their appearance and demeanor. Says Babets, "When [one of
the boys] didn't get his way, he slugged. He hit me a couple of times. He
clocked his brother. He clocked the kid next door, and he had to stand in
the corner for that. I talked to one of the women in my church, herself a
former foster child, and I asked, 'What do you do with a kid who is punching?' She said, 'Get a punching bag.' The night before he was removed, he
made the connection. He went to hit his brother, and he stopped himself
and said, 'No, no. He-Man.' And he ran over and hit the He-Man punching
bag. That's what made Thursday even more terrible."

*   *   *

Jean and Babets had heard rumors that *The Boston Globe*, following up on a
neighbor's complaint, was about to run a story about their foster children,
but a phone call from Deputy Commissioner Collins reassured them that
the department was prepared to stand behind its placement. The children's
mother, who had voluntarily placed them with DSS, had even signed a

statement giving her approval of her sons' placement with the two men. However, within hours of the story's appearance on May 9, Jean and Babets were informed that the children would be immediately removed from their care. The stated reason for that decision was that "public attention and attendant media convergence constituted an immediate endangerment to the physical and emotional well-being of the children at this placement." Indeed, television crews landed on Jean and Babets' front porch the afternoon the story appeared. (Concern arose in the black community that minority children had been placed with white foster parents. This proved groundless, however, as the two boys were white.)

A few weeks later, at a formal grievance hearing on the men's request for a return of the boys, DSS officials noted the "exceptional care given by the grievants and the clinical benefits accrued therefrom. . . . The Department does not refute the clinical gains made during placement at grievants' home nor the potential clinical efficacy of returning the children, *if* one could reasonably assume that the notoriety which resulted in the removal were absent or could be constrained."

Jean and Babets feel the media attention didn't affect the children and that the real reason for their removal was homophobia. Babets points to the amount of publicity surrounding another foster care controversy several weeks later. Although that case did involve a long-term placement and adoption proceedings, the name and even photographs of the child in question were made public without DSS mention of removing him from the heat of that "media spotlight."

Says Jean, "Whatever happened to us, we can deal with that. It's the pain I saw in the two kids that we felt was unforgivable." Adds Babets, "The baby was too small; he really didn't know what was happening. [The older child] was really angry. He wouldn't even talk to me. How do you explain to a kid who thinks that you as an adult have control over things, that you have nothing to say about this? I saw the pain in him. I knew the pain in me. What could I say? What could I do? Nothing."

Commenting on David Jean and Donald Babets' story, Governor Michael S. Dukakis said, "No citizen of the state ought to be treated that way."

*   *   *

The removal of two small boys from Jean and Babets' home was just the beginning of a series of events that will affect the lives of many children and families touched by the Department of Social Services—including but not limited to cases where the sexuality of the caretakers is an issue. The day after the children were taken to a temporary placement before being settled with relatives, Governor Dukakis ordered a review of state foster care and a specific policy on the placement of foster children in gay households.

One day before that policy was announced, the Massachusetts House of Representatives approved a rider to the proposed state budget that equated homosexuality with a threat to children and, if enacted, would have compelled DSS to "not knowingly place or knowingly continue the placement of any child under its jurisdiction in the care of person or persons whose sexual preference threatens the psychological or physical well-being of the child." This would have been a retrospective as well as prospective restriction extending to adoption, guardianship, family day care, and respite care as well as foster care. The amendment passed with an overwhelming vote of 112–28.

However, an amended version passed by the state Senate struck all references to homosexuality and called upon DSS simply to place children with people whose sexual orientation "presents no threat to the well-being of the child." The Senate's nonspecific language was eventually adopted by a joint legislative budget committee and has been enacted as law.

On May 24, Philip Johnston, secretary of human services, announced a policy that contains no mention whatsoever of homosexuality but establishes clear priorities for the future placement of all foster children: "This administration believes that foster children are served best when placed in traditional family settings—that is, with relatives or in families with married couples, preferably with parenting experience and with time available to care for foster children.

"In exceptional circumstances it may be necessary to place a child in a nontraditional home—that is, with an unmarried couple or with a single person. Any such placement will henceforth require the prior written approval of the commissioner."

The policy announcement met with a variety of responses. It was widely understood as insuring that placements with gay foster parents would not be approved and was applauded by one state legislator as a step toward preserving "the traditional American family [as] a pillar of our society." Gay-rights groups attacked the policy as a crassly political ploy by the governor, intended to appeal to conservative voters at the expense of children's unmet needs for foster homes. Child-welfare professionals and advocates, by and large, questioned the administration's decision on clinical grounds. Deputy Commissioner Collins, who originally approved the placement and who stated that he was "personally and professionally opposed to the removal," has announced his resignation effective January 1.

The administration denies charges that its actions were an attempt to diffuse criticism from conservatives and moderates and to modify the governor's liberal image on matters of social policy. Still, when it was announced, no attempt was made to correct the perception that the DSS policy would restrict placements in "nontraditional" homes. While claiming the policy did not represent a "categoric exclusion," Johnston said that future placements with gays appeared "highly unlikely." And once the policy was announced, people high in the Dukakis administration expressed their expectation that the issue was moot, and that it was time to get on with other business.

Nearly four months after the policy was announced, controversy persists. The Civil Liberties Union of Massachusetts and Gay and Lesbian Advocates and Defenders are preparing a legal challenge to the policy regulations. According to GLAD spokesman Kevin Cathcart, arguments will focus on two issues: equal protection for homosexuals and, more emphatically, the state's interpretation of the "best interest of the child" standard. Says Cathcart, "The policy makes distinctions between classes of people for reasons that have no relationship to their ability to be foster parents or provide foster care. It impinges on the rights of children in foster care to have decisions made on their individual best interests, and also limits the pool of potential foster parents available, which is not in the children's best interest."

A number of plaintiffs will be named in the case, among them David Jean and Donald Babets. Cathcart expects that the final list will include heterosexuals as well as lesbians and gay men; "single parents who have applied to become foster parents and were not approved, or people who were approved but don't have children placed with them; and people who have had children removed." The case may also be pleaded on behalf of families with children in the foster care system.

The legal challenge does not assert any inalienable "right" to be a foster parent. However, Cathcart says, "It's clear in the circumstances that led to its promulgation what the intent of the policy was. I think we will see, as it is in operation for a time, that it was not only intended as an anti-gay policy but is also functioning that way." He claims, "It has a chilling effect by its existence. People—lesbian or gay or single or in any way 'nontraditional'— will be less likely to apply in the first place."

Secretary Johnston and DSS Commissioner Marie A. Matava say the state's policy is fair and nondiscriminatory. "No group is excluded," says Johnston, who began his career as a social worker in the Department of Public Welfare. "Nothing is said about sexuality. People will be asked about sexual preference because it's a relevant issue but by no means the only issue." According to Johnston, "The only question here is, in the best of all possible worlds, how should a social worker who is about to make a placement of an abused and neglected child for whom the state has a responsibility, how should that social worker go about making a decision as to the most appropriate placement? I believe the policy we came up with represents good casework. I also believe, in the absence of the politics, that if you went to other states and talked to professionals . . . or if you talked to professionals six months ago in this state, most of them will agree pretty much with the way this policy reads."

Matava further explains that the new policy has been in the works since last December. "This is not a policy that focuses on any one issue. . . . If there were two key words in the policy, they'd have to be 'relatives' and 'parenting experience.'" She hopes to see the number of foster placements with relatives double in the coming year, from the current 5 percent. As far as making placements with couples or single people is concerned, she says, "Parenting experience is the key."

The administration insists that concerns and fears raised by the state's action in Jean and Babets' case, and in the development of its foster placement policy, are entirely the result of misinterpretation and distortion. Matava and Johnston say they regret alarm among social workers, single parents, or in the gay community, and they claim any worry is premature. Says Johnston, "Read the policy and watch how it's implemented."

As put forth in regulations drafted to implement the new policy, there are two major procedural changes in the way DSS now makes foster placements: First, all applications for prospective foster parents—married couples included—contain a question about sexual preference. And second, since July 1, any nonrelative or "nontraditional" placement with single parents or unmarried couples requires that an "exemption application form" (with the sexual preference query) must be approved by the commissioner. (Placements with relatives or traditional families do not require permission from the central office.) This is the first time routine decisions about foster care have been made at the commissioner's level.

Many DSS social workers feel the new policy is having a negative effect on a small number of children, because some placements that might be in their best interests are not being made. In some instances, single parents with years of foster-care experience have refused to answer or have given what DSS considers an "inadequate" reply to the question about sexual preference. One veteran foster parent, a clergyman, answered by saying he had taken a vow of celibacy. In that instance, the case worker was told by a supervisor to find out *if* that foster parent *were* to have sex with someone, with whom would it be? He refused to answer and was not approved for placement. Says Commissioner Matava, "None of the information on the application is really optional."

A social worker from the western part of the state who asked that her name not be used says, "If I have a 15-year-old girl who has been sexually abused by her father, and we have a single mom or two single women, and they don't want to answer the sexual preference question, I may be forced to place that child in a two-parent [traditional] home that may not be the best for her. I feel . . . I'm making more and more decisions not on what the child needs but on political considerations and administrative policy."

Social workers in Boston report that there is a general hesitancy to find out whether the department will actually approve placements in a gay or lesbian home. Apparently, individual supervisors and administrators at all levels are discouraging case workers from recommending such placements, to avoid the anticipated rejection or notoriety, or both. At least one caseworker who said she would like to test the policy's position on homosexual foster parents worries about putting information concerning individuals' sexuality into the DSS computer system.

By and large, department social workers are discouraged, upset, or insulted by the new policy. Local 509 of the Service Employees International Union that represents 7,800 Massachusetts human service workers passed a motion soon after the policy was announced "resolved that the commonwealth should select foster parents based upon their ability to parent rather than their race, sex, religion, family constellation, sexual preference." Despite Matava's insistence that the new procedures do not place additional burdens on workers, some caseworkers disagree. "Getting permission [for nontraditional placements] involves a lot of documentation on the worker and supervisor level," says one supervisor. "It involves a lot of person-hours and a lot of people. It also undermines the field professional who has, up to this point, been able to draw on his or her own clinical judgment and knowledge of the case to make a decision."

The most common criticism of the policy is that it is out of touch with the realities faced in the field. The new emphasis on relatives makes one worker remark wryly, "It's not like you have time to put an ad out, like the treasurer's office [does]. If someone walks into the office at 4 o'clock in the afternoon, freaked out and needing some respite care, where are the relatives?"

*   *   *

But the most pressing concern for many DSS workers is the ranking of single-parent families—behind relatives and two-parent households—as a third priority requiring central office approval. Although state figures show that 67 percent of children in foster care live with "traditional" families, in some urban areas single parents constitute more than half of all foster parents. A recent survey in one Boston area office showed that of 250 approved homes, only 17 fulfilled the department's definition of a "traditional" home, which means that virtually all placements in that office now require approval from the central office. Johnston says that while he has heard of concerns from single parents that "we're sending them the message that they're not good parents, nothing could be further from reality."

Still, that message has been received and has helped create a coalition of gay-rights groups, church organizations, professional associations, and child-welfare advocates who are on record as opposing the policy. The policy's distinction between "traditional" and "nontraditional" families has particularly stung members of the black community. Barbara Simmons, president of the Greater Boston Association of Black Social Workers, says she was "surprised at the policy," saying it was a case of "apples and oranges, tying all these things together." While her organization has no comment on the subject of gay foster parents, its letter to Secretary Johnston stated, "The implications of such a policy on the lives of Black families and children have the potential to be devastating. The policy ignores the important role that Black single females have played throughout our history."

Simmons says, "we've done a lot in the area of getting single parents recognized, and we don't want people getting the message they're not as valued. [This policy] is going to make people have second thoughts; they are now a third priority. Why put yourself out to be rejected? If it was me, I'd have second thoughts."

*   *   *

In preparation for a meeting with Governor Dukakis and members of his administration, Diana Waldfogel, dean of the Simmons College School of

Social Work, asked the school's librarian to seek out the available research and literature pertaining to the subject of gay and lesbian parenting. Based on nearly 75 citations, she says, the research is all either "neutral or positive" regarding the impact of homosexual parents on children's development. Waldfogel was one of 30 speakers at a June 21 forum of social workers, psychologists, psychiatrists and agency workers who decried the state's policy. She says, "That group was unanimous for the first time in history on any issue—that the foster home policy should be as flexible as possible."

Waldfogel feels the state's policy was made "without professional investigation and too quickly," and adds, "I felt they operated on information that was more appropriate 15 or 20 years ago." Waldfogel, whose own clinical background is in child guidance, says, "In the '40s and '50s, the typical case was an intact family with difficulties. The world isn't like that anymore—for good or for bad. In the '70s and '80s, in the agencies where our students work, it's rare to even find a two-parent family."

The demographics of the American family have changed drastically in the past decades. According to a study by the Joint Center for Urban Studies of MIT and Harvard University entitled "The Nation's Families: 1960–1990," in 1960, 41.5 percent of all American households consisted of a married couple with young children. By 1990—even accounting for the current population swell created by the postwar baby-boom generation—that category will have dwindled to slightly more than 25 percent. The categories of households that have grown most are those headed by single people; by 1990, these are expected to account for 45 percent of the population.

Changing demographics have led to a reassessment of normative family structures in the social sciences and the helping professions. According to Waldfogel, much of this reassessment grew out of the sociological and political debate during the 1970s, when the absence of fathers in black families was "blamed" for generational patterns of welfare dependence. The question was raised, says Waldfogel, "How is it that some people who come out of these settings do very well? How does it work? How do people cope?" Studies of neighborhood networking and extended-family relationships made for a revised view of the single-parent, usually female-headed household, "which was no longer understood as a deficit model." Indeed, Waldfogel says, "These families were recognized as having positive coping mechanisms. What the state ranks as being second- or third-best may be better in some cases. In this very diverse society, there is probably no one 'best model' that applies to everyone."

*   *   *

After five weeks with the new policy in place, Commissioner Matava's office reported having approved 174 placements of 220 children in single-parent foster homes. The first "test case" regarding a gay foster placement had yet to appear, since, at that time, no application stating homosexual preference had been submitted.

However intended by the administration, the state's new foster care policy and these specific changes have had an impact on individuals and communities. In the wake of the Massachusetts discussion, New Hampshire has banned all foster care placements in gay or lesbian homes. Some of the repercussions within the commonwealth have been reported in the media, but much of the fall-out is diffuse, harder to document—the stuff of feelings and fear.

The most notorious development, which came within a few days of the DSS policy's announcement, was the decision by a private foster care agency under contract with the state to remove a teen-ager from the home of a gay man in Woburn—a person with 20 years of foster parenting experience. In a letter to the governor (which was reprinted in the *Gay Community News*), this foster parent wrote, "You should know how your edict given to protect foster children . . . really affected two foster children and their families."

According to his account, a teen-age boy charged with burglary who had been in his care for a month was abruptly removed and placed, without explanation, in another foster home where an abused teen-age girl had been living. The girl was sent back to live with her natural family, a move "not clinically indicated," nor welcomed by her. The boy eventually landed in a Department of Youth Services lockup facility, "even further geographically from his family—a placement that was initially considered ill-advised, and the reason [he] was placed in foster care originally."

While the governor's reply was sympathetic and a DSS spokesman called the foster care agency's decision "a misinterpretation and misapplication of the policy," that action was a swift response to some of the visceral, unarticulated beliefs involved in the current discussion of foster care.

Alan Tweedy, clinical director of Gay and Lesbian Counseling Services in Boston, says, "The whole issue has reinforced basic homophobic attitudes and myths. It has raised the pervasive fear that gay men are obsessed with sexuality; that people are 'converted' to homosexuality as children by an older person; that gay men are unable to have meaningful relationships; that homosexuality is a deviance due to a problem in the family, that it's a sickness. Would you want to put kids with anyone like that? I wouldn't." Tweedy says, "The worst thing is, this situation has reinforced these fears without even naming them," and, he adds, "homosexuals are good scapegoats for [the public's] not dealing with the fact that most sexual abuse takes place by heterosexual men—mostly family or friends of family—against female children."

                              *   *   *

Because the current controversy developed in response to a placement with a gay male couple, and because male homosexuality is a particularly volatile subject, the much greater impact of the DSS policy on lesbians has received little attention. A far more numerous though less visible constituency among foster parents, many lesbians are divorced or have borne children of their own, or both.

"In some ways," says Faith, a foster mother, "from DSS' point of view, except for being single I'm an ideal candidate. I'm educated, a professional with an adequate income, and I'm a person of color." Faith is currently involved in adoption proceedings for a girl she has raised in foster care since infancy, together with her lover, Marie. (The women's names have been changed at their request.)

The two women took responsibility for the baby after one of the mother's relatives asked them to care for the neglected, frightened child.

Faith remembers that when the foster placement was made, "We were asked pointedly about our relationship and sort of urged to come clean. Even though the worker had been open and seemed like an ally, we decided that up the line, it was risky." Marie insisted she "lived upstairs," and things were left at that. This was not, however, an omission Faith was comfortable with. "Up to that point [when the Jean and Babets case came to light] I felt sort of dishonest. This was a major life decision, and you don't want to make it in a shady way." Now, she says, she is relieved that she didn't reveal her sexual preference. "It really is a question of what's best in the long run" for the child.

Faith, herself a trained social worker, says, "I can predict what would have happened to her if we hadn't gotten involved; she wouldn't have gotten very far in life. With her mother, or even in another foster home, there would be more of a chance she'd become the stereotypical kid of color, on welfare, with kids of her own in 15 years." Faith's expectations for her "daughter" are sky-high. "When I look at her, I see [author] Alice Walker and [athlete] Wilma Rudolph all in one.

"I feel blessed to have her," says Faith, "and no way any state or anyone will take her without all the people in her life putting up a fight." But, she says, if the opportunity and challenge of taking on a foster child had occurred in the current climate, she probably would have chosen not to do so—arguably, a loss for some child.

* * *

Back where this drama began, at David Jean and Donald Babets' house in Roxbury, stuffed toys still sit on the beds for the two foster children long gone. Jean and Babets are increasingly resigned to the fact that they probably will never see those little boys again, but the two weeks they spent with them has reaffirmed their desire to be parents.

Says Jean, "There used to be a billboard in the city that said, 'Kids are born colorblind. Let's keep them that way.' Don and I talked about how we would describe our relationship to a child. We would want to say, "There are all types of relationships between people, and all of them can be good. The important things are caring, honesty, respect; those things cut across whatever kind of relationship or family.'

The thing is to not be part of any . . ." Jean pauses, groping for the right word, which Babets supplies: "prejudice."

COMMENTS AND
RECOMMENDED READINGS

Just as individualism resurges periodically in the United States, so does its critique. After Tocqueville, perhaps the most compelling statement is John Dewey's *Individualism: Old and New* (New York: Minton, Balch & Co., 1930 [reprinted by Capricorn Books, 1962]). Recent efforts include Elizabeth Fox-Genovese's *Feminism Without Illusions: A Critique of Individualism* (Chapel Hill: Univ. of North Carolina Press, 1991), which reproves the individualist strain in the feminist movement, and Philip Selznick's *The Moral Commonwealth: Social Theory and the Promise of Community* (Berkeley: Univ. of California Press, 1992).

The federal government's principal welfare program, Aid to Families with Dependent Children (AFDC), was originally introduced as part of the Social Security Act of 1935 and was designed primarily to address the needs of widows and orphans. It was thought that, as Social Security established itself and expanded, AFDC would gradually disappear. There was also no expectation that mothers would join the labor force, even if their children were no longer young and dependent. This conception of AFDC changed radically, however, as new forms of dependency emerged and the role of women in society was transformed. See Daniel Patrick Moynihan, *Family and Nation* (San Diego: Harcourt, Brace, Jovanovich, 1987). The essays collected in *The Politics of Social Policy in the United States* (Princeton: Princeton Univ. Press, 1988), eds. Margaret Weir, et al., look at the historical evolution of New Deal policies and assess future prospects. For a careful evaluation of recent workfare programs, see Judith M. Gueron and Edward Pauly, *From Welfare to Work* (New York: Russell Sage Foundation, 1991).

For several decades, welfare case workers enjoyed considerable discretion in determining the size of grants to their clients. In the 1960s, there was a movement to constrain this discretion by establishing uniform rules to determine grant amounts. Even then, little auditing occurred, and the rules were often not followed. In the 1970s, more systematic auditing was introduced, thus providing an important part of the context for "The Hearing of Mrs. G." See Evelyn Z. Brodkin and Michael Lipsky, "Entitlement Programs at the Local Level: Quality Control in AFDC as an Administrative Strategy," *Social Service Review* 34:3 (1983), pp. 22–43. See also Evelyn Z. Brodkin, *The False Promise of Administrative Reform: Implementing Quality Control in Welfare* (Philadelphia: Temple Univ. Press, 1986). For a general critique of "oppression exercised in the name of management," see Simone Weil, *Oppression and Liberty* (Amherst: Univ. of Massachusetts Press, 1979), discussed by Jean

Bethke Elshtain in "The Vexation of Weil," in *Power Trips and Other Journeys: Essays in Feminism as Civic Discourse* (Madison: Univ. of Wisconsin Press, 1990).

Contrary to widespread belief, the percentage of births to teenagers has been steadily declining. In 1987, it was 12 percent of births, down from any other year in recent decades. However, two-thirds of those teenage mothers were not married and that number is higher than it has ever been. Half of the births were to 18- and 19-year-olds, half to teens below 18, nearly all unmarried. One needs to add only that the poverty rate among unmarried teen mothers is over 75 percent. The most authoritative volume on this issue is *Risking the Future: Adolescent Sexuality, Pregnancy, and Childbearing* (Washington, D.C.: National Academy Press, 1987), edited by Cheryl D. Hayes. Central to any assessment of the type of policy described in "Buying Time" is the distinction between a threat and an offer. For a careful conceptual analysis, see Alan Wertheimer, *Coercion* (Princeton: Princeton Univ. Press, 1987), especially Chapters 12 and 13. Aside from attempts to enforce child support regulations, policymakers have generally neglected the contributions of males to producing the problems addressed. This neglect has lent a gendered cast to all welfare programs, including those aimed at teenage pregnancy. See the essays in *Women, the State, and Welfare* (Madison: Univ. of Wisconsin Press, 1990), edited by Linda Gordon. On the relation between public policy and conceptions of fatherhood, see Frank F. Furstenberg, Jr., "Good Dads—Bad Dads: Two Faces of Fatherhood" in *The Changing American Family and Public Policy* (Washington, D.C.: Urban Institute Press, 1988), edited by Andrew J. Cherlin.

Providing shelter to battered women is only one strategy of assistance—and at best a temporary one—but of great importance given the well-known inadequacies of the criminal justice system in prosecuting batterers, on the one hand, and insufficient support services for meeting women's financial and emotional needs, on the other. These difficulties are noted in *Under the Rule of Thumb: Battered Women and the Administration of Justice*, A Report of the United States Commission on Civil Rights (Washington, D.C.: January 1982). A sustained analysis is offered by Susan Schechter in *Women and Male Violence: The Visions and Struggles of the Battered Women's Movement* (Boston: South End Press, 1982). See also *Feminist Perspectives on Wife Abuse* (Newbury Park: Sage Publ., 1988), edited by Kersti Ylló and Michele Bograd. On the legal consequences for women of resorting to self-help, see Cynthia K. Gillespie, *Justifiable Homicide: Battered Women, Self-Defense, and the Law* (Columbus: Ohio State Univ. Press, 1989).

In April 1991 a Florida appeals court upheld the first conviction in the United States of a woman charged with delivering cocaine to her newborn child through the umbilical cord. But in the same month (a week or so earlier) a Michigan appeals court reversed a trial court ruling that had ordered a woman to stand trial on the same charge. This divergence reflects the current controversy over punitive versus therapeutic approaches to drug-addicted pregnant women. For a discussion of the issues, see Jan Hoffman,

"Pregnant, Addicted—and Guilty?" *New York Times Magazine*, August 19, 1990, pp. 33ff. To understand the issues from the point of view of the women themselves, see Vicki D. Greenleaf, *Women and Cocaine: Personal Stories of Addiction and Recovery* (Los Angeles: Lowell House, 1989).

Foster parenting is just one among many areas of concern where gay men and women have experienced systematic discrimination, including sexuality (e.g., the Supreme Court's 1986 decision in *Bowers v. Hardwick* upholding a Georgia antisodomy law), the military (where exclusion is based solely on status rather than conduct), and public and private responses to the AIDS crisis. For a thorough review of the issues, as well as an extensive resource guide to services and organizations, see Joy A. Schulenburg, *Gay Parenting* (New York: Doubleday, 1985).

PART VI

MANAGERIAL STYLE AND GOVERNANCE

INTRODUCTION

As women take on new roles in public institutions, they often find themselves with unanticipated obligations. Some have to do with their status—or presumed status—as representative women. For example, Lynn Martin, in the case "Among Friends" (Section D), entered Congress with the desire (as she put it) to be a mainstream political player. Substantively, she was interested in tax and budget issues, and she sought out and obtained a position on the House Budget Committee. More generally, she was eager to play a leadership role in the Republican Party. But as she pursued her objectives, she found that she could not ignore—largely because others would not let her forget—the fact that she was a woman. In internal deliberations, she was asked by her House colleagues to speak about "women's issues" on the assumption that, being a woman, she must be an authority. In relation to the public, her visibility in the Republican hierarchy served the party in dealing with an apparent "gender gap" among voters (women being more inclined than men to favor Democratic candidates). Indeed it quickly became clear to Lynn Martin that highlighting the fact of her womanhood was—whether she liked it or not—strategically advantageous for the pursuit of her own objectives. But she was never entirely comfortable with that fact; in many ways, she was a reluctant role model.

Could women who attain leadership positions reasonably be reluctant to become role models, or do they have special obligations to other women such as advancing a common agenda or serving as mentors? One obvious reason for reluctance is that role modeling leads to unfair burdens. The high visibility of token women within an organization subjects them to a greater degree of scrutiny and leads to performance demands not imposed on others. They are more vulnerable to criticism if they should make a mistake, even while they have to work harder just to have their achievements noticed. Organizations with few women often exploit them as showpieces. And, internally, they receive extra assignments—for example, to all important decision-making committees—to get "a woman's point of view." These burdens lead to legitimate resentment. Another reason for reluctance is that women feel pressured to speak for their gender rather than just themselves. Women who are pioneers within an organization are looked to by other women, especially those lower in the hierarchy or on the outside trying to break in, to represent the interests of women generally. They are obliged to make public proclamations of their commitment to causes that may have little relation to their self-identity. Finally, women may be reluctant because adopting the burdens of role modeling appears to relieve other members of the organization—specifically, the men—of their obligations to reach out, to become mentors, and to support women's equal participation in organizational life.

Is it reasonable to expect women who enter public life to act *as women* and not just as members of their organizations, whether it be Congress, or a police force, or a juvenile detention facility? Are there gender-based qualities that women bring to these activities that lead them to value things differently and to conduct themselves differently? In answering this last question, we should first distinguish it from the question of whether women need to (or ought to) act differently because of pervasive gender stereotypes. For example, in running for political office, a woman will have to take account of public perceptions of women if she hopes to project an image that will persuade citizens to vote for her. But her aim as a candidate may be no different from a man's: She wants to maximize the number of votes in her favor, and she exploits public perceptions to that end. Similarly, as noted in the case on policewomen's use of deadly force (Section B), gender stereotypes influence the way suspects react to police activity. Male suspects rarely attack female officers, and female suspects often resist male officers, because it is understood, in both cases, that "men are not supposed to hit women." Again, in "Taking Charge" (Section A), the remarkable "desk incident" (in which the newly appointed Rose Washington has to do battle with her deputy to get access to her own desk) may turn partly on the deputy's stereotypical assumption that women are weak—an assumption of which he is eventually disabused.

In short, there is no doubt that gender stereotypes influence how people conduct themselves. But stereotypes do not necessarily correspond to actual differences. Of course, the reflexive use of stereotypes may produce differences. To the extent that males and females consciously conform to dominant stereotypes, they may exhibit just the conduct one would expect if there were deep gender differences. This kind of conscious gender-identification may make it difficult to separate entrenched differences from ones that are self-consciously exploited but shallow. Carol Gilligan shows appreciation of this point in her recent work. Whereas initially she took at face value the gender differences that seemed to reveal themselves in her interviews, she now says that the spontaneous choice of moral voice that people make is not necessarily the same as—and not necessarily to be preferred to—the choice they make after reflection.[1]

Nonetheless, as we mentioned in Part III, many people believe deep differences exist and therefore that women will tend to act as women if given favorable opportunities. How should we expect these differences to exhibit themselves? We can begin with the dichotomy of traits that Gilligan associates with the two moral voices. The justice perspective, exhibited mostly by males, is characterized by the valuing of autonomy. The individual is primary, and relations with others are entered into for mutual advantage. Rules are restraints on the self and are considered fair as long as they apply equally to all. Moral reasoning is principled, and conflicts are seen as matters of competing rights. By contrast, the care perspective, exhibited mostly by females, values attachment. Relationships are primary, and separation or isolation from others are threats to self-identity. Responsibilities to others are extensions of the self, not externally imposed burdens, and are valued for sustaining interdependence and connection. Moral reasoning is contextual, and conflicts are seen as matters of competing responsibilities.

This enumeration simplifies somewhat the moral voices Gilligan describes. But applications of the hypothesis of gender difference to styles of organization and management are typically elaborated in the same manner. Thus, the male style is usually characterized as rational, competitive, hierarchical, adversarial, authoritative, and product-oriented. The female style is empathic, collaborative, participatory, mediative, supportive, and process-oriented. Of course, for these terms to serve as more than buzzwords, they need to be translated into concrete behavior. Many of the cases in this section provide vehicles for attempting such applications. For example, among the many innovations Rose Washington introduced to "take charge" of her institution, one of the more striking was moving her office from the top floor—tellingly referred to as the penthouse—to the third floor, where she was near the staff as well as the juvenile detainees. That may be construed as a move away from hierarchy and toward collaboration. Similarly, in "Among Friends," when Lynn Martin gets one of her first opportunities at leadership because of a (male) colleague's illness, many people observe that her unexpected success is based on her more "receptive and inclusive" style.

Of course the cases are sufficiently rich in detail to confound easy generalizations. Moreover, the dichotomy of gender traits may raise more questions than it answers. In particular, one has to confront the normative question of how the two sets of traits relate to one another. There are four main possibilities. (1) One could regard one set as morally superior to the other. Those who defend the hypothesis of gender difference often argue that male traits now dominate organizations and need to be replaced by female traits. One difficulty with this view is the lack of a vantage point from which the judgment of superiority is made. If it is from the standpoint of the female voice itself, it is vulnerable to a like judgment from the male voice and the result is a moral standoff. If it is from outside both voices, the third (neutral) standpoint would seem to be not gender-related. (2) One could regard both voices as complete and sufficient in themselves, and neither as superior to the other. Then the choice between them would simply be, perhaps, which voice one is more comfortable with. No one defends this view. (3) One could regard them as both incomplete and in need of each other, thus complementary. This view is attractive because it suggests that the present problem is one-sidedness—males have been unfairly dominant—and the proper corrective is diversity in the workplace so that both (or all) viewpoints are represented. The difficulty is that because they employ incompatible frameworks of analysis, it is not clear how the different voices communicate with one another. (4) Finally, one could regard the moral ideal as a synthesis of the two voices. So, for example, the ideal manager would embody the best traits of both voices: fairness as well as compassion, sensitivity to rights as well as readiness to meet responsibilities—exhibiting whatever trait is fitting for the occasion. Thus, a kind of androgyny would be preferred, in which gender-difference would be submerged in an encompassing ideal, with women and men conducting themselves as whole, integrated people.

NOTES

1. Carol Gilligan, "Moral Orientation and Moral Development," in *Women and Moral Theory*, edited by Eva Feder Kittay and Diana T. Meyers (Totowa: Rowman and Littlefield, 1987), p. 27.

SECTION A

Leadership

Taking Charge: Rose Washington and Spofford Juvenile Detention Center

Anna M. Warrock

Since her arrival in August 1983, Rose Washington, executive director of New York City's Spofford Juvenile Center, had worked to turn around a facility beset by problems. Spofford was the city's secure detention facility for juveniles accused of serious crimes. Over two decades it had developed a reputation as an unsavory and dangerous holding pen. "The name alone was . . . synonymous with the worst in youth institutions—dilapidated and poorly staffed—a warehouse offering few services," recalls Barry Krisberg, president of the National Council on Crime and Delinquency. Child abuse by staff, suicide attempts by children, runaways, staff burnout leading to chronic understaffing, a deteriorating building, all plagued the largest facility run by the city's Department of Juvenile Justice (DJJ). Legal aid lawyers could convince judges to release accused delinquents to even the most tenuous of family situations rather than keep them in Spofford awaiting a court date.

The persistent problems had proved too much for a string of directors—Washington was the 27th director in Spofford's 25-year history. The revolving door for those at the top had contributed to a staff perception that management was, at best, a transient nuisance. Left largely to their own devices as director after director departed, Spofford's 300 juvenile counselors had come to feel that they ran the institution. They distrusted change, believing it would be only temporary. They resented the repeated attempts at reform by those who represented what they regarded as an aloof and indifferent central administration—which Spofford staff members referred to somewhat contemptuously as "downtown."

Washington was hired to fulfill a mandate for reform by DJJ Commissioner Ellen Schall, who herself had taken office in January 1983. Schall wanted to change Spofford from a warehouse to a facility that provided the services troubled youths needed to change the direction of their lives as they made their way through the juvenile justice bureaucracy: the courts, detention centers, and follow-up services. She had improved medical services and proposed educational reforms at Spofford but knew she needed a strong leader to guide Spofford out of its problems.

Washington also believed in the reform agenda but had her hands full battling to get the Spofford staff to participate in more basic programs she believed essential to ending the facility's problems with security and care. As each problem at Spofford demanded attention, Washington began to walk a narrow line between forcing needed changes into the relatively fragile new environment she had created since she arrived at the facility, and stepping back from management reform lest she alienate those staff on whom she had to rely.

BACKGROUND: SPOFFORD

Spofford Juvenile Center is an eight-story, white brick secure detention center for youths aged 10 through 15 (the really young children, 7 to 10 years old, are housed not in Spofford but elsewhere in DJJ's non-secure detention facilities; the median age at Spofford is 14.5 years). Built in 1958, the facility is located in Hunts Point, an industrial section of the South Bronx, across Long Island Sound from La Guardia Airport. Of the 12,000 youths arrested annually in New York city, about one-third pass through Spofford before court dates or on their way to long-term detention upstate. At any one time, the center houses between 150 and 200 kids; 75 percent are accused of violent crimes, including robbery, assault, rape, and murder. More than 90 percent of the youths are black or Hispanic, 95 percent are male, and virtually all of them are poor.[1]

Spofford had started out in the 1960s and early 1970s as a secure facility but without bars on the windows. It housed both accused delinquents and children known as PINS (persons in need of services), who had sometimes done nothing more than run away from home. "We'd have kids who'd broken windows just to get picked up and brought in, so they'd have a warm bed," recalls Cleophus Glass, a former juvenile counselor who later became a unit director. Those days were remembered fondly by long-term juvenile counselors. "This job used to be fun," recalls Shirley Lewis, for 30 years a juvenile counselor and unit director. "When we had PINS kids we'd take them to the theatre—these kids had never seen a play—or we'd take them to the beach."

But by the mid-1970s, more juveniles were being picked up for felonies, including armed robbery and murder. Escapes from detention were common, and although the character of the clients had changed over time, there was little consensus on how to treat youngsters who were accused of violent crimes. Many states, including New York, enacted laws to treat such juveniles more like adults. The Juvenile Offender Act, which took effect in New York in September 1978, required that juveniles accused of violent crimes be held in a secure detention facility—essentially a jail—while they waited for court dates. In New York City, Spofford was that jail.

As a secure facility, Spofford was a bleak place. It had bars on the windows and locked doors sectioning off corridors, stairwells, dormitory areas and each dorm room. Staff walked down the dim linoleum-and-brick halls accompanied by the jangle of keys as the heavy metal doors closed with a thud and the keys scraped in the locks. The dormitory rooms facing off a narrow corridor were also narrow, with a single metal bed frame, a small night table, and a window high up in the wall. Detainees wore colored coveralls that indicated their dorm assignments; upon admission to Spofford, detainees were issued yellow coveralls which they called "banana suits." Their street clothes, used for their court appearances, were stored in a special room.

Problems at the facility were exacerbated by an ongoing administrative debate over whether Spofford should be closed. At different times, several proposals to close the building had been put forward, making directors wary of spending money on its upkeep. Maintenance during some administrations had been minimal, and by 1983 Spofford had only a skeletal maintenance staff—two of the three elevators didn't work—and a minimal cleaning schedule.

The transition from a facility for a mixture of youths to a jail holding only delinquents was fraught with problems, and, overwhelmed, many Spofford directors apparently just gave up. No director had stayed long enough to follow through on programs that would help juvenile counselors handle the new population. Most of the new directors had stayed less than a year; one stayed less than a week after a background check proved unfavorable, a second simply walked out after a month at the facility. "It was a crisis atmosphere," Glass says. "If there was a need, something was done. If not, nothing was done." With no management stability, the balance of power had shifted to Spofford's long-time staff, who knew more about the facility's operation than many of the directors. Old-timers—by 1983, about 40 percent of the juvenile counselors and dorm managers had 10 to 25 years of experience—were the only source of continuity at the facility. "This place was run from the bottom," says David Martin, a juvenile counselor for 17 years and later a unit director. "The only fortunate part was that old-timers cared about the quality of care for the kids."

They had a difficult population to serve. About 65 percent of the youths stayed less than ten days; others stayed a month or more. Given the transience of the majority of the population, it was very difficult to design a program. Also, because these children were accused but not yet judged delinquent nor convicted of a crime, some human service administrators felt that detention should be kept brief and that "treatment" without a judge's decision was inappropriate.

In July 1979, in an effort to address some of the problems facing juvenile detention, New York City's Mayor Edward Koch removed detention services from the city's enormous Human Resources Administration and placed them in a new, autonomous department. The Department of Juvenile Justice would manage Spofford, which housed up to 215 youths and employed three-quarters of DJJ's 643 employees; non-secure detention, comprising five group homes and eight foster home placements for a total of 68 beds; court services, responsible for taking children to and from their court dates and supervising them in the family court detention rooms; and Aftercare, which was at that time only an idea that after detention, children should be helped to re-enroll in school and connect to services in their community.

But the managerial transience continued. Commissioner Schall's predecessor was caught in a political snafu over a proposed decentralized system to replace Spofford and left in November 1982. Three other executives in the central office were also fired; Rose Washington's predecessor quit the week Schall took office.

Schall wanted to be careful with Spofford. "There was a strange push-pull around Spofford," she recalls. "The history of commissioners with a reform agenda for a major institution is that it's hard to stick to the agenda if you get swept up and pulled under by the enormous problems. At the same time, part of me, when I see something, wants to fix it. I knew that there was a set of operational issues that needed to be fixed"—security, educational program, follow-up on the clients—"and I knew that I wanted to do something for the kids." Yet to remain an effective commissioner, "I didn't want to get sucked in," she says.

"Every commissioner had been brought down by Spofford," says John Isaacson, a partner with Isaacson, Miller, Gilvar, Boulware, an executive search firm hired to help Commissioner Schall find a director for Spofford. "Someone would come in, skim across the surface, make pronouncements, sound good, and then there was a scandal and you fire the commissioner." Or the Spofford director.

SURVIVING AT SPOFFORD

Rose Washington had heard that Spofford was out of control. Feeding off the palpable air of violence and tension, the youths delighted in keeping tension high. When eating, they'd drop their utensils or trays with a clatter, keeping everyone on edge. Fights were common; some counselors felt that the only way to control the youths was through equally physical tactics, which led to charges of child abuse. In April 1980, four juvenile counselors had been suspended and arrested on charges of beating up four teenaged boys. In November of that year, a 15-year-old boy had hung himself. In May 1981, five youths, including a convicted murderer awaiting transfer, had escaped.

Given such an atmosphere, the staff had devised their own ways of surviving. "Administrators came here with their bags packed," says Glass, so consequently, he, like other staff, "was focusing on myself." Because counselors were poorly paid—juvenile counselors (the entry-level counselor position) made $17,000 in 1983 about $4,000–$5,000 less than city corrections staff—many staff, including Glass, had two jobs. "I probably didn't give [the Spofford job] all the attention I should have." In some cases, a counselor would punch in to Spofford, go to a second job, and come back to punch out at the end of the shift, or have a friend punch out. Night-shift counselors would come in after a full day's work elsewhere and be prepared to sleep for the night. Others would not show up at all, availing themselves of the full extent of a variety of leaves permitted them. "They would take sick leave, annual leave, death leave," says Washington. "Sometimes they'd call in right before the shift and say they had something called 'emergency personal business' and not show up." As a result, says Washington, other employees would work extensive overtime hours, escalating costs.

The juvenile counselors had come to feel that they, not the commissioner downtown or the directors who came and went, were on the front lines caring for increasingly violent clients in an atmosphere of constant transition. That attitude was compounded by an identification with their clients. Many felt they were a minority staff taking care of minority kids for a white bureaucracy. The staff was 75 percent black and 16 percent Hispanic. All had high school educations, some had college degrees. (To be hired as a juvenile counselor required a high school degree and four years of experience or a college degree and one year's experience.) Because of the problems, turnover among new staff was high. Those who stayed felt that the facility "belonged to them," according to Washington.

Both out of distrust and a sense of power, the juvenile counselors had evolved a method of handling attempts at reform. "We got real good at maybe doing something [new] halfway the first time, then half-way again, and then half again, and so then you go and do it the old way," says Romaine Howard, formerly a unit manager and later in charge of Spofford's accreditation efforts. The staff also had become skeptical of any change. "A new director would come in and want you to move your desk from the front to the back of the dorm," recalls Delores Wade, a juvenile counselor for 26 years. "Moving the furniture was important to them. Well, okay, let them move the furniture around, and when they leave, you know, we'll just move it back." Observes Washington: "There was a 'take care of each other' attitude, a distrust of outsiders and 'downtowners.' They felt they had to be protective against those who would disrupt the status quo."

ROSE WASHINGTON

Rose Washington, 43 at the time she was hired as director of Spofford, was born in Daphne, Alabama (population 1,500). She was raised by her grandmother in a house with no electricity and no running water. Herself the daughter of slaves, the grandmother instilled in her children and grandchildren a respect for education and pride in their achievements, relying on the church and school to reinforce those values. "She was so proud that she was able to send her son to Tuskegee Institute," Washington says. "She told these stories about picking velvet beans to send him to college. So part of my upbringing was hard work, and the other part was, you did all of this and you did not let this interfere with your education."

Washington, too, picked cotton, corn, and beans for three cents a bushel to make school money. "I had goals when I was out there, to make enough money to buy books and clothes, even though it wasn't enough to last a whole year." In the fields Washington also faced racism. "I'd pick 25 bushels in a day, but you know the person keeping count, who was white, would say I'd picked 10. But I'd continue to work, you know, I had set these goals."

Washington dropped out of eleventh grade but eventually graduated and, after starting a family, started college. When she and her husband moved to Sidney, in upstate New York, so he could take a better job, she took night courses and worked part-time as a teacher's aide at Camp Brace, a delinquent youth facility run by New York State's Department for Youth (DFY)[2] in nearby Masonville. She got her BS in early secondary education and English in 1968.

It was as a teacher's aide at Camp Brace (most of whose residents came from Spofford) that she began to understand the problems of New York's delinquent children. "Our program consisted of English, science, math, and social studies," she says. "But these kids couldn't read." Washington along with other counselors lobbied for remedial reading classes, and then had to find innovative ways to motivate the youths. Her experiences taught her that "if people want to work with kids, and they take the time to find a way, there is a key to that kid, I don't care how difficult he is."

Washington decided she wanted to continue helping delinquent youths. When she was asked to become a senior youth division counselor, the first woman to be a counselor in one of DFY's male facilities, she took the job. She ran into resistance from some co-workers—"There was a feeling, women couldn't make these boys work, you had to manhandle them, what if they didn't want to get up in the morning"—and to meet it, "I was determined I was going to earn their respect. I can't say I overcompensated, but maybe I worked harder or something so it became a challenge for me, and then I got where I liked those challenges."

By 1978 Washington was named assistant director under a new camp administrator and then became acting director three months later when the director became ill. "At the time I didn't want [the job of director]; and also women had not been directors of facilities in the Division for Youth," Washington says. "But after I had tried on some new things and had been very successful, I decided I would continue. I liked controlling the whole program, having an effect in every area." After two years, Washington became director of the Tryon School, also in upstate New York. Tryon was the division's largest facility at 100 beds, which, under Washington, increased to 200.

Even though she first interviewed for the Spofford director's position mostly out of curiosity, Washington impressed Commissioner Schall. Schall knew she needed someone who would lead Spofford, who would not blame "downtown" and would take authority for changes. Washington's experience indicated many positive points. "I knew she was self-motivated, sane, mature, and sensible," Schall says, "that she was tough-minded and doesn't give up. I was less clear on who she relies on and what her relationship to bosses was. I knew she had a good . . . theory about it, but I was less sure about how she carried it out." Schall was also unsure about how much patience Washington had, but "I knew she was a leader in the charismatic sense and had a very good sense of vision."

For her part, in a second meeting with Schall, Washington tried to establish that it was she, and not the executive team or the planning department, who would run Spofford. Washington wanted to make sure she had the authority to make changes on her own. "One of the things I had learned as I checked around about DJJ was, people said that the agency was top-heavy and that maybe I would not be able to be involved in planning as much," she says. "Everything was done as a team so I would not be able to function autonomously and that I needed to know what, as director, was expected of me." Schall's answers during interviewing satisfied Washington that "I would be able to function and yes, I would be a team member but my contributions would be really valued and that I would run Spofford." At that second meeting, the two women made a personal connection that convinced them they could share a vision of a new Spofford. It wasn't until after she had accepted the position, however, that Washington learned she was 27th in the line of Spofford's directors.

TAKING CONTROL

On her very first day as head of Spofford, the staff made clear to Washington both their distrust of their new manager and their resistance to change. At a ceremony in Spofford, Washington was sworn in as director and the man who had been acting director (and applied unsuccessfully for the director's position) was sworn in as deputy executive director. "The staff knew him, he'd been a juvenile counselor and come up through the facility, and they didn't know me," Washington recalls. Along with gifts came welcoming speeches. "They told him, 'We're so proud of you, we're glad you've come through, you're one of us, and we have these gifts,' in fact it was two huge gifts. Then the director of social services gave me a gift and a plant and said, 'How happy we are that you are joining us, Miss Washington, and we are going to work you to death, but we're going to be right there working along beside you.'"

When Washington went to her eighth floor office, she faced a second challenge from the former acting director. Her predecessor had worked his way up from juvenile counselor in 20 years at Spofford. Schall, impressed with his sense of caring for the youths, had appointed him acting director but told him she was going to conduct a national search for the strongest possible administrator. When he did not get the job, he was disappointed, but Schall felt that making him deputy executive director would help smooth relations between Washington and the staff and help Washington handle such difficult issues as union relations and staff management.

Right away, however, the deputy challenged Washington's position. "I was sworn in on August 15th, and then the next morning, I came in, and he was sitting in my office behind the desk. And—here's my *deputy* you know, and I didn't want to come in confrontational—so I put my things on a little table in the office, and I started talking to him about what we were going to do, and so forth, and he kept sitting there. We must have sat like an hour or so, and I had to go to the personnel office, and different things that day, and then go back to the director's office. When the phone would ring he would answer it and hand the phone to me across the desk. We went on like this for about three days. I started coming in early, but at 7:30 he was there, 7:00 he was there, 6:30 he was there. So I finally said, 'Could I have my desk, please?' And he said, 'Well, where am I going to go?' I said, 'Well, we could look for an office for you, maybe [the director of programs'] office.' 'Well, where is he going to go?' I said, 'I don't know, but I do have to have my desk.' So he got up and walked out—he was angry then."

That testing relationship was to continue. "When I talked to [the deputy director] about why plaster was falling in the cafeteria, he talked to me about feeling castrated by me, and I wanted some accountability, I wanted things taken care of, addressed," she recalls. Those first few months, says Washington, "I couldn't speak nice enough to (him)," she said. "I needed to say, 'Please, would you do this?' It's not 'I want this done,' it is, 'Could you please take care of this,' and take any excuse for it not being done."

Nonetheless, the deputy, who often accompanied Washington to meetings at the DJJ office downtown—where he sat on the executive committee of DJJ—portrayed Washington as a tool of the white commissioner. When the possibility of dismissing staff members was raised at senior management staff meetings, the deputy told Spofford's counselors, according to Washington, "that I was about firing people, and I didn't care about the staff, and I didn't know how to work with kids—all I wanted to do was fire staff."

The accusations fed into broad resentment of Washington's position. The juvenile counselors often identified more with their charges than with anyone in management. Although she was black, Washington represented the white bureaucracy, the white administrators who were an hour away and far removed from the day-to-day reality of Spofford. Washington says staff had characterized Schall as "'this white woman up at the big house . . . she hardly ever comes here.' Well, I said, 'I am in charge of Spofford. The commissioner doesn't have to come up here, she supports us through me.'"

Conversely, the staff also charged that Washington was "soft." The Spofford style in the past used strong language and threats to keep the youths in line. Washington handled fights differently. "If a kid was out of control, I'd begin to role model with the staff—pull the kid aside, talk to him, find out what was wrong, and if the kid needed discipline, he would be disciplined, but it would be handled in a fair way," Washington recalls. "Many times you could defuse the situation by getting [with] the kid." The staff felt she was coddling youths at the expense of their ability to discipline. "So I was being portrayed as being this soft, coddling person, liking only the kids [and not the staff]."

THE FIRST CRISIS

Despite the initial difficulties over her desk, Washington decided she had to try to work with her deputy. He was Schall's appointee, and Schall believed he had the experience that would help Washington get acclimated. Washington told him that for the first three months, she wanted him to be in charge of day-to-day business while she learned how things operated. The arrangement did not last long. Within a month after her arrival, Washington and a deputy were at a meeting in Schall's office when a call came in that there was a "riot" going on in the Spofford cafeteria, where some 180 youths were gathered for dinner. Schall, Washington, and her deputy drove to the Bronx with Washington leaning out a window, as they headed down FDR Drive, attaching an antenna to the car so she could use a two-way radio. At that moment, "I made the decision that I needed to take over," Washington remembers, "I couldn't wait."

As they travelled, Washington made radio contact with the associate executive director. "He said they had managed to get the majority of the kids into their dormitories, but there were still a few fighting," Washington said. "And I wanted to know if he deemed it to be out of control. He said, no, but the police were there. And so I said at that point, 'You are not to allow the police to come into the facility. If you deem it to be under control, then I want the staff to get the kids into their rooms.'" Washington called for a lock-down: the juvenile counselors were to lock the youths in their rooms.

After an hour's drive in heavy traffic—the trip normally took 40 minutes—the group arrived at a noisy facility; the youths in one dorm were beating on their doors "so you could hear this noise ringing in the building." She quickly called senior staff together to learn the details: 180 kids had been eating together in the cafeteria when an apparently pre-arranged fight broke out. Washington knew that during mealtimes "the tension was so thick you could cut it with a knife." The crisis made it clear to her she had to act immediately. "That night I said, 'Never again will these 180 kids be programmed together.' I made the decision—only three dormitories are going to eat together in the cafeteria, and they're going to come down in shifts."

At that point, Washington called a halt to her staff meeting because the noise was "reverberating all over the building, and I'm sure it could be heard out in the community." She headed to the dorm. Staff didn't even want her to open the room doors, but she insisted on talking to each youth. "I thought it was very important to establish with the staff that I could manage these kids, because I was the first female head of the facility, from upstate New York and from Alabama. So I went down to the dormitories where the kids were, I walked through the corridors, and I said to the kids, 'This is Ms. Washington. I run the place. I want to talk to you.' And you know how kids yell: 'Ms. Washington! They did this to us!' and so forth and so on. So I said, 'I can't talk to you with all this noise. You're going to have to be quiet. I'm going to come into your rooms and talk to you." The youths told her only a few were responsible for the disturbance, but because of the lock-up they didn't get their bedding and would be deprived of their night-time snacks. "I told them that I run a fair facility, and they would get their snacks and to make up their beds, and that I would be back to talk with them." In her position as executive director, she knew it was a violation of children's rights to withhold food as a punishment, despite the measures staff felt were necessary. Even then, Washington recalls, "You see how I was set up in this situation? They'd told the kids, no snacks, and here I was, giving them snacks. It made me seem soft." (The next day Washington put the principal culprits under restrictions and put mild restrictions on the two dorms most involved in the melee.)

Washington, Schall, and other senior staff worked all night to arrange a schedule for mealtimes. That night Washington learned the details of Spofford's organization. "I knew there were 12 dormitories and there were people called unit coordinators, and I asked, well, what does that mean? 'Well, we have unit coordinators, but they only manage the day shift,'" staff explained to her. "The night shift is supervised by the deputy director for operations." To Washington, it seemed needlessly complex and afforded little accountability or control. For the near-term, however, she focused her efforts on avoiding a repeat of the cafeteria problems. "Three dormitories make up a unit. I said only three dormitories will eat at once. They will eat in a half-hour and the next three will come. Of course, that gave me the reputation of a person who made snap decisions without knowing what was going on."

The juvenile counselors warned that it would take too long to move dorm groups in and out of the cafeteria, and that not only counselors but the kitchen staff would waste time with this new attempt at organizing. Ultimately, however, they acquiesced. The first week the plan didn't work— the shifts moved too slowly through mealtimes and the schedule began to back up again. Then Washington, who had noticed Romaine Howard's drive and energy, put her in charge of calling the dorms. Howard wanted the mealtimes changed. "I thought it sounded good to me," she says, "because I felt it was crazy the way we were eating anyhow." She circumvented any attempts to disrupt the schedule. By November, when the staff began to realize the difference staggered mealtimes made, Howard says, "they said, 'Hey, this isn't so bad.'" At least the tension at mealtimes had been reduced.

Not that things went smoothly, even with people who began to support Washington. Howard became furious when she heard from another staff member that Washington was "writing her up," compiling a report on her performance. She marched in to the cafeteria wearing union buttons and a union hat. At a hastily-called meeting in Washington's office, Howard vented her anger, only to learn that the staff person had evidently misinterpreted, perhaps deliberately, Washington's note-taking during a meeting. Further, Washington told Howard, if there ever was a question she should come to Washington directly, her door was open. "That impressed me, you know," Howard says.

Another move Washington made almost immediately was to switch her office from the eighth floor to the third floor, where both the entrance level and the dining rooms for staff and for youths were located. Staff called the director's eighth-floor office "the penthouse," recalls Washington. "Beautiful view of the World Trade Center and the Empire State Building—through the bars you could see that. And they kept the floors up there spic-and-span." Some staff were skeptical, telling Washington that the noise level on the third floor would be too loud. Others approved the move. "She was saying, 'I'm down here with you,'" says Glass.

Washington took to walking through the facility at any time of day or night, seeing how each shift operated, or coming in on holidays to play cards with the kids. In this way she discovered that some of the night shift were coming in, "rolling up their hair in curlers and going to bed," she says, instead of keeping watch on the dormitory. She also found out "it was incest in here in terms of professional behavior, people supervising their cousins and things like that." She knew she would have to make some staff changes.

FUTURE AGENDA

Staff Issues: "Getting Over"

As she began to take steps toward her goal of greater staff accountability, Rose Washington had to confront not only the shortcomings of individuals but her own mixed feelings in disciplining staff members. "Part of what I had to overcome in here, working with a predominantly black staff, was my need to nurture," Washington recalls. "I understand the circumstances under which . . . well, how far our people have had to come, and so it was very hard to fire somebody." Yet Washington perceived a conflict within the juvenile counselors also. "They *loved* some of the kids," she says, but with no direction from management, many felt they were "getting over"—taking advantage of a situation in which there was little direct supervision, enjoying the apparent security of their post but doing the minimum or little more.

"They called [Spofford] a 'country club.' They were really 'getting over.' People would come in, and they figured that they were black and this white administration in this city owed it to them . . . and this was another way of getting back at the establishment, was to get over," to do a half-hearted job despite their concern for the youths. Although reluctant to confront staff members, she also believed that "they had mixed emotions" about what they were doing. She hoped that if she held them more strictly accountable, they would "grow in their respect for themselves."

To get the best employees, however, Washington believed she had to take action—and she believed that would have to include firings. She began to dismiss provisional staff, who were not protected by civil service regulations, if they did not measure up to her new standards. Those fired were dismissed both for child abuse—"They would take a kid in a dormitory and punch him out; one threw keys at kids and cut their lips"—as well as the abuses of "getting over," such as sleeping on the job or "clocking in" but leaving the building. Her actions sparked concern, however, even among those with civil service protections—especially when Washington began to hold a series of general staff meetings at which she specified that such abuses would not be tolerated by long-term civil service staff either and would be documented in writing.

Organization

Washington believed that long-term improvement hinged on reorganization and simplification of Spofford's multi-layered supervisory structure. When she arrived, management consisted of Washington herself, her deputy executive director, and the three deputies whom he—not she—supervised: one for programs, one for support services, one for operations. Everyone else at Spofford belonged to a union. (Even some of those who were in the small group of upper management had formerly been ranking union officials.) Each of four "units" at the institution had, at its head, a "unit coordinator"—not a management employee but a ranking (or "principal") juvenile counselor. The unit coordinators reported to the deputy for programs. Ostensibly, the coordinators and program deputy were to decide policy matters—e.g., what kind of clothing should be worn, how many should sleep in a dorm. In practice, however, the influence of this group was limited to the first of the three 8-hour shifts. A parallel organization, under the supervision of the deputy for operations, was responsible for evening and night shifts—and employed its own juvenile counselors of various ranks. (See Exhibit 1.) Each of the four units was divided into three dormitories, housing an average of 16 youths; two dorms on the intake unit might go up to 21 or 24, however, if there were an influx of youths. On an individual shift—in part because of chronic absenteeism—one counselor might be responsible for supervising all 16 or 24.

As she examined the organizational structure, she found that "if I wanted to have any impact on the child, I needed to go to my deputy director first, who went to the deputy of programs, who went to the deputy of operations, who went to the unit coordinators, who went to the principal juvenile counselor, who went to the senior counselor, who told the juvenile counselor, and [then] *maybe* that thing would get carried out," Washington recalls. She wanted to create accountability and to remove layers of command that she felt interfered with her knowledge of what was going on at the youths' level. She believed, moreover, that education and recreation programs were artificially separated from the housing and counseling functions of the dormitories. And she had learned, in dealing with the cafeteria riot, that unit coordinators were not given the ultimate responsibility for overseeing their units. All of this disturbed Washington. She particularly wanted to bring the unit coordinators into management and make each accountable for an individual unit.

In seeking to increase her ranks of managers, Washington ran the risk of alienating Spofford's unions. Under what had been transient management, the Spofford staff looked to its unions for continuity. Of 13 unions representing Spofford employees, the largest was District 37, Local 1457, of

EXHIBIT 1   Spofford Juvenille Center Organizational Chart, 1983.

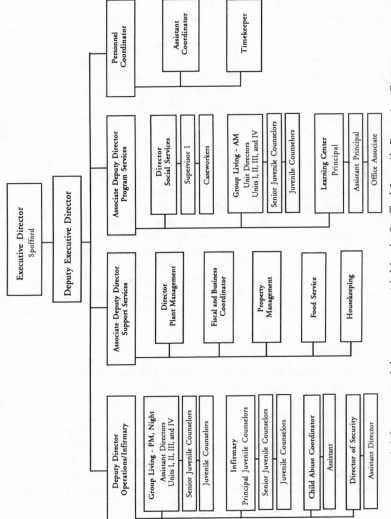

Source: Compiled from original documents provided by the Spofford Juvenile Detention Center.

the American Federation of State and Municipal Employees, which represented about 300 juvenile counselors. Some felt that the union wielded too much power because it seemed important to be "in good" with the union to get ahead. To many of the staff, however, the union was the only organization that seemed to take the employees' welfare seriously. An adversarial relationship with transient management had developed. According to Andrew Holman, a senior juvenile counselor and president of the local, "There [had been] a kind of hysteria on the part of management: 'We don't want to give the union the upper hand.'" Communication with directors had been so bad, "the union didn't find anything out except through the grapevine."

In planning any changes, however, Washington faced the constraints of union work rules. Specifically, a unit coordinator could not supervise recreation or social service staff members who reported directly to a deputy director. At a DJJ executive staff meeting, Washington proposed that unit coordinators become "unit managers"—and take on 24-hour supervisory responsibility for their units. She was warned, however, that such a course was administratively difficult and would be resisted by union officials, who would object to losing a high-ranking position in their ranks. She faced further union complications if she attempted to decentralize social service and recreation programs and make them part of the dorm structure. She was advised, though, that it might be possible for her to promote the unit coordinators to existing, unfilled civil service positions—as "head counselors"—as which they would remain in the union but could be asked to take on more management-type responsibilities. They would also have to be paid more. It might also derail the long-term goal to which she continued to cling: making the coordinators part of the management team.

Physical Conditions

As she contemplated the overall organization of the institution, Washington had to consider, as well, the dingy, dirty and, at times, frightening conditions around her. She had enjoyed some "small wins," such as the improvement in the cafeteria routine. But deep problems remained. The maintenance staff did not include a full-time, permanent plumber or electrician. The cleaning staff was inadequate. Dorms were dirty—and budget constraints made the hiring of additional cleaning crews unlikely. Possession of contraband—including weapons—was common, as were incidents such as the dorms' metal furniture being thrown by angry youths. Counselors believed such conditions could trigger violent behavior even in those who might otherwise not be given to it. "When a kid doesn't feel safe, he starts to act out," observes one counselor. Conditions for the staff left much to be desired as well. The staff dining room was austere and uncomfortable.

Relations with Central Office

Finally, Washington found herself under pressure from the central DJJ office. She had already had one tussle with central office over Spofford's education program. Schall's deputy commissioner of planning, Kathy Feely, had two jobs, supervisor of aftercare and non-secure detention, and department planner. She was told by Schall to "fix" Spofford's education program in the autumn and spring of 1983 and 1984, so she asked an education planner to look at Spofford's program. This created two immediate problems. The mere presence of the planner aroused the staff's resentment. "We were tired of outside people coming in and telling us how to do the job we'd done for years," Delores Wade says. Feely adds that "nobody in the school wanted to let the planner see the files. . . . I was from City Hall." Also without realizing it, Feely had begun to undercut Washington. When the planner reported that there was no pretesting to check education level, for example, Feely told Schall, her boss. "But then Ellen had something that even Rose didn't know about," Feely says. Washington "straightened that out very fast," Feely says, and insisted that she be told first what the planners found. Feely agreed.

But the dynamic continued. During the summer, Feely and Washington were discussing a program intended for children with developmental disabilities. Schall and Feely supported the program, but Washington felt her plate was full. From Washington's point of view, simply bringing in more planners went against her team-building efforts. "Staff would reject something if they are not a part of its development," she says. Feely as a counterpressure felt that "Ellen wants the work to get done and yet doesn't want Rose to feel imposed upon."

At times Washington did not feel imposed upon as much as misunderstood. "Sometimes for us black managers, working in an agency whose head is white, you wonder if there is really a realistic view of what you are dealing with," Washington says. "Many times when I was downtown I talked about what was going on up here. That it was difficult, painful work for us, to see kids hurt or be afraid that a child was going to be hurt, . . . and how much pain we have to take in order to continue to be patient, continue to go back and be there for a kid who is constantly testing to see if you really are real, because so many people have not been there for them. It is really emotionally draining."

NOTES

1. Actions of the court, as well as the demographics of those arrested may have reinforced Spofford's client profile. Attorneys for white youths stressed that in addition to being violent, Spofford was viewed as a place for minority youths, and judges were reluctant to send white youths to the facility.

2. DFY provides 50 percent of Spofford's detention-related expenses and sets up guidelines, such as the staff-youth ratio, for detention centers state-wide.

The Use of Force

A Policewoman's (Non)use of Deadly Force
Jillian P. Dickert

Officer Tinsley Guinn-Shaver lay in a hospital bed. Memories of the previous night's events pounded in her brain, mixed with the painful throbbing of her bodily injuries. Late in the night on March 7, 1990, Tinsley had become the first woman police officer in the Houston Police Department to shoot a suspect to death while on patrol.

The shooting had been traumatic. At the hospital, she seesawed between extreme nervous reactions, crying uncontrollably or laughing hysterically. Later, recurring nightmares of the shooting would haunt her, as she relived the incident in slow motion—the bullet wound, the betrayed look on the suspect's face, his arms limp against his sides as he fell to the ground. In these dreams she could hear exactly what he screamed at her before she pulled the trigger, but when she awoke his words were unintelligible. In sleep, she returned to these nightmares in search of his lost words, as if they alone would bring her peace.

Several fellow officers offered her assistance and support during her hospital stay. They told "dead suspect" jokes and generally made light of the shooting. Still, they called her a hero. While this peer support was reassuring, Tinsley felt troubled. Her act was not heroic; regardless of the circumstances, she had killed another human being.

POLICE AND DEADLY FORCE

Sociologist Egon Bittner has written that "the role of the police is to address all sorts of human problems when and insofar as the problems' solutions may require the use of force at the point of their occurrence."[1] The public expects—indeed has authorized—the police to intervene in their problems when force (or the threat of force) is needed to keep a situation from getting worse. Police officers are thus granted a latitude in choosing solutions not available, legally, to other citizens. Most often an officer's mere presence in a situation will suffice; other times deadly force is required.

The exact number of US citizens killed by police each year is not known with any certainty. Educated guesses fix the number anywhere between three hundred to six hundred. The large majority of shootings are considered justified by police departments, and very few officers are referred for criminal charges. While most shootings are reported to have been in self-defense or in defense of another person's life, substantial numbers have occurred, by the officers' own accounts, in situations where the victim did not present an imminent threat to anyone's life, including flight "without other resistance," a stray bullet, or mistaken identity.[2]

The rates of shootings by police officers vary considerably among cities and across neighborhoods within the same city. These variations may be explained by levels of crime and arrests, income inequality, "social cohesion" (such as divorce, unemployment, suicide rates), and gun density within the community.[3] Police departments also differ widely in their policies and review procedures regarding the use of deadly force. No single set of standards dictating when an officer may use a firearm is universally accepted. Despite a clear national trend for police departments to enact written policies governing the use of firearms, many of these policy statements are poorly written and confusing. An increasing vulnerability to civil suits has discouraged many police departments from adopting firearms policies more restrictive than state law.[4]

The policy of the Houston Police Department is very exacting. It permits officers to use deadly force if and only if there is imminent fear of death or bodily injury for the officer, the officer's partner, or a citizen. Further, officers are not permitted to shoot fleeing felons. According to Tinsley Guinn-Shaver, this deadly force policy is formally taught during training at the Houston Police Academy. Thereafter, an officer learns on the street when deadly force is warranted. The street credo is: "If someone pulls a stick, then you pull a bigger stick. Never lose control of the situation."

THE HOUSTON POLICE DEPARTMENT

Historically, the Houston Police Department was known for its aggressive, confrontational style of policing. As recent commentators have noted, the department "long prided itself on taking names and kicking ass."[5] At times, policing was not easily distinguished from harassment, especially of the city's varied minority populations. Even in cases of genuine criminality, officers' reactions were often out of proportion to the needs of the situation. According to department lore, for example, "in the good old days a burglar caught in a house was likely to die there."[6]

In late 1989, a rash of incidents aggravated the already-damaged relations between the department and the citizens of Houston. One Houston police officer was under indictment for murder. Another was called before a grand jury for a questionable shooting. Still others had been charged with crimes ranging from drug use to trading leniency for sexual favors.[7] In one particularly controversial incident, a policeman shot and killed a black man after stopping him for speeding. Police said the man was shot six times— four times in the back, once in the abdomen and once in the arm—when the officer said it appeared the man was reaching for a .357 magnum revolver on the passenger seat of his car.[8] This was the third person the officer had killed in his seven years on the force. Fellow officers admitted the officer had grown more aggressive since he had begun using steroids for body-building several years prior to the incident.

In December, the family of Ida Lee Delaney, a black woman who was shot to death in October by an off-duty police officer, filed a lawsuit claiming the city of Houston and the Houston Police Department had a history of tolerating and inciting the use of excessive force "to such extent that it [had] become custom and habit."[9] Citizens brought their rage over the Delaney case to the streets. Protesters, demanding swift action, carried signs bearing the names of Joe Campos Torres and Randall Allen Webster, two young men who came to symbolize the Houston department's reputation as a brutal police force.[10] In 1977, Torres, 23, was severely beaten by several officers and tossed into a local bayou, still handcuffed. They taunted him to swim, and watched him drown in agony. Two officers were brought to trial and convicted but received only a year's probation. Webster, 17, was shot the same year after he led the police on a chase with a stolen van. Later, it was revealed that the officers had planted a "throw-down gun" next to his body to make it appear they had acted in self-defense. Not since those two cases and an ensuing riot had citizens so angrily demanded reform of the Houston Police Department.

A few years after the Torres and Webster incidents, Mayor Kathy Whitmire appointed Lee P. Brown, a black man and an outsider, to head the department. It was hoped that Brown's innovations as director of public safety in Atlanta could be introduced in Houston, improving police service and relations with the community. Toward that end, Brown pioneered neighborhood-oriented policing in Houston and established progressive minority hiring and promotion programs—programs that have been imitated in police departments around the country. To ease tensions in the community, Brown designed a "six-point plan" that included a summit on crime-related women's issues and random drug testing for officers.[11] Brown also instituted a firearms policy stipulating that police officers could not *draw* their weapons unless their lives, or someone else's, were in danger.[12]

Despite Brown's successes, however, police attitudes regarding the use of force resisted change. In 1989, police shootings of civilians in Houston rose to 40, twelve of them fatal, more than doubling the 1988 total of 17 shootings with four fatalities.[13] This was the highest number of shootings since 1982—itself a record year—when officers fatally shot 14 people in the line of duty and wounded 35 others.[14]

Houston legislators reflected their constituents' anger over these incidents in public statements deploring police violence. Representative Debra

Danburg (D-Houston) called for stiffer psychological screening to prevent the hiring of individuals unable to control their violent behavior. Representative Al Edwards (D-Houston) asked Governor Bill Clements to call a special legislative session to establish a civilian panel to review violent incidents by police.[15]

A NEW POLICE CHIEF

In January, 1990, Chief Brown left Houston to become police commissioner in New York City. Mayor Whitmire replaced him with Elizabeth Watson, who had directed Houston's West Side Command Station—the site of Brown's initial experiment in neighborhood-oriented policing. Watson was a protege of Lee Brown, who confided that he had been grooming her for the position.[16] Watson became the first woman police chief in the history of the department—and only the second in charge of a major police force across the US (the first was in Portland, Oregon).

Chief Watson was to supervise approximately 4,000 officers—less than 10 percent of them women—in this 580-square-mile city (the fourth largest in population in the US), plus 1,100 civilian employees, with a $177 million budget, and about one million calls for police service each year.[17] According to Joyce Hersh, president of the Houston-area National Organization for Women, one of the keys to Chief Watson's success would be her ability to control a small number of "cowboy groups" within the department who regularly flouted department policy and violated citizens' constitutional rights.[18] Clearly, among them, acceptance of a woman police chief would be slow. As one female officer reported, "Male officers were coming up to me and curtsying after they heard the announcement about Watson's appointment. They asked me if curtsying would be the policy now instead of saluting."[19]

THE POLICE ACADEMY—
A WOMAN'S EXPERIENCE[20]

The first women went on patrol for the Houston Police Department in 1975. When Alice Appleby entered the Police Academy for training, she found that women were considered to be "problems"—or, as one male instructor said, "women are a waste of skin." Alice's class began with ten female cadets; four months later, she was the only remaining woman. To her it was clear that the treatment of women—not the rigor of the training—thinned the number of women cadets.

Ironically, Alice felt that much of the negative attention she received at the academy was the result of her superior performance. She scored better than any of her male peers in marksmanship, high-performance driving skills, physical endurance, and classroom instruction. The resentment was evident even among men her own age. The male cadets felt that women could be police officers only because the law demanded it, not because women might be better than men at the job. Twice in her defensive tactics class, Alice was viciously attacked by two different male cadets who were determined to prove that no woman could arrest a man if he did not permit it. Both times she ended up with bruises and busted lips—and a hand-cuffed, prone, and embarrassed male cadet.

In shotgun training, one of the male instructors surreptitiously loaded the weapon with slugs instead of standard shells. A slug packs such a powerful blast that it can penetrate the front end of a standard-sized vehicle, travel through it, and penetrate and exit a second vehicle. The recoil of a gun loaded with slugs is also powerful. On the first shot, Alice was knocked to the ground. She took it as another initiation rite women had to endure.

Just before the academy graduation ceremony, the instructors proudly presented Alice with a pair of brass balls. They explained that since she was female, it was their responsibility to "alleviate her shortcoming." "It takes balls to be a cop," they snickered. Alice shocked everyone at the ceremony by delivering the brass balls to the police chief and members of the command staff—in front of the cadets' family members and several high-ranking members of the city administration—and requested formal action against the instructors for sexual harassment. Disciplinary action was taken and the tradition of supplying female cadets with brass balls came to an end.

HOUSTON POLICEWOMEN ON PATROL

Many patrolwomen felt that, when they graduated from the Houston Police Academy, their male co-workers questioned whether they could do the job. But sometimes a single incident made believers of the critics and earned the women acceptance.

"When I first went on the street, the male officers seemed very receptive to the female officers," Alice explained. "But, in effect, they like many men had become more adept at masking their prejudices. Acceptance of men into the fold of police culture is automatic, with rejection only occurring after a man makes a grievous error. Women, in order to be accepted, first have to prove themselves worthy of inclusion." After claiming credit for an arrest Alice had made, one of her male partners even boasted to a detective, "Yeah, I'm going to teach her to do the job just like a man, even if I have to teach her to piss standing up!"

Alice experienced a double standard among police officers in their response to mistakes committed by male officers in contrast to those made by female officers. "Mistakes by female officers seem to receive greater derision and informal commentary than those made by male officers," she observed. "Thus, one mistake early in a woman's career can be very costly to her reputation among the troops for years to come. Or, more commonly, the refusal to demonstrate the behaviors adopted by male officers can create a great deal of alienation between a female officer and her peers."

Often female officers find themselves in compromising situations because of their male colleagues. Alice explained: "Every injury I sustained and fight I was in resulted from an over-reaction or mistake committed by a male officer. In hindsight, it seemed as though brawn was much more of a liability than an asset in police work."

A female sex crimes sergeant at the Houston Police Department recalled patrolling with a short male officer with a chip on his shoulder. "I was sick and tired of coming home with my clothes all ripped up," she said. Her partner became defensive when she questioned his methods. "If you know a better way of doing it, do it," he told her. So for the next two weeks he stood back as she handled the prisoners. "And for two weeks, we weren't in any fights," she observed. Finally, they talked it over, and he admitted he sometimes used unnecessary force. "We were the best of friends from that day forward," she said.[21]

Policewomen at the Houston department claim they balance a patrol team because men and women react differently when confronted. Though at a disadvantage in a physical confrontation, a woman can often calm a tense situation with some well-chosen words. Also, men will rarely attack female officers. "The training is still ingrained there that they usually won't hit a woman," one female officer said. At the same time, female offenders often resist male officers because "women know men are afraid to hit them."[22]

HOUSTON POLICEWOMEN
AND DEADLY FORCE

Most research on police use of deadly force has been compiled in the last ten to fifteen years. Because of the closed culture of policing and non-standardized reporting practices, knowledge gained from such studies is at best sketchy. Not only is it difficult to gain an accurate count of fatal shootings by police, it is virtually impossible to determine the nature and number of incidents in which deadly force would have been justified but was not used as a result of the officer's skill at apprehending suspects without it.

Some have suggested that patrolwomen, when confronted with danger or violence, will use their guns more frequently than male patrol officers. If an individual policewoman is not able to handle a violent situation, she may be forced to use her weapon in self-defense. Yet none of the various studies on policewomen show any indication of policewomen either firing or unholstering their weapons more frequently than male officers.[23]

When Alice Appleby conducted a review of shootings involving Houston police officers over the fifteen years since women began patrol duty, she discovered that no female officers were involved in any way. Women never discharged their weapons to kill, injure, or apprehend a suspect. When asked why they had never used deadly force in the course of their work, Houston policewomen responded:

"*Patience . . . I think that women tend to be more patient in these situations than men.*"

"*I don't like to generalize. I would say that women tend to have a larger menu of choices than men and use those more often. Face it, we have to use more finesse. And I think everyone, citizens included, benefits.*"

"*I don't panic, never have in any situation. If someone, a suspect, is acting in a threatening way, I try to look beyond what's on the surface and try to think about what's causing him to act that way. I have always been able to talk people down and cool everybody off."*

"Women can read interpersonal signals like body language better, which helps them avoid dangerous situations and act quickly when they occur. Men are slower to read signs of aggression towards them, and often feel invincible and overconfident in their strength, thereby setting themselves up for a confrontational situation. Men fear their peers' perceptions of them more. The use of force—even deadly force—becomes like an initiation into a club, so to not use force makes the male cop seem less of who he should be in front of who he works with."

"Women have a different perspective on the nature of humanity. I think most of the male officers believe that most people have malevolent intentions. But I think, being a woman and peace officer, that the majority of people are good and will do what is right if they have the chance. I mean, if someone is pointing a gun at you and is upset and irrational, you can still maintain control. You make them aware of what they're doing and give them an alternative . . . they'll usually take it."

"In this job they try and make you do everything like a man. You try for a while and then you say, 'screw it, what made them experts anyway?' I think they make a lot of mistakes because they're always trying to prove something. I don't have to prove anything; there's a lot of freedom that comes with that."

Some argue that perhaps the situations patrolwomen respond to are not as dangerous or life-threatening as those involving male officers. Thus, male officers would have to resort to deadly force more frequently. However, in Appleby's study of felony and misdemeanor arrest statistics for a Houston patrol division over a five-year period, it turned out that every female police officer was ranked in the top 15 percent of all officers for arrest averages. This suggests that policewomen face their fair share of danger.

In what situations did Houston policewomen choose not to use deadly force? Consider Alice Appleby. Alice was able to earn the rank of "distinguished expert," a level of marksmanship very few men attain. Although being a "good shot" is an important badge of prestige for any police officer, this distinction caused those officers who value force over finesse to seek Alice as a partner.

During a routine felony stop, Alice and her first partner—a male— pulled over a moving van. Using a loudspeaker, Alice ordered the suspects out of the van. The first suspect, the driver, came out while the male officer covered him. Due to the height of the van, Alice was unable to see him, but both officers were protected by the open doors of the cruiser. Next, two other men exited from the passenger side of the cab. One of the men had a pistol and drew down on Alice. She immediately ordered him to put the gun down, informing him that she had a cover, and that he would be the loser in a shooting match. Reason prevailing, he put the gun down. All of the men were placed under arrest.

Alice's partner was incensed that she did not shoot the suspect the minute he drew his gun, lamenting that she "passed up a perfect opportunity to kill some scum." He told her about some shootings he had been involved in and claimed it was simple for an officer to get away with "teaching people a lesson." He reminded her that "dead men don't talk." When Alice asked if other officers felt the same, her partner nodded. Apparently, killing a suspect was considered by some Houston officers as fitting and honorable, even when it was not necessary to resolve a situation. Alice never rode with this officer again.

On another occasion, Alice rode with a female officer, and her experience was very different. At the time, neither woman knew the other very well, much less each other's views about their jobs. Around 2:00 a.m. one night, they received a disturbance call. Two shots had been fired from a residence in the midst of a Houston warehouse district. The policewomen surveyed the scene and requested backup units. In the front yard, an elderly man shouted obscenities at a man on the ground who was crab-crawling away from him. The older man was energetically waving a pump shotgun.

While their arrival on the scene distracted the older man, the younger man—who appeared to have been shot in the leg—crawled around the building to safety. Now the policewomen were the target. The older man drew down his gun and threatened to kill them. They were protected by the patrol car, which bought them some time. Although deadly force would have been appropriate and legal, they were able to convince the older man to lower his gun in a matter of minutes. He presented himself to be handcuffed. There was no conflict between the policewomen about how to handle the situation.

Alice maintained one of the highest felony arrest averages in her division at the Houston Police Department. Although she responded to many volatile incidents where she could have legally committed homicide or maimed a suspect, she never found it necessary to use deadly force. And, until March 7, 1990, no other female officer at the Houston Police Department had done so either.

TINSLEY GUINN-SHAVER

After two years as a civilian police dispatcher in Houston—her hometown—Tinsley Guinn-Shaver decided she wanted to become a police officer. She was sworn in at age twenty. That was in the early 1980s, when Chief Lee Brown was engaged in his efforts to improve the department's service and reputation. Honest and hard-working, Tinsley was the type of person the department wanted to recruit and retain within its ranks.

When Tinsley completed her probationary training, she was assigned to patrol duty on the night shift of Houston's West Side Command Station. Houston's West Side was known for its high-rent neighborhoods, expensive restaurants, shopping malls, glitzy nightclubs, and extensive social drug use. Yet beneath the veneer of conspicuous wealth, the West Side was plagued by nightly knifings and shootings, crack and cocaine trafficking, and an epidemic of auto thefts and drunk driving. Tinsley maintained one of the highest felony arrest records among her peers on the night shift, earning the respect of both residents and colleagues for her efforts to "clean up" the neighborhood. Residents of the West Side even nicknamed her "Miss Lucy," for Lucifer.

In 1986, Tinsley became the first patrolwoman to be named "Officer of the Year." This followed a particularly daring arrest after three men had stabbed a security guard to death at a local nightclub. With Tinsley's arrival on the scene only minutes after the brawl, the suspects fled the bar. Tinsley pursued them on foot. When she caught up with two of the men, she tackled both of them with a flying dive, striking them with her nightstick. The third suspect, however, was hidden in nearby shrubs. He crept up behind her and stabbed her in the back. Thinking that she had only been bitten, Tinsley continued to subdue and handcuff two of the men with little further struggle. She did not realize she had been stabbed until some backup officers arrived and pointed it out to her.

After the necessary surgery and recovery, Tinsley was back on the beat and patrolling with no less tenacity than before the stabbing. Her male co-workers were impressed, her reputation as a tough street officer secure. But on the night of March 7, 1990, this toughness was tested in the extreme. The following is Tinsley's personal account of what happened, supplemented by background information.

MARCH 7, 1990

"I'm a cop on the beat, night shift patrol. I have been a police officer for nine years and am not unaccustomed to working alone; however, this night (a balmy night) we were exceptionally short-handed. I was the only unit in my beat, and for the night I was responsible for the adjacent beat as well. Knowing that there were no backup units immediately available to me, I decided to be a reactive, rather than pro-active, unit.

"I slowly cruised along Fondren Street, leaving the junkies, huddled in the shadows, to their own destruction. A white 1976 Chrysler sedan pulled in front of me. Because it's unusual to see a middle-aged white male in this area at night, I checked the license plate on the mobile data terminal in my patrol car, and found that the out-of-state (Oklahoma) plate had expired five years ago.

"I hit the button for the lights, and immediately the area was illuminated in brilliant, flashing strobes. The suspect pulled unhesitatingly over and stopped. I approached the vehicle with caution, but the driver was very polite and cooperative. I advised him of the status of his plates and asked him for his license and insurance. He provided the documents, and I hurriedly returned to my car to check the subject on the computer.

"Suddenly my computer flashed a warning message. Apparently, my simple traffic stop was really a felony stop as the driver (now identified as James Greene, age 44) was wanted on two different charges, from two states. I verified a felony warrant out of Kentucky for parole violation and a felony warrant out of Oklahoma for probation violation (connected to a cocaine conviction).

"I greatly desired a backup unit to effect this arrest; however, a stolen auto chase was in progress and that left no units and no radio air time to ask for assistance. (It is standard practice among police officers to stay off the air during high stress situations; failure to do so might seriously jeopardize the safety of other officers.) Therefore, the radio dispatcher was the only person who knew of the felony arrest I would have to make.

"I hesitated to approach this man alone. Years of experience had taught me that a person's demeanor can change drastically in a matter of seconds. I procrastinated as long as I dared (about thirty minutes), hoping for a break in air traffic. The suspect was getting restless, so I decided to go ahead and approach him alone. I feared that if I did not, he soon would confront me.

"I advised the suspect that he had a warrant out; however, I attempted to convince him that it was a simple municipal warrant rather than the felonies I had verified. He mumbled under his breath that it was impossible for him to have an outstanding ticket. I asked him if he knew he had a couple of traffic warrants, and he said, 'I don't remember getting them.'

"He exited his car as I instructed, his demeanor meek and polite. The suspect placed his hands on top of his car as advised; however, as I began to take him into custody, he threw his body back into mine, knocking me momentarily off balance. He swung his arm out, smashing me in the face. I recovered quickly as the force he hit me with was not strong enough to break my grasp. I held on to prevent him from fleeing. We danced around in the middle of the street, with me attempting to maintain my hold and him attempting to break it. He was very wiry and agile, and I was unable to effectively restrain him.

"Unexpectedly, he escalated his force against me, ramming his head into my face like a raging bull. The pain blinded me and tears came to my eyes. In that instant, he fled. I immediately pursued him, and much to both of our surprise, I caught up with him within the block. [Tinsley tried to give second-by-second details over a hand-held police radio throughout the foot chase.]

"Once again we struggled, and once again he managed to elude my grasp. As he ran from me this time, he kept looking frantically over his shoulder, and while he was gauging me, he tripped on an unseen grassy incline on the side of Crossview Street and fell into the gravel. I was on him in an instant, yet this time, as I fought to hold him, his attack became vicious. I saw the rage in his eyes. His fists rained a torrent of blows on my face and chest. His foot caught me, and I crashed to the ground. Wrenching the police radio from my hand as I fell, he jumped astride me and smashed the radio down on my head and face repeatedly. He hit me with such force that he lost his grip (his hands were covered with sweat and blood from the fight). The radio bounced crazily off my head and fell to the ground out of our reach.

"With one hand I was fending off his blows, and with the other I was protecting my gun. I bucked my body to get him off me, but I was unable to dislodge him. Still sitting on top of me, he struck me with his fists until his hand fell on my flashlight, which I had dropped to protect my gun. I read his intention in his eyes even before he picked up the light. I fought with renewed vigor, but he brought the flashlight down into my face with brutal viciousness. I felt my teeth break, like fragile china. Blood sprayed us both. Again the flashlight thudded on my face and head. I heard bones give way and felt my nose shift with the blows. My focus was no longer clear, yet I could still see him with his eyes wide in frantic hostility. His mouth was hanging open and saliva was drooling down his chin. I could see that he was screaming something, but the pounding of my own heart blocked out his words. In that moment, I knew that he might kill me.

"I calmed down and took control of my senses. With a strength fueled by fear, I threw him off me, kicked at him, and with a scissor-like grip threw him to the ground. He landed with such force that the air was knocked out of him. I watched as my flashlight fell harmlessly into the gutter. I rolled over and crawled to my radio. I tried to make my lips form the words as I called for an ambulance, but they were split open and bleeding and speech was painful. The dispatcher was unable to understand me. I shakily got to my feet; all I could think of was getting back to my patrol car three and a half blocks away.

"I was disoriented and dizzy, and as I stood there trying to gather my wits, I realized that the suspect I had been struggling with had just run by me. I remembered that I was trying to arrest him, so I pursued him again. I didn't realize I had dropped my handcuffs in the middle of Fondren Street during our first encounter.

"I caught the suspect in a parking lot of an apartment complex. This time, as I grabbed him, I think I saw fear in his face. He couldn't believe that I was still capable of pursuing him. His fear, however, seemed to fuel his hostile energy. He struck me hard in my already-battered face. I dropped my radio and struck him back with such force that we both fell against a car. He grabbed me with one hand and began a rapid strike motion with the other into my head, face, and chest. I felt myself sinking beneath the blows. I believed that if I passed out, he would beat me to death in his rage. [She finally spotted a backup unit, but it drove past without seeing her.] Time was running out.

"Out of desperation, I pulled my gun. I saw his expression register the presence of my weapon. I struck him several times with the gun. Blood ran down his face as the barrel ripped at him, yet still he fought. I begged him to just get down on the ground or simply walk away. I knew I would not be able to pursue him again. He said, 'O.K., O.K., you win,' but he kept fighting, punching. He would not relent; he pummeled me with the force that only a crazy man could possess. I stood there struggling to maintain my consciousness and my life. I pointed the gun at him, only inches from his body, and pulled the trigger. The bullet pierced the left side of his chest. The silence was overwhelming. I watched his arms fall helplessly to his sides, and his lips mouthed unknown words. 'Oh my god, I'm gonna die,' he screamed as he crumpled to the ground, my hand still clutching his collar.

"My eyes were like a movie camera in slow motion. I saw my finger pull the trigger. I faintly heard the gun as it went off and saw a hole appear in his side as the flame from the muzzle burnt away his shirt, leaving powder burns on his skin. He hit the concrete on his face, his hands limply at his sides. I stood for a second, then fell to the ground choking. I began to fight for air as I spat up blood, grass, and teeth fragments. I could faintly hear the suspect as he lay crying for his life. Then I saw flashing lights as the backup units found me. Eight minutes and thirty-five seconds after my initial contact with the suspect, I finally had help. I wept—in pain, fear and relief.

"A backup officer approached. 'Are you all right?' he asked. 'No,' I replied. 'Roy, I shot him.' I thought to myself 'get a grip,' but I was bawling uncontrollably, choking on teeth fragments. My friends gently loaded me into a police car to transport me to the hospital. I stared out the window, watching as the suspect, still alive, was loaded into an ambulance. I saw the blood stains on the ground where his life had begun to run out of him. So violent in life, yet so vulnerable and helpless in death.

"It started to rain."

AFTERMATH

At the hospital, Tinsley remained almost delirious for the rest of the night. She was unable to stop crying for several hours. Her body was covered with bruises, and she had lost four upper teeth. Still feeling the surge of adrenalin and not yet cognizant of the seriousness of her injuries, Tinsley went home at approximately 6 a.m., to avoid the media. She did not want to be on camera, but more than that she feared that they would label her just another "trigger-happy cop" at the Houston Police Department.

James Greene died during surgery at Ben Taub Hospital, five hours after he was shot. Although Tinsley remembered shooting him in the lower left side of his chest from approximately twelve to fifteen inches away, the autopsy showed that the bullet was fired less than an inch away from his upper chest, wounding him just above his heart. The bullet had lodged in his spine and paralyzed him immediately. Someone announced Greene's death over the city-wide police channel. For several minutes, police officers across Houston responded by intermittently tapping the transmit buttons on their hand-held radios, blocking all transmission with the resulting clicking noises. This clicking is the police equivalent of applause.

Meanwhile, Tinsley was at home and in the shower. She could hear her friends cheering in the living room at the news of Greene's death. At the time, their cheers did not bother her—she was glad he would not be able to sue her! Later, however, she felt guilty for not feeling guilty. Throughout her career, Tinsley had worked hard not to act or be perceived as hard or callous. So when she initially felt no pain or remorse over Greene's death, it frightened her.

The citizens of Houston made Tinsley a local hero. Area radio and television stations were deluged with over two hundred get-well faxes, and

Chief Watson received numerous letters commending Tinsley's dedication. Tinsley made guest appearances on talk shows, receiving praise from news people and celebrities alike. In the eyes of the public, her substantial injuries helped justify the shooting. At the Houston Police Department, Tinsley's male colleagues lavished her with back-slapping support. Most asked why she did not shoot sooner, and a few inquired about her psychological well-being.

Her female colleagues reacted differently. To them, the press, the public, and the male officers misinterpreted the event by calling it heroic. As one policewoman put it, "Killing anyone should be a matter of pure survival. Women know that, but men miss the point. They make a sick game of it. Don't get on that track because it's a mind fuck, and it will end you up in hell or prison, whichever comes first." The bottom line was that she had killed a human being. Regardless of how "bad" he was, he was still a human being.

Tinsley, too, was disturbed by the glorification of the shooting. Although it was her conviction that Greene meant to kill her, and she shot him only to remove that threat, Tinsley felt she had let the community down. She thought she should have been able to gain control of the situation without shooting Greene. To use deadly force was to fail as a police officer.

After extensive dental work, "Miss Lucy" was back on patrol and training rookie officers by mid-April. In August, a Harris County grand jury declined to indict her for the shooting.

NOTES

1. Egon Bittner, "The Capacity to Use Force as the Core of the Police Role," in *Moral Issues in Police Work,* eds. Frederick A. Elliston and Michael Feldberg (Rowman & Allanheld, 1985), p. 21.

2. William A. Geller, "Police and Deadly Force: A Look at the Empirical Literature," in *Moral Issues in Police Work,* eds. Frederick A. Elliston and Michael Feldberg (Rowman & Allanheld, 1985), p. 205.

3. Ibid., p. 211.

4. Catherine H. Milton, Jeanne Wahl Halleck, James Lardner, and Gary L. Albrecht, *Police Use of Deadly Force* (Police Foundation, 1977), p. 10.

5. Malcolm K. Sparrow, Mark H. Moore and David M. Kennedy, *Beyond 911: A New Era for Policing* (New York: Basic Books, 1990), p. 90.

6. Ibid., p. 90.

7. S.K. Bardwell and Felix Sanchez, "Watson Reportedly Ordered 'Tight Lid' On Beating Charges," *Houston Post,* 5/17/90, p. A-24.

8. S.K. Bardwell and David D. Medina, "Officer More Aggressive Since Steroids, Colleagues Say," *Houston Post,* 11/17/89, p. A-13.

9. David Elliston, "Ida Delaney Family Sues HPD, 3 Officers, City and Club," *Houston Post,* 12/5/89, p. 1.

10. Jane Grandolfo, "New Disputes Reopening Old HPD Wounds," *Houston Post,* 11/19/89, p. A-22.

11. S.K. Bardwell and David Plesa, "How Watson's Command Might Affect Key Programs Under Way Within HPD," *Houston Post,* 1/21/90, p. A-33.

12. Jane Grandolfo, "New Disputes Reopening Old HPD Wounds," *Houston Post*, 11/19/89, p. A-22.

13. S. K. Bardwell and Andrew Kirtzman, "HPD's '89 Civilian Shootings Rise to 40," *Houston Post*, 1/11/90, p. A-23.

14. Jack Douglas, "Fatal Shootout on Freeway Brings Police Killings to 9," *Houston Post*, 11/2/89, p. A-19.

15. Mary Lenz, "Lawmaker Seeks Special Hearing on Police Violence," *Houston Post*, 11/18/89, p. A-21.

16. Walter Shapiro, "Reforming Our Image of a Chief: Elizabeth Watson Did Not Start Out as a Feminist Pioneer, but Houston's New Top Cop is Stubbornly Working for Change," *Time*, 136:3 (1990), p. 80.

17. Jane Grandolfo, "Nation Watches Houston's Women Leaders," *Houston Post*, 5/13/90, p. A-16.

18. William Pack, "Women Applaud Nomination of Houston's First Female Chief," *Houston Post*, 1/20/90, p. A-20.

19. Paul Harasim, "A Woman Who Knows Her Place," *Houston Post*, 1/20/90, p. A-19.

20. The following three sections are based on essays written by a student at the Kennedy School of Government who wishes to remain anonymous. She is disguised in the text as Alice Appleby.

21. Michael Haederle, "Policewomen Gaining Acceptance Slowly," *Houston Post*, 11/4/84, p. A-14.

22. Ibid., p. A-14.

23. Peter Horne, *Women in Law Enforcement* (Thomas, 1980), p. 168.

SECTION C

War and Peace

Army Women and the Saudis:
The Encounter Shocks Both

James LeMoyne

IN SAUDI ARABIA, Sept. 24 [1990]—Maj. Jane S. Fisher hopped into her jeep and drove out to the flight line at a military air base here, where American F-15 jets and C-5 cargo planes kicked into the sky above a Saudi desert now filling with convoys of American troops.

For Major Fisher, it was a short drive to another long day's work supervising the handling of American jet fighters before takeoff. But her duties here reflect one side of a wide cultural chasm that American Army women and their Saudi hosts are still struggling to comprehend.

"IT IS SO STRANGE"

Saudi Arabia is, after all, a conservative Islamic country where women wear black veils, walk on the streets two steps behind their men and are prohibited from driving and from doing a great number of other things.

"Being here makes me glad to be an American," Major Fisher said in an interview. "I'm thankful I'm not a Saudi woman. I just don't know how they do it."

But it is just as easy to find Saudi women who are every bit as grateful not to be American.

"It is so strange," said Aisha Ala-Suwaida, a Saudi doctor, speaking of the sight of American Army women here, who make up roughly 10 percent of the more than 150,000 American troops deployed in Saudi Arabia and the region.

"I am glad not to be an American woman," she said. "Women are not made for violence with guns."

Najat Al Fadel, a Saudi medical internist, agreed.

"I did not expect women to come with the troops and live together like this," she said, almost stammering to express her amazement. "It is, it is—surprising to us."

That is probably a great understatement. Still, it is not easy for outsiders to understand the shock felt by Saudis on seeing American Army women working and living as equals, and in many cases the military superiors, of men here.

Sgt. Sherry L. Callahan, 25 years old, described what she and other Army women felt after arriving in Saudi Arabia.

"At first we were angry," said Sergeant Callahan, the assistant crew chief tending the lead F-15 fighter of the First Tactical Fighter Wing at the base. "We were deployed here to save these people and, like, they don't want us because we're women."

Sergeant Callahan said that at the base, whose precise location cannot be disclosed under Pentagon ground rules for journalists, she still notices the reaction of Saudi soldiers when they see her elbow next to a man to work on the innards of her jet fighter or, even worse, order one of her men to carry out a task.

"They're shocked to see me work beside American men," she said. "And when I tell a guy to do something, you see them staring and saying to themselves, 'Hey, that's not right for a woman to be ordering around a man.'"

A HANDSHAKE SHOCKS

But Sergeant Callahan said that after a month of working in the same hangar with Saudi Air Force crews, there had been a decided thaw in Saudi feelings.

"At first they just didn't know what to say to me," she recalled. "But sometimes now they even ask me to help on their aircraft if they're behind."

In Saudi society, women appear to be prohibited from having authority over men, except in rare cases among physicians, for example, or within the private confines of some homes.

Public physical contact is equally rare. Many Saudi women not only cover their head and face, but also wear gloves to insure that they do not touch men.

When a reporter shook the hand of one Saudi woman, she seemed stunned for a second to have had physical contact, even in formal greeting. To photograph a woman invites the wrath of her husband, the family and the police.

There is no dating or dancing here. Premarital sex remains the object of enduring family shame and social censure. Infidelity can be, and is, punished by execution.

A MEASURE OF LIBERALIZATION

Within those strict confines, however, Saudi women appear to have won a measure of liberalization. Most go to school and many aspire to be doctors, teachers, designers, architects and office workers in banks and businesses that cater to women.

Recently King Fahd, in a statement prompted by Iraq's invasion of Kuwait, said he would encourage Saudi women to participate more fully in national life. But the occupations that he mentioned as befitting women, particularly teaching and nursing, are those already open to women. Both Saudi and Western officials did not consider the King's statement signaled a radical change for women.

Inside the home, several Saudi men and women said, wives and elder daughters can exercise great authority, often controlling family finances and organizing the men's lives.

"Saudi Arabia is not a tent with a man inside with four wives," declared Hadiah Al-Shammary, a notably out-spoken 25-year-old Saudi woman who is a doctor at the King Fahd teaching hospital here. "We're a developing country and a pretty good one."

A BROAD RANGE OF DUTIES

Dr. Al-Shammary might be called a variant of the new Saudi woman. She said she would never marry a man she did not love, and she would leave her husband if he took another wife. Under Islamic law, a Saudi man may take as many as four wives, but few do because of the expense and because more and more women refuse to countenance a second wife in the household.

Nor does Dr. Al-Shammary wear a veil over her face, a practice she calls a matter of personal choice. "We are changing faster than many people think," she said. "You can see the difference."

Yet even she said she thought it a little strange that American women should want to become soldiers, though she added that "American women have the right to choose for themselves."

That choice has been made by tens of thousands of American women, many of whom are being deployed here. They serve in a broad range of duties, as pilots, mechanics, logistics supervisors, armed guards and military police officers.

"I have 150 women out here and they do an outstanding job," said Col. Ted Reid, commander of a combat unit of the 24th Infantry Division deployed far out in the desert. "I would not want to operate without them."

A HAZY LINE ON COMBAT

Under current American law, Army women are barred from direct combat roles, but the line between combat and noncombat duties here seems hazy. Many women here are in positions on the front lines and at the rear where they will be subject to attack if war breaks out. Women are deployed in the desert with combat units and are armed.

The 24th Supply Battalion of the 24th Infantry Division is the most forward-deployed American supply battalion in Saudi Arabia. According to its officers, nearly a quarter of its approximately 400 troops are women.

A visit to the battalion found armed American women driving trucks, manning radios, standing guard duty and ferrying water and gas tankers.

Capt. Cynthia Mosley, 29 years old, from Mobile, Ala., lined up her supply unit of women in a driving wind of heat and dust. Several of the women complained at the tough conditions, but Captain Mosley did not.

"I think it's important that I'm out here because I am about the best there is at what I do," she said. "It shows that not only are we women willing, but also that we're able to fight for our country."

Saudis do not see most of the American women, who are on bases and in the desert. But they are very aware of others moving from dock loading areas and to air bases and local hotels as they do their work in rear areas. Contact with Saudi civilians is infrequent, but contact with Saudi men on the bases is constant.

The experience of the American women will be a testament to the changes that the sexual revolution has wrought in American society and its military.

Major Fisher, who is 34 years old, is a 12-year veteran of the Air Force and is married to an Air Force pilot. They have two children, a young son and a daughter.

"YOU'VE GOT A JOB TO DO"

When ordered to Saudi Arabia from Langley Air Force Base in Virginia, she had two days to get ready, she said. Her husband was away on Air Force business but got back just in time for a hurried one-hour farewell at the terminal, she added.

Saying goodbye to her children was perhaps harder.

"My 10-year-old son knew something was wrong," Major Fisher said. "I told him there was a crisis and I had to go—that it was my job."

She arrived with one of the first groups of American soldiers, expecting to be at war with Iraq almost immediately. Conditions on the ground in Saudi Arabia were decidedly cramped, she said, as more troops poured in.

"I looked over and saw a guy taking a shower in the stall next to me," Major Fisher recalled. "We just laughed. You can't get hung up about it. You've got a job to do."

According to several Army women here, they are discouraged from dating men in their units. If romance blooms, the United States military ordains that it should occur within military rankings: enlisted women are not to date officers, noncoms are not to date privates.

Although the Saudis have learned to accept American Army women driving and working in military areas, they still prohibit jogging and they are far more strict about what American women can do outside of a military base.

A VICTORY AT THE GYM

"We can't drive and we have to wear long sleeves and pants or a long dress to cover our legs," Major Fisher said.

A major victory for American Army women here was to be granted access to the formerly men-only gym at the local air base—with the proviso that they enter through the back door and leave after their two-hour time limit is up.

Major Fisher speculated that a kind of sexual revolution would come to Saudi Arabia too, even if slowly.

"If I were a Saudi woman I'd look at the American women here and ask 'Why can she do this and I can't?'" she said. "They're going to have to fight their own battles."

In Saudi and US Women, Common Feeling Is Pity
Colin Nickerson

DHARAN, Saudi Arabia—The American servicewomen arriving by the thousands to this desert kingdom, where men may still take four wives, look sadly on their Saudi sisters cloaked head-to-toe in black abaay, eyes invisible behind the veils prescribed by Islamic custom.

"Even when you see them, they seem invisible. I simply cannot imagine their lives," said Navy corpswoman Kim Kanode, 31. "You feel lucky to be from America, where women may have a way to go but have still come a long way. These women are centuries behind. I just pity their lives."

Saudi women, meanwhile, admit to being amazed—stunned, really— by the spectacle of US troop carriers rumbling through their streets carrying rifle-bearing women in combat helmets. But even the most progressive among them feel no envy.

"I feel pity for these American girls with their guns," said a female engineer in her 30s. "Saudi women so often have looked to the West for inspiration. But how can we believe training women to kill and destroy is progress?"

Saudi Arabia, birthplace of the Prophet Mohammed and most conservative of Islamic nations, denies women rights that are taken for granted in other Moslem lands. Women cannot drive cars, must adhere to an ultramodest dress code enforced by religious police, and are barred from public places, including most restaurants and all swimming pools.

It is a country of sexual paradox, where over the past two decades women have been encouraged to pursue advanced degrees and enter professions ranging from medicine to economics. Yet it is also a country where a female surgeon, say, or a full university professor requires written permission from a male "custodian," husband, father, brother, even teen-age son, before she can travel abroad.

Dating is unknown. Premarital sex, if discovered, would bring public censure and shame not only to the woman involved but to her extended family. Adultery may be, and occasionally is, punished by death.

A female doctor in Jeddah recalled the humiliation of having her pay docked for two weeks when religious police discovered her making medical rounds in a long dress that police charged revealed too much ankle.

"The long beards harass housewives and doctors alike. It is very democratic," she said, alluding to the whiskered imams, the religious teachers who oversee enforcement of Saudi morals.

Yet the doctor, who requested anonymity like most of the Saudi women interviewed, said she would never want to see her country become "liberalized" in the same way as the United States, where she lived for several years and earned her undergraduate degree.

"Saudi may be one extreme, and much change is needed here, especially for women," she said. "But America is another extreme, and it also is in need of change. An American woman can drive and has many freedoms. But she cannot walk the city streets in safety. If she has children she must always worry about drugs and molesters. Are sex movies and homeless people on the street a sign of liberty?

"Americans confuse permissiveness with freedom. There should be a balance," she said. "Saudi Arabia, at least, is not a kingdom of crime and fear. I may be required to wear a certain clothing, but in my country I walk in serenity and peace."

She cited the strong bond of the family as one of the Saudi culture's great strengths. "Everywhere I go in my country there is some cousin or uncle or friend who will take me in, feed me, and let me feel I am at home. Saudis care for one another in a way I do not believe Westerners do."

Combat Barrier Blurs for Women on the Front Line
Colin Nickerson

. . . Never before has the United States fielded so many servicewomen performing such a variety of military jobs to a potential war zone. After a slow start, the level of women among the more than 220,000 American troops in Saudi Arabia and the Persian Gulf is reaching the same proportional level as in the 2-million-member armed forces as a whole: 11 percent.

Women repair the engines of fighter jets, pilot supply planes, command complex communication centers, track ships and planes on radar, serve in secret intelligence units, perform surgery in field hospitals, oversee logistics and do such ordinary grunt work as standing night guard, driving trucks and ladling out unsavory meals of hash and reconstituted eggs.

"American women have always gone to war in one way or another," said Marine Lance Cpl. Melanie Robert, 20, an M-16 assault rifle slung over her shoulder as she patrolled the perimeter of a supply dump. "But I don't think our role has ever been so obvious as here. Whatever happens, women are going to be in the thick of it."

. . . Meanwhile, the presence of so many women in a relatively small theater of operations is making a mockery of the military rules, and US law, that forbid females from serving in combat. Those rules are already bending nearly double, like oasis palm trees in the ferocious "shamal" winds of November.

"You could say the theory of keeping women out of harm's way does not quite match the reality," said Army Sgt. Barbara Bates, 28, a military meteorologist from Nashville.

Bates is the sole woman serving among more than 700 artillerymen with a forward-based mobile howitzer battalion of the 24th Infantry Division. Like all servicewomen, Bates holds a noncombat "military occupation and specialty." Only men can be assigned jobs defined as combat specialties, whether slogging with the infantry, commanding a battle tank or bucking the G-forces of a tactical fighter jet.

There is, however, a Catch-22: Women can be "attached" to combat units so long as their duties match their noncombat service specialty.

. . . Hence, meteorologist Bates finds herself attached to a field artillery battalion in a role every bit as vital and dangerous as that played by the gun crews serving the big 155mm howitzers.

Her job, when the guns start to fire, is to provide swift, precise readouts of local wind speed, temperature and other weather conditions that can make the difference between a killing shot or a wasted shell. A strong wind can bend the trajectory of a 95-pound artillery shell so much that it can land hundreds of yards off target.

Come war, Bates would be no less exposed to danger than her male comrades. "When the shells start coming downrange, I will be counting on my flak jacket and foxhole for protection, not my MOS," she laughed.

Like many women here, Bates found some irony in the notion of "defending democracy," as President Bush recently described the US mission here, in a country that permits few rights to women.

"I know it is a different culture. Still you have got to wonder about a society that won't even let women drive a car or show their faces in public," Bates said. "So I just focus on our mission of deterring Iraqi aggression and leave it at that. The Saudis will have to solve their social problems. . . . "

Politics

Among Friends: Lynn Martin, Jerry Lewis, and the Race for the Chair of the House Republican Conference
David M. Kennedy

Publicity is usually the very stuff of a modern political campaign. Media strategies, advertisements, and polls consume vast energies in an attempt to win and shape the recognition of a distant electorate. But when the electorate is not so distant—when politicians campaign among themselves, for posts in their own hierarchies—the game changes. George Mitchell, Maine Democrat, won a hotly contested race for Senate majority leader late in 1988, and Bob Dole (R-Kan.) was reelected minority leader; Jim Wright (D-Texas) and Bob Michel (R-Ill.) were reelected to the parallel positions on the House side. All four ran vigorous campaigns, but without slogans, consultants, rallies, advertisements, or any of the other trappings of an ordinary political contest. Inside Congress (or state legislatures or other similar bodies) there is no need to fight for name recognition or to project a simple image. By the time members have the standing to make credible runs for leadership positions, their colleagues know very well what they have done and are likely to do. The issues are always parochial and internal, often entirely private and hidden. Campaigning is subtle and face-to-face. The resulting contests are intense, personal, and obscure.

House Republicans Lynn Martin of Illinois and Jerry Lewis of California waged a hard-fought race in 1988 for the chair of the Republican Conference, the third rung (below leader and whip) on the House Republican leadership ladder. Both were promising young members, both held lower-level leadership posts already, and for both it was up or out. The winner would join the ranks of such prominent Republicans as John Anderson and Jack Kemp, both of whom had parlayed the conference chair into presidential bids. The loser would be out of the leadership altogether. The choice was difficult and the handicapping close. "You had two excellent candidates," says Texas Republican Tom DeLay. "For me, as for a lot of members, it was not an easy or a comfortable choice: something we don't like." Personal and political relationships and gender politics complicated the race immensely. The contest would be hotly contested right down to the day of the December 5 election.

THE CONTENDERS

Lynn Martin and Jerry Lewis were, in many important ways, more like than unlike. Martin, 49, a bluff, informal, rapid-fire Chicago native, was elected in 1980 from her solidly Republican district in northern Illinois (the same one that sent John Anderson to the House) after serving in the Illinois senate. Lewis, 54, smooth, carefully coiffed and elaborately courteous, went to Congress in 1978 from his equally solid district in southern California, before which he'd been in the California assembly. Both were in their party's conservative mainstream. "Neither one of them is off the graph in any way," says a House Republican leadership aide. "Lewis is not an extreme conservative and Martin is not a liberal. He is conservative to moderate and she's moderate to conservative." Martin had taken several more liberal positions in favor of such things as the equal rights amendment, abortion rights and gun control, but she did so without calling much attention to herself, and they had not poisoned her with her colleagues. Lewis was thought of as conservative without being nearly as fire-breathing as the likes of Newt Gingrich (R-Ga.) and his confrontational Conservative Opportunity Society. "I describe myself," he says, "as a person who is not a bomb-thrower."

Neither was a substantive heavyweight in the mold of Les Aspin (D-Wis.) on defense issues, or former member David Stockman (R-Mich.) on taxes and the budget. Martin sat on the Budget Committee from 1981 until 1987, where she had been a consistent voice in favor of lower taxes and the Reagan economic program, and on the Armed Services Committee, but when she stood out she did so not as an expert or theorist but as a party activist. In 1986, in particular, when ranking Republican committee member Delbert Latta (Ohio) fell ill, she took over and managed the writing of the Republican budget alternative in such a receptive and inclusive way—according to many members—that it did far better on the floor than usual. She also gained an enviable reputation for a quick wit (particularly after being tapped by George Bush to stand in for Geraldine Ferraro in rehearsals for the 1984 vice-presidential debates) and a sharp, partisan, and quotable tongue, and became a staple Republican guest on the Sunday television panel shows. The honors mounted quickly. In her third term, she was the first woman to break into the Republican leadership when she won a race for the vice-chair of the Republican conference—a not particularly powerful but still prestigious post—and she was asked early to co-chair Bush's 1988 presidential campaign. By the time of her race for the conference chair, Lynn Martin was without question one of the leaders of her party, and perhaps its most prominent woman.

Jerry Lewis had a similarly eminent but rather lower profile. He sat on the Appropriations Committee, but his chief victories were won on the obscure battlefields of party politics. He won, successively, the chairs of the House Republican Research and Policy committees, which put him on the House Republican leadership ladder. In both jobs, he worked hard, but almost entirely out of the public eye, crafting positions for his fellow Republicans to use against the Democrats, both on the House floor and in their districts. He served on the 1988 Republican Platform Committee. And, most obscure but not by any means least important, he won the right to represent California on the House Republican Committee on Committees, where he voted for the entire delegation—18 votes, the most of any state—when it came to making Republican committee assignments. Like most of Lewis' other jobs, it was made to order for the exchange of favors. It was, unabashedly, how he preferred to work.

Immediately after Labor Day, 1988, as soon as outgoing conference chair Dick Cheney (Wyo.) announced his intent to move up to the whip post vacated by Senate-bound Trent Lott (Miss.), Martin and Lewis threw their hats in. Their basic campaign pitches reflected what both the candidates themselves and their colleagues viewed as their strengths. Lynn Martin presented herself, to colleagues hugely frustrated by the party's permanent House minority status, as a woman whose time had come: an antidote to the party's male, country-club public image; closely tied to the incoming Bush administration; and able, through her intelligence and combativeness, to propel House Republicans toward parity with the Democrats. Jerry Lewis presented himself as a known and positive quantity: someone who had for years sought and found opportunities to help Republican members in a variety of creative ways, and who would—armed with the greater power that came with leadership—continue to do so in the future. They were both, many members found, very attractive platforms. "I'm an old friend of Jerry's, he's done me a lot of good, and I started out supporting him," says one who vacillated until the end. "And then I listened to Lynn, that we could have a smart woman in the Republican leadership, and I thought, hey, we need some of that. I didn't know what to do."

THE PROBLEM AND THE PRIZE

Both Martin and Lewis had in large part been driven to seeking the conference chair by the Democrats' seemingly perpetual domination of the House. "If you're in the minority here," says Martin, "and I am—as a Republican, I'm not talking about as a woman—the most you can accomplish after X number of years would be ranking minority member of some committee. Realistically, although ranking minority member of the committee can be important internally, it is not often that you look in a paper and read about a committee's ranking minority member. You read about a committee chairman." Her position was even worse than most. Since the Budget Committee imposed a six-year limit on its members' tenure, she rotated off in 1987. "I don't regret joining that committee, because it was incredible during those

first Reagan years," she says. "But it meant that not only was that choice
going to limit my rise on that committee, it was going to limit my chances
for seniority on *other* committees: because once off Budget I was going to be
coming in, in effect, after both my [elected] class and the class to follow." To
her, the implication was so clear she can't really remember when she first
saw it. "Running for leadership was literally the only route for a while, to
be part of things," she says. "I'm not sure I ever went through this step by
step, but it doesn't take long to figure out."

In consequence, Martin had been running for or in the leadership almost her entire time in the House. She mounted a token run for the chair of
the Research Committee in her second term, more as a way of announcing
her arrival than anything else, then contested and won the conference vice-
chair in the next round of House Republican elections. She could have
stayed safely in that seat, but it was neither powerful nor visible enough for
her taste, and she was determined to move up.

Lewis felt no less bound by his minority status. It was "very frustrating
for a guy who likes to view himself as a policy player," he says. "You can
participate in the subcommittee discussions once in a while, but you're rele-
gated, essentially, to working on issues that affect your district. If you want
to address yourself to policy, you have to do it by way of rhetoric on the
floor. That's very, very disconcerting for a person in the minority. I had a
number of years in the California state legislature, which is a highly professional one that allows a person to get really involved in policy, in depth. I
came that close to leaving the Congress after one term. It was very imper-
sonal, and very partisan. The frustration goes on, serving in the minority.
So I focused upon how you go about imparting better balance between our
two parties, where I feel there is a great need for balance, and the only way
to get at that was by way of leadership." He started early too, at Research
and Policy, and he too was determined to move up.

The conference chair they both coveted, while still but the third-ranked
leadership position, was in some ways even more attractive than the leader
and whip posts. The conference itself was simply the body of House Republicans, which met more or less weekly in closed session to thrash out legislative issues, frame strategy, receive messages from the White House, air
grievances, and whatever else might come up. (House Democrats have in
recent years called their equivalent the "Caucus.") The conference chair was
guaranteed a certain prominence and influence through setting the agenda
and running the meetings. More important, perhaps, the chair often enjoyed more autonomy than the top leadership, since the leader's job (at least
a Republican leader with a Republican White House) was primarily to deliver on the president's policy, and the whip's, as chief vote-getter, was,
literally, to follow the leader. That often meant forging working arrangements with the Democrats, no matter how much private teeth-grinding they
might cause. The chair, more identified with the membership itself, often
had more latitude to speak out for members—Dick Cheney, normally a man
of moderate tone, made use of it in 1987 when he quite publicly called House

speaker and Republican nemesis Jim Wright "a heavy-handed son of a bitch"—and to follow a personal agenda. Jack Kemp (R-NY), who was conference chair from 1984 to spring 1987, pushed his economic program to great effect within the House, to the public, and even to the president in the Republican leadership's standard weekly sessions at the White House (Dick Gephardt (D-Mo.) used his equivalent chairmanship of the Democratic Caucus to advance his ideas prior to *his* run for president).

There were more tangible perks as well, chiefly a budget for conference operations and staff. Some of the money was effectively earmarked, as for publishing a weekly legislative digest, but there was enough left over for about six positions, to be spent more or less as the chair pleased. "In effect, the chairman gets extra staff, and believe me around here that's nice," says an outgoing member of Cheney's conference staff.

Both Martin and Lewis—prominent, respected, and already demonstrably successful in leadership campaigns—were well positioned to mount credible races. Both had very strong ideas about how to present themselves. And both knew that running would be an uncommonly intricate and sensitive undertaking.

THE FIELD OF BATTLE

Leadership races are subtle and opaque entirely because they are aimed at an extraordinary electorate. Members of Congress are proud and independent, have a bewildering array of public and private interests and ambitions, and are used to forming the most fluid and momentary political alliances. When they vote, they do so in private—all leadership balloting is secret—and for their own reasons. No matter how thorough and sophisticated the campaigning, when the elections are over, very often little is known of just why the winners and losers fared as they did.

For all that, there were a host of powerful attractions and fault lines at work within Lewis and Martin's House Republican electorate. The most basic was probably the natural internal loyalty of state delegations. Neither could simply assume the support of the other Republicans from their state, but each had a large edge on winning those votes. It was a rich harvest indeed for Lewis; 18 California votes was a nice head start on the roughly 88 he would need to win. Martin's gain was smaller and more problematic. The Illinois Republican delegation was only nine strong, and minority leader Michel, the dean of her delegation and one of Martin's biggest fans, felt obliged to stay scrupulously neutral in the conference race. She could presumably count on his vote, but she could not ask him to work on her behalf.

Also strong, if less constant and predictable, were the House's perennial bonds and tensions between regions and different-sized states. The West, the Midwest, the South and the Northeast have always had distinct political interests and styles, and their House representatives have a certain tendency to hang together. In the conference race, this seemed to mean that

Lewis' Western, and Martin's Midwest, colleagues would be more likely to vote for them and that the East and South would be up for grabs. If either candidate had been Eastern or Southern, things might have been different: those regions, with their strongly identified politics, are more likely to excite actual opposition. Like-sized states have a similar tendency to hang together. Given the widely varying size of House delegations, a coalition of, say, California, Texas, and New York can easily run roughshod over the likes of Rhode Island, Wyoming, and North Dakota, particularly on internal matters like leadership selection and committee assignments. Delegations from small states consequently have a long-standing interest in supporting each other, or, failing that, in blocking the ascent of members from big states (this is a dynamic, predictably, largely absent in the Senate). Lewis could expect to suffer. "Illinois is not a small state, but California is definitely a big state," Lewis says. Fortunately for him, delegations also generally have an interest in preventing any one state from getting too powerful, and if Martin won, two of the three top Republican leadership posts would belong to Illinois. "That helped," he says, "but nonetheless the California circumstance is a reality I live with."

Any number of more personal bonds also pertained. Members of the same committee were often inclined to support one another, giving Martin something of a base among her Armed Services and old Budget colleagues and Lewis one through Appropriations. Representatives who had first been elected to the House the same year—members of the same "class"—tended to feel some loyalty toward one another. Members of the House's many unofficial associations were natural allies; Martin was likely to benefit from her participation in the Wednesday Group, a moderate Republican policy committee. Personal friendships counted for a great deal. Henry Hyde (R-Ill.), for instance, was rather more conservative than Martin, and except for the Illinois bond might have been inclined to weigh in with Lewis, but they were famous friends and his vote was never in question.

Such ties often conflicted. Conservative Texan Tom DeLay, for instance, served with Lewis on Appropriations and both liked and respected him. He was also a member of a small, long-standing once-a-month dinner club with Martin, whom he found most impressive and considered a very close personal friend. To complicate things, another member of the club, and another close friend, was Colorado Republican Hank Brown, one of Martin's strongest and earliest supporters. DeLay, uncharacteristically, found himself seriously torn.

To all these time-honored bonds and schisms, the conference race added the new and uncertain twist of gender politics. Lynn Martin's candidacy had galvanized the 11 Republican women in the House. If she won, she would be a Republican star; if she lost, she would be out of the leadership she had broken into two years before. "I was surprised by how they lined up for me," Martin says. "Virginia Smith from Nebraska said, 'I will support you anytime you want to run: for anything, anytime.' She was just unequivocal about it. We're not that close; she just said, 'It's time.'" Olympia Snowe (Maine), who had nominated Lewis in his last run for the Policy Committee, became one of Martin's strongest supporters. Many in the mostly male House Republican membership were themselves clearly attracted to the political symbolism of putting a woman near the top of their party. Others, more privately, apparently were not. "A lot of the old-timers, really senior members, went with Lewis because for one reason or another they don't want a woman running the show," says a conservative Republican aide. "You won't hear it said out loud, but it's true." Just how important an issue Martin's sex was would not be apparent until election day: if then.

Most important of all, in the end, would be House Republicans' overall sense of what they had already gotten from Jerry Lewis and Lynn Martin, and would get in the future if they elected one or the other to preside over them. Most members would ultimately vote from some mixture of personal debt and personal and partisan interest. They would look not only, or perhaps even primarily, to the candidates' campaigning, but to the record both candidates had forged. "If you want to be in leadership, you come in here and from day one you'd better know where you're going," says one Republican. "Once you cast that one vote, take that one action, that sets you apart from your colleagues, it can mark you." Lewis and Martin had crafted quite different characters for themselves, as their fellow Republicans knew very well. Much would turn on them.

JERRY LEWIS: THE INSIDE MAN

If Jerry Lewis won, it would be because he had made all the right and traditional moves. "Lewis is a guy who has just been coming up through the ranks," says a member of Michel's staff. "He was research chairman, policy chairman, and now he's just continuing to climb the ladder. He's been very effective in all of his roles. He's redefined them to suit his own needs. He's taken on innumerable projects, he's just carried a lot of water. So his strength within the conference is that he's done it the old-fashioned way, he's earned it. "He's earned a step up." That was just how Lewis wanted it. He leaned, by skill and inclination, toward the quiet deal, the political favor, the collected debt, and his colleagues knew it and respected him for it. "Jerry is, I think," says one, "masterful in working within the system."

His tenure on the Policy Committee was a typical example of how he worked. Officially, the committee was simply charged with developing party positions on important issues (an increasingly important task as Republicans worked to redefine themselves as the "party of ideas"). Lewis found a way to do the job that redounded to the personal benefit of many of his fellow Republicans. Rather than have the committee and its staff issue papers itself, he created a number of report-writing subcommittees, as on Science and Technology, chaired by minority members of the corresponding standing House committees, who thus had an opportunity to put their names forward in a way otherwise forbidden by their minority status. "They could put it on their letterhead, or substitute these task force papers for committee assignments on an issue," says a leadership aide. "It wasn't exclusively his idea; the Research Committee does that too. But he did it while he was there, and a lot of people appreciate what he did for them."

There was steel in Lewis' makeup as well. He valued his abilities and his reputation as an operator, and when he felt he'd been crossed he got both mad and even. In his first year of sitting on the Republican Committee on Committees, his sole assignment from his delegation being to hold the Appropriations seat of a retiring California member for her successor, he lined up enough support early to secure the assignment. Or so he thought. When the Committee on Committees met, someone else got the seat. "I was not happy with that," Lewis says, by all accounts an understatement. "I went about putting together a coalition that would make sure that wouldn't happen again." Two years later, in the next round of committee assignments, Lewis' big-state coalition got the seat back. He paid a price: resentful small states organized against him, in the Committee on Committees and elsewhere, and mounted a stiff challenge to his bid for the policy chair. He still won, but not easily. He could expect some resistance still in the conference race.

Lewis' knack for such maneuvering held a powerful attraction for the Republican membership. "Jerry's appeal is that he is an excellent strategist," DeLay says. "He is one of the best vote-counters I have ever seen, and that is a talent that doesn't happen very often around here. There aren't very many good vote-counters: able to talk to another member about an issue and either change his mind or be able to read that member as to where he is really coming down. A lot of members—some members—will tell you, 'Yeah, I'm with you,' when they're never going to be with you. Or they will twist a phrase, and you think they're with you, and they're really not. You've got to be able to read that, and Jerry can read it better than most. The present leaders that we have I'm sure are good vote-counters, but they are more policy-oriented. They are more into deciding which way we should go on an issue, how to work that issue, but the nitty-gritty of counting votes, putting together a meeting, running a meeting properly, making sure that the conclusion of whatever you are doing comes out the way that you set it up to begin with: Jerry is excellent at that, excellent. Jerry is more of a wheeler-dealer than Lynn, he figures the angles and then goes after the angles. That's a good quality in a congressman."

The presumption in House Republican circles was that Lewis had been working the angles toward the conference chair for some time, in particular using his Committee on Committees votes to accrue debts in strategic states. Those deals weren't signed and sealed, and nobody could name names, but nobody doubted it. "You know it's happening," a leadership aide says. "You just hear it, feel it." He'd done a measure of campaigning for other members, though his comparatively low public profile limited his impact, and he'd raised and distributed over $50,000 in 1988 campaign funds for House Republican races. He had, all seemed to think, laid his groundwork classically and well.

LYNN MARTIN: A WOMAN OF SUBSTANCE

If Lynn Martin won, it would in large part be because she had accepted and turned to her own advantage a role she probably would not have chosen for herself. "I did not come here with any emphasis on women's issues," she says. "In fact, I used to joke that as a member of the Illinois legislature I had voted on the Equal Rights Amendment more than any other member of Congress, and I thought that finally, when I got here, I was done with it: you know, in the Illinois house, people were chaining themselves up. I thought, oh, boy, I am finally free of that." It was not to be. By the time of the conference race, Martin was entirely identified not so much with women's politics—though she played a larger role than she'd anticipated—but as a political woman, both in her own mind and those of her colleagues. Her own ambitions, and national and congressional Republican politics, had left her little choice.

Martin was elected in 1980 to a House that counted only nine women among its 192 Republicans. No woman was or ever had been in the leadership, and none, it's probably fair to say, was particularly prominent or influential in party affairs. Sexism, say many Republican congresswomen, was generally subtle, but still pervasive. At least one longstanding party discussion group refused to admit women. "There's a tradition of courtesy here, so you didn't have people saying things to your face," says one. "But you could feel it: particularly in the vacuum of opportunities for women."

At the same time, Republicans were seriously concerned about the newly-identified "gender gap," and eager to find some way to close it. That meant that when Lynn Martin, concerned about her minority status and the ceiling on her tenure on the Budget Committee, started to look to leadership, her candidacy was inevitably viewed, significantly if not primarily, as a woman's candidacy: both trailblazing and politically symbolic. Martin herself felt so to some extent—"I thought it was time for a woman," she says—but only to some extent. She was still far more interested in tax, budget, and party issues than in any particular women's issues.

Nonetheless, the political context was such that gender politics dominated her strategic thinking. Her first leadership race was for the chair of the Research Committee in 1983, and her run was purely symbolic. Her eye was really on the vice-chair of the conference, which she expected to come open in the next term, but she felt she had ground to prepare. "I got into the race very late, only three days before the election, not to win it but to get them used to the idea that shortly a woman was not only going to run seriously but expect to win," she says. "I had waited quite deliberately, knowing that it's like the kid who doesn't do his homework and then fails:

he says, well, if he had studied, he would have done well. I ran knowing it wasn't the right time, but so the signal would be clear, so that everybody could say, 'Well, I already committed to somebody, I can't vote for you, but next time, next time.' Then, boom, next time was there, and they've said it, and everybody knows it's time to do this. It was like a Lamaze course. It was time to get ready for us."

The next time was in 1984, when Abraham Jack Edwards retired both from politics and his post as conference vice-chair. Martin ran, and won easily. Normally, she thinks, she would have had more trouble. "I'd only been here two-and-a-half terms, and that's awfully soon to move into leadership," she says. "But the woman thing was just so overpowering that nobody said, hey, wait a minute, you haven't been here long enough. It was very clear to everybody that they were electing the first woman to leadership. They knew that; it was time. The gender gap was a big thing in the news, and I think that was very helpful."

More ordinary political currents were helpful too, most particularly the continuing support of fellow Illinoisan Minority Leader Michel. Or his perceived support. House Republicans saw Michel, a long-time Martin supporter, as more or less anointing her for vice-chair, which counted for a lot. Martin and her office saw things quite differently. "He didn't want me to run, particularly," she says. "I had that pretty strong feeling. It could mean change, conflict, in Illinois' position, though he didn't actively try to talk me out of it." She knew perfectly well, though, that her colleagues thought she was Michel's protégé, and she didn't try to change their minds. "Michel's support has been much overstated, but it doesn't do that much harm to have everybody believe it," says one of her aides. "So we never fed it, but we never argued it either." The myth, if that is what it is, remains strong in Republican circles.

Once elected, Martin faced the discouraging reality that vice-chair of the conference—a largely symbolic post with no assigned duties, no staff, and no real power—was really not much of a job, particularly under energetic chairs like Jack Kemp (and then Dick Cheney, who took over when Kemp withdrew from the conference to mount his 1988 presidential bid). Once again, gender politics offered an out. As the first Republican woman leader, Martin was a standout in GOP circles, and her House colleagues were quick to capitalize. "In the beginning, it was, 'My district's women's group is coming to town, will you come talk to my women?" says an aide. "So she did a lot of talking to the women's groups in the beginning. Then it was, 'My interns are coming to town. Will you talk to my interns?' And then finally, the invitations started saying, 'My Chamber of Commerce is coming to town, will you talk to my Chamber of Commerce?' So it went from speaking to the women's board of whatever was in DC—oh, and the wives need someone to speak to too—to, the Chamber is here. Of course it was patronizing, but you also understand that you walk before you run and before that you probably crawl, but if that's the first step you take it. Sure, you can sit back and say, 'Patronizing, I want to talk to the generals about national defense,' but let's be realistic, if Lynn wanted to talk to the generals back then it just wouldn't have happened. So she always took what was there and built on it."

Martin's strategy for these meetings, whatever got her in the door, was to deal with anything but women's issues. "I never talked about them," she says. "I was talking about budget authority, what we were going to do in agriculture in terms of where we were going to find cuts to reach the Gramm-Rudman guidelines, about the Bush campaign. That's a very different thing." Her clear intent was to come across as a core, mainstream policy and political player. At the same time, she found herself speaking up more and more on women's issues in the leadership's own councils. "There's no question that, when certain issues came up in leadership, even though they weren't my issues—child's issues or women's issues I didn't have any particular expertise in—I was automatically turned to," she says. "I didn't automatically have the answer. I mean, I know the human problems of child-care, but I may not know anything about a particular piece of legislation. You get that additional burden; nobody looks at all the men on the committee and assumes automatically that they know everything about veterans' affairs. It's delicate. On the one hand, you can't deny you're a woman. On the other, you can't be there to speak only as a woman; I never featured myself in that role. So I used my entrée when I could, and disabused them occasionally: sometimes, in leadership, I say that I don't know anything about whatever it is. Sorry. You know, 'Guess what!'"

Her major piece of legislative activity in this period helped cement her reputation as an equal rights advocate. Early on in her House tenure, Martin noticed, while helping make up the budget for the chamber's own committee system, that there was a significant gap between male and female committee staff's average salaries. She noted further that female staff had no legal recourse on the matter, since Congress had routinely exempted itself from its own civil rights and affirmative action legislation. She repeatedly introduced legislation to fill the gap; it stayed bottled up in committee until 1988, when it passed (in watered-down form) in the wake of front-page scandals about working conditions in the House print shop and several members' offices.

The popular perception of Martin's bill as the product of a crusading spirit was not entirely on the mark, however. It was at least as much, perhaps more, the product of a finely honed partisan instinct. "She started realizing that even though the House was under Democratic control, and they were the great civil libertarians, it was not carrying over to their own committees," an aide says. "She was very political, and saw that as a useful partisan issue. Do the Democrats practice what they preach? Obviously, they did not. It didn't reflect much on the Republicans, because Republicans don't control committees." Martin played it nicely enough that even though there was Republican opposition to her legislation, Michel came on board and it became official Republican policy. "It was a fairly class piece of work," says a conference aide.

Things seemed to be falling her way. George Bush, an old political friend, asked her in 1987 to be co-chair of his presidential campaign, and she accepted immediately. All through that year and next she campaigned for him nationwide, which increased her visibility and prominence; whenever she could she also campaigned for local Republican congressional candidates, stacking up political favors to be called in later (some saw her as particularly useful campaigning for Republican men running against Democratic women, a role she was perfectly willing to fill). She raised and distributed some $30,000 in campaign funds. And, at least to some eyes, she began building bridges to the far House Republican right that was her least natural ally. In one telling incident early in 1988, she mounted a vehement House floor defense of the extremely conservative California Republican Robert Dornan, with whom she normally had very little in common, when he felt that he had been cut off in debate by the presiding Democrat. "She was just blistering about his right to be heard," says one observer. "That was when I knew she was running for the conference chair." She too, in her own way, had laid her groundwork well.

THE RACE

The race for the conference chair began officially on Labor Day 1988, when Cheney announced his run for the whip post Trent Lott was vacating. Both Lewis and Martin sent letters to every one of their colleagues formalizing their candidacies. Martin's was distinctive for its clear emphasis on her public persona. "Our wars are fought not just in committee rooms and on the floor of the House; our battles have to be won before the American voter," she said. In the nicest possible way, she claimed that standard as her own. "The skill of Bob Michel and the calm wisdom of Dick Cheney say much about our party and its strength," she said. "I think I would bring something else to the mix: understanding of our Conference's views and an ability to communicate them."

Both set up steering committees of House colleagues, chosen on the basis of personal relationships and political advantage. Martin's was chaired by her good friend from Colorado Hank Brown; not only did they get on well together, but "I'm east of the Mississippi, he's west of the Mississippi," she says. Andy Ireland rang in for the South and opened a bridge to his large Florida delegation; triple threat Bill Clinger represented the East, the large Pennsylvania delegation, and, as ex-chair of the Wednesday Group, House moderates. The committee members lobbied their delegations and their friends, but neither group had too much impact on the strategies Martin and Lewis followed, or the messages they tried to get across. "There was no mystery about what we had to do," Martin says. "We had people divided geographically, and we sat down and talked about what the letter should say, and who should say what and when. But everybody kind of agreed on what the job was."

The job, more baldly than in almost any other kind of campaign, was to line up votes. Both Martin and Lewis talked face-to-face with almost every one of their colleagues, often many times. Unlike almost any other congressional business, staff was almost entirely uninvolved. "These races are the toughest kind of personal politics," Lewis says. "Eyeball-to-eyeball contact is the best way to communicate your arguments as well as to convince people they should vote for you; if you are going to be able to measure how people are going to vote, you have *got* to talk to them in person if at all possible. My campaigns for leadership posts have been highly personal, almost entirely one-on-one, and whenever possible in person." Martin felt she was running, in some real sense, a separate campaign for every member. "People have all sorts of reasons for making their choices," she says. "You tailor your approach to the person you are speaking to. Sometimes it's regional. Sometimes it's friendship. Sometimes it's ideas. You're courting votes just as you do at home, but it's a much more delicate process, and one that requires that you add a little more salt, a little less pepper, to what each person wants for dinner. You're preparing a different plate for each."

Some members knew their minds from the beginning. "I've supported Lynn Martin for leadership positions since she first ran, so when she said, 'Going to support me again?' I just said yes," says one. "Lewis said, 'Are you still supporting Martin?' and I said yes; nothing against you, Jerry, you're a fine man and all that, but I think we should have a woman in our leadership and Lynn's a very able and articulate person." Lewis had his stalwarts as well. The remaining Republicans had to be persuaded.

Martin's basic tack was to emphasize her ability to do good for House Republicans and their party. One prong was a pledge to buck the party structure on behalf of the conference when needful. "She saw herself trying to get a position on issues early and get to the White House with it," an aide says. "Say, 'OK, let's make sure we get this in the mix,' be their advocate, when Bob Michel and Dick Cheney will have to be the administration's advocate, coming the other way."

The other was to elaborate her appeal as a prominent Republican woman. She spoke not about gender politics as such but rather about political perceptions. "She said that she was probably a better spokesman for the Republicans, needed to be out there in order for them to become a majority, so that we'd lose the three-piece-suit country club image," her aide says. "That she was something a little different than that, not necessarily philosophically different but presenting a different image. She didn't criticize Jerry directly, because he has the same image as all the other males whose votes she was trying to get. She just said, I can promote an image that will bring more credibility to Republicans as the party that cares. How can you stand there in a three-piece-suit talking about why you have to cut some program? You need a grandmotherly type explaining why you have to; you need a woman with two kids explaining how it works." Everybody got the message, and many bought it. "I felt like we needed a woman in leadership," one member says. "I really feel like our women are superior to the Democratic women, and we ought to showcase them. It's good for the party."

Jerry Lewis believed that this line of argument was the chief threat to his candidacy, but he didn't try to block Martin's thrust. "It was not an item that was sensible to address because it is a point that is correct," he says. He tried, at most, to parry it. "I did say that Barbara Vucanovich from Nevada has been, during this last Congress, the chairman of the Republican Study Committee, which is a significant level of responsibility," he says. "And I was quick to say that we have several fine women in the House who happen to be members of Congress—no small accomplishment in politics for a woman—who are articulating women's concerns extremely well, and we should not denigrate the role they are playing on behalf of the Republican Party. Now, I didn't get any women's votes, but I think I might have turned some men."

Primarily, though, Lewis tried to build on his own strengths. He had his own schemes for bolstering the conference's influence and strengthening House Republicans' claims on national campaign resources, and he pushed them fairly hard. More than anything else, though, he had a history and a persona as a doer of favors, and he worked hard to collect what he was due and to promise more of the same. "What I got from him was, he's done a lot for members," DeLay recalls. "That he has proven he can handle the job. He did remind me of how well he did for Texas when we had six freshmen needing committees. And he did, he took care of them; I was there, on the Committee on Committees at the time, and he came through. In hearing from some of the other members, I think he used that kind of argument a lot. That was his money, if you will, and he spent it; that's what we do up here."

Martin watched all this in some frustration. "I would have done that if I could," she says. "You know, all through the years here, I've never been able to do anything for anybody; my committee assignments haven't been right for it. It's not wrong to do things for people, it's kind of nice. I mean, you end up talking more esoterically: if you elect me good things will happen in general. Well, if you can say a specific good thing will happen to *you* if you elect me, that has got a lot more interest. *That* has an effect."

Lewis' challenge was to get his point across without seeming too base about it. "If you link people's ambitions, or your committee assignment responsibilities, to their leadership support or nonsupport then I think you have crossed a line that is unacceptable to me," he says. What that meant in practice was no explicit promises. "It's only legitimate to let people assume that there is a relationship, by reason of the fact that you are on the Committee on Committees and might be able to help them if they have some future ambition, but you don't have the conversations in any linked way," he says. "I mean, an awful lot of people talk to me about the Committee on Committees shortly after—in the same conversation, really—my talking about the chairmanship. Many, many of the members do. I just have to be responsive to their desires and objectives, but make sure that I don't get myself in a circle where I am linking, because that just isn't acceptable." Martin was amused by such delicate sensibilities. "I don't think anyone ever promises explicitly," she says. "But you can hint, you're there, it's a fact."

For all their different backgrounds and approaches, Martin and Lewis' vote-counting showed them very evenly matched as the election approached. "I think if you went in and looked at classes, looked at committees, looked at regions, we were both competitive in all of those," Lewis says. Not everything went smoothly. Lewis' life was complicated when fellow California Republican William Dannemeyer announced that he, too, was going to run for the chair. Dannemeyer, a confrontational conservative, has a reputation among his colleagues for marching to his own drummer, and few members seemed to have any real idea of why he was running. Dannemeyer's staff says that he entered because neither previous candidate was a sufficiently activist conservative; Lewis is convinced that he came in as a spoiler because Lewis refused the unswervingly antigay Dannemeyer's demand to disassociate himself publicly from a gay Southern California AIDS group. In either case, his candidacy was potentially troublesome, threatening both to siphon off some of Lewis' more conservative backers and split the California delegation. Martin's life, ironically, got more difficult when President-elect George Bush's transition team started to mention her for several different cabinet posts. House Republicans started to worry whether, if elected, she'd even be around to serve. "It was sort of the worst of all worlds," she says, and she eventually sent a letter to all her colleagues insisting that the conference chair was what she really wanted (though she didn't remove herself from cabinet contention or pledge not to serve if called on). It didn't entirely quell the speculation.

The race remained one of individual votes. Lewis in particular essayed some deals with other leadership candidates, in particular a scheme to deliver California support to Joe McDade, senior member of the Pennsylvania delegation and candidate for House Republican secretary, in exchange for McDade's commitment of Pennsylvania votes (McDade's entry into the race made a mess of Bill Clinger's work to line up Pennsylvania for Martin). The deal seemed to have some life to it when, just a week before the election, the *Wall Street Journal* sank McDade's candidacy with a front-page story alleging financial improprieties. Martin didn't even try such maneuvers, knowing that it wouldn't work for her and figuring that the people she might win that way were probably constitutionally such that she'd lost them already. "It would never occur to me to sell my Illinoisans," she says. "California's just so big that you can say, 'I can deliver four people.' Well, maybe I could have delivered four Illinoisans, I don't know, but the Midwest is different, it just doesn't work that way. It doesn't make it right or wrong, but the people I was going to get, that isn't the way I'd get their votes. If people were inclined to work like that—and that's not a bad way—they were already going to be on the other side. It's just a difference in types."

As the campaign entered its last week, Lynn Martin cleared her calendar, locked herself in her office, and commenced to call, one last time, every Republican member of the House (Congress was in Christmas recess, which meant that many members were out of town). Lewis did much the same. It was a sign that both campaigns were strong and that neither was secure. "It went down to the wire," says Tom DeLay, who remained undecided right up to the election. "If either of them, Lynn or Jerry, had broken down in any area, it would have been a walk-away, but they didn't. They both accomplished what they needed to accomplish. But neither one of them, believe me, the day of the vote, knew that they had won. Jerry was scrambling all over the place, and so was Lynn, right up to the very vote. I was approached by two of their people right at the very end. The message of that, to me, was that neither one of them knew that they had the votes. They were relying on that group of 'don't knows' to get them over the top." In fact, both candidates' vote-counting showed them winning, but by very slim margins. Both knew that they could expect a certain number of defections, and that some of their committed votes would be pledged to both sides (Lewis used a full 20 percent fudge factor). Neither was sanguine. Both were extremely optimistic.

THE ELECTION

It took two ballots. William Dannemeyer's six-vote showing on the first was weak—"We were all embarrassed for him," says a member—but still enough to deny either Martin or Lewis victory. On the second, his votes split four to Lewis and two to Martin, and Jerry Lewis was the new chair of the House Republican Conference. Martin's disappointment was sharper for the fact that of seven members who stayed away from the elections, she'd counted five as her votes. Her count, in the end, was ten off, four of which she knows were double-pledges because they called and confessed after the election, which she and her staff found surpassingly odd. Though the West went solidly for Lewis and the Midwest for Martin, both siphoned some votes from the opposing regions. Jerry Lewis gave a very generous acceptance speech crediting speculation about Martin's cabinet status for his narrow victory.

Martin took her defeat philosophically. Her main second guess, she says, has to do with whether she and her team may have soft-pedaled the political appeal of her gender. "I think maybe we were a little too subtle," she says. "I think there's a tendency to think everybody's thinking sort of the same way you are, and that may just not be true. Maybe you have to hit them on the head a little more. Maybe we should have said, 'The Democrats are going to elect a black or a woman to their leadership. Isn't it time we do something?'" The Democrats did; Mary Rose Oakar (Ohio) and black Budget Committee chair William Gray (Pa.) were part of a three-way race for chair of the Democratic Caucus, and Gray won, the first black to break into congressional leadership. Lynn Martin, meanwhile, was out. Others in the Republican leadership showed real concern, partly for personal reasons and partly, clearly, for political ones. One called up immediately after her defeat and said, "We'll find something for you, we can't keep on doing this to ourselves." What, if anything, the something will be is still unclear.

Martin made a point of being a particularly good loser. "It struck me, not as a burden, not even a responsibility, I don't know what I'd call it, as my job to go on," she says. "I think women don't necessarily learn to compete, to win and lose gracefully. I think that when you haven't done something, and then you try it as an adult, it's harder to risk it. A little boy has played football and other sports, he's won, he's lost, he's cried, so he's learned to go on. I think that it's harder for women to risk failure because they've had so little practice. So when something is this close, it's not as good as a win—I'm not going to suggest that—but you don't go back to the corner. Even some men go back to the corner, I'm not suggesting you don't if you want to. But I thought it was very important that I sent out a letter telling everybody how much I thought of them and telling them I was still with them, and that I went to the first meeting of the conference after the election. Because that is what my supporters would have expected and the people who didn't vote for me too. There is a mode of behavior that you owe it to others to adopt, because a woman's chance will come again. Something will have to give. I actually do believe this."

COMMENTS AND
RECOMMENDED READINGS

In the 1970s most studies of women in management were gender minimalist, either in their assumptions or in their conclusions. What differences existed between women and men were explained not by characteristics of the two sexes but by their relative position in organizational networks. Thus, the salient questions had to do with structures of opportunity, degrees of power or powerlessness, and the consequences of tokenism. This view was persuasively elaborated by Rosabeth Moss Kanter in *Men and Women of the Corporation* (New York: Basic Books, 1977).

In the 1980s a dramatic shift to gender maximalism occurred, especially as Carol Gilligan's work in moral psychology became more widely known. Under this view, women and men bring different qualities to the workplace and these qualities manifest themselves in different managerial styles. Though anecdotal, the contrast is vividly portrayed in Sally Helgesen's *The Female Advantage: Women's Ways of Leadership* (New York: Doubleday, 1990). See also the symposium on "Women in Management" in the *Journal of Business Ethics* 9:4–5 (April-May 1990). Gilligan's views are most fully elaborated in *In a Different Voice* (Cambridge: Harvard Univ. Press, 1982). For more recent reflections on the nature of the gender difference, see her essay "Moral Orientation and Moral Development" in *Women and Moral Theory*, edited by Eva Feder Kittay and Diana T. Meyers (Totowa: Rowman and Littlefield, 1987), pp. 19–33. An excellent overview and critique is offered by Owen Flanagan in *Varieties of Moral Personality* (Cambridge: Harvard Univ. Press, 1991), Chapters 7–11.

In his reporting on the encounter between Saudi women and American women soldiers, James LeMoyne quotes one Saudi woman as saying, "Women are not made for violence with guns." At first glance, this statement appears to reflect what Sara Ruddick calls "maternal thinking," the idea that the practice of mothering provides an experiential foundation for resistance to militarism and other forms of violence. See Sara Ruddick, *Maternal Thinking: Toward A Politics of Peace* (Boston: Beacon Press, 1989), p. 174. Yet Ruddick does not pose a simple opposition between "maternal work" and "military work." She says: "Peacekeeping is the art of avoiding battle; the challenge is to recognize when peacekeeping should end and battle begin." For a subtle treatment of women's attitudes regarding war, see Jean Bethke Elshtain, *Women and War* (New York: Basic Books, 1987). On policewomen and the use of deadly force, see the relatively early study by Susan Ehrlich Martin, *Breaking and Entering: Policewomen on Patrol* (Berkeley: Univ.

of California Press, 1980). A more recent empirical study is reported by Sean A. Grennan in "Findings on the Role of Officer Gender in Violent Encounters with Citizens," *Journal of Police Science and Administration* 15:1 (1987), pp. 78–85. Martin also offers a comprehensive review of women's progress in policing in her book *On The Move: The Status of Women in Policing* (Washington, D.C.: Police Foundation, 1990).

Historical perspectives on women in politics—from Anne Hutchinson and Abigail Adams to Margaret Sanger and Sojourner Truth to Angela Davis and Sandra Day O'Connor—are offered in the collection of essays *Women Leaders in American Politics*, edited by James David Barber and Barbara Kellerman (Englewood Cliffs: Prentice-Hall, 1986). Another comprehensive collection on the variety of political roles women have entered, both historical and contemporary, is *Women, Politics, and Change*, edited by Louise A. Tilly and Patricia Gurin (New York: Russell Sage Foundation, 1990). For reflections on the intersection of race and gender issues in politics, see the works of bell hooks, especially her *Yearning: Race, Gender, and Cultural Politics* (Boston: South End Press, 1990).

About the Book
and Editors

A rich collection of lively and accessible readings and case studies, *Gender and Public Policy* is the first text of its kind and the ideal choice for the teaching of public policy issues as they relate to women and gender. The readings range widely over topics on family and reproductive issues, on economics and culture, and on women's issues in management and government. They include personal stories, court decisions, historical narratives, and several cases prepared especially for this volume. All were chosen for their demonstrated value for facilitating and focusing classroom discussion.

Although the book as a whole reflects a firm commitment to feminism and the welfare of women, the selections represent a variety of views and ideologies, giving students the opportunity to reevaluate traditional gender roles in different ways. Editorial introductions, comments, and suggestions for further reading appear throughout the book to help students place issues in an appropriate context.

Gender and Public Policy will make an invaluable contribution to teaching in women's studies programs, schools of public policy, and business schools as well as in departments of political science, sociology, and philosophy that feature courses on women's issues.

Kenneth Winston is professor of philosophy at Wheaton College. He taught for many years at the Kennedy School of Government, Harvard University, and he has published many articles and reviews on law, ethics, and public policy issues. **Mary Jo Bane** is currently on leave from the Kennedy School of Government while serving as commissioner of social services for the State of New York. She is the author of *Here to Stay* and numerous papers on poverty, the family, and social policy.